BEIJING

William Lindesay

and

Wu Qi

© 1999, 1997, 1995, 1992, 1988 Odyssey Publications Ltd
Maps © 1999, 1997, 1995, 1992, 1988 Odyssey Publications Ltd

Odyssey Publications Ltd, 1004 Kowloon Centre, 29–43 Ashley Road,
Tsim Sha Tsui, Kowloon, Hong Kong
Tel. (852) 2856 3896; Fax. (852) 2565 8004; E-mail: odyssey@asiaonline.net

Distribution in the United Kingdom, Ireland and Europe by
Hi Marketing Ltd, 38 Carver Road, London SE24 9LT, UK

Distribution in the United States of America by
W.W. Norton & Company, Inc., New York

Library of Congress Catalog Card Number has been requested.

ISBN: 962-217-603-8

Grateful acknowledgment is made to the following authors and publishers:

University of Hawaii Press for *The Venerable Schoolmaster Gao* by Lu Xun, translated by William A Lyell ©
1990 University Press of Hawaii; The University Press of Hawaii for *Rickshaw* by Lao She, translated by
Jean M James © 1979; Cambridge University Press for *The Travels and Controversies of Friar Domingo
Navarrete 1618–1686* edited by J S Cummins, © 1962 The Hakluyt Society; George N Kates for *The Years
That Were Fat* by George N Kates © 1966 George N Kates; *City of Lingering Splendour* by John Blofeld ©
1961 by John Blofeld, reprinted by arrangement with Shambhala Publications Inc, 300 Massachusetts Ave,
Boston MA 02115; Chatto & Windus Publishers and Peters Fraser & Dunlop for *The Gunpowder Gardens*
by Jason Goodwin © 1990 Jason Goodwin; Random Century Group and Jonathan Cape Ltd for *Destination
Chungking* by Han Suyin

Editor: Frank Davies
Series Editor: Jane Finden-Crofts
Design: Bobby Chan
Maps: Bai Yiliang and Tom Le Bas
Cover Concept: Margaret Lee

Front cover photography: China Photo Library Limited
Back cover photography: James Z Huang
Photography/illustrations courtesy of Magnus Bartlett 13, 16 (bottom), 69, 93, 96, 108, 112; Kevin Bishop
8–9, 16 (top), 43, 114, 127 (bottom), 143; Don J Cohn 76–7; Richard Dobson 30, 49, 68, 123; James Z
Huang 46, 52, 127 (top); William Lindesay 34–5, 60, 131, 138; Ingrid Morejohn 65; James Montgomery
5, 139; John Warner Publications 22–3, 71; The Commercial Press Ltd 64, 105; Wattis Fine Art 73, 88–89

Production by Twin Age Ltd, Hong Kong
Printed in Hong Kong

The Gate of Heavenly Peace (Tiananmen), entrance to the Imperial Palace

Contents

(Previous pages) A Building in the Summer Palace (Yiheyuan)

PEKING VERSUS BEIJING: WHAT'S IN A NAME?

First, let's learn to pronounce the name of the city. *Bei* sounds like 'bay' with the B pronounced harder than an English *B* but softer than a *P*; and *jing* sounds like the second syllable of 'paging' or 'staging'—there is a bit of friction in the initial consonant. The *j* in Beijing is *not* the equivalent of a French soft *j*, as in *jardin*.

'Peking' is the English version of the earlier French 'Pékin', which is the name of a city in Illinois, USA.

Until the 1970s, nearly all English publications used the 19th-century Wade Giles romanization system to render Chinese names in English, except in the case of certain place names which used the French-influenced postal spellings, such as Amoy (for Hsia-men or Xiamen), Chekiang (for Che-chiang or Zhejiang), Chungking (for Ch'ung-ch'ing or Chongqing), and Tientsin (for T'ian-chin or Tianjin). In the early 1970s, China declared its own *pinyin* romanization system official. *Pinyin*—literally 'spell the sounds'— had been developed in China based on the Russian Cyrillic alphabet, hence the use of eye-crossing *x, zh* and *q* not followed by a *u*. *Pinyin* is less unwieldy than Wade Giles, but like any romanization system, depends more on the inner ear than the eye. Most of the world adopted the *pinyin* spellings for Chinese place names, but some newspapers and publishers boldly refused to adopt the *pinyin* spelling of a city that to anglophones has been Peking for about 300 years. What would happen if the Italians asked us to write Roma, and the Spaniards España?

Some pedants went so far as to suggest changing China to *Zhongguo*, as the name of the country is written in *pinyin*. 'China isn't a Chinese word,' they say, 'it was made up by foreigners.' Shall we then have a Zhongguoish meal at a Zhongguoish restaurant where the waiters speak Zhongguonese?

Further questions arise over such neologisms as Beijing opera, Beijing duck and, perhaps a contradiction in terms, Old Beijing.

Libraries throughout the world were also thrown into a quandary about how to catalogue their Chinese books, and some of the great libraries in the West which hold large Chinese collections have two separate card systems, one for *pinyin* and one for Wade Giles. As card catalogues are computerized, the difficulties will lessen.

Introduction
Beijing and its People
—by William Lindesay

Beijing is unlike any other city in China, totally unrepresentative in grand capital style, a true centre at the edge. Home to 1 in 100 Chinese, or 12 out of China's 1,200 millions, power emanates over its high walls, through its sentried gates, and from ministerial motorcades as they speed along the city's boulevards.

This notorious officialdom diminishes in direct proportion to distance from the capital, if popular doggerel is anything to go by: 'If you don't go to Beijing, you won't realize how small your local officials are; if you don't go to Shanghai you won't know how small your ideas are; if you don't go to Shenzhen you won't know how small your wallet is, and if you don't go to Hainan you won't realize the bad state of your health.'

But even though Shanghainese have the most radical ideas, Shenzheners the most money and Hainan islanders provide 'exhausting' nightlife, for better or for worse, richer or poorer, Beijing rules them all. And it's been like that for most of the last 900 years.

Conquest dynasties from the north first favoured the site for settlement, at the edge of the North East China Plain in the lee of the Yanshan mountains. Jurchens, Quitans, Mongols and Manchus either overran each other or Han rulers to establish, destroy and rebuild, or occupy cities here.

All who came, saw and conquered left their marks, monuments and memories. The Liao (916–1125), made the site their secondary capital, naming it Yanjing, the city of swallows; the birds still dart around the eaves of Beijing's ancient buildings every summer. Nothing remains from the Jin Dynasty (1115–1234) capital, Zhongdu. Besieged by the invading Mongols for 6 years, it was finally razed to the ground for the building of Genghis Khan's Dadu. Remains of the Yuan dynasty city wall, which had impressed Marco Polo, can be seen between the northern legs of the third and fourth ring roads. Buildings, monuments and relics from the Ming and Qing capital of Beijing, being more recent, are relatively abundant.

Yet in today's sprawling Beijing the past is well hidden by the present and future. Cranes and scaffolding are never far, and arriving at the city's airport, or the new monolithic West Railway station, and making the trip into town, it is difficult to see anything of antiquity. Guidebooks, tour brochures and the foreign press tend to portray an image of a benighted populace, dressed in green Mao suits and caps, living in the shadows of quaint pagodas and eaved pavillions. Nothing could be further from the truth.

Be prepared to see huge hoardings advertising Hitachi, Motorola and Hennessy Cognac, smoke-glass fronted skyscrapers, real estate developments, 4-lane

Residents of Beijing brave winter weather in Tiananmen Square

expressways and ring roads jammed with traffic. See women flaunting femininity, with the aid of make up, mousse and designer fashions which were frowned upon for decades; see men flashing their fortunes by posing with mobile phones. This is Deng Xiaoping's legacy of reform and opening.

It's all the more remarkable when you realize that many of the other great sites of the city are reminiscent of times when reactionary politics, isolationism and, seemingly, xenophobia were in command.

Mao's portrait still adorns Tiananmen, the Gate of Heavenly Peace, from where he proclaimed the foundation of the People's Republic on 1st October 1949 with a speech and raising of a new flag. Later, in 1966, he received millions of fanatical red guards in the square below at the height of his cult status. Fittingly, or unfittingly, depending on one's judgement of history, the late chairman still presides over the raising of the Chinese flag every day. The 'Sentry of the Motherland' march out through the archway under his portrait at dawn, halt the traffic and raise the flag. And 400 metres south is Mao's mausoleum where his remains are on show in a crystal sarcophagus.

Tiananmen is an architectural, and therefore historical interface. Austere, Stalinesque buildings rim the square to the east and west, while to the north lies the largest collection of ancient palacial buildings in the world: the Imperial Palace.

The maze of golden-roofed buildings and courtyards was home to every Ming and Qing emperor from 1420 until Pu Yi, the last emperor, left in 1921. In this citadel isolated by a moat and high perimeter walls that no ordinary person saw behind, some 23 emperors, their families, ministers, eunuchs and concubines lived in a world apart from the masses, with emperors believing themselves to possess the mandate of heaven for ruling the vast Middle Kingdom outside.

As if a mile were a foot, Ming emperors regarded their huge empire just like a palace ground which needed a boundary wall for security, and with millions of subjects under their direction ordered the construction of the strongest Great Wall in history through the Yanshan mountains to the north of Beijing. US President Richard Nixon, walking on the Wall in 1972, summed up its magnificence with masterly understatement: 'Yes, it really is a *great* wall.'

China has changed beyond recognition since that Ping-Pong diplomacy brokered between Beijing and Washington in the early 1970s. Perhaps the most remarkable transformation has been in the people. They are one, or rather many, of the great sights of China.

In Beijing's downtown areas a foreign face hardly causes a head to turn, except from those brothers and sisters from outside, the term for migrant workers from labour-exporting provinces such as Sichuan, Anhui and Henan, who flock to the capital to work as construction workers and domestics.

Individualism is the backlash to enforced collectivism that was imposed for so long. More people want to be different, crave to be successful and show it off. The country has suddenly become a land of businessmen, and Beijing has its unfair share. Kickbacks are essential operating costs to grease the palms of obstructive bureaucrats into giving their permission to make things happen.

The economy finds itself somewhere between a semi-dismantled, centrally-planned system, and a semi-constructed, market economy. Many Beijing families are microcosms of the national situation: typically, one spouse sticks with the state employer for the socialist life preserver of an apartment and eligibility to a host of state benefits, while the other will *xia hai*, or plunge into the commercial sea, and try to make a fortune. But another plunge, *xia gang*, into unemployment, is now being inflicted on surplus staff by Premier Zhu Rongji's restructuring of state enterprises.

Money is the hottest topic of conversation. At the advent of Deng's economic reforms in the early 1980s, it was stressed that a good communist did not have to be poor, and to get rich was glorious. Wealth seeking suddenly became politically correct. On the streets these maxims were popularly summarized as *xiang qian kan*, looking ahead and looking at money, quoted in a recent social survey of Beijing urbanites as being the philosophy which best describes their aim in life.

But all work for money and no play makes Wang a dull comrade. That socialist salute, by the way, is totally out of fashion, having been replaced by the genderless *shifu*. The Nineties also sees *zhao le*, or having fun and pleasure seeking, gathering momentum. Restaurants are everywhere. A walk down a Beijing street is akin to a culinary tour of China. And there are some foreign concessions worth visiting. McDonald's and KFC burst at weekends as Beijing's parents cater to their little emperors' needs, while granny looks on dotingly. Nights are livelier, too. While most of Beijing becomes increasingly addicted to TV, the young, beautiful, rich, curious and bad go out to play. Entertainments range from rock and roll to jazz gigs, from karaoke to song-and-dance-hall action. Some establishments are more than just venues for social intercourse, a chat and a tipple.

Vices which Mao fought ruthlessly for so long to eradicate are now rampant again. Deng opened China's door to the world and gave the people more than they ever had. Now departed, the side-effects of his reforms—money worship, hedonism, rising corruption and crime—are being targeted by Communist Party Secretary Jiang Zemin's recently-launched 'spiritual civilization' campaign which aims to put the good heart back in the nation.

But for all these problems, China today is much more human and relaxed than it was, even a decade ago. As any visitor to Beijing will quickly find out, most Chinese are friendly, flexible and fun loving. And their likes are making China less of a People's and more of a people's republic with each passing day.

Men all over China commonly keep songbirds and take them to parks at dawn. This bird, one of the most popular, is called a Huamei, meaning 'painted eyebrows'

Decorative gate in the Imperial Palace protected by two door lions

Getting to Beijing

Visas

Tourists travelling in a group enter China on a group visa—a single document listing all members of the group. The visa is obtained by the tour operator on behalf of his clients, and individual passports will not be stamped. Individual visas can be obtained at Chinese embassies and consulates and perhaps certain travel agencies in your respective countries; from the Chinese Ministry of Foreign Affairs visa office in Hong Kong; or through several Hong Kong travel agents including branches of CITS and CTS (*see* page 29). Just one passport photograph and a completed application form are necessary. The visa gives you automatic entry to the more than 1288 open cities and counties in China.

Visa fees vary considerably depending on one's nationality, the source of the visa and on the time taken to get it. In Hong Kong, for instance, you would pay around US$30 for a three-month visa granted within a few hours, while a standard one-month tourist visa processed in three days will cost around US$20.

An application for a business visa should generally be accompanied by an invitation from the appropriate host organization in China. In Hong Kong, all that is needed is a letter from the applicant's company confirming that he wishes to travel to China on business. Multiple re-entry visas are available for regular business visitors.

Visas can normally be extended by designated Public Security Bureaus dealing with the entry and exit of aliens. Extensions are granted for a maximum of one month, on no more than two successive occasions. The PSB office in Beijing is located on Beichizi Dajie, east of the Forbidden City. Visa difficulties are best solved via a consultancy which advertises its services in the office.

By Air (see Useful Addresses, pages 164–5)

Most major international carriers now fly to Beijing and have ticket offices in the city. Prices for outbound tickets purchased in Beijing tend to be more expensive than tickets bought in Europe or North America due to price controls imposed by Civil Aviation Administration of China (CAAC). However, a few ticket agencies have opened in the last year. They offer discounts of around 20 per cent on airline-office quoted prices. Contact Daqing Air Ticket (tel. 65922705), Bridge to China (tel. 65912283) or Yanmei (tel. 64155825) for details.

Chinese airlines operate more than 100 international routes to 38 countries, most of them by Air China, which has a 43-year-long safety record. Five other regional airlines, China Eastern, China Southern, China Northwestern, China Southwestern and China Northern operate the bulk of domestic services and a few

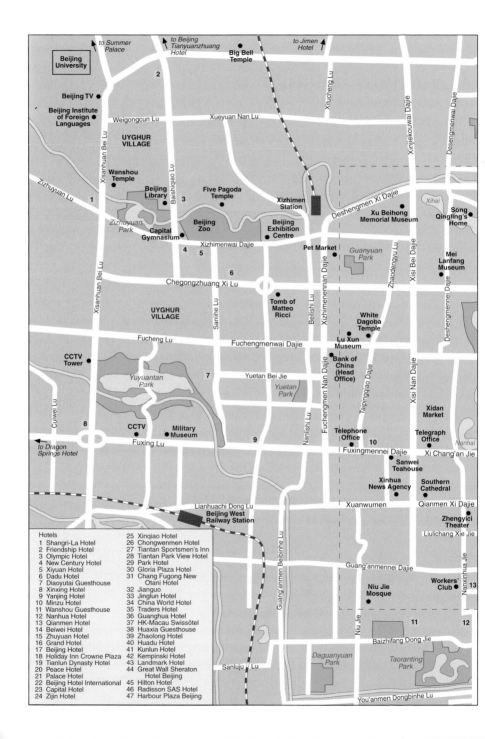

to Summer Palace

Beijing University

to Beijing Tianyuanzhuang Hotel

to Jimen Hotel

Big Bell Temple

2

Beijing TV

Beijing Institute of Foreign Languages

Weigongcun Lu

Xueyuan Nan Lu

UYGHUR VILLAGE

Wanshou Temple

Xisanhuan Bei Lu

Baishiqiao Lu

Beijing Library

3

Five Pagoda Temple

Xizhimen Station

Xitucheng Lu

Xinjiekouwai Dajie

Desengmenwai Dajie

Deshengmen Xi Dajie

Xihai

Xu Beihong Memorial Museum

Song Qingling's Home

Zizhuyuan Lu

Zizhuyuan Park

1

Capital Gymnasium

Beijing Zoo

Beijing Exhibition Centre

Xizhimenwai Dajie

Pet Market

Guanyuan Park

Zhaodengyu Lu

Xisi Bei Dajie

Mei Lanfang Museum

4

5

6

Chegongzhuang Xi Lu

Sanlihe Lu

Xizhimennan Dajie

Beilishi Lu

UYGHUR VILLAGE

Tomb of Matteo Ricci

White Dagoba Temple

Deshengmennei Dajie

Fucheng Lu

Fuchengmenwai Dajie

Lu Xun Museum

CCTV Tower

Yuyuantan Park

7

Yuetan Bei Jie

Yuetan Park

Fuchengmen Nan Dajie

Bank of China (Head Office)

Taipingqiao Dajie

Xisi Nan Dajie

Xidan Market

Cuiwei Lu

8

CCTV

Military Museum

Fuxing Lu

9

Nanlishi Lu

Telephone Office

10

Telegraph Office

Nanhai

to Dragon Springs Hotel

Fuxingmennei Dajie

Xi Chang'an Jie

Sanwei Teahouse

Xinhua News Agency

Southern Cathedral

Xuanwumen

Qianmen Xi Dajie

Zhengyici Theater

Lianhuachi Dong Lu

Beijing West Railway Station

Guang'anmen Beibinhe Lu

Liulichang Xie Lu

Guang'anmennei Dajie

Niu Jie Mosque

Workers' Club

13

Nanxinhua Jie

Niu Jie

11

12

Baizhifang Dong Jie

Sanluju Lu

Daguanyuan Park

Taoranting Park

You'anmen Dongbinhe Lu

Hotels

1 Shangri-La Hotel
2 Friendship Hotel
3 Olympic Hotel
4 New Century Hotel
5 Xiyuan Hotel
6 Dadu Hotel
7 Diaoyutai Guesthouse
8 Xinxing Hotel
9 Yanjing Hotel
10 Minzu Hotel
11 Wanshou Guesthouse
12 Nanhua Hotel
13 Qianmen Hotel
14 Beiwei Hotel
15 Zhuyuan Hotel
16 Grand Hotel
17 Beijing Hotel
18 Holiday Inn Crowne Plaza
19 Tianlun Dynasty Hotel
20 Peace Hotel
21 Palace Hotel
22 Beijing Hotel International
23 Capital Hotel
24 Zijin Hotel

25 Xinqiao Hotel
26 Chongwenmen Hotel
27 Tiantan Sportsmen's Inn
28 Tiantan Park View Hotel
29 Park Hotel
30 Gloria Plaza Hotel
31 Chang Fugong New Otani Hotel
32 Jianguo
33 Jinglun Hotel
34 China World Hotel
35 Traders Hotel
36 Guanghua Hotel
37 HK-Macau Swissôtel
38 Huaxia Guesthouse
39 Zhaolong Hotel
40 Huadu Hotel
41 Kunlun Hotel
42 Kempinski Hotel
43 Landmark Hotel
44 Great Wall Sheraton Hotel Beijing
45 Hilton Hotel
46 Radisson SAS Hotel
47 Harbour Plaza Beijing

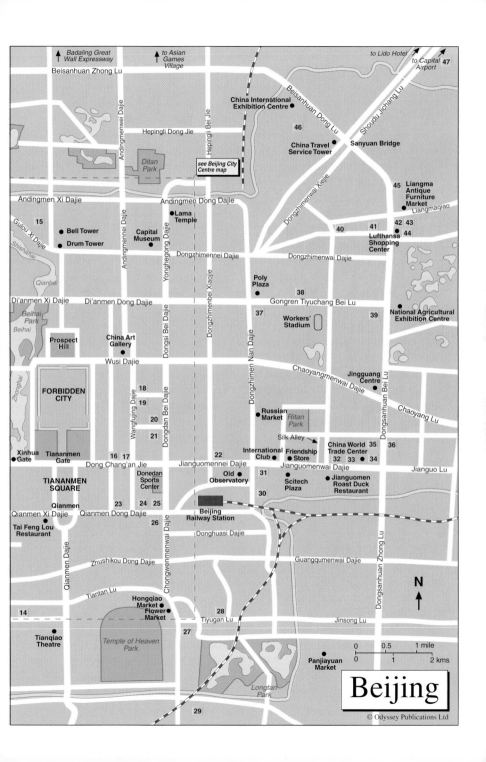

Badaling Great Wall Expressway
to Asian Games Village
to Lido Hotel
to Capital Airport 47

Beisanhuan Zhong Lu

Beisanhuan Dong Lu

Shoudu Jichang Lu

Hepingli Dong Jie

Hepingli Bei Jie

China International Exhibition Centre

46

Ditan Park

see Beijing City Centre map

China Travel Service Tower

Sanyuan Bridge

Dongzhimenwai Xiejie

45 Liangma Antique Furniture Market

Liangmaqiao

Andingmen Xi Dajie

Andingmennei Dajie

Andingmen Dong Dajie

Lama Temple

40

41

42 43
44

Lufthansa Shopping Center

15

Gulou Xi Dajie

Shishahai

Bell Tower

Drum Tower

Capital Museum

Yonghegong Dajie

Dongzhimennei Dajie

Dongzhimenwai Dajie

Qianhai

Dongzhimenbei Xiaojie

Poly Plaza

38

Di'anmen Xi Dajie

Di'anmen Dong Dajie

Gongren Tiyuchang Bei Lu

39

National Agricultural Exhibition Centre

Beihai Park

Beihai

37

Workers' Stadium

Prospect Hill

China Art Gallery

Wusi Dajie

Dongsi Bei Dajie

Dongzhimen Nan Dajie

Chaoyangmenwai Dajie

Jingguang Centre

Zhonghai

FORBIDDEN CITY

18

19

Wangfujing Dajie

Dongdan Bei Dajie

20

21

Russian Market

Ritan Park

Silk Alley

China World Trade Center

35

36

Dongsanhuan Bei Lu

Chaoyang Lu

Xinhua Gate

Tiananmen Gate

16 17

Dong Chang'an Jie

22

Jianguomennei Dajie

International Club

Friendship Store

32 33 34

Jianguomenwai Dajie

Jianguo Lu

TIANANMEN SQUARE

Donedan Sports Center

Old Observatory

31

30

Scitech Plaza

Jianguomen Roast Duck Restaurant

Qianmen

23

24 25

Qianmen Xi Dajie

Qianmen Dong Dajie

26

Beijing Railway Station

Tai Feng Lou Restaurant

Qianmen Dajie

Chongwenmennei Dajie

Donghuasi Dajie

Zhushikou Dong Dajie

Guangqumenwai Dajie

Dongsanhuan Zhong Lu

N

Tiantan Lu

Hongqiao Market Flower Market

28

Tiyugan Lu

Jinsong Lu

14

27

Tianqiao Theatre

Temple of Heaven Park

0   0.5   1 mile
0   1   2 kms

Panjiayuan Market

Longtan Park

29

Beijing

© Odyssey Publications Ltd

international routes. After a dreadful year in 1994 when a spate of hijackings to Taiwan and several crashes occurred, CAAC, once dubbed China Airlines Always Crashes, tightened up security, maintenance and administration throughout the industry. Now, with the big six Chinese airlines using entirely modern aircraft, and ticketing agencies in China having more than 100,000 computer terminals networked to CAACs reservation system, air travel to and within China on Chinese airlines is more convenient and reliable. Foreigners, once obliged to pay surcharges on their air tickets, now enjoy equality as all tickets are single priced.

Air China's main office is located at 15, Xi Changan Jie (tel. 66013366 domestic, or 66016667 international). Air China also has branches in the Beijing Hotel and Lido Holiday Inn. Most large hotels have travel desks which offer a computerized reservations service and flight confirmations. Note that airport tax is levied on international departures at 90 *yuan*, and 60 *yuan* for domestic departures.

The most popular air route to Beijing from Hong Kong is the two daily flights on Dragonair. Flying time is just under three hours. Hong Kong Dragon Airlines Ltd (Dragonair) is located in Hong Kong at 9th Floor, Worldwide House, Des Voeux Rd, Central (for reservations, telephone 25901188) and in Beijing at A710 Henderson Centre, Chang'an Avenue (tel. 65182533). The second choice is Air China, which has four daily flights. Air China's Hong Kong agent, CNAC (China National Aviation Corp.) has a new ticket office at CNAC Building, Ground Floor, 10 Queen's Road, Central. (For reservations, telephone 28610322). When direct flights are full, there is an alternative route via Tianjin which adds a minimum of one hour to the journey. Both Dragonair and Air China have flights to Tianjin, but only Air China operates a service which involves no change of plane. Alternatively, one could travel to Shenzhen or Guangzhou airports and fly to Beijing.

With the air travel boom, Beijing Capital airport finds itself inundated at most times of the day. Trolleys are in short supply and queues for taxis sometimes lengthy. Fares into town range from 90 *yuan* in small red Charades, and up to 150 for Toyota Cedrics or Santanas when meters are used. A ten *yuan* surcharge is payable if the airport expressway is used, but there are no baggage extras. At night many rogue drivers will refuse to use their meters. An alternative is the Air Bus, running every 20–30 minutes and costing only 16 *yuan*. There are two routes: Route A (8am–10pm) from the airport to Sanyuan Bridge (near Hilton Hotel), Kunlun Hotel, then the subway stations of Dongzhimen, Dongsishitiao and Chaoyang, terminating at Beijing Railway Station, then returning to the airport (6.30am–7.30pm) via World Trade Center bridge and Jingxi bridge. Route B: (8.00am–10.00pm) from the airport to the China International Exhibition Centre, Anzhen Bridge, Beitaipingzhuang, the Friendship Hotel, Beijing TV, Shangri-La Hotel terminating at Xinxing Hotel then

(6.30am–6.45pm) returning via the Friendship Hotel, Beitaipingzhuang and Anzhen Bridge.

By Rail

Beijing can be reached by rail from a handful of international destinations including Moscow, Ulan Bataar, Hanoi and in theory, Pyongyang in North Korea. For train tickets to these places contact CITS at the Beijing International Hotel (tel. 65120509). Since July 1997, following China's resumption of sovereignty over Hong Kong, a new service runs from Kowloon to Beijing. The *Jingjiu* line has been specially built and allows express trains to make the more than 2,500-kilometre trip in around 36 hours. Besides this line, of course, once in China almost all railway routes lead to Beijing.

Train accommodation is available in soft sleeper, hard-sleeper, soft-seat and hard-seat carriage. Sleeper accommodation provides a berth in either a 4-bed compartment with door, or a 6-bed without a door. All soft sleeper carriages en route to Beijing have air conditioning, as do most hard sleepers.

Beijing's ticket offices are computerized, as are those in most provincial capitals. This makes ticket purchasing much quicker than it was a few years ago. Also, the Ministry of Railways has been a prime mover in the abolition of dual pricing: now everyone, foreigners and Chinese alike, pays the same. At least one long train journey by sleeper is highly recommended during your stay in China, as it provides foreigners with probably the only chance they will ever have of living among the locals. Food is available on the train and from platforms en route, and boilers for hot water exist in every third sleeper carriage.

Incoming trains terminate at either the aging Beijing Station, or the modern Beijing West Station, which opened at the beginning of 1996. Beijing Station serves routes with termini in the north, north-east and south-east, namely the provinces of Heilongjiang, Jilin, Liaoning, Inner Mongolia, most of Ningxia (Yinchuan), Hebei, most of Shanxi (Datong, Taiyuan), Tianjin, part of Henan (Luoyang), Shandong, Jiangsu, Anhui, Shanghai, Zhejiang, and parts of Fujian. Beijing West Station serves termini in Xinjiang, Gansu, Qinghai, Sichuan, Chongqing, Yunnan, Guizhou, Guangxi, Shaanxi, part of Shanxi, part of Hunan, Hubei, Jiangxi, part of Fujian and Guangdong. For any rail enquiries telephone 65633662.

Taxis outside both stations are a problem, and the traffic regulations concerning the setting down and picking up of fares only compounds the situation. Some drivers demand exorbitant fares from baggage-laden arrivals, whether they be foreign or Chinese. If you can walk a few hundred metres you will be treated more respectfully. Beijing Station is conveniently located on the subway system (*see* page 40). Outside

The central street in the Chinese Quarter of Peking, photographed by John Thomson, 1879

the West Railway Station to the east (right) there are a number of bus stops with regular departures.

Regarding the purchase of tickets for travel out of Beijing, bookings can be made up to 5 days ahead of departure, but things are changing, with the selling of tickets up to 20 days in advance being tested. Both stations have special ticket offices for foreigners. At Beijing Station it is located on the ground floor in a room off the soft sleeper waiting room in the south-east corner of the main hall. At Beijing West Station, the ticket office is on the east side of the first floor. Office hours for both are the same, 5.30am to 10.30pm, and closed for lunch from 12.00pm to 1.00pm, daily.

Facts for the Traveller

CUSTOMS

Four bottles of alcohol, three cartons of cigarettes, unlimited film and unlimited medicines for personal use may be brought into the country.

Antiques up to the value of Rmb 10,000 may be taken out of China as long as each article bears a red wax seal which indicates that it may be exported. You are well advised to keep the relevant sales receipts for possible inspection at customs on departure.

MONEY

■ CHINESE CURRENCY

The Chinese currency is called 'Renminbi' (meaning 'people's currency') and this is abbreviated to Rmb. It is denominated in *yuan*, but referred to as *kuai* in everyday speech. The *yuan* is divided into ten *jiao* (colloquially called *mao*). Each *jiao* is in turn divided into 10 *fen*. There are large notes for 100, 50, 10, 5, 2, and 1 *yuan*, small notes for 5, 2 and 1 *jiao*, even smaller notes for 5, 2, and 1 *fen* and coins for 1 *yuan*, 5 and 1 *jiao*, 5, 2 and 1 *fen*. Rmb can be reconverted when you leave China, for which you will need to show exchange vouchers. A Rmb exchange service is available at banks and money-changers in Hong Kong.

■ FOREIGN CURRENCY

There is no limit to the amount of foreign currency you can take into China. In the major cities, all freely negotiable currencies can be exchanged for Rmb at branches of the Bank of China, in hotels and the large stores. If you need more cash during your stay, one way to get it is to have money wired in your name to the local main branch of the Bank of China. The remittance will arrive in four to six working days. A few credit card companies allow their card-holders to draw a cash advance of up to US$100 from the Bank of China. American Express card-holders may cash personal cheques for up to US$1,000 on payment of a charge. Otherwise, personal cheques, cashier's cheques and international money orders require 45 days' clearance.

■ CHEQUES AND CREDIT CARDS
All the major European, American and Japanese traveller's cheques are accepted. International credit cards may be used in a limited number of Friendship Stores, hotels and banks, and you should check with your credit card company or bank before you rely on this form of payment for your purchases.

■ TIPPING
Attitudes toward tipping, once forbidden, now reflect the hybrid market-cum-centrally-planned economy. While washroom staff in hotels hover expectantly, waitresses in some restaurants will follow you out into the street to give you the few *yuan* change that you left as a tip.

■ TWO-TIER PRICING
Chinas State Pricing Commission implemented a regulation on 31st December 1997, outlawing all forms of dual pricing, the bane of China travel ever since the country opened its doors to tourism in the late 1970s. Foreigners can now buy travel tickets, accommodation and gate tickets at the same rates as local Chinese. However, the overcharging mentality, common throughout world tourism, lives on in the minds of many in the industry, especially in state-operated hotels where travellers are still often overcharged with management sanction.

LOCAL TIME
The whole of China operates within one time zone. Beijing time is eight hours ahead of GMT and 13 hours ahead of EST.

PACKING CHECKLIST
The electricity supply is 220 volts and the sockets are mostly two-pin. Take a selection of adaptors for your electrical appliances but you may not be able to use them at all outside the larger cities. It is also wise to bring along sufficient supplies of any prescription medicines you are taking, and an extra pair of prescription glasses, if only to save time and trouble, in case you lose or break them.

Station to Station

News was always passing, being digested and commented upon; and obvious-ly it kept coming promptly and fresh from its source. This was specially true of the messengers who delivered "chits," the local name for our notes that replaced Western telephone calls. When foreigners were in close relation, such messengers might be on the road constantly. Each chit was entered into a chit-book (I have mine yet); and its receipt was attested, if the master was away from home, by a rubber stamp or else by the ordinary house seal pressed into it. The latter was esteemed more formal and therefore in better taste. If the message was received personally the master might scrawl his initials, foreign fashion, beside his own name. In this way we could nearly always tell quite accurately what had happened to every document.

When only a word of acknowledgement was needed, it was often added in this place. "Would you perhaps like to come picnicking on the lakes next Thursday evening?"—"With pleasure."—"Do you care to see the Devil Dancers tomorrow in the Lama Temple?"—"Drop by my house first!"

These messengers came from other households; they were all known to each other; and they usually sat quietly in the kitchen, chatting and sipping tea while a return message was being devised within. Chits were often frisky; nearly everyone enjoyed the arrangement, not least the messenger himself. Sensing his role, he sat recounting the latest, or hearing our own news; and it never took long for anything of remark to spread over the town. A messenger with five notes to deliver knew by heart who had dined with whom the night before, how it had all gone, and so on, in the whole of his master's circle, by the time he returned home with his chit-book again. Further, since we were all said to have nicknames in these regions, the literal sentences must at times have been somewhat curious. One Westerner, who had a weakness for visiting hostesses just before meal hours, was known simply as the "Want-Food One." There were "Old Virgins" and Great or Small "Very-Verys" (older or younger married women) in numbers.

If that special rupture of the amenities commonly known as a "Peking quarrel" were bubbling, and they often did, the messenger's role would become more active. I do not know whether these altercations sprang from pride confronting pride, since on however small a scale each was sovereign in his own scrap of kingdom; or from exasperation when an adversary of one's own kind began to set bounds, to limit one's power. These were traits that life in courtyards engendered. Even the Chinese were aware of a common temptation to "bolt the door and set oneself up as Emperor."

Here I stumbled upon what must have been a wellspring of classical Chinese intrigue. Especially during love affairs, the messenger had a chance to make so much personal face, which he was not at all loath to seize, that drama sprang into being full-fledged. The household servants were informed: "As she wrote that chit, her amah [maid] told me that she appeared to . . ." etc. This would be relayed within; and although I sternly discouraged such gossip, from time to time the situation would explode if my servants felt that I ought to know something of importance to myself (as they considered it), and therefore to all of us—before I penned my reply. After all they were my small army, and in the world ambush was inevitable. One must be prepared.

Or perhaps some genial party was going forward, perhaps arrangements were being made in fine weather for an excursion to a distant temple; and the preparations—food, crockery, and transportation—were being divided. A message would come, and after domestic consultation I would select a sheet of paper. Finally I would put my envelope into the chit-book, adding on my line the words "Reply herewith." Meanwhile the messenger had kept his own liaison unbroken, sitting comfortably in the kitchen. The oral system worked quite as well, on his level, to keep him in touch with such affairs, as did for us our own writing. Connection was therefore double, and from the Chinese point of view now secure.

George N Kates, The Years that Were Fat

COMMUNICATIONS
■ TELECOMMUNICATIONS

Beijing's telephone system has improved markedly since city numbers went 8-digit in 1996. Local, long distance and international calls are all loud and clear, and can be made from post offices, payphones, private roadside kiosks and of course, hotels. The latter two alternatives slap on service charges between 15–30 per cent. Domestic calls are half price after 9pm, but international calls are the same price 24 hours-a-day. Phone cards can be bought in 10, 20, 50, 100 and 200 *yuan* denominations from large post offices and hotel front desks. Mobile phones can be hired on a daily basis for 350 *yuan*, or 310 *yuan* per day for weekly rental, with a 4,000 *yuan* deposit from Phone Rent, (tel. 84229335).

Your hotel operator is probably the best source of up-to-date numbers, but in even the best hotels, may require some urging to chase after that number that has changed twice! Or you could try dialling information on 114 (local calls), or 116 (long distance). *The China Phone Book,* published in Hong Kong, and available in many hotels in China, is the best source for business telephone numbers. The red-covered China Telephone Directory, bilingual edition, published annually by the Ministry of Posts is a good, cheaper alternative for 150 *yuan* and available at most large post offices.

USEFUL TELEPHONE NUMBERS

China international dialling code (from abroad)	86
Beijing international dialling code (from abroad)	8610
Fire	119
Police	110
Beijing Emergency Centre (medical)	120
Beijing directory inquiry	114
International operator	115
Domestic long distance operator	113
Domestic long distance inquiry	116
Time (in Chinese)	117
Weather (in Chinese and English)	121
Beijing suburban operator	118
Tourist Hotline (24 hours)	65130828

Most major hotels offer International Direct Dialling (IDD) to dozens of countries, and domestic long-distance calls (even to Lhasa). For AT&T USA Direct, call 10811.

There is a 24-hour telecommunications office at Xidan, for telephone calls and faxes. Other Post and Telecommunications offices are given in Useful Addresses on page 162.

Nearly every hotel in Beijing has a fax machine and offers the service for a three-minute minimum charge. After adding the service charge, which can range from 10 to as much as 30 per cent, the minimum cost for sending a fax to Hong Kong is around 40 *yuan* and overseas around 80 *yuan*. Most hotels also charge a small fee for receiving faxes, in addition to a 'paper charge'.

Several international courier services now operate out of Beijing and the other major Chinese cities. Their addresses and those of other Post and Telecommunications offices are given in Useful Addresses on page 162.

■ ENGLISH-LANGUAGE MEDIA
China Daily (http://www.Chinadaily.net), launched in June 1981, has grown to 12 pages on weekdays and is a good insight into reforms-promoting journalism, with noteworthy spice in the form of its pun headlines courtesy of a team of foreign copy editors. Provided gratis to guests in star-rated hotel rooms, it can also be picked up from front desks, as can *Beijing Weekend*, the city's what's on published on Fridays. *Business Weekly*, published on Sundays, is of interest to the business-minded. Entertainment tabloids such as *Metro* and *City Edition*, are available free from bars, cafes and airline offices. Fighting for slices of the lucrative advertising market, they focus on the city's arts scene. Also worth looking out for is *Beijing This Month*, a travel magazine available at hotel front desks, and often a good source of ideas for unusual side trips. In cyberspace, visit http://www.cbw.com/icic to see the *China Business World—International Community in China* web page, a good source of pre-arrival information, business, travel and regularly-updated cultural magazine features. Hotel bookstores carry *Time*, *Newsweek* and Hong Kong papers. Satellite TV, both CNN and Star, are available in 4-star hotels and upward, while domestic TV puts out News in English on CCTV 2 at 11–11.15pm nightly. Beijing TV also broadcasts news in English at 11.45pm. On the radio, China Radio International (FM 92 MHz) has a current affairs-cum-news magazine broadcast in English every morning from 7–8am, followed by Easy Listening FM for a couple of hours at noon with an expat DJ.

TRAVEL AGENCIES
Long-established and state-owned China International Travel Service (CITS) and China Travel Service offer reliable but pricey travel services ranging from rail ticket purchasing to tours elsewhere in China. For a more personal and reasonable service, try a smaller agency such as Beijing Blue Sky or Beijing Tradewinds (*see* page 166).

Delivering honeycomb coal briquettes, still used for cooking by many people in Beijing

With little to do after their retirement men often gather for a game of dominos

HUTONGS

Beijing's *hutongs*—back alleys—are where Chinese life can be seen at its most typical and traditional.

Mostly doomed to be torn down and redeveloped for modern housing blocks, these fascinating little streets form a miniature grid of walled courtyards and passage ways, in between the sweeping boulevards which are the main traffic arteries. Often blessed with picturesque names—Knitting Yarn Hutong, Sea Transport Granary Hutong, Performing Music Hutong, Little Trumpet Hutong and Big Trumpet Hutong–the *hutong*s are essentially residential areas where the informality of ordinary life can be witnessed. Pot plants nod at the visitor passing by, and a canary in a cage mocks the rare cat which slinks over an old, grey-plastered wall. Old men dawdle with their long-stemmed pipes, and grandma takes the well-padded baby out for a stroll.

There is much debate about the origin of the word *hutong*. The most convincing argument is that *hutong* derives from a Mongol word, *hotlog*, that means 'water well' and suggests a small geographical area of the city that may have been served by a single well. It is likely that during the Yuan dynasty, when the Mongols established their capital Dadu in an area that generally coincides with the limits of the later Ming and Qing capitals, they dug many wells. However as most of the well water was brackish, and eventually proved insufficient for the growing city's needs, canals were dug to supply the city with water from several sources in the western suburbs and link up the Grand Canal to the urban waterway system. In this way the imperial granaries could be filled directly from the barges that transported tribute rice from southern China, whereas transhipment had previously been necessary. The names of some Beijing *hutong*s have changed several times, and underwent a major anti-feudal whitewashing during the Cultural Revolution. One choice example from that period can be rendered in English as 'Red-to-the-end-of-the Hutong'.

Sometimes a commune donkey-car loaded with vegetables seeks passage along the narrow lanes, and teenagers loaf around joking. The walls are daubed with slogans such as 'Observe Hygiene' and 'Look After Soldiers' Families Well' but the air of perpetual afternoon overpowers propaganda.

The Beijing Tourist Bureau has set up a **24-hour tourist hotline**, with operators who speak English, Japanese and Chinese. Their telephone number is 65130828.

CLIMATE AND CLOTHING

Beijing has four clearly defined seasons. From November to March, winter is usually dry and clear but winds from the northwest can bring temperatures down to –15.5°C (–4°F). In November and the first half of December, the weather is crisp and cool and the cerulean blue of the dawn sky intensifies to the point where it appears like a vast turquoise lens. Locals describe the early winter sky as 'tall' or 'high' or 'deep'. The best winter clothing is layers of warm garments including thermal underwear, sweaters and coats, in addition to warm boots and fur hats with earflaps. Heating in the hotels can be very fierce, while heating in some public buildings can be inadequate or nonexistent. China follows a system of 'command heating'. North of the Yangzi River the heat in many public buildings and residences is turned on 15 November and turned off 15 March, regardless of the temperature. And in many local apartment buildings, the heat goes on for a few hours in the morning and is turned off during the day to conserve fuel. The Chinese produce good winter clothing such as thick cotton underwear, padded jackets and furs, all at reasonable prices.

Spring usually lasts from mid-March to mid-May and is a good time for a visit, with trees and flowers coming into bloom and the occasional shower to wash the city. Clothing should include a warm coat and sweaters as well as some light-weight clothes, and possibly a raincoat.

Late spring is the season for Beijing's notorious dust storms. They don't blow in every year, but when they do you will certainly know it! The atmosphere is filled with a near-pudding of yellow to orange dust from the Gobi Desert that finds its way into everything from sealed closets to your closed mouth. No amount of tree planting seems to be able to reduce the amount or density of the dust. It is also dusty in Beijing whenever it is dry.

Beijing summers are very hot and humid. Temperatures reach 40°C (104°F) and rainfall can be heavy. Light cotton clothing is recommended. Visitors will often be in places without air-conditioning.

Autumn is the best season in the capital. From September to mid-October it is warm, sunny and dry. There is a wealth of colour in the parks, and fruit and flowers in the markets. Dress as you would for autumn in southern Europe or northern California.

Beijing has a large diplomatic community of more than 17,000 including dependents, some 50,000 foreign business people and 20,000 overseas students, who have combined to influence the Chinese and their dress. Informality is ubiquitous, and only mosque visitors need to worry about what they wear. Meanwhile, Beijing has a good number of classy, swanky and chic dressers, especially in the central business districts of the China World Trade Center, Jianguomenwai and Lufthansa Center.

■ AVERAGE TEMPERATURES IN BEJING

		°C	°F		°C	°F		°C	°F
Average		−4.4	24.1		18.9	66.0		19.1	66.4
High	JAN	1.7	35.1	MAY	25.3	77.5	SEP	25.5	77.9
Low		−9.7	14.5		11.9	53.4		12.2	53.8
Average		−2.1	28.2		23.9	74.5		12.2	53.9
High	FEB	3.8	38.8	JUN	29.6	85.3	OCT	18.7	65.7
Low		−7.2	19.0		17.7	63.9		6.8	44.2
Average		4.7	40.5		25.6	78.1		4.3	39.7
High	MAR	11.0	51.8	JUL	30.3	86.5	NOV	10.0	50.0
Low		−0.9	30.4		21.5	70.7		−0.2	31.6
Average		13.0	55.4		24.0	75.2		−2.5	27.5
High	APR	19.4	66.9	AUG	28.9	84.0	DEC	3.0	37.4
Low		6.5	43.7		19.9	67.8		−7.0	19.4

HEALTH

Foreigners wanting to stay in China to work or study must go to the local quarantine station for health examinations and an AIDS test before their residence permits are issued by the Public Security Bureau.

Consult a physician or a government health authority (in the USA, the US State Department) for their recommendations on vaccinations for China. In recent years, the US Consulate in Hong Kong has suggested inoculations against hepatitis A and B, Japanese encephalitis (not available in the USA), tetanus, polio, cholera and malaria. However, this terrifying list should be considered alongside the specifics of your itinerary. For a fall trip including visits to Beijing, Xi'an, Shanghai, Suzhou and Guilin, for example, the possibility of contracting any of these diseases is minuscule. It is only when travelling to southwest or northwest China in the summer or to very out of the way areas that such a regimen should be considered. Long-term residents in Beijing often take the series of inoculations against encephalitis, a mosquito-borne disease.

(Following pages) Snow covers the Forbidden City

The most common ailments contracted by tourists in China are upper respiratory infections—in other words, chest colds. Some physicians prescribe a quarter-dose of an antibiotic like tetracycline as a mild preventative. Beijing is extremely dry and cold in the winter, and it is necessary to dress properly and drink lots of fluids all the time. Beijing residents tend to dress much more warmly than seems necessary during the transitional seasons of fall and spring, and are often amazed to see foreigners wearing short sleeves and short pants when they are still wearing long underwear. Chinese people seem to believe that overdressing is the key to staying healthy during these seasons.

Never drink unboiled water in Beijing. Hotel rooms are normally supplied with thermos flasks of boiled water—both hot and cold—which are replenished daily, although many hotels now have internal water-treatment facilities that render the tap water potable. Because Chinese standards of sanitation lag behind those of the West—you will note, for instance, widespread spitting—it makes good sense to wash your hands carefully before eating anything. Peel all fruit and avoid raw leafy vegetables unless you are in an upmarket restaurant.

Beijing has a number of hospitals for foreigners, emergency clinics, and international medical evacuation offices. (See the listings in Useful Addresses, page 162.) The telephone numbers for the **Beijing Emergency Centre** are 120 and 66014433. If you are in a hotel, tell the front desk that you need an ambulance. Several hospitals have emergency services for foreigners.

Peking Union Medical College Hospital (PUMC) *Xie He Yi Yuan* (comprehensive hospital with a large clinic for foreigners) Dongdan Beidajie Tel. 65127733

Sino-Japanese Friendship Hospital *Zhong Ri You Hao Yi Yuan* Hepingli Beijie Tel. 64221122

Sino-German Policlinic *Zhong De Zhen Suo* (privately run 24-hour ambulance service; performs minor surgery) Basement, Landmark Tower, 8 Dong Sanhuanlu Tel. 65011983, 65016688 extn. 20903

Beijing Friendship Hospital Yong'an Lu, Tianqiao Tel. 63014411

Clutching at Straws

High on the Venerable Schoolmaster Gao's list of gripes was the gall of the man who had edited A General Textbook of Chinese History *in not taking the classroom teacher into account when putting this text together. Though some of it did tally with Liaofan's Shorter History, there were large chunks that didn't, so that it was impossible to weave the two books together into any kind of coherent lecture. The Venerable Schoolmaster Gao glanced at a slip of paper that had been left in the textbook, and his smouldering resentment against the teacher who had quit halfway through the course was fanned into a full blaze, for the note read: Begin at Chapter Eight—The Rise and Fall of the Eastern Jin Dyansty [317–420]. If that clod hadn't already finished lecturing on the Three Kingdoms Period [220–65], Gao himself wouldn't have had nearly so much difficulty preparing. He knew the Three Kingdoms Period up one side and down the other: The Triple Oath of the Peach Garden, Kong Ming Borrows Arrows, Zhou Yü Thrice Angered, Huang Zhong Beheads Xia Houyuan at Dingjun Mountain, and any number of other such incidents.* [1]

And if it had only been some later period—let's say the Tang Dynasty [618–907]—well, then you had material like Qin Qiong Sells His Horse. [2] *Yes, he could have told stories like that in a pretty entertaining way, too. But no! It couldn't be the Three Kingdoms or the Tang, it had to be that damned Eastern Jin right in between! Once more, Gao sighed in exasperation; and once more too, he made a dive for* Liaofan's Shorter History.

[1] *All of these episodes are contained in the popular historical novel* Romance of the Three Kingdoms. *In a Western setting, a character like Gao might consider familiarity with Dickens'* Tale of Two Cities *and Hugo's* Ninety-three *sufficient qualification for offering a course on the French Revolution.*

[2] *Qin Qiong was a military hero who helped the first Tang emperor found the new dynasty. Again, Gao's knowledge is derived from popular fiction.*

Lu Xun, The Venerable Schoolmaster Gao,
translated by William A Lyell

For more on *Lu Xun* see Lu Xun Museum (p.149) and Recommended Reading (p.154)

It is impossible to generalize about the quality of the Chinese medical services, but Beijing doctors tend to be thorough and reliable, particularly in geriatric medicine; just think of all the octogenarians they have to keep on their feet! Most long-term foreign residents, however, prefer to go abroad for major medical and dental treatment.

A handful of foreign embassies provide limited medical service for their own nationals, but as a rule embassy medical staff are not permitted to practise in Chinese hospitals, and thus they should be brought into emergencies on a consulting basis only.

GETTING AROUND

Just 15 years ago Beijing's wide boulevards were empty save for buses—both petrol driven and electric trolley—and a few lace-curtained Soviet cars. Now the city is grid locked with vehicles of every conceivable shape and make, and in one of the world's most populous cities that spells environmental trouble. Town planners gasped in awe at the pace Beijing built its ring roads (it now has four, with a fifth planned), but only in heavy traffic did they realize what chaos broke out as vehicles met when they joined and left the orbitals: the same place is used causing queues to build up around every slip road. If this doesn't put you off, Beijing Jeeps and VW Santanas can be hired from Capital Auto Leasing (tel. 64915258) or CVIK Car Rental (tel. 65123481) on production of a passport and Chinese driving licence.

Most tour groups will travel by coach. Only the lucky will make a trip on the subway, the best way to beat the jams in the city centre. Tickets are two *yuan* for any trip, with trains running every 5 minutes or so from 5am–11pm. Platforms are simply bi-directional and station names are posted in both character form and *pinyin* on signposts affixed to pillars facing the tracks. Maps on the tunnel wall indicate the name of the next station down the line. Once aboard, announcements are made via a bilingual recording. Overall, the Beijing subway is one of the easiest in the world to use, but it only consists of a loop and a leg with one interchange between, and just 30 stations. A new line, extending from Xidan via Wangfujing and Jianguomen to the China World Trade Center, will be completed by 2000.

There are basically three kinds of taxi available. Microvans (*miandis*) mainly yellow-coloured, are the cheapest at ten *yuan* flagfall, which is good for the first ten kilometres, thereafter 1.5 *yuan* per kilometre is charged. Most *miandis* are decrepit. Next up are Charades, the red or yellow economy cars. Flagfall is 10.4 *yuan*, which is good for the first four kilometres, thereafter 1.6 *yuan* per kilometre is charged. Imported cars, mainly Toyota Cedrics and VW Santanas, are the most expensive rides at flagfalls of 12 *yuan* and rates of 1.8–2 *yuan* per kilometre. In 1996, as waiting-in-jam time increased, taxis installed new meters with timers. Now you pay for time spent crawling along or standing still.

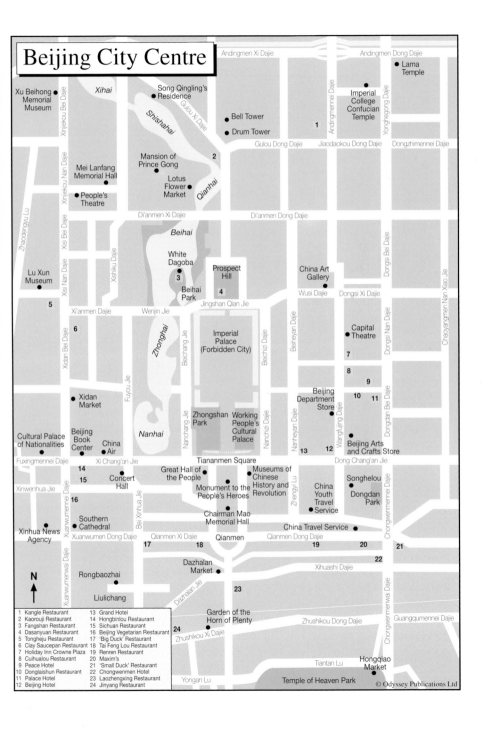

Beijing City Centre

Andingmen Xi Dajie   Andingmen Dong Dajie

Lama Temple

Xu Beihong Memorial Museum

Xihai

Song Qingling's Residence

Imperial College Confucian Temple

Bell Tower

Drum Tower

1

Shishahai

Gulou Dong Dajie   Jiaodaokou Dong Dajie   Dongzhimennei Dajie

Mansion of Prince Gong

2

Mei Lanfang Memorial Hall

Lotus Flower Market

Qianhai

People's Theatre

Di'anmen Xi Dajie   Di'anmen Dong Dajie

Beihai

White Dagoba

3

Prospect Hill

China Art Gallery

Lu Xun Museum

Beihai Park

4

Wusi Dajie   Dongsi Xi Dajie

5

Xi'anmen Dajie   Wenjin Jie   Jingshan Qian Jie

6

Zhonghai

Imperial Palace (Forbidden City)

Capital Theatre

7

8

9

Xidan Market

Beijing Book Center

China Air

Nanhai

Zhongshan Park

Working People's Cultural Palace

Beijing Department Store

10   11

Cultural Palace of Nationalities

13   12

Beijing Arts and Crafts Store

Fuxingmennei Dajie   Xi Chang'an Jie   Tiananmen Square   Dong Chang'an Jie

14

Concert Hall

15

Great Hall of the People

Museums of Chinese History and Revolution

Songhelou

Xinwenhua Jie

16

Monument to the People's Heroes

China Youth Travel Service

Dongdan Park

Southern Cathedral

Chairman Mao Memorial Hall

Xinhua News Agency

Xuanwumen Dong Dajie   Qianmen Xi Dajie   Qianmen   Qianmen Dong Dajie

China Travel Service

17   18   19   20   21

22

Rongbaozhai

Dazhalan Market

Xihuashi Dajie

Liulichang

23

Garden of the Horn of Plenty

Zhushikou Dong Dajie   Guangqumennei Dajie

24

Zhushikou Xi Dajie

Tiantan Lu

Hongqiao Market

Yongan Lu   Temple of Heaven Park

N

1 Kangle Restaurant	13 Grand Hotel
2 Kaorouji Restaurant	14 Hongbinlou Restaurant
3 Fangshan Restaurant	15 Sichuan Restaurant
4 Dasanyuan Restaurant	16 Beijing Vegetarian Restaurant
5 Tongheju Restaurant	17 'Big Duck' Restaurant
6 Clay Saucepan Restaurant	18 Tai Feng Lou Restaurant
7 Holiday Inn Crowne Plaza	19 Renren Restaurant
8 Cuihualou Restaurant	20 Maxim's
9 Peace Hotel	21 'Small Duck' Restaurant
10 Donglaishun Restaurant	22 Chongwenmen Hotel
11 Palace Hotel	23 Laozhengxing Restaurant
12 Beijing Hotel	24 Jinyang Restaurant

© Odyssey Publications Ltd

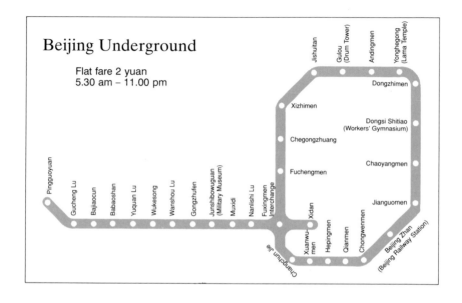

Beijing Underground

Flat fare 2 yuan
5.30 am – 11.00 pm

Jishuitan
Gulou (Drum Tower)
Andingmen
Yonghegong (Lama Temple)
Dongzhimen
Xizhimen
Dongsi Shitiao (Workers' Gymnasium)
Chegongzhuang
Chaoyangmen
Fuchengmen
Jianguomen
Pingguoyuan
Gucheng Lu
Bajiaocun
Babaoshan
Yuquan Lu
Wukesong
Wanshou Lu
Gongzhufen
Junshibowuguan (Military Museum)
Muxidi
Nanlishi Lu
Fuxingmen Interchange
Xidan
Xuanwu-men
Hepingmen
Qianmen
Chongwenmen
Beijing Zhan (Beijing Railway Station)
Changchun Jie

Buses, both single and double deckers, trolleybuses and minibuses are difficult to use because of gross overcrowding, troublesome ticket purchasing and uncertainty of where one should alight. But if you have time to get lost it is worth experiencing the push and shove. (Warning: pickpocketing is rampant on crowded buses so put valuables in a wallet around your neck and inside your clothing!) If the bus stop notice has 'Ticket Vendor' posted, then you should enter the bus via the middle door only and have prepared the correct fare of 5 *mao* or 1 *yuan* to drop in the box. No change is given. Some other buses have conductors to take fares and give change. City maps, published annually, are the best source of information on bus and trolley-bus routes. They can be bought for about 3 *yuan* from roadside newsstands.

Minibuses, charging much higher fares than the public buses since they offer passengers more chance of a seat and choice of places to alight, follow conventional bus routes and have the number of the route they follow posted in their windscreens. Fares are between one and five *yuan*.

The bicycle remains the average Beijinger's main transport: for the environment's sake, the later the masses swap their bike lock keys for ignition keys, the better. Bikes can be hired on an hourly, half-daily or daily basis from many hotels geared to taking foreign tourists. Deposits are usually required.

RELIGION AND WORSHIP

Although religious practice in China has been restricted or discouraged in the past, visitors to Beijing can worship in a wide variety of churches and temples, many of which are of great architectural and historical interest.

Catholicism in Beijing dates back to the 17th century, when the Jesuits Matteo Ricci, Adam Schall and Ferdinand Verbiest brought the word of God and the rationality of Western science and astronomy to the Ming and Qing imperial courts. Masses are held daily at 6.30am and several times on Sunday. There are four major Catholic churches: the **Nantang**, or Southern Cathedral, standing on the site where Ricci once lived (Xuanwumen, tel. 66056470); the **Beitang**, or Northern Cathedral (Xisi, tel. 66015214); the **Dongtang**, St Joseph's (Baimiancao, Wangfujing); and the **Nangangzi** Mass Hall (Yongsheng Xiang, Xingfu Jie, Chaoyang District). The Jesuit Cemetery, including the tomb of Matteo Ricci, is now in the grounds of the Beijing Communist Party School on Chegongzhuang. Visiting arrangements must be made in advance via the sisters at Nantang.

Protestantism was established in China somewhat later than Catholicism by British and American missionaries. Services are conducted at the **Chinese Council** (181 Dongdan Beijie), originally occupied by the YMCA and the Chinese Bible Society; **Chongwenmen Church** (Xiaoshun Hutong, Chongwenmen, tel. 65242193); **Gangwashi Church** (57 Nanxisi Jie, tel. 66034027); **Zhushikou Church** (Qianmen Dajie, tel. 63016678); and **Haidian Church** (Haidian, tel. 62551392).

Islam came to China over 1,000 years ago by sea and via the Silk Road. In Beijing there are some 200,000 Moslems or *Hui* (as they are known in China), and 50 mosques for them to worship in. The largest are the **Niu Jie** (Ox Street) **Mosque** (tel. 63032564) in the southern part of the city (*see* page 103), formerly a Moslem quarter, and the **Dongsi Mosque** (tel. 65257824), which dates back to the Mongol or Yuan Dynasty.

Taoism was practised in many monasteries in the city, the majority of which have been closed since 1949. The largest remaining city monastery, the **White Clouds Taoist Monastery**, the Baiyunguan (Binhe Jie, Guang'anmenwai, tel. 63467179 and 63463887), also houses the China Taoist Association (*see* page 103 for details).

Buddhism came to China around the time of Christ and has had a profound influence on Chinese thought, art, architecture and cuisine. Buddhist temples in the urban and suburban areas are described in the Sights section of this book. Listed here are three places of active worship: **Guangjisi** (Fuchengmennei Dajie, tel. 66160907); **Fayuansi** (Fayuansi Qianjie, tel. 63034171); and the **Yonghegong** or Lama Temple (72 Yonghegong Jie, tel. 64049027).

Noble House

Pao's home and mine were in the same street in Peking, a half-street that ambled leisurely along the bank of a canal in the Forbidden City: on the one side blank, secret walls and roofed gateways flanked by curled and grinning carved stone lions; on the other side the willows and the water. Pao's house was very important, much the richest and most noble in our street. Great gates opened upon a vista through courtyard after courtyard, spacious, imposing. Pillared pavilions supported wide roofs that swept in stately curves against the sky. Gold leaf and lacquer and deep-cut carving made splendid the doors and pillars. My home at the far end of the short street was quite modest by comparison—a single courtyard surrounded by small, unpretentious rooms.

This great house of Pao's family was in a continual stir of magnificent activity, fascinating to all the children in our street. We would gather about the gateway, watching, listening. It was a pageant for our benefit and we missed none of it. In the morning we came running to see the departure of Pao's father for the yamen, where the government offices were. The mounted body-guard would be drawn up at the gates, waiting. The lord of the house would issue forth, take his place in his carriage, and drive away, with the solemn clatter of many hoofs accompanying him.

Later in the forenoon came merchants. It might be a slender, smart young clerk, carrying some small and valuable parcel. It might be the proprietor of a shop himself, plump and prosperous, idly wafting his fan, followed by apprentices loaded with bundles and boxes. For the women of this household preferred not to soil their satin shoes, running about the streets. They lived for the most part secluded within their own inner courtyards, and when they wished to purchase anything—whether silks, or thin porcelain bowls and cups, or ear-rings of silver-gilt set with jade or coral—a selection was brought for their choice.

At noon in the winter we watched the "doing of good works". Files of the poor and beggars would come on the hour as though summoned. They would stand at the gates with their cracked bowls and pots, waiting for the gift of

The dramatic costumes and make-up of Beijing Opera

food each day distributed. The stewards of the household then came out, carrying huge crocks of jow, the soft-cooked rice, steaming in the frosty air. They would ladle out the jow into the bowls held out to them by gaunt and dirty hands, and the beggars would warm their hands on the bowls as they sucked up the scalding hot rice.

Most dazzling of all the glories of Pao's house, to the watching children, were feast nights, when guests came riding to the gates in rickshaws and four-wheeled open carriages, all tinkling with bells on the harness, with footmen attending before and behind. We edged into the outer courtyards, as close as we might come to the centre of festivity in the high court beyond. Here we could see and hear and even smell of things sumptuous, as gorgeously robed ladies passed us almost close enough to touch, smelling of flowers and sandalwood and musk; and hurrying servants crossed and recrossed the courtyard bearing great bowls and platters that left on the air a trail of exquisite savour to make the mouth water.

Creeping still closer we would watch, enchanted, the actors brought to entertain the company, the best in Peking (and that meant the best in China!). Emperors and heros of long-ago dynasties came to life in their song and pantomine, to the brazen music of gongs and cymbals, the intricate beat of drums, the shrill quaver of stringed instruments. We knew by heart each play and legend; we hailed by name the characters as they appeared, recognizing Tsao-Tsao by his treacherous, skull-white face and loyal Kung by his green robe and scarlet complexion, and the clowns with a tiny white patch over the bridge of the nose. Before a word was spoken we knew what scene was to be played. We were endlessly fascinated by the gold-encrusted robes, the helmets plumbed with yard-long pheasant feathers. And even to us, children though we were, there was significance and beauty in the stylized acting. There was excitement and meaning in the dance combat with spears and swords whirling, gowns and pheasant feathers whirling, drums and cymbals clashing, lights glancing gold and violet and crimson over the rich embroidered robes. . . .

Han Suyin, Destination Chungking

ENTERTAINMENT

Just five or six years ago, if you wanted a cup of coffee you had to go to a coffee shop in a luxury hotel; if you craved a cold beer you had to retreat to a hotel bar, and for music all that was available was Richard Clayderman in lobbies. Even close dancing among Chinese themselves was taboo, and largely confined to dawn encounters in parks where safety was certain with the world looking on. Things are totally different now, and changing fast.

■ HOTEL LOBBIES AND BARS

The ground floor of the Beijing Hotel used to be the social hub for foreigners in the city, a place where residents and long stay travellers would tentatively entertain their Chinese colleagues, acquaintances and lovers while tourists wrote postcards home and African and Arab students impressed timid waitresses with their flair for languages. But those days of waiting for a warm beer, cup of coffee without a saucer and a stale, dry sponge cake have long since gone.

The bustling **Jianguo Hotel** lobby has a most interesting atmosphere. It is a good place to relax, people watch and listen to piano or chamber music. For more intimate surroundings, the hotel's **Charlie's Bar** is a favourite. They have weekly bar-food specials of fish 'n' chips (served in *China Daily*) and a curry night.

For a drink with a view, try the appropriately-named **Palace View Bar** (open June to October, 7–10pm) on the top floor of the Grand Hotel. It is the closest luxury hotel to the Forbidden City, and a well-timed aperatif here comes with a bonus of the sun setting over the golden roofs of the palace.

Hotels with pubs attached worth a look-in include the **Paulaner Brauhaus** in the Kempinski where home-brewed German beer, dark and light, is served in a Bavarian atmosphere with sausages and sauerkraut to boot. For a British style pint, there is the **Red Lion** atop the China World Tower, or the very popular **Pig and Whistle** in the Holiday Inn Lido.

Many hotels bars have live music, among them **Piccadilly** at the Palace Hotel, the **Club Bar** at the China World and the **Gallery Bar** at the Holiday Inn Lido. Other favourite and well-established expat haunts include the **Mexican Wave**, Dongdaqiao Lu, south of Guanghua Lu crossroads, and **Frank's Place** opposite the Worker's Stadium east gate, Gongren Tiyuguan Donglu.

■ CAFE SOCIETY

Johnny's Coffee, across the traffic-jammed north Third Ring Road from the China International Exhibition Centre, is the place for a good flavoursome brew, especially for those who have drunk all the tea in China they possibly can. Out on the old airport road and opposite the Holiday Inn Lido main drive-in is the **Libresso Bistro**,

open 24 hours, serving good coffee and wholesome food with a splattering of local abstract art on its walls. Hard to find but worth the hutong searching is **Cafe Cafe** at Dongdaqiao Xiejie in Sanlitun; if missed there are many other alternatives in the vicinity. **Hard Rock Cafe** has come to Beijing: look for the chevvy, red of course, halfway up the building alongside the Great Wall Sheraton on the east Third Ring Road. Fascinating tastes of Western pop culture await those treating Chinese guests, as the walls are covered with pop memorabilia under a dome mural which juxtaposes Mao with the Fab-Gang of Four, the Beatles.

■ TEA CULTURE
Sanwei (tel. 66013204), nestled above the bookstore of the same name and just across Chang'an Avenue from the Minzu Hotel serves tea all day in a timeless, studio setting. Jazz shows and classical Chinese music recitals are held some evenings. Meanwhile, down in the Qianmen area south of Tiananmen on the third floor of 3, Qianmenxi Dajie there is the **Lao She Teahouse** (tel. 63017529), named after the author of *Rickshaw Boy*. Tea and snacks are served to accompaniments of storytelling, cross talking, conjuring, magic and ballad singing. Book ahead for evening shows between 7.30–9.00pm. For similar folk acts to tea and Beijing roast duck there is the **Tianqiao Happy Teahouse** (tel. 63040617) at Al, Beiweilu in the Xuanwu District. For a modern teahouse-pub experience that appeals to younger Chinese and expats, try the **Teahouse** at Sanlitun Nanshilou (tel. 64165676), just off the main bar strip.

■ PUBS & DISCOS—(*see* Beijing Nightlife on page 51)

■ PERFORMING ARTS
Bai tian kan miao, wan shang shui jiao, look at temples during the day and sleep in the evenings, used to sum up Beijing's cultural entertainment scene in the 1980s, but now a mixture of local and imported diversions are on offer in relative abundance every night of the week. Check the Friday editions of both *China Daily* and *Beijing Weekend* for listings, and the fortnightly *City Edition* for its what's on pages. And remember, the Chinese have been starved of music, dance, theatre and movies for so long that a veritable culture-vulture society hovers to swoop down on tickets when they go on sale. So be sure to scan the press for the shows and book fast. If you find a box office is sold out, but still really want a ticket, scalpers usually loiter outside venues touting tickets at small premiums.

■ ACROBATICS AND PUPPETRY
The wonderful talents of Chinese acrobats should not be missed during any stay in China. If it's breakable, valuable, heavy or dangerous then it gets tossed by an acrobat somewhere in Beijing. Most provinces have their own troupes. Sichuan, noted for its

China's female rock vocalist Wei Hua

short people who lend themselves well to acrobatics, have a troupe performing daily, 7–8.40pm at the **Chaoyang Theater** (tel. 65072421), at 36, Dongsanhuan Beilu. Admission is 30 *yuan*. **China Puppet Theater** (tel. 64243698) at Anhuaxili, Chaoyang District is a popular venue for shows by the Chinese Acrobatic Troupe, 6.30–8.30pm daily. Admission is 30 *yuan*. During the day at the same venue, 10–11.30am and 2–3.30pm, the theatre puts on shadow puppet shows. Admission is 20 *yuan*, half price for children.

■ DANCE, MUSIC, FILM

A mixed bag of Western contemporary, ballet, Chinese revolutionary and ethnic folk dance can be found in Beijing. The premier **Central Ballet of China** (tel. 63538505) performs both Chinese ballets and foreign ones: in recent years there has been a nostalgic revival of interest in *The Red Detachment of Women* and *The White Haired Girl*, while *Swan Lake* and *Giselle* always pull in the romantics. The troupe may perform at any of several venues including the **Poly Plaza** (tel. 65001188 ext. 5682) at Dongsishitiao subway station. For Chinese folk dances look out for the **Oriental Song and Dance Ensemble** (tel. 64674431) playing at various venues. Classical music's main venue is **Beijing Concert Hall** (tel. 66055812) at 1, Beixinhuajie. Chinese and touring foreign orchestras give concerts here.

Chinese movies have taken the world by storm with productions including Chen Kaige's *The Big Parade* and *Farewell My Concubine*, and a string of Zhang Yimou-produced and Gong Li-starred epics such as *Red Sorghum*, *Judou* and *Raise the Red Lantern*. Over the last few years all these and many more domestic gems have been screened with English subtitles on Friday evenings at **Cherry Lane** (tel. 65224046) based in the Sino-Japanese Youth Exchange Centre, 40 Liangmaqiao Lu, Chaoyang District. Also, tune into CCTV 6 on your TV to find a satellite-cable movie channel screening six Chinese movies and two foreign ones every day.

■ BEIJING OPERA

In the early Nineties it seemed that Beijing opera—a unique blend of acting, singing, dancing, music and acrobatics—was on its deathbed. Movies and video rentals were largely to blame for its demise, and then came along karoke with what seemed like the final, fatal blow. Only a miracle could save the unique artform from being demoted to a mere tourist attraction. The miracle did come in the form of the genre's megastars: 1994 was the centenary of the birth of Beijing opera's two most famous actors, Mei Lanfang and Zhou Xinfang. Thanks to their everlasting, shining stardom, a revival swept through Beijing opera's hometown. Further help came when the capital's premiere venue, the **Zhengyici Theater**, closed for years and facing a fleet of bulldozers, was saved by a multi-millionaire opera fan, Wang Yuming. Originally built as a temple in 1620 during the reign of Wanli, it became a theatre in 1713. Later, the great Mei acted countless female *dan* roles on its stage. Now there are performances nightly, starting at 7.30pm at 220, Xiheyan Dajie, Xuanwu District. (tel. 63189454 for details). Admission to an opera is 150 *yuan*, or 50 *yuan* for genuine students, which includes tea and snacks. For 260 *yuan*, a Beijing roast duck feast is thrown in. But the real banquet is on stage. The Lao She Teahouse and Tianqiao Happy Teahouse both put on shorter opera excerpts (*see* page 47), **Liyuan Theater** within the Qianmen Hotel (tel. 63016688, ext. 8986) has a pick of famous opera scenes, but for a spit and sawdust experience among mainly local opera buffs try the **City Worker's Club** (tel. 63535390) at 7 Hufanglu, Xuanwumen for just opera with no tea or soft seats and only five *yuan*.

Performance at the Lao She Teahouse

Afternoon Tea

For the elderly who do not want to sit in tenements all day there is a tea-house under the arcades. Tables and stools spill onto the pavement: the stools are bamboo, and barely a foot high, chiefly to assist squatting; they are very comfortable. The proprietor lurks behind a clay oven, where a kettle hisses on a coal grate. Soot blackens the chimney breast, the wooden ceiling, the dingy walls. All around the tea man there are shelves and niches stacked with earthenware teapots, none larger than a plum, and thimble-sized tea-cups (without handles, of course) standing on ceramic trays. A great tin caddy, bald with wear, and dented in a thousand places, stands with them.

The tea-equipage is brought to the table. It is absurdly small—everything is so small that were it not for the soot and the old men and the grumpy proprietor, you could easily believe yourself attending a dolls' tea-party in a Wendy house. The owner stomps up with the kettle. He takes the lid from the miniature teapot, which is stuffed to the brim with tea, and fills it with a swing of the kettle. Four tiny cups surround the pot; he picks up the dainty pot between his thick fingers and pours out the tea in a circle over the cups. When the pot is drained he empties the cups onto the tray. This is called washing the leaves, a customary practice which is supposed to remove the bitter edge and encourage the leaf to expand, as well as warming the tiny cups. He refills the teapot, and leaves you to pour the liquor into the cups, with a circular motion, to maintain an even strength.

The water sits briefly on the leaves, and the pot must be emptied completely on each round: four cups are provided, even if only two people are drinking. The first brew after the washing should last about half a minute; subsequent brews are given a few seconds. There is a limit to how much tea can be drunk like this before your heart races and your mouth begins to fur. It's tea's answer to espresso.

Jason Goodwin, The Gunpowder Gardens

BEIJING NIGHTLIFE

—by Calum MacLeod

As the once grey streets at China's heart burst with neon pulses, Beijing soars inexorably up the global karaoke index. "The Chinese are hedonists *par excellence*," declared the classic 1935 guide 'In Search of Old Peking'. Mao's revolution somewhat curbed the capital's pleasures, and lowered its bedtime, but today's visitor finds a city relishing anew a booming entertainment industry. So, when your tourist or work day is done, the opera over and duck digesting, strike out of your pleasure dome perchance to ride the cultural maelstrom of the late, great Deng Xiaoping.

For many Beijingers, the escapist screams of **karaoke** shape the premier evening out, the chance to express and impress in a make-believe, music-video world. If tempted, bring a fat wallet—the more glittering the **KTV** palace, the more remarkable the price per song. For those seeking more melodious sounds, the good news is jazz and plenty of it. The annual **Beijing International Jazz Festival**, drawing top names worldwide, has nurtured a number of fine Chinese bands and jazz bars, where live music, food and drink combine.

Combos like venues come and go, but look for saxophonist Liu Yuan, his Jazz Quintet and seedy ambience at the **CD Café**, south of the Agricultural Exhibition Centre on Dongsanhuanlu (65018877, ext. 3022); Tien Square at the **Sunflower Jazz Café** at 1, Guanghua Lu, near Ritan Park's south gate (65940515); Wide Angle at the **Sanwei Bookstore** teahouse (*see* Tea Culture, page 47); or Guys at the **Shadow Café** (*see* below).

Besides jazz, blues and covers bands also frequent many of Beijing's watering holes, a whole strip of which now lines Sanlitun Lu at the heart of the Sanlitun embassy zone. Post-movie, pre-boogie pitstops here include **Public Space**, at 50 Sanlitun Beilu (64160759), the more refined **Jazz Ya**, at No.18 (64151227), **La Terrasse** nearby (64155578), and two others tucked off to the west—the cheerful **Peking Chalet**, at Bldg 1, Sanlitun Beilu (64164631), and the liberal **Half & Half** at Bldg 15, Sanlitun Nanlu (64166919). The Dongdaqiao Xiejie *hutong* just to the southwest conceals the busy **Minders** (65006066), Nashville (65024201) and the trendy **Hidden Tree** (65093642). Further north, find the ever popular **Schillers** (64619276), and live bands at the **Keep in Touch** (64625280), opposite the Kempinski Hotel, and lighter sounds at the **Amazon Bar**, 100m south of the Hilton Hotel (64600726).

Whereas jazz has assumed a certain respectability, the rougher-edged music scene perseveres bravely amid official displeasure. Like the young artists harrassed out of their Old Summer Palace village in the mid-90s, rock's hardy

hedonists inhabit the fringes of society. While occasional stadium concerts are approved for the bands that have followed seminal rocker Cui Jian, short-notice, small-scale gigs remain the norm. Studentland in Haidian to the northwest is as promising a hunting ground as any, notably **Shadow Café & Club X**, Beijing's first fusion of café-bar and disco cum moshpit, at 31, Kexue Nanlu, opposite Shuangan Market on Beisanhuan Xilu (62618587).

Elsewhere in Haidian, find alternative music at the **Angel Bar**, 1, Wudaokou (62059580), and drinks and dance at **Bluejays**, 44, Chengfu Lu, (62533432). To catch the bohemian set over a quieter pint and game of chess, choose the **Moon House**, a cosy newspaper and candle-clad den nestling in the second *hutong* south of Beijing University's west gate. The **Solution Pub** nearby (62558877) offers live music diversion, or go truly underground, and accord with conservative economist Chen Yun's birdcage theory (fly freely within limits) at the **Pretty Bird Club**, avant-garde bar/restaurant in a nuclear bomb shelter, 3, Anhuali Xiqu (64277025).

The arrival of mega-discos has transformed the dance front—no-holds-barred, supra-warehouse bopping, wild dressers, foreign DJs and extravagant light shows. Expect entrance charges from 50–100 *yuan*, weekend queues and an eclectic hitlist tailored for a city still assimiliating disco heritage. For cosmic dirty dancing, try the cavernous **NASA Disco Club** where strobes stab the sky and army jeeps double as bars at 2, Xitucheng Lu (62032906). The infamous JJs Shanghai has spawned a Beijing branch so vast it is dubbed the **JJ Disco Square**. Locals flock to the challenge so weekends offer writhing room only at 74 Xinjiekou Beidajie (66189305). In similar vein is **Nightman Disco**, opposite the west gate of the International Exhibition Centre (64662562).

Among newer challengers are the vast **Oriental No.1** up in the Asian Games Village (64994088), Japanese techno palace **V-One** in the Wangfujing Grand Hotel (65223931), **Jacksons** up in Haidian (62017285) and **Dance Agogo** (65953589) on Dongsanhuan Zhonglu. Stalwarts include the **Kunlun** hotel disco (the Glass House) and the venerable British-style **Poachers Inn**, a socio-musical hotpot and your best post-midnight bet, offering a mixing clientele of Beijingers and foreign residents jumping joint discos and rocking bands on Friday and Saturday nights. Weekdays feature a slower tempo of jazz and the unusual. Find it north of the Sanlitun strip, above the small Friendship Store at 7, Sanlitun Lu (65323063).

These are but the more obvious tips of a fast moving iceberg, frequently in and out of hot water; some will die and others fly, so ask around, and check *City Edition*, for the place to be.

Cui Jian, China's most famous rock singer

SPORTS

'Running water never goes stagnant, and a door which is often opened never has a rusty hinge,' sums up the Chinese attitude to the importance of keeping fit. But tradition never took into the account Beijing's increasingly polluted air, especially during the often cloudy summer season.

For vigorous exercising, it is essential to get up and out at dawn before fumes are choking. College campuses always have sports fields and tracks, and being a few hundred metres away from the nearest roads, have cleaner air to breathe. Social joggers can run with **Beijing's Hash House Harriers** (tel. 65126622, ext. 340): check *Beijing Scene* for the week's venue. For a peaceful run make a bid for the Western Hills. The gates of the Summer Palace are open free to dawn patrollers before 6.30am, while a little further out west, Fragrant Hills, for just 5 *yuan* admission, is a great place for a jog or a brisk hike up Incense Burner mountain. Getting there by bicycle could make the outing into a bi-athlon: for longer rides just head northwest. Serious cyclists can find good quality frames with Japanese Shimano components and accessories including helmets at **Giant** (tel. 68351287), 300 metres west of Beijing Zoo. For social long-distance cycling contact **Bellas Bicycles** who ride from the deli-bistro of the same name (tel. 64148785).

Most parks turn into realms of martial arts exercisers at dawn. *Tai chi* (shadow boxing), various forms of sword and spear play, and *qigong* in which adherents stand, flap their arms and breathe deeply can all be seen, as well as dance groups comprising mainly the middle aged and elderly. Ballroom dancing also happens in Chinese parks. Whether you take part or not, it is a great photo opportunity.

Still in the city, but off the streets, several luxury hotels offer sports facilities. The **Friendship Hotel** (tel. 64898888, ext. 32), within a garden complex, has two swimming pools, one indoor one outdoor, two tennis courts, a golf driving range, snooker tables and a mini gymnasium. For Clark Hatch-style fitness equipment, head for the **Hilton**. Other first class indoor facilities can be found in the **Great Wall Sheraton Hotel, China World Hotel, Shangri-La, Swissôtel** and **Holdiay Inn Lido**—all of which have indoor pools. To swim some serious mileage, full-sized indoor pools can be found in the **Asian Games Village** (tel. 64993435) or the centrally-located **Dongdan Sports Center** (tel. 65231241). Outdoor swimming in lakes is enjoyed all over Beijing, most notably at Shishahai, outside Song Qingling's former home and on the east shore of Qianhai. These are also famous winter swimming spots where clubmembers from groups such as *Bei Xiong*, Polar Bears, break the ice and enjoy a few minutes chill. All are welcome. Ice skaters look on: skates and sleds can be hired for use on specially-prepared cordoned off stretches of ice. The season is usually December and January and is most idyllic on the Summer Palace's Kunming Lake and on Beihai.

The great outdoors can take on a special meaning for those with hiking boots heading out to the wilds of Beijing's Great Wall country. **The Great Wall Hiking Club**, based at the Great Wall Sheraton Hotel (contact PR Dept. tel. 65905455) , holds three hikes per year for members, while **Great Wall Reach** (wildwall@public.netchina.com.cn) has a farmhouse below the Wall in Huairou County and offers accommodation and personally-guided hikes of various lengths and difficulty on the Wall throughout the Beijing region to individuals and small groups.

Golfers fed up with bucket and net practice can have a downtown 9-hole round at **Beijing Chaoyang Golf Club** (tel. 65001145) for 250 *yuan* weekdays, 340 *yuan* weekends. For a full round, head out to the Ming Tombs. You know you are nearing the **Beijing International Golf Club** when local peasants seemingly jump out of the bushes into the path of your car waving bags of the latest cash crop: Dunlop 65s, Penfold Aces and Titleist golf balls—fished from a lake on the course. This is Beijing's St. Andrews. Green fees are 1,200 *yuan* weekdays, 1,400 *yuan* weekends and holidays. Maximum time allowable for a round is 4 1/2 hours. An alternative, near the airport, is the 36-hole **Beijing Country Golf Club** (tel. 69441108), with green fees of around 900 *yuan*.

For watchers, not players, national and international competitions are held at the Worker's Stadium, Capital Gymnasium and Olympic Center: check the English-language press for details. On TV, CCTV 5 is an all-day sports channel.

SHOPPING

Before the reforms-based consumer revolution broke out in China, visitors to Beijing were fascinated by the contents of almost every shop and market in the city. While speciality shops offered arts, crafts and native products, ordinary Chinese department stores with their old-fashioned austerity goods had a definite curiosity, and bargain, value. Most of the latter have gone: shopping streets have been redeveloped Hong Kong-mall style and invaded by the shops and franchised restaurants one would find at home. The Jeans West–McDonald's phenomenon is lamented by the visitor but welcomed by locals, for whom *mai dongxi* (shopping) has become a major activity. At the same time, selling to local Chinese has become such big business that selling to occasional pennywatching tourists pales into insignificance. Many arts, crafts and native-product stores have changed their business lines entirely. Typical of this trend is the recent reorganization of the Beijing Friendship Store. Just taken over by the Xidan Department Store, its management says, and the majority of its merchandise tells you, that selling to locals with the cash is now king. And this for a store which as recently as eight years ago prohibited access to Chinese without passports themselves. Nevertheless, Beijing remains an oriental shopping wonderland, but in order to find what you want you may have to shop around. That takes time, especially since bargaining everywhere (apart from joint-venture department stores and hotel shops) is the norm.

■ SHOPPING IDEAS AND RECOMMENDED GOODS

Bargain Souvenir Goods: chopsticks; name seals (chops); porcelain cups; painted wooden combs; printed T-shirts; sports goods (table tennis bats, badminton rackets, leather footballs); domestically-published books and maps (novels in foreign languages, pictorials); thermos bottles; bamboo, cane and straw articles; clay plant pots; medium-format 120 roll film cameras (Seagull brand); cassettes or CDs of Chinese classical and folk music; army clothing and gear (drill pants, green plimsolls, water bottles, multi-pocketed waistcoats, rucksacks); patchwork quilts.

Clothing: Fake designer clothes in outdoor markets; straw hats; silk material and made-up garments (underwear, blouses, skirts, polo shirts, shirts, ties, bath robes, pyjamas); cashmere clothing (sweaters, cardigans, scarves, berets, gloves, long johns, overcoats); leather and fur (jackets, coats, hats).

Children's Goods/Gifts: Cuddly toys (pandas, camels); kites (paper or painted silk) plus reels of thread; Chinese stamps; dolls in minority national dress; leather footballs; plastic relief maps of China; ornamental swords and daggers used for martial arts, necklaces.

A Taste of China: Various types of tea in caddies; various liquors in ornate bottles; Chinese cooking utensils and crockery.

Bargains: Silk carpets; cashmere overcoat; lacquer screen; period furniture embroidered/openwork/appliquéd tablecloths.

■ SHOPPING ADVICE

1. Like the locals, always examine the article you intend buying. Items are often well-wrapped, not just to keep them clean, but to hide their shoddiness. Don't be afraid to unwrap goods for close inspection. If something doesn't satisfy you, ask for another, and another. Beware: lack of quality control in Chinese factories is notorious. Also, shopkeepers and market vendors commonly buy faulty goods or seconds to sell.

2. Ask for a receipt, especially from larger stores. If you don't get a receipt you should get an extra discount of six per cent for the sales tax dodge you are playing a part in.

3. Always bargain, especially in tourist souvenir shops, clothes and curio markets. If 100 yuan is the starting price quoted for an article, you should be able to obtain it for between 50 and 70 *yuan*.

Exterior of the Beijing Silk Store, established in 1840

4. If you want to buy more than one of something, first bargain for the single item to establish an acceptable price. Then say you want to buy two or three and negotiate a discount for your multiple purchase.

5. To get the best deal you need time. Walk away and be reluctant to return. Don't show immediate interest in the item which you really want.

PLACES TO SHOP

Up until the 1990s there were just a couple of main shopping areas, in Wangfujing and Xidan. Recent development has answered the needs of Beijing's near-14 million population with the construction of shopping centres in all parts of the city which feature prominent department stores.

■ WANGFUJING

Beijing's most famous shopping street is unrecognizable even before its ongoing redevelopment has been completed. Once called Morrison Street after the Australian-born London Times correspondent who lived at number 98, the street is largely occupied by uninteresting commodity shops and international franchises within modern shopping malls. Nevertheless, while the street's name draws in provincial visitors, few Beijing locals go there unless they are guiding relatives and guests from outside. Of certain interest are: **Beijing Shi Baihuo Dalou** (literally Beijing City 100 Buys Big Building), which though having undergone modernization still carries many local lines and a vast array of goods. Nowhere is the impact of the arrival of Western culture more vividly illustrated than on the ground floor, where Beijing girls have face packs and volunteer for make-up demos offered by the world's biggest cosmetics makers. Elsewhere, check out the redeveloped **Beijing Arts and Crafts Store**, the city's largest **Foreign Languages Book Store**, **Lisheng Sports Goods Department Store** and a couple of stores between the aforementioned two specializing in the sale of culinary equipment, a must for foodies who want to prepare authentic Chinese food back home.

■ LIANGMAHE

Just ten years ago the Liangmahe moat marked the edge of town with fields beyond. Now the district is a fashionable shopping, eating and hotel and business district. Here, between the Hilton Hotel in the north, the Kempinski Hotel in the centre and the Great Wall Sheraton in the south, are dozens of local privately-owned restaurants, the Hard Rock Cafe, a handful of bars, the **Liangma Antique Furniture Market** and the enormous **Lufthansa Shopping Center**. The latter has perhaps the widest choice of imported goods in Beijing. Particularly worth checking out are the cashmere selections, especially *King Deer, Erduosi* and *Snow Lotus* labels; stunning silk materials and a large books section, containing one of the best English-language selections in the city.

■ XIDAN

Along with Wangfujing once the top shopping street in Beijing. Extensively redeveloped, the street holds little of interest to the visitor as it is now occupied with characterless malls and international franchises. Around the Xidan crossroads (see the bike jams here during the rush hours), however, there are several wedding photo stores where newly-weds dress up to the nines in Western matrimonial splendour to take romantic portfolios.

■ CHINA WORLD TRADE CENTER

Beijing's futuristic tall and gleaming hotel, apartment, office, cafe and shopping complex at the eastern end of Jianguomen Avenue. Contains a well-stocked **Foreign Languages Bookstore** and several arts and crafts stores. Nice and reasonably-priced **China World Deli** and **Daily Grind** coffee shop in the basement. Several boutiques stock modern designs with classic Chinese characteristics.

■ QIANMEN

South and southwest of Tiananmen Square is one of the oldest, cheapest and busiest shopping centres in Beijing. Alleyways off to the southwest are particularly crowded by market stalls and droves of mainly visitors from the provinces in search of bargains. But the area has several shops worth being jostled for, providing you have battened down your valuables—Qianmen always was, and still is, a happy hunting ground for down and outs. Look out for **Beijing Silk Store** with its ornate shopfront (see photo page 57), **Ruifuxiang Silk Store** and **Tongrentang Drug Store**.

■ JIANGUOMEN

The area along the eastward continuation of Beijing's main thoroughfare of Chang'an Avenue and known as Jianguomen is a popular and busy shopping and business district. Five hundred metres east of Jianguomen subway station is the **Friendship Store** with **Scitech Plaza** across the avenue. A further kilometre east is **Silk Alley** and **Guiyou Department Store**.

■ LIULICHANG

The charming old street known as Liulichang (Glazed Tile Factory) is Beijing's best known shopping street for good quality antiques, books and paintings. It has been

completely restored, and the high concentration of shops, many privately owned, make it an attractive place to wander in, even if you do not intend to buy anything.

Liulichang was established over 500 years ago in the Ming dynasty. Initially it was the site of a large factory which made glazed tiles for the Imperial Palace. Gradually other smaller tradesmen began to cluster around, and at the beginning of the Qing, many booksellers moved there. The area became a meeting place for intellectuals and a prime shopping district for art objects, books, handicrafts and antiques.

In 1949, Liulichang still had over 170 shops, but many were quickly taken over by the state. Inevitably, much of the street was ransacked during the Cultural Revolution. Following large-scale renovation of the traditional architecture, the street reopened in 1984 under the policy that the shops should only sell arts and crafts and cultural objects. The street is a mixture of state-run and privately-owned shops. You will be encouraged by owners of the latter to step inside, browse and bargain. Staff in state-run shops have a minimum price for stock so it is acceptable to bargain here as well.

■ MARKETS

Beijing has dozens of markets or streets specializing in the wholesale or retail sale of specific commodities. While some are of great interest to the visitor, others are sector vignettes showing the development of the economy. Among the most useful and interesting are:

Beijing Gardening Market, West side of Tiantan Lu on the perimeter of Tiantan (Temple of Heaven) Park. Sells plants, pots, flowers and everything related to gardening.

Guanyuan Pet Market, between park of same name and Second Ring Road, southeast of Xizhimen. Cages, buckets and bowls, often on the back of tricycles or handlebars of bicycles, full of pets. Plus pet feeds and other needs.

Zhongguancun Computer Village, around the Zhongguancun-Haidian Lu cross-roads in northwest Beijing. Computer Mecca; sidewalk hawkers selling fake VCDs and flagship software copies for a dollar or two.

Photography Shops, clustered around Xuanwumen crossroads, outside subway station of same name. Ten or so photo stores stocking professional equipment, good ranges of accessories, most films and offering repair services. Note, high quality print films are widely available and often at good prices. Slide films can be obtained around Xuanwumen, but stocks tend to be dated. APS (Advanced Photo System) films and processing can be found at only a few places, namely Lily, Ground Floor of CITIC Building or on the second floor of the Beijing International Hotel.

Panjiayuan Antique Market, south of Jinsong Nanlu, southwest Beijing. On Saturday and Sunday mornings, from dawn. Mainly in open air, most on offer is of curio-value or fake, but great buys have been made by those in the know.

A large bronze ding, or cauldron, in the Forbidden City

Russian Market (Clothes), Yabao Lu, north of Jianguomen International PO and between Second Ring Road and Ritan Park. Streets packed with cheap clothes stalls, popular with Russian and Mongolian traders.

Silk Market, alleyway between Jianguomen and Guanghua Lu. Silk and cashmere garments galore.

Stamp Market, 200 metres west of Anhua Qiao on the Third Ring Road. A covered market, open every day, but best attendance at weekends. Mainly Chinese stamps of the People's Republic, including valuable Cultural Revolution issues, and some of China's earliest Large Dragons. Modern commemoratives can often be bought at below face value. Coins, bank notes and telephone cards are also traded here.

■ TEMPLE FAIRS

In Old Peking, religious rituals at Taoist and Buddhist temples were often accompanied by temple fairs, basically street markets where everything from food to antiques to jewellery was sold by pedlars who set up stands or simply spread their goods on a cloth on the ground. In this century, the fairs gradually shed their religious appurtenances and became purely commercial ventures where the average Beijing citizen could buy things at low prices.

Major fairs took place at five Beijing temples from three to ten or more days per month. In recent years, these fairs have been revived, although they are held only during the Spring Festival, the lunar New Year which usually falls in late January or early February. The fairs feature traditional toys and snacks, performances of feats of strength, ballads and opera, and general merchandise. The principal sites for these fairs are: Ditan Park, White Clouds Temple (Baiyunguan), Longtanhu Park, Temple of Confucius, Big Bell Temple, former Imperial College (Guozijian), and the Drum and Bell Towers.

SHOPPING SUGGESTIONS

■ ANTIQUES

Antiques which can be exported must bear a red seal, although the red seal does not guarantee that an item is necessarily an antique worthy of the name. On the whole, the oldest pieces date from the middle to late Qing period—between 100 and 150 years old. Many pieces sold as antiques may be no more than 50 or 60 years old, but the shop assistants in the State-run stores are generally truthful about the period of any particular item, when asked. The **Yueyatang** in Liulichang is the exception. Here it is possible to purchase much older *objets d'art* such as Ming porcelain, Tang carvings, Zhou coins, and very old paintings and calligraphy.

Most antiques for sale already have a red export seal on them—be sure to keep these on, as you may be required to show the items as well as the receipts to customs on departure. Should you buy antiques which do not have a seal, it is advisable to have one fixed. This involves a visit to the Beijing Arts Objects Clearance Office situated in the compound of the Friendship Store, open 2–5pm on Mondays and Fridays. A small fee per piece is charged.

The best-known antique shops in Beijing are in Liulichang. **Yunguzhai** at 80 Liulichang East, is famous for its antique ceramics—vases, plates, bowls, bird-feeds and jars, bronzes and stone Buddhist carvings as well as jade and ivory carvings.

On Zhushikou Dajie, just opposite the Fengzeyuan Restaurant, is another shop, the **Zhenyunge**, which has antique porcelain vases, pots and dishes, lacquer boxes, cloisonné, jewellery and miscellaneous objects of interest.

Another shop of particular interest is the **Huaxia Arts and Crafts Store** at 12 Chongwenmennei Daijie. Foreign residents call this store the 'Theatre Shop' because of its collections of old Beijing opera gowns and costumes. Although not strictly an antique store, the assortment is fascinating. The first floor has sections selling embroidered linen, old fur coats, carpets and restored pieces of old Chinese furniture. Upstairs are elaborate blue kingfisher-feather hairpins, children's silver pendants, brass ink-boxes and incense burners, Buddhist mantra beads, small old pieces of embroidery and braid and odd pieces of pure kitsch of Chinese, Russian, Japanese or European origin.

A similar bazaar where old, but not quite antique furniture and other antiquities are sold can be found in the two large buildings that make up **Chaowai Market** north of Ritan Park near the diplomatic district. A less formal market where used goods are sold is located at **Dong Huanchenggen**, a north-south street between the Forbidden City and Wangfujing.

■ BOOKS

All 4 and 5-star hotel bookstores carry a selection of books with particularly good selections being available at the Great Wall Sheraton, Kempinski and China World hotels. The **Foreign Languages Bookstore**, 219 Wangfujing, stocks books in a number of languages printed by Beijing's Foreign Languages Press, as well as some foreign paperbacks, guidebooks and news magazines. Art books on many aspects of China's culture and her treasures are handsomely reproduced. Translation of Chinese novels and short stories, both modern and classical, are most reasonably priced, as are dictionaries, booklets and pamphlets on a wide range of subjects.

The **Friendship Store** has the largest selection of books and magazines, and the better hotels also carry guidebooks, as well as newspapers. The best collection of art books in Liulichang is at **Zhaohua Calligraphy and Paintings House**, 4 Liulichang Xijie.

Maps of every province of China can be purchased at the **China Cartographic Publishing House** on Baizhifang Xijie in Xuanwu District.

The largest bookstore in town is the newly-built **Beijing Book City** on the north side of Chang'an Avenue just east of the Xidan crossroads. Though stocking mainly Chinese books, titles in foreign languages are available on the second and third floors. The store is more user-friendly than most with benches provided for browsers to sit and read. Elsewhere, there is **Haidian Book City**, actually a congregation of bookstores and a good source of materials for those studying Chinese. **Lufthansa Shopping Center**, fourth floor, has a very good range of travel and history books.

The most pleasant place to shop for books in Beijing is **Liulichang**. The large traditional compound on the east side of the intersection of Liulichang Dongjie and South Xinhua Jie called Haiwang Cun (Village of the Sea King) has been taken over by the **China Bookstore** (Zhongguo Shudian). The store sells mostly new Chinese books, but there is a large selection of used Chinese, Japanese and Western books in the building lining the east side of the courtyard.

■ CARPETS

New Chinese carpets of all sizes, in classical and contemporary designs in wool and silk, may be seen at the **Friendship Store** and at the carpet pavilion in the Round

Records of medical prescriptions for Emperor Guangxu and Dowager Empress Cixi, Palace Museum Collection

City at the entrance to Beihai Park. **Beijing Arts and Crafts**, 200 Wangfujing, also has a good collection of both Chinese and Central Asian carpets, but prices are high. Prices at **Jinchang**, in 118 Liulichang East or at the Beijing No.5 Carpet Factory on Xiao Liangmaqiao Lu are marginally better than at the Friendship Store and Beijing Arts and Crafts. Several stores in the west section of Liulichang sell old carpets, as does the Huaxia Arts and Crafts Store at 12 Chongwenmennei Dajie.

■ SILK

The **Yuanlong Embroidery Silk Store**, near the north gate of Tiantan Park, has a history of more than 100 years of handling silk and embroidery and offers a tailoring

Sundial, Imperial Palace

service. The **Beijing Silk Store** at 5 Zhubaohi in Dazhalan started business in 1840 and also undertakes tailoring orders at reasonable prices.

■ FURNITURE

The widest selection of renovated original furniture is available at the **Liangma Antique Furniture Market** in northeast Beijing, opposite the entrance to the Kempinski Hotel. The Friendship Store and department stores such as Lufthansa offer reproduction period furniture. A wide selection is available at the **Huaxia Arts and Crafts Store** (*see* page 63). Plainer Ming-style chests and cupboards with attractive brass fittings, upright chairs and cabinets are to be found at the **Donghuamen Furniture Shop**, 38 Dongsinan Dajie. Most of the pieces here are reasonably old and have been restored in the workshop located behind the store.

A very wide selection of old furniture in various states of repair can be seen at the **Chaowai Market** to the north of Ritan Park. Be advised that the cost of shipping an item abroad is often greater than the cost of the item itself.

■ JEWELLERY

Modern and traditional styles of jewellery set with semi-precious stones are for sale in many of Beijing's tourist shops. You may find old pieces of silver in the form of pendants which were traditionally worn by children as good luck charms, small needle-holders which women wore hanging from their jacket-button, pill-boxes, or bells. Chinese skill in cutting and working jade is seen in the artistry or carved figurines, vases and medallions.

Wenfangsibaotang at 99 Liulichang Xijie has a good selection, and **Peiwenxuan** at 37 Liulichang East is a small, charming shop selling attractive jewellery and small trinkets.

■ PAINTING AND CALLIGRAPHY

Fan paintings, embroideries, original old scroll paintings and calligraphy by some of China's master painters are found in the famous **Baoguzhai**, in picturesque premises at 63 Liulichang Xijie.

A favourite shop is **Rongbaozhai** at 19 Liulichang Xijie. Here reproductions of old paintings, rubbings and the works of modern painters may be found. This shop specializes in art materials, and its clients are mostly artists, amateur or professional, who lovingly feel the quality of the reams of handmade paper and discuss the merits of the squirrel-hair brush as opposed to the fox-hair brush. Decorative blocks of ink are for sale as are the various porcelain accoutrements of Chinese painting. Behind the shop are block-printing workshops well worth investigating.

Moyuange, at 61 Liulichang East, is another good shop for paintings, and **Beijing-Anhui Sibaotang** on Liulichang East, is a specialist dealer in the 'four essentials' of Chinese calligraphy: paper, ink, brush, inkstone.

Contemporary Chinese painting, including oil painting now commands great interest and high prices on the international art market. Regular shows and sales are held at the joint venture **Red Gate Gallery** in the Deshengmen gate tower and the **Wan Fung Art Gallery** at 136 Nanchizi, east of Tiananmen Square. Tel. 65233320.

The **Beijing International Art Palace** in the Holiday Inn Crowne Plaza Hotel in Wangfujing also holds regular shows of contemporary painting in a small, attractive gallery. Although not a salesroom *per se*, purchase of works on display can be arranged with the management. Tel. 65125063, 65133388, ext. 1208.

■ PORCELAIN

While wandering about the streets the visitor will find many small local shops stocking cheap, everyday porcelain and pottery, rice bowls, storage pots and small ornaments which are often quite appealing. In Qianmen Dajie are two shops selling modern porcelain. The **Hunan Pottery Products Store** (No.99) has tea sets, bowls, plates, vases and ornaments all made in Changsha, capital of Hunan Province. The other, the **Jingdezhen Porcelain Shop** (No.149/151) has products from the principal porcelain centre in China, Jingdezhen in Jiangxi Province. Pottery has been made there since the second century BC and during the Northern and Southern Dynasties (317–589) its porcelain graced the tables of the imperial Court. Both Chinese and Western dinner services are for sale in various designs, including the famous blue and white rice pattern.

■ SEALS AND INKSTONES

Seals or chops engraved with one's name are a good and useful purchase. While scholars of old paid large sums for rare stones with well-cut characters, visitors can buy cheaper ones at many arts and crafts stores in the city. The cheapest stones, including the carving of your name in both scripts, plus a box, start at about 15 *yuan*. Most expensive *chicken blood stones* can cost thousands of *yuan*. Orders can sometimes be fulfilled on the spot in less than ten minutes. Cutters have dictionaries at hand to translate foreign names into Chinese.

■ OTHER SPECIALITY SHOPS

The **Beijing Chopstick Shop**, 160 Xidan Bei Dajie, has a wide selection of chopsticks, some forming sets. Strangely, this shop also specializes in walking-sticks and fans.

At the **Nationalities Friendship Store**, Nationalities Palace (Minzugong), beside the Minzu Hotel, there are handicrafts produced by some of China's minority peoples; embroideries from Yunnan, saddle-bags from Xinjiang, decorated wooden saddles from Inner Mongolia and sets of colourful minority costumes. You can even buy a nomad yurt. The **Dazhalan Hat Shop**, 9 Dazhalan, off Qianmen Dajie, has hats traditionally worn by the Tibetan, Mongol and Central Asian minorities.

The **Nationalities Musical Instrument Shop**, 104 Qianmen Dajie, not only has Chinese traditional musical instruments such as the two stringed *erhu*, elegant *pipa*, drums and clappers, but also Central Asian long-stemmed guitars, tambourines and Tibetan horse-headed banjos.

Pavilion of Viewing Scenery, the Summer palace

The inspiring shapes and faded colours of Beijing's Forbidden City

IMPERIAL EXAMINATIONS

Northwest of the junction of Jianguomen and the north-south highway, in the vicinity of the present Chinese Social Sciences Institute, is the site of the Ming and Qing Examination Hall (Gongyuan). Nothing is left of it now; its existence is recalled only by the streets—Gongyuan Dong Jie and Gongyuan Xi Jie—and a few *hutongs* named after it.

The system of imperial examinations, by which candidates were recruited into the ranks of the civil service, had its origins in the Han dynasty (206 BC–AD 220). As the government of a united and increasingly less feudal China grew more complex, an established, non-hereditary, corps of officials and administrators gradually became the accepted basis of political organization.

The competitive examinations originally tested competence in a broad range of subjects— economics, philosophy, administration—but by the Ming these had narrowed to a highly formalized syllabus based on interpretations of the Confucian classics. The increasingly orthodox responses demanded by examiners culminated in the very stylized 'eight-legged essay' (*ba gu wen*), a rigid literary form later critics condemned for its tendency to inhibit originality and creative writing.

During the Ming and Qing, examinations were held not only in the capital but also in provincial centres during the autumn. By March, thousands of hopeful candidates would be assembling for the triennial examination in Beijing. For nine days they would be confined in row upon row of tiny cells, being fed meagre meals brought in from outside and closely guarded by invigilators, to scribble away at their 'eight-legged essays' in the hopes of dazzling rewards. Success meant being received by the emperor in one of the sumptuous halls of the Imperial Palace and the privilege of joining the ruling elite. Indeed, by 1400, the examination was the only guaranteed means of entry into the imperial service. While the system was not immune to corruption—invigilators were bribed, cribs were smuggled in, sometimes in the form of minute embroidery on the cuffs of a robe—it did furnish scores of talented sons of peasant families with brilliant careers and political advancement.

The ideal of the loyal scholar-official has remained a figure of awe to the Chinese to this day. Stories of their erudition and civilizing influence on warrior-emperors abound. They tell of dutiful ministers who expounded the moral precepts and historical precedents set down by ancient sages, and related them to the political issues of the day. By gentle reminders that an emperor's mandate to rule depended on 'government by righteousness,' they curbed the worst excesses of their arrogant sovereigns.

This system of competitive entry to the civil service came to be adopted by countries outside of China but, by the late 19th century, profound scholarship was no longer an adequate qualification for statesmanship. The debâcle of the Boxer Rebellion in 1900 forced Empress Dowager Cixi to initiate a number of reforms. These included abolishing the imperial examinations in 1905.

Chinese ministers of state (left to right)
Shen Kwei Fen, Tung Hsun and Mao Chang Hsi. *Photographed by John Thomson, 1870*

History of Beijing

Beijing is both an old and a new city—old in its cultural heritage, and new as the capital of the People's Republic of China. Today, a first impression is of fast development in preference to reverence for the past. Even so, many of the buildings here are steeped in the history of China over the last 800 years and it becomes rapidly obvious to any visitor how integral the city's development is to the rise and fall of dynasties, and indeed, to Chinese civilization itself.

Peking Man The story of Beijing starts a long time before recorded history. Fragments of the bones of 'Peking Man', dated to a period about 300,000–500,000 years ago, were discovered at the village of Zhoukoudian, outside the present city (see page 139).

Capital of Conquerors During the Zhou (1027–221 BC) and subsequent dynasties, a series of large established settlements grew around Beijing. But as the area was the focus of an unsettled frontier region far from the capital—Chang'an; now Xi'an—and other centres of power further south, it suffered a turbulent history.

For part of the period dominated by the Liao Kingdom (916–1125), the city was a secondary capital enjoying the pretty name (which is still used from time to time) of Yanjing, the City of Swallows. In the 12th century the 'Golden Tartars' swept down from Manchuria and wrested the city for their own, and established the State of Jin.

When Kublai became Great Khan of the eastern part of the Mongol empire in 1260, he decided to develop Beijing as his winter capital, calling it 'Dadu', or Great Capital, and took up residence in a palace in what is now Beihai Park.

By the time the Venetian explorer Marco Polo reached Beijing at the end of the 13th century, it was called Khanbaliq, the City of the Khan, and was already one of the world's great metropolises. From his long detailed description of the city, it is clear that Marco Polo was utterly overwhelmed by the size and opulence of the Mongol capital.

■ **UNDER THE MING**

The Ming dynasty, founded in 1368 upon the defeat of the Mongols, first established its capital in Nanjing, and on account of its relegation Dadu was renamed 'Beiping' (Northern Peace). With the accession of the dynamic third Ming emperor, Yongle, the dynasty entered a period of vitality and expansion. He re-established Beijing as the capital in 1421, giving the city its modern name, which means Northern Capital, and which Europeans later romanized as 'Peking'.

Much of present-day Beijing was built during the period that immediately fol-

Showroom of a lantern merchant, Peking, Thomas Allom, 1804 – 1872

lowed. In contrast to the unplanned, sprawling cities of the south, traditional concepts of town-planning were employed, and nowhere was this more evident than in the grid layout of Beijing. The foundations of Khanbaliq were, of course, already there, but they were now extended; walls were built and moats were dug. As Beijing flourished, the city originally established by the Tartars became too small, and in 1553 a new outer wall, or Chinese City, was built to enclose the suburbs that had burgeoned out to the south.

Within the boundaries, a massive building and renovation programme created some of the most striking testimonies to Ming confidence and power. Over 200,000 workmen laboured to build the imperial palace between 1407 and 1420. Though the palace buildings have been restored and rebuilt many times since then, the plan remains essentially the same. The Temple of Heaven (a magnificent example of Ming architecture) and the Altar of Agriculture (which no longer exists) were erected in the Outer City. Mindful of their mortality, the early Ming emperors planned and prepared their own burial grounds in the same methodical and grandiose fashion as can be seen at the Ming tombs. Nor was the defence of the realm neglected: the finest sections of the Great Wall to the north of Beijing were constructed during this period.

■ UNDER THE QING

For a century after Yongle, stability was maintained in the empire. But weak rulers and corruption eventually fragmented the authority and drained the energies of the state. The last Ming emperor hanged himself on Prospect Hill (Jingshan) behind the Imperial Palace in 1644, when rebels and Manchu forces were already at the city gate.

The Manchus, founders of the Qing ('pure') dynasty that came to rule China, were descendants of those Tartars who invaded Beijing in the 12th century. This time they were to stay for 267 years.

The Qing were more interested in maintaining the existing capital and administrative systems than in making any radical changes. As they themselves became culturally assimilated (to the extent that they lost their own language), their improvements to Beijing and its environs tended to preserve the styles and techniques of the Ming period. The most interesting contributions the Qing rulers made to their adopted capital were the various summer palaces that they built outside the city.

Notable Qing rulers included Kangxi (reigned 1661–1722), Qianlong (reigned 1736–95) and the Empress Dowager, Cixi (ruled 1861–1908). Kangxi's reign was the longest in Chinese history; he was a contemporary of Louis XIV of France and Peter the Great of Russia (both of whom he had contact with). During the long reigns of Kangxi and Qianlong, China enjoyed peace and prosperity. The 18th-century European ideal of the Chinese nobility as a highly cultured people dressed in gorgeous silks and much given to splendid ceremonies derived from Western travellers' accounts of this land of plenty.

But the ideal was an elaborate façade; the Manchu court had, by the 19th century, become enervated and stagnant. Clinging rigidly to ancient systems of thought and rituals, the ultra-conservative officials rejected all original ideas or innovations as seditious. Attempts by reformers to modernize China were invariably quashed.

■ THE COMING OF THE BARBARIANS

The history of the late Qing empire is a sorry account of unsuccessful resistance to Western encroachment from without, and to domestic rebellion from within. The First Opium War (1840–42) pried open China to foreign trade. In a second round of the conflict (1858–60), Beijing was actually captured by Britain and France, whose troops burned down the Summer Palaces, and whose representatives established embassies in a Legation Quarter (southeast of the Imperial Palace, in the area bounded by Dong Chang'an Jie, Chongwenmennei Dajie and the Inner City wall) over which the Chinese had no jurisdiction. It was this legation quarter that the men of 'The Society of the Harmonious Fists', the Boxer rebels, besieged for two months in 1900 in protest against the growing influence of the foreigners.

Piecemeal reforms, reluctantly conceded by Cixi, came too late. Her successor Puyi, who ascended the throne at the age of six, was the last emperor of China. For some years after the collapse of the Qing, he continued to live in the rear quarters of the Imperial Palace, while the front portion was turned into a museum. He finally moved from the palace in 1924.

■ UNDER THE REPUBLIC

Following the 1911 Revolution, Beijing became the stage for important events in the development of modern republican China. On 4 May 1919, Tiananmen Square was the arena of an historic mass demonstration: students and patriots, in what became known as the 'May Fourth Movement', passionately denounced the humiliating terms for China under the newly-signed Treaty of Versailles. It was a show of solidarity that started many Chinese on the road to socialism. In 1928, when the political centre of the Republic was moved to the Nationalists' power base at Nanjing, the old name of 'Beiping' was restored to the abandoned capital. The Nationalist old guard in Taiwan continue to use that name to this day.

Emerging from its Japanese occupation between 1937 and 1945, the city had to wait another four years before regaining its paramount status. The communists entered Beijing unopposed in January 1949. On 1 October, Chairman Mao Zedong proclaimed the establishment of the People's Republic of China from the rostrum of the Gate of Heavenly Peace, and a new era for Beijing, indeed for the whole of China, began.

■ MODERNIZATION

Since the founding of the PRC, Beijing has become the country's political and cultural centre and has experienced many drastic changes. In the spirit of the revolution, many of the city's major monuments went the way of the city's walls and were pulled down in the late 50s. By the late 60s, Beijing was awash with the many political currents of the Cultural Revolution. At the height of this highly charged period, a trip to Tiananmen Square became a requisite pilgrimage for thousands of zealous young Red Guards who journeyed to Beijing from the farthermost reaches of China as a demonstration of their revolutionary ardour and commitment to the cult of Mao.

Political struggles, public purges and mass campaigns rent the society for a full decade before popular outrage was vented at what was to become known as the Tiananmen Incident. On 5 April 1976, 100,000 people gathered at Tiananmen Square to protest the removal of memorial wreaths which had been laid at the Monument to the People's Heroes as a tribute to the late Zhou Enlai. This public mourning for the moderate premier is now seen as a turning point in the political tide, a clear denunciation of the last years of Mao's rule and of Jiang Qing, his widow. Within six months, Mao Zedong had died, and subsequently, the 'Gang of Four' and the political structure of the Cultural Revolution were dismantled.

With Deng Xiaoping as its new leader, China embarked on a programme of adapting Maoist thought through a reform movement known as the 'Four Modernizations'—

76

■ REIGNS OF MING AND QING EMPERORS
Ming Dynasty (1368–1644)

Hongwu	1368–1398
Jianwen	1399–1402
Yongle	1403–1424
Hongxi	1425
Xuande	1426–1435
Zhengtong	1436–1449
Jingtai	1450–1456
Tianshun	1457–1464
Chenghua	1465–1487
Hongzhi	1488–1505
Zhengde	1506–1521
Jiajing	1522–1566
Longqing	1567–1572
Wanli	1573–1620

Celebrations of Emperor Kangxi's 60th birthday (scroll), 1713

Taichang	1620
Tianqi	1621–1627
Chongzhen	1628–1644

Qing Dynasty (1644–1911)

Shunzhi	1644–1661
Kangxi	1662–1722
Yongzheng	1723–1735
Qianlong	1736–1795
Jiaqing	1796–1820
Daoguang	1821–1850
Xianfeng	1851–1861
Tongzhi	1862–1874
Guangxu	1875–1908
Xuantong	1909–1911

Shades of Summer

The time to take incense to the temple on Miao Feng Mountain had come again and it was very hot. Sellers of paper fans seemed to have emerged from somewhere all at once with boxes hanging from their arms and strings of jingling bells to attract attention hanging from the boxes.

Many things were for sale in the streets; green apricots were heaped in piles while cherries gleamed redly and brightened your eyes. Swarms of bees swooped over bowls of roses or dates and the agar jellies on porcelain plates had a milky glow. Peddlers of cookies and jellies had their wares arranged with remarkable neatness and spices of every kind and color were also set out on display.

People had changed into brighter and more colorful unpadded garments and the streets were suddenly filled with their colors, as if many rainbows had come down into them. The street cleaners worked faster, going down the road sprinkling water without a pause, but the light dust soon flew around as before and vexed people. There were longish twigs of willow in the slightly dusty air and lightly and delightfully swooping swallows as well which made people feel cheery in spite of themselves. It was the sort of weather that really made you wonder what to do with yourself and everyone yawned great lazy yawns while feeling tired and happy too.

Processions of various kinds set out for the mountains continuously. Lines of people beating on drums and gongs, or carrying baskets on shoulder poles, or waving apricot yellow flags went by one on the heels of another, lending an unusual kind of bustle to the entire city, lending an elusive and yet familiar thrill to the people and lingering sounds and fine dust to the air. Those in the processions and those who watched them all felt a kind of excitement, devoutness, and exuberance.

The hurly-burly of this chaotic world comes from superstition; the only solace the stupid have is self-deception. These colors, these voices, the clouds filling the sky, and the dust in the streets made people energetic and gave them something to do. The mountain goers climbed mountains, the temple goers went to temples, the flower gazers looked at flowers. Those who couldn't do any of these things could still watch the processions from the sidelines and repeat the name of Buddha.

It was so hot it seemed to have roused the old capital from its spring dream. You could find amusements everywhere but everyone wondered what to do. Urged on by the heat, the flowers, grasses, fruit trees, and the joy among the people, all burgeoned together. The newly furbished green willows along the South Lake enticed harmonica-playing youngsters; boys and girls tied their boats up in the shade of the willows or floated among the lotuses. Their mouths sang love songs and they kissed each other with their eyes.

The camellias and peonies in the park sent invitations to poets and elegant gentlemen who now paced back and forth while waving their expensively decorated paper fans. They would sit in front of the red walls or under the pine trees when tired and drink several cups of clear tea, enough to draw out their idle melancholy. They'd steal a glance at the young ladies of wealthy families and at the famous "flowers" of the south and north who strolled by.

Even places which had heretofore been quiet had visitors sent to them by the warm wind and bright sun, just as the butterflies were sent. The peonies of the Ch'ung Hsiao temple, the green rushes at the T'ao Jan pavilion, the mulberry trees and rice paddies at the site of the Zoological and Botanical Gardens, all attracted the sounds of people and the shadows of their parasols. The Altar of Heaven, the Temple of Confucius, and the Lama temple had just a little bustle in the midst of their usual solemnity as well.

Students and those who like short trips went to the Western Hills, the hot springs, and the Summer Palace. They went to sightsee, to run around, to gather things, and to scribble words all over the rocks in the mountains.

Poor people also had somewhere to go: the Hu Kuo temple, the Lu Fu temple, the White Pagoda, and the Temple of Earth. All the flower markets were busier. Fresh cut flowers of every sort were arranged colorfully along the streets and a penny or so could take some beauty back home.

On the mats of the soybean milk vendors fresh pickled vegetables were arranged to look like big flowers topped with fried hot peppers. Eggs were

continues

really cheap and the soft yellow egg dumplings for sale made people's mouths water.

T'ien Ch'iao was even more fired up than usual. New mats had been hung for tea sheds, one right next to another. There were clean white tablecloths and entrancing singing girls who waved to the ancient pines above the wall at the Temple of Heaven. The sounds of drums and gongs dragged on for eight or nine hours and the brisk heat of the day made them sound especially light and sharp in a way that struck and disturbed people's hearts.

Dressing up was simple for the girls. One calico frock was all they needed to go out prettily dressed and it revealed every curve of their bodies as well.

Those who liked peace and quiet also had a place to go. You could drop a fishing line at the Chi Shui reservoir, outside the Wan Shou temple, at the kiln pits east of town, or on the marble bridge west of town. The little fishes would bump into the rushes now and then, making them move slightly. When you finished your fishing, the pigshead meat, stewed bean curd, and salted beans you ate with your baigan *could make you both satiated and drunk. And afterwards, following the willow-edged bank and carrying fishing pole and little fish, you entered the city at a leisurely pace while treading on the beams of the setting sun.*

There was fun, color, excitement, and noise everywhere. The first heat wave of summer was like an incantation that made every place in the city fascinating. The city paid no attention to death, paid no attention to disaster, and paid no attention to poverty. It simply put forth its powers when the time came and hypnotized a million people, and they, as if in a dream, chanted poems in praise of its beauty. It was filthy, beautiful, decadent, bustling, chaotic, idle, lovable; it was the great Peking of early summer.

Lao She, Rickshaw, (1936), translated by Jean M James

of agriculture, industry, science and technology, and national defence. The result of China's opening to the outside world has been a marked increase of cultural exchanges, joint-venture projects and direct investment from a multitude of foreign sources. International-style hotels and office high-rises now line major thoroughfares. Private enterprise markets are commonplace. The affluence of the *ge ti hu*—individual small-time entrepreneurs—is apparent as more and more families purchase computers, cars and their own apartments.

But with this reform, China has inevitably experienced pangs of growth. Breaking the 'iron rice-bowl' has meant that employment is no longer guaranteed, and so the voices of the discontent and dispossessed have become louder. China today also boasts a huge, nomadic army of employment-seekers who inundate the capital after the Lunar New Year.

The upside of all of this is the gradual resurgence of a commodity economy geared more or less to consumer demand. Tourists and local residents alike have benefited from a broadening of the service economy to include private taxis, restaurants, guest houses and travel services, although letting out the reins in this regard has in some cases led several years later to the imposition of strict regulations which have finally brought a sense of order to these small scale enterprises.

An upsurge in domestic tourism has also changed the face of the city. The major tourist spots are crowded with sightseers from every corner of China. So successful has the campaign to encourage Chinese people to travel that the railways report running at 140 per cent of capacity, and tourist hot spots like the Forbidden City and Temple of Heaven are restricting access to certain centuries-old flights of steps and marble pedestals because they are beginning to be chafed away by vast numbers of well-shod feet, some wearing high heels and steel taps. The market economy, coupled with the necessity of reducing domestic tourist deluges to the main sites, struck in April 1994. Sharp gate ticket hikes were announced, asking local Chinese for tens of yuan, rather than just a few *mao* or *kuai* of the socialist days.

On the other hand, cultural sites formerly closed to the public are being rehabilitated; one effect of which is to reduce the pressure on the most popular destinations. Notable among the new attractions is the Beijing Art Museum, which has found a home in the Temple of Longevity (Wanshousi) to the east of Purple Bamboo Park in the Haidian district (*see* p.149). To satisfy those domestic tourists who cannot globetrot, a World Park was opened in Spring 1994 at Fengtai, in the south of the capital. Crowds flock to see the scaled-down replicas of the Wonders of the World, and famous Chinese sights.

Even so, while the skyline of Beijing is being changed out of recognition by skyscrapers, swaths of the city laced with *hutongs* and courtyard houses are being preserved in the traditional manner. New Beijing and Old Peking will continue to mature hand in hand, as China enters the 21st century and its people face modern challenges.

Sights in Beijing

TIANANMEN SQUARE

The enormous square facing the Gate of Heavenly Peace—Tiananmen—is the heart of modern China. During the centuries of the Qing empire the square did not exist. There were originally buildings on either side of a central thoroughfare leading northwards to the entrance of the Imperial Palace.

Gradually cleared during the first half of the 20th century, this huge area, covering about 40 hectares (98 acres), has witnessed crucial developments in China's history. A number of important political demonstrations took place there during the Republic (1911–49). On 1 October 1949, Chairman Mao proclaimed the establishment of the People's Republic of China from the rostrum of the Gate of Heavenly Peace. Twenty-seven years later, the Tiananmen Incident—when masses demonstrated their support for the late premier, Zhou Enlai—heralded the end of Mao's reign and the downfall of the Gang of Four. In the spring of 1989 the square was the site of student demonstrations for democracy in China, which culminated in a military crackdown.

The **Gate of Heavenly Peace** itself is an imposing long red structure with a double roof of yellow tiles on the northern side of the square (*see* picture on page 5). Since 1 January 1988, tourists have been allowed to enter the gate and climb to the rostrum from which emperors handed down edicts over the centuries and Mao Zedong declared the founding of New China. Besides being steeped with historical significance, this rostrum, overlooking the museums of Chinese History and Revolution, Tiananmen, and the Great Hall of the People, provides one of the finest views of Beijing. The 30 *yuan* entrance fee is best spent in the early morning or late afternoon to avoid the glare of Beijing's bright sun. Open from 9am to 6pm, with the last tickets sold at 5pm.

On either side of the gate's rear portion are two parks. To the east is the **Working People's Cultural Palace**. Over 550 years old, this was an imperial ancestral temple and now contains a park, a library, a gymnasium and other recreational facilities. On the western side is **Zhongshan Park**, dedicated to Dr Sun Yat-sen, the leader of the 1911 Revolution and founder of modern China.

On the eastern side of Tiananmen Square are two major museums, the **Museum of Chinese History** and the **Museum of the Chinese Revolution**.

In the centre of the square is the **Monument to the People's Heroes**, an obelisk in memory of those who died for the revolution, with inscriptions by Mao Zedong and Zhou Enlai, as well as a dozen stone carvings.

At the far southern end of the square (beyond Chairman Mao's Memorial Hall) is the **Qianmen**, or Front Gate, a massive double gate which controlled entry to the northern section of the city.

■ GREAT HALL OF THE PEOPLE

On the western side of the square, this monumental building, completed in 1959, houses the People's Congress. It may usually be visited on Monday, Wednesday and Friday mornings, however, visits cannot be made when party meetings (which naturally take precedence) are scheduled. The 15th Communist Party Congress was convened here in October 1997 and National People's Congresses are held every March.

The Great Hall of the People is built round a square, very much in the solid 'revolutionary-heroic' mould. It is worth going inside where, even if the decor is not to everyone's taste, the sheer scale of the rooms is breathtaking. From the huge reception room, the Wanren Dalitang (Ten-thousand People Assembly Hall) leads off to the west, the banquet wing to the north, and the offices of the standing committees of the national congress to the south. The Assembly Hall is over 3,000 square metres (3,600 square yards), containing more than 9,700 seats on three tiers, all installed with simultaneous interpretation equipment. Overhead, the vaulted ceiling is illuminated by 500 recessed lights radiating outwards from a gleaming red star. Some 500 guests can sit down to dinner in the banquet room, which is half the size of a football field. Gilded columns and brilliant lighting combine to produce a sumptuous if overwhelming effect. In addition to the formal public rooms, the Great Hall has 32 separate reception rooms, named after each province, provincial-level city and autonomous region of China (including one for Taiwan).

■ CHAIRMAN MAO'S MEMORIAL HALL

Standing behind the Monument to the People's Heroes is Chairman Mao's mausoleum. It was built in only one year by teams of volunteers and inaugurated on 9th September 1977, the first anniversary of his death, by his successor to the Communist Party leadership, Chairman Hua Guofeng. This imposing two-tiered edifice resting on a foundation of plum-coloured Huangang stone is supported by 44 granite columns and topped by a flat roof of yellow glazed tiles. It bears a striking resemblance to the Lincoln Memorial in Washington, D.C.

There are three main halls on the ground floor, one to the north, one to the south, and the Hall of Reverence in between. Entering the first, a vast reception area capable of accommodating over 600 people, the visitor will be confronted by a seated statue of Mao carved in white marble. Behind it hangs a painting of Jingganshan in Jiangxi Province.

Inside the Hall of Reverence, the embalmed body of the late chairman draped with the red flag of the Chinese Communist Party lies in a crystal coffin. The dates '1893–1976' are engraved in gold on a plaque.

Leaving the mausoleum by the south hall, the visitor will see a celebrated poem by the late Mao Zedong inscribed in gold on one of the walls. The walk-through will

THE IMPERIAL PALACE

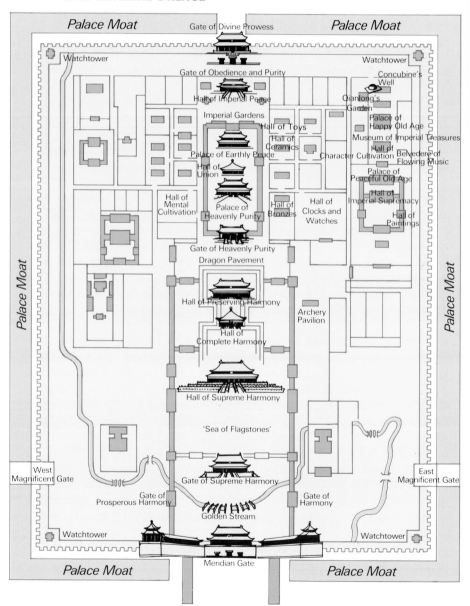

Palace Moat

Gate of Divine Prowess

Palace Moat

Watchtower

Watchtower

Gate of Obedience and Purity

Concubine's Well

Hall of Imperial Peace

Qianlong's Garden

Imperial Gardens

Palace of Happy Old Age

Hall of Toys

Museum of Imperial Treasures

Hall of Ceramics

Hall of Character Cultivation

Belvedere of Flowing Music

Palace of Earthly Peace

Hall of Union

Palace of Peaceful Old Age

Hall of Mental Cultivation

Palace of Heavenly Purity

Hall of Bronzes

Hall of Clocks and Watches

Hall of Imperial Supremacy

Hall of Paintings

Gate of Heavenly Purity

Dragon Pavement

Hall of Preserving Harmony

Archery Pavilion

Hall of Complete Harmony

Hall of Supreme Harmony

'Sea of Flagstones'

West Magnificent Gate

East Magnificent Gate

Gate of Supreme Harmony

Gate of Prosperous Harmony

Gate of Harmony

Golden Stream

Watchtower

Watchtower

Meridian Gate

Palace Moat

Palace Moat

Palace Moat

Palace Moat

take less than five minutes, since stopping is not allowed. Security is very strict, and handbags and cameras must be checked in before entry. There is no entrance fee.

A bustling shopping area near the exit of the hall on the south side of the building offers a wide range of new Mao memorabilia. For more valuable Mao souvenirs from the Cultural Revolution, visit the Panjiayuan market.

THE IMPERIAL PALACE (GUGONG)

Centre of the Chinese world for nearly 500 years, the Imperial Palace today remains the most complete and best preserved collection of ancient buildings in China. Also called the 'Purple Forbidden City' (Zijincheng) for the exclusive nature of the emperors who built and inhabited it, the Palace is a vast complex of halls, pavilions, courtyards and walls. It is within these walls that 24 emperors of two dynasties, aided by their ministers, eunuch guards, concubines and servants, acted out the drama of ruling imperial China from the early Ming in 1420 to the fall of the Qing in 1911.

'Gugong', as it is known to the Chinese, is also a masterpiece of architecture. An extraordinary sense of balance is maintained between the buildings and the open spaces they surround. The scale is monumental but never oppressive; the design symmetrical but not repetitive. True to the Chinese predilection for harmony over diversity, the Palace makes use of a single style of building in an awe-inspiring combination of geomantic planning and aesthetic beauty. All the buildings are carefully laid out on a north-to-south axis, but there is no sense of rigidity to them. Like the Louvre or the Taj Mahal, the Imperial Palace is a monument that can be visited with pleasure again and again.

Originally built in 1420 by over 200,000 workmen at the direction of the third Ming emperor, Yongle, the Palace was almost burnt to the ground in 1644 during the Manchu takeover. Rebuilt and renovated many times, it nonetheless retains the initial design set down 500 years ago.

The Palace can roughly be divided into three parts. In the foreground are four gates, each of which may look large enough to the first-time visitor to be a palace by itself. Beyond these gates, at the centre of the complex, are three principal halls, of monumental size and scope, where the emperors conducted important State ceremonies. In the rear are three lesser halls, still of notable size, and many smaller courts where the emperors and their families and attendants lived.

Occupying an area of over 74 hectares (183 acres), the complex was indeed more like a city than a palace. The visitor entering for the first time may be surprised that each gate and hall leads to yet another, seemingly grander one, at its rear. The effect can be overwhelming and the similarity of design in buildings throughout behoves the visitor to note the special functions of each in order to gain an appreciation for the complexity of the whole. One can, with little imagination, easily understand how the emperors who

An Echo of the Past

While I was picturing the scene, an unknown voice said quietly:
"In her day there was no electricity. The attendants carried lanterns of scarlet gauze."

I swung round startled. I had been so sure I was alone; the soft, almost feminine voice, emerging unexpectedly from the darkness and seeming like a continuation of my thoughts was disturbing.

"I beg your pardon?"

A shadowy figure, his face barely visible above a dark robe which blended indistinguishably with the night, was standing so close to me that I might have touched his hand. Perceiving he had startled me, he apologized and added:

"I saw you gazing across at the pavilions by the landing-stage. They are beautiful, are they not? But that yellowish light is out of place and garish—like so many things these days."

"Do you mean to say you were here then?"

He laughed, or rather tittered, musically, his voice so feminine that, could I have believed it possible in Peking to encounter a woman walking alone in a solitary place at night, I should certainly have taken him for one. (The Manchu-style gowns of men and women were, even when seen in daylight, not greatly dissimilar.)

"Yes, indeed I was here then. You are a foreigner, but you speak Chinese well. Doubtless you have heard of the T'ai Chien?"

"The imperial eunuchs? Of course. But they vanished long ago."

"Long as a young man sees things; short enough to one well into the autumn of his life. I was already middle-aged when the Revolution dispersed us. Now I am sixty."

"Were you with them long? In the Imperial Household, I mean?"

'Not long. I was castrated in the seventh year of Kuang Hsü [1882], so I had only twenty-nine years in the Forbidden City. How quickly the time passed!"

"Castrated by your own choice?"

"Why not? It seemed a little thing to give up one pleasure for so many. My parents were poor, yet by suffering that small change I could be sure of an easy life in surroundings of beauty and magnificence; I could aspire to intimate companionship with lovely women unmarred by their fear or distrust of me. I could even hope for power and wealth of my own. With good fortune and diligence, I might grow more rich and powerful than some of the greatest officials in the empire. How could I foresee the Revolution? That was indeed a misfortune. I have sacrificed my virility and my hope of begetting children for a dream which, passing fleetingly, stopped short and can never return."

"And so now you come here sometimes in the darkness to recapture an echo of your dream? But how do you live?"

"I manage well. I am a guide—not one of those so-called guides who live by inventing history for foreigners and by making commissions on things they purchase. I have not yet fallen to that. Discriminating Chinese gentlemen arriving from the provinces prefer to obtain their guides through the Palace Eunuchs' Mutual Prosperity Association. Often they have heard my name from their friends and are kind enough to ask specially for my services. I charge highly, for I am able to tell them many things they could scarcely learn from other sources."

After chatting with him longer, I asked if he and his fellow eunuchs were happy in their old age.

"Happy? How could that be? We have no wives, no sons to bear us grandsons and sacrifice at our tombs. We manage to live. We are not often hungry. We dare not ask for happiness."

John Blofeld, City of Lingering Splendour

The Western Gate, Peking, *hand-coloured engraving by Thomas Allom, adapted from an original drawing made by William Alexander during Lord Macartney's Embassy to China in 1793.*

ruled this Forbidden City could consider themselves at the centre of the universe.

It is often stated that there are 9,999 'rooms' in the palace; one room less than the great palace in heaven, which has a perfect 10,000 rooms. Actually, there are many fewer than 9,999 rooms, but there are nearly that number of bays (in Chinese, *jian*). A bay, in Chinese architecture, is defined as the square or rectangular space between four columns. Columns do all the work of supporting the roof in Chinese buildings as no weight is borne by the walls.

■ TICKETS

Foreigners and 'compatriots' from Hong Kong, Macau and Taiwan can buy their tickets at either the front or back entrance to the palace, but for dramatic effect the only choice is to enter from the Meridian Gate, Wumen.

Entrance to the Forbidden City is 20 *yuan*, while the Accoustiguide recording is 30 *yuan* for foreign languages and 10 *yuan* for Chinese. This gives an interesting general introduction to 17 sites within the palace. The English tape is narrated by Roger Moore; likewise other famous voices speak in the ten other languages, including Chinese. Acoustiguides are available at both the north and south gates. The palace is open from 8am–5pm; the last ticket is sold at 4pm.

Generally, tour groups are not offered the Acoustiguide service. It takes about 90 minutes to cover the most popular destinations in the palace, and would be best used in combination with a detailed guide book which directs you to other interesting corners of the palace.

Tickets are also sold in a kiosk in the parking lot at the rear (north) of the palace near the Gate of Divine Prowess. If you divide your visit to the palace into two sessions and wish to save time, you might enter from here on your return visit and go directly to the specialized collections of Chinese art that can be found in the vicinity of the Palace of Heavenly Purity in the residential quarters. But you would be sacrificing the dramatic effect of entering the palace through the awe-inspiring gates and courtyards that sealed the emperor off from the rest of the world.

■ THE PALACE GATES

By passing through the **Gate of Heavenly Peace** (Tiananmen) and the **Upright Gate** (Duanmen), one arrives at the imposing **Meridian Gate** (Wumen), which is the traditional entrance to the Forbidden City. The horseshoe-shape of the Meridian Gate's massive fortress walls, topped with five towers, seems to draw the visitor submissively forward through the entrance to the inner precincts. This gate was originally used for impressive functions such as reviewing victorious troops and announcing the lunar calendar. Only the emperor himself was permitted to pass through the central opening of the gate.

Beyond this gate lies a courtyard leading to the fourth and final gate, the **Gate of Supreme Harmony** (Taihemen), a huge open porch supported by red lacquered pillars. One crosses a stream by one of five marble bridges, beautiful pieces in their own right that are dwarfed by the enormity of the surrounding courtyard and palace walls. Two striking bronze lions guard this entrance, the female with a cub beneath her paw, the male with a ball. They symbolize the power of the emperor and the subservience demanded by him.

■ THE PRINCIPAL HALLS

The next courtyard, called the 'Sea of Flagstones' by the Chinese, was designed to accommodate 90,000 people during an imperial ceremony. In its centre stands the **Hall of Supreme Harmony** (Taihedian), the largest and grandest structure in the Palace. Here were held the most solemn of ceremonial occasions, such as celebration of the New Year and the emperor's birthday, or announcing the successful candidates of the imperial examinations. This hall is filled with many treasures, including bronze incense burners, musical chimes made of jade, and a nine-dragon screen behind the throne.

Behind the Hall of Supreme Harmony are the halls of **Complete Harmony** (Zhonghedian) and **Preserving Harmony** (Baohedian). In the former, the emperor donned formal regalia before proceeding to the Hall of Supreme Harmony, or performed lesser State functions like inspecting seeds for a new planting. The Hall of Preserving Harmony was used for a time as the site for the highest level of the imperial examinations (*see* page 70). Behind this hall, between the descending staircases, is the '**Dragon Pavement**', an exquisitely carved block of marble said to weigh over 200 tons.

■ THE INNER COURT

The three rear halls, the **Palace of Heavenly Purity** (Qianqinggong), the **Hall of Union** (Jiaotaidian) and the **Palace of Earthly Peace** (Kunninggong), were also the site of lesser State functions. During the Ming dynasty, emperors lived among these buildings, but later the Qing rulers moved to smaller, less formal parts of the Palace. They nevertheless continued to use the Palace of Earthly Peace to consummate their marriages. The last emperor, Puyi, who ascended the throne as a child and formally abdicated in 1924, was allowed to use this chamber on his wedding night. However, intimidated by the colour scheme of gaudy red (the traditional colour of joy), he fled to his usual quarters.

The east and west sides of the Palace's rear section contain a dizzying succession of smaller courts where the imperial families, concubines and attendants lived, schemed for power and engaged in their many intrigues. In the far northeast corner of the complex, behind the **Palace of Peaceful Old Age** (Ningshougong), is the famous well down which the Pearl Concubine was cast (*see* page 104). Several of the eastern palaces have been converted into exhibition halls for the collections of the Palace Museum (*see* page 144).

A Portrait of Empress Dowager Cixi

Every year, on her birthday, at an auspicious hour, the Empress Dowager would set free 10,000 caged birds. It must have been a spectacular sight to see her and her entourage in the snow-covered grounds of the Summer Palace as she opened cage after cage of exotic and brilliantly coloured birds and then prayed fervently that they would not be recaptured. By doing this, she hoped that Heaven would be good to her in her next life. She did not realize that her eunuchs were waiting on the other side of the hill to resell as many of the birds as they could catch.

Most of what is known about the Court of imperial China concerns the late 19th and early 20th centuries, for it was only then that eyewitness accounts were written. Before that, Court life was meticulously hidden from the curious eyes of outsiders, whether Chinese or foreign.

It was the Empress Dowager Cixi, effective ruler of China from 1861 to 1908, who began, in her 60s, to invite the ladies of the foreign legations to visit her at Court. Moreover, her chief Lady-in-Waiting was Der Ling, daughter of a Manchu official, who had been brought up in France. In Der Ling, Cixi found someone who could bridge Chinese and Western cultures, and explain to her the many puzzling features of Western ways.

In 1903, Mrs Conger, wife of the American Minister to Beijing, persuaded the Empress Dowager to allow her portrait to be painted so that it could be shown at the World Exposition of St Louis. This was a novel idea to the Chinese whose portraits were painted only after death. The American artist Katherine Carl, sister of the Commissioner of Customs in Chefoo, thus became the first foreigner since Marco Polo to stay in the Imperial Palace, and the first foreigner ever to enter the ladies' quarters. The portrait, measuring six foot by four—disappointingly small in Cixi's opinion—is now owned by the US Government and hangs in the Freer Gallery of Art in Washington. Two or three other paintings of the empress were left with her in Beijing.

Miss Carl wrote an account of her unique experience, of her impressions of her surroundings—her surprise at the 85 clocks in the Throne Room, where she painted the portrait—and of the kind and considerate treatment she received from Cixi. But it is only on reading Der Ling's recollections that we see how anxious Cixi was that Miss Carl should not become too well acquainted with Court life. Der Ling was charged to remain constantly with Miss Carl and specifically commanded not to teach the American any Chinese. Cixi was concerned that Miss Carl should not see the eunuchs punished, lest she should consider the Court officials savages.

Cixi's secretiveness pervaded all her dealings with foreigners. A special court language was used when in the presence of foreigners who understood Chinese. On one occasion, entertaining some American ladies at the palace, she invited them to see her private sleeping quarters. Unknown to them, however, the previous day had been spent in totally altering the furnishing and fitting of the bedroom so that her real taste and intimate surroundings remained unknown. Chinese subjects were also traditionally forbidden to look at members of the imperial family. Cixi was greatly surprised to learn from Miss Carl that Queen

Victoria, whom she very much admired, took walks and carriage rides in public places where she could be seen by the populace at large.

The Empress Dowager was never alone, for even while sleeping she was attended by eunuchs and ladies-in-waiting who were forbidden to fall asleep. She rose early between 5.30 and 6 am. Every morning, with Emperor Guangxu, her adopted son, she would receive her ministers and generals and deal with matters of State. The rest of the day would be given over to diversions. Both Katherine Carl and Der Ling describe walks in the palace grounds, boat trips on the lake and games of dice. There were also theatrical performances of which the empress was particularly fond.

If the day was filled with diversions, the year at the Court was punctuated by festivities. Birthdays, the New Year, weddings, accessions and the seasonal festivals were celebrated with fireworks, day-long performances by eunuchs and Court troupes, presentation of gifts and extravagant banquets at which glittering gold, silver and jade tableware would be heaped with hundreds of delicacies. On these occasions the imperial family and their officials wore their grandest robes and the usual business of the Court was suspended for several days.

Pavilion of Buddhist Incense at the Summer Palace

Two sections in the eastern palaces are worth seeing. One is the **Qianlong Garden**, built for the retirement of the aging emperor (reigned 1736–95). It is a quiet, secluded rock garden with a central pavilion made of fine wood brought from the forests of Sichuan and Yunnan provinces. One of three smaller pavilions was specially constructed for elaborate drinking games with strong Chinese liquor, a favourite pastime of the emperor.

The **Belvedere of Flowing Music** (Changyinge) is a three-storey theatre, the largest in the Palace, and a favourite haunt of the Empress Dowager Cixi. Magnificently carved and painted eaves set off the stage where dramas often depicted Buddhist worthies and Taoist immortals swarming all over the boards, dropping from ceilings and popping out of trap doors. The building opposite, where Cixi watched the dramas, has a rich display of silk costumes, stage properties and scripts used by the imperial troupe. There are also drawings of famous productions of the 60th birthday celebrations of Qianlong and Cixi. The latter affair is said to have continued for ten consecutive days.

Beyond the rear palaces, by the northern gate of the Palace, are the **Imperial Gardens**. Landscaped with cypress and pine trees that are now hundreds of years old, this is a perfect spot for a rest or a casual stroll.

Before leaving the palace, you might visit an interesting exhibition of palace architecture and construction located in the tower of the **Gate of Divine Prowess**. Here there are blueprints, tools, colour schemes, roof tiles and old photographs that are highly informative despite the frustrating absence of labels in any language except Chinese. Tickets for the exhibition are sold in the kiosk on the east side of the courtyard inside the gate. You reach the tower by a long incline once used by the soldiers guarding the palace.

PROSPECT HILL (JINGSHAN) OR COAL HILL (MEISHAN)

Just north of the Imperial Palace, the site occupied by Prospect Hill was a private park reserved for the use of the emperor in the Yuan dynasty (1279–1368). During the Ming (1368–1644), an artificial hill with five peaks was made, utilizing earth excavated when the moat of the Imperial Palace was dug. There is an old but fallacious story that an emperor kept supplies of coal hidden under the hill, hence its other name, Coal Hill (Meishan). A pavilion was erected on each peak, and five bronze Buddhas given pride of place in them. Four of the statues were removed by the troops of the Allied Expeditionary Force when they came to Beijing to relieve the Siege of the Legations in 1900. Prospect Hill was opened to the public in 1928. Designated as a park after 1949, and closed during the Cultural Revolution, it can now be visited between 6 am and 8 pm.

At the southern approach is the **Gorgeous View Tower** (Qiwanglou). Previously visited by emperors coming to pay their respects at an altar to Confucius, it is now an exhibition venue for displays of paintings, porcelain and calligraphy.

The best view of Beijing is from the **Pavilion of Everlasting Spring** (Wanchunting) perched on top of the middle peak, which used to be the highest point in the city. Northwards, one can see the Drum and Bell Towers, a traditional feature of old Chinese cities. To the northwest, the two slabs of water of the Shishahai and Beihai Lake are intersected by Di'anmen Dajie. To the south, the golden roofs of the Imperial Palace can be seen stretching into the distance.

On the eastern slope there used to be an old tree (said to be cassia) from which Chongzhen, the last Ming emperor, is supposed to have hanged himself in 1644. According to one version of the incident, the emperor decamped to the hill upon hearing that rebels intent on overthrowing the dynasty had already stormed the city. He had evidently retreated in some disarray: he wore no head-dress, had only one shoe, and the sleeves of his robe were freshly stained with the blood of his consort and two princesses. The story goes that he committed suicide with his own belt. The spot was once marked by a stone tablet. Later emperors in the early Qing, passing this place to go to the Hall of Imperial Longevity behind the hill, were required to alight from their sedan-chairs and proceed past the tablet on foot, perhaps in order to show more humility when contemplating the salutary example of an unpopular predecessor. Part of the Hall of Imperial Longevity is now the **Beijing Children's Palace**.

BEIHAI PARK

To the west of Prospect Hill is one of the most beautiful places in Beijing. Beihai Park is open from 6 am to 8 pm (extended to 9 pm in the summer), and is a popular place for skating in the winter and boating in the warmer months. There is a jetty on the northern shore, in front of a botanical garden, from which boats can be easily hired. The extraordinarily beautiful lotus blossoms make late summer a favourite time for visitors.

A lake was first dug here during the Jin dynasty (12th–13th century); a palace, an island—Qionghua or Hortensia—and pleasure gardens together created a retreat for the Court.

The retreat was refurbished three times during the Yuan dynasty, and again overhauled in the 15th century by Emperor Yongle, the architect of Beijing. The lake was divided into two: the central and southern lakes to the south, Zhongnanhai, is now reserved for senior members of the Chinese government. Dubbed the 'new Forbidden City' by Beijing residents, **Zhongnanhai** contains the villa where Mao Zedong lived and worked. The complex is off-limits to foreigners but Chinese tours are occasionally admitted. The northern part, Beihai, is open to the public. By the south entrance to the park is the **Round City**, which contains the enormous jade bowl, with fine carvings of sea monsters around the outside, that was given to Kublai Khan in 1265. The bowl went

missing for several centuries, and was functioning as a pickle vat in a monastery in the northern part of the city until the Qianlong emperor rescued it and brought it here in the 18th century. The carved inscriptions on the bowl date from this time.

The building that stands in the centre of the Round City, the **Hall of Receiving Light**, contains a large, white, jade Buddha image that resembles the statue in the Jade Buddha Temple in Shanghai. It was here that the Guangxu Emperor met with the British ambassador in 1893. Former emperors would rest and change their clothing in the Round City on their way to the palaces in the western suburbs. The Round City is open to visitors from 8.30 am to 4.30 pm.

■ QIONGHUA ISLAND

The dominant landmark on Qionghua Island, also called Hortensia Island, is the **White Dagoba**, a Buddhist shrine of Tibetan origin, built in 1651 in honour of the visit of the Dalai Lama to Beijing. Terraces lead down the southern slope, near the bottom of which is the White Dagoba Temple, now known as the **Temple of Everlasting Peace** (Yongansi).

Fangshan Restaurant (*see* page 185), famous for its imperial dishes, is located among the buildings that form the **Hall of Rippling Waves** (Yilantang), a former palace, at the northern end of the island. Not far from this, to the west, is the **Pavilion for Reading Ancient Texts** (Yuegulou), which is a storehouse of 495 stone tablets, engraved with calligraphy during the Qianlong period, including samples of writing from 1,500 years ago.

■ THE NORTHERN SHORE

Over a period of 30 years, Emperor Qianlong embellished several pavilions, halls and terraces along the northwestern shore of the lake. To commemorate his mother's 80th birthday, he had erected the **Ten-thousand Buddha Tower** (Wanfolou) at the western end of the cluster of buildings and gardens. Sadly, the little Buddhas have all been stolen.

Nearby, in front of the former Temple of Expounding Fortune (Chanfusi), now the site of a botanical garden, stands the **Iron Screen**, a Yuan-Dynasty wall of volcanic stone carved with strange mythical creatures. A later version, the **Nine-Dragon Screen**, made of glazed tiles in 1417, can be found further east, scaring evil spirits away not from the temple that used to stand behind, but from the Beihai Sports Ground.

Some of the old buildings around Beihai Lake have been converted to modern use; one of the most well-preserved is the **Study of Serenity** (Jingxinzhai) near the northern apex of the lake. This, deservedly called a garden within a garden', comprises a quiet walled enclave with a summer house, which now accommodates a literary research institute.

The Empress Dowager Cixi used to go to Beihai for picnics on the lake, and today the park continues to be a favourite with citizens enjoying a snack either from some of the small pavilions serving food, or a full meal at the Fangshan Restaurant.

The White Dagoba, Beihai Park

THE DRUM AND BELL TOWERS (GULOU AND ZHONGLOU)

Drum and Bell Towers are a traditional feature of an old Chinese city. In Beijing they are located to the north of Prospect Hill. The Drum Tower (Gulou) dates from the Ming period. Rising from a brick podium, the multi-eaved wooden tower is pierced on two sides by six openings. In Imperial times, 24 drums would beat out the night watches; now only one of them remains. The tower has been renovated, and it may be entered and climbed. Not far north of the Drum Tower is the Bell Tower (Zhonglou), a structure 33 metres (108 feet) high. The present tower was constructed of brick in 1747. The copper bell, which replaced an earlier iron bell that is still intact, rang out over the city at seven o'clock every evening until the practice was stopped in 1924. The towers are open every day from 9 am to 5 pm.

SONG QINGLING'S HOME

Song Qingling (Soong Ching-ling), born in 1892 in Shanghai, was married to the famous Republican, Dr Sun Yat-sen, and became an active political figure in her own right after his death in 1925. Though initially aligned, through her husband, with the Nationalist Party (Guomindang), whose leader Chiang Kai-shek married her sister Mei-ling, she eventually split with the right wing and, after spending several years in the Soviet Union, became a supporter of the Communists.

The Chinese accord Song Qingling enormous respect not simply because she held several high offices in the government of the People's Republic; she was also, in a very prominent way, a convert from the 'class enemy', coming as she did from a powerful and wealthy Shanghai family.

Her former residence at 46 Beiheyan, overlooking the Back Lake (Houhai), originally belonged to a member of the Qing royal family. Song Qingling occupied it from 1963 to her death in 1981. It may be visited daily between 9 am and 4.30 pm, and provides a relaxing diversion from Beijing's major sights. The house is enclosed by a lovely garden filled with pine, cypress and flowering shrubs, as well as traditional pavilions linked by winding corridors. The Fan Pavilion (Shanting) gives a view of the whole garden.

The living quarters have been turned into a modest museum displaying memorabilia of the former occupant's eventful life. Song Qingling was educated at Wesleyan College in Macon, Georgia and the bookshelves contain an impressive collection of English-language books.

THE MANSION OF PRINCE GONG (GONGWANGFU)

Located at number 17 Qianhaixi Jie in the Rear Lakes (Shichahai) district, the Mansion of Prince Gong is one of the largest and best preserved prince's mansions in

Beijing. Prince Gong was the younger brother of the Xianfeng emperor, whose short rule lasted only ten years (1851–1861). When Xianfeng died and the young Tongzhi emperor mounted the dragon throne at the age of five, Prince Gong served as regent along with Xianfeng's principal concubine and Tongzhi's mother, the notorious Empress Dowager Cixi. Prince Gong offended Cixi when he had An Dehai, her favourite eunuch, killed. Prince Gong also represented the Chinese government in negotiations with Lord Elgin in 1860, and was a key player in Chinese politics during the troubled decades of the late 19th century.

The mansion is divided into three sections. There is the residence itself, with a large banquet hall now used for evening shows. The spacious garden has several artificial hills made of heaped Lake Taihu stones, grotesquely eroded chunks of limestone that were transported from the Yangzi delta region. Atop one of the hills there is a pagoda that was used for gazing at the moon. There is also a large square fishing pond with an island in its centre.

A number of literary scholars in China have suggested that Prince Gong's mansion was the model for the mansion and garden, the Prospect Garden (Daguanyuan) described by Cao Xueqin in *The Dream of the Red Chamber* (*Honglou Meng*), the 18th-century novel generally regarded as China's greatest. Indeed several details of the mansion correspond with the descriptions in the book, especially the layout of the buildings. In the 1980s, the mansion was rescued from the clutches of the Public Security Bureau, which was using the grounds as a residence for retired officers. It is now fully restored and open to the public every day from 8.30 am to 5 pm.

A modern Prospect Garden was built in the southwest district of the city, based closely on the novel. It was used in the filming of the television series based on the book, and is now open to the public as a park (see page 106).

Xu Beihong Memorial Museum

This quiet little museum at 53 Xinjiekou Bei Dajie is one of the few public places in Beijing not crowded on a Sunday. It is dedicated to the renowned modern Chinese artist Xu Beihong (1895–1953), who is known internationally for his paintings of horses, and whose style has been widely imitated.

The museum was originally located at Xu Beihong's old home, but that building was demolished to make way for Beijing's subway. The present museum displays Xu's collection of oil paintings, sketches and watercolours simply but effectively. It is an enjoyable place to visit; hours are 9 am–12 noon, 1 pm–5 pm (closed Monday). Tel. 62252187.

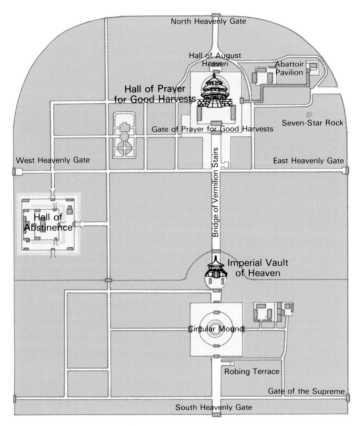

Temple of Heaven

Southern Districts

THE TEMPLE OF HEAVEN (TIANTAN)

The Temple of Heaven has been called 'the noblest example of religious architecture in the whole of China'. Begun in 1406, in the reign of Emperor Yongle, it was completed in 1420. The huge site—twice the size of the Imperial Palace—is reached by going south along Qianmen Dajie, following a route traversed by past emperors and their entourages in splendid procession from which the commoner had to avert his eyes.

The emperors came to Tiantan at the winter solstice to offer sacrifices to Heaven—

momentous occasions for which the temple's grandeur and simplicity provided a fitting background. The temple's design symbolized certain tenets of their beliefs. The altar and temple buildings are located within a wall which is half-circular to the north, and square to the south. During the Yongle period, annual sacrifices to the earth at the summer solstice were also performed here; the outline of the enclosure represented the imagined shapes of heaven (curved) and earth (square). Note that the roof tiles of the **Hall of Prayer for Good Harvests** (see below) are a deep blue, the colour of the sky. Moreover, each of the main structures in the temple has three tiers, making a total of nine, a number in Chinese cosmology representing Heaven. A separate Altar to the Earth (Ditan) was later constructed to the north of the city.

From the entrance at West Heavenly Gate, an avenue leads to the **Hall of Abstinence** (Zhaigong). For three days before the rites began, the emperor would have forsworn meat and wine, and the last day of his fast would be spent here. For his safety, the hall was enclosed by a moat.

From there visitors can walk up to the **Circular Mound** (Yuanqiu), an open altar set on three round marble terraces, built in 1530. The emperor used to come here to commune with Heaven and, interestingly, there is a curious acoustical effect to be heard from the centre of the Circular Mound.

Next to the Mound is the **Imperial Vault of Heaven** (Huangqiongyu), a wooden structure roofed with blue tiles and built entirely of wood in 1530. Tablets used in ceremonies held on the Mound were stored here. The Imperial Vault is surrounded by a round wall, popularly known as the **Echo** or **Whispering Wall**, because of its remarkable acoustics. If the round courtyard is relatively quiet—something it has not been in several years due to the rising tide of domestic tourism—two people standing out of earshot at any point along the wall with their heads at approximately the same distance off the ground can hear each other talking.

A second acoustical phenomenon is the '**echo stones**', which refer to the first three rectangular stones at the foot of the staircase that leads up to the Imperial Vault. If you stand on the first stone at the foot of the stairs and clap your hands once, you will hear one echo. If you clap once on the second stone, you will hear two echoes. And a single clap from the third stone will produce three echos. Again, this 'works' only if the courtyard is quiet enough for the vibrations to resonate in peace.

Leaving the Imperial Vault, there is a fine walk along a raised approach called the **Bridge of Vermilion Stairs** to the main building of the park, the magnificent **Hall of Prayer for Good Harvests** (*see* picture on page 108). This round wooden hall is surmounted by a triple roof covered in blue tiles and crowned with a gilded ball. The walls are resplendently painted in rich colours—red, blue, gold and green. It stands on three marble terraces.

The original Hall of Prayer for Good Harvests was built in 1420, but burned down in

1889 and was later reconstructed. At the time, there were no trees in China tall enough to supply the wood for the four tall columns, and thus these pillars, representing the four seasons and four directions, were imported from Oregon in the USA by the American shipping magnate, Robert Dollar—a fact that appears in no guidebook published in China since 1949. This showpiece of architectural ingenuity, 39 metres (125 feet) high and supported by 28 wooden pillars, stands without the aid of nails. The Hall was last used in 1914 by Yuan Shikai, then President of the infant Republic, who had imperial ambitions.

Two rectangular buildings stand in the courtyard before the Hall. The one to the west is a large comprehensive gift shop, while the one to the east now contains a display of the musical instruments, both authentic and reproduction, used in the imperial rituals.

Both the Altar and the Hall of Prayer are circular structures enclosed by square courtyards, a design symbolizing the journey from earth to heaven as the supplicant approached the place of worship. Behind the Hall of Prayer for Good Harvests is the **Hall of August Heaven** (Huangqiandian), where many of the objects used in the ceremonies are now exhibited.

None of Beijing's other three altars can compare with the Temple of Heaven, but potentially the finest is the **Altar of the Earth** (Ditan), built in 1530, and set in a wooded park in the northeast of the city. The Hall of Abstinence there has already been renovated. Some of the buildings of the **Altar of the Sun** (Ritan), built in 1531, as well as the altar it-self, still exist in a pleasant park near the Friendship Store. The **Altar of the Moon** (Yuetan) on the opposite side of the city, also built in 1531, is now the site of a television tower.

THE SOURCE OF LAW TEMPLE (FAYUANSI)

Situated in Fayuansi Qian Jie off Niu Jie in the Xuanwumen district, this temple is in the southwest quarter of the city. It was built by the Tang emperor, Taizong, in AD 654 in memory of troops killed in a battle with the Koreans and has been restored many times since. Two pagodas used to stand beside the temple, but they were destroyed by fire in the middle of the Tang period. It was at Fayuansi that the Song Minister Xie Dieshan, brought under guard by Yuan troops to Beijing, chose to starve himself to death rather than submit to the Mongols.

The Fayuansi comprises six courtyards planted with lilac trees. In the past, the temple was obliged to lay on a series of vegetarian banquets every spring for local dignitaries, for it is an age-old Chinese custom to spend a convivial evening wining and dining with crowds of friends on the pretext of admiring the season's new blooms.

The present occupants belong to the Chinese Buddhist Theoretical Institute, and the temple buildings now provide accommodation and classrooms for a number of novice monks. The temple is open daily from 8.30 am–11 am and 1.30 pm–4 pm.

Niu Jie Mosque (Niu Jie Qingzhensi)

Of the 80-odd mosques in Beijing, this one, right in the centre of the city's Moslem district, is the largest and oldest—it was built in AD 996 by Nazruddin, son of an Arab priest. The mosque is open daily from 8 am to 5 pm.

The exterior gives very little hint that it is other than a temple, but inside the gate there is a hexagonal Tower for Viewing the Moon, serving an Islamic purpose. This structure enables the imam to determine the beginning and end of Ramadan according to sightings of the moon. Grouped round courtyards behind the tower are the main prayer hall with its entrance facing west towards Mecca, a stele pavilion, the minaret from which the muezzin calls believers to prayer, a bath-house and some classrooms. The prayer hall is decorated in bright red and gold, with a section reserved for women behind a screen.

Islam was introduced to China in the Tang dynasty (618–907) and today the religion is embraced by several racial minorities in the country as well as the Hui, a more widespread community of Moslems often distinguishable from the ethnic Chinese only by the faith they profess.

White Clouds Taoist Monastery (Baiyunguan)

Located approximately one kilometre south of the Yanjing Hotel on Binhe Lu off Baiyun Lu, the White Clouds Taoist Monastery is one of the most important Taoist temples in China. The first Taoist monastery was built on this spot in the eighth century, but the present incarnation is the result of two overhauls that took place in 1956 and 1981.

The most famous inhabitant of the monastery was the Yuan-dynasty monk, Qiu Chuji, to whom one of the halls is dedicated. The period during which Qiu rebuilt the monastery, around 1230, is regarded as its golden age.

Like all other religious institutions in China, the White Clouds Monastery was hard hit during the Cultural Revolution, but now 100 monks, including young adepts, live on the premises, all of whom belong to the *chuanzhen* sect of Taoism. The monastery is the headquarters of the China Taoist Association, and thus is actively involved in 'foreign affairs'. The monastery performs a number of traditional Taoist ceremonies for a fee, and is crowded with believers and curiosity seekers on the two dozen Taoist holy days every year. In the old days, a major three-day ritual including horse races in the street took place here during the first lunar month, but this practice has long ceased.

The monastery is laid out on three parallel axes, with the most important structures on the central axis. There is a peaceful courtyard containing an ordination platform that resembles a miniature outdoor stage in the rear section of the western axis. Immediately inside the main gate, there is a stone-lined pond spanned by a bridge with an oversize Chinese coin hanging from it. Good luck is accorded to whoever can hit the giant coin

The Concubine in the Well

If the walls of the Forbidden City enclosed a dazzling Court presided over by enlightened emperors, they also—down the centuries—hid the innumerable plots, intrigues and betrayals that were played out in the struggles for power. It is said that the Forbidden City is a graveyard of souls; within its tortuous precints, inexplicable deaths and suspected murders were almost a familiar feature of Court life. There were always, at one time or another, the conflicting interests of pretenders, concubines, eunuchs and ministers to be resolved, especially when questions of succession were involved, or when weak emperors—either because of extreme youth or sheer incompetence—could be manipulated by self-seeking regents and corrupt officials.

The method of exterminating rivals by secret murder was employed with particular frequency, even finesse, by the Manchu Empress Dowager Cixi. This venal and selfish woman, who was supreme ruler of China for nearly half a century (1861–1908), has been regarded with such horror and fascination that, in the popular mind, the facts of her life have become blurred by legend.

As a young woman, Cixi entered the palace as a low-ranking concubine to Emperor Xianfeng (reigned 1851–61). On producing a son, she was promoted to Concubine of the First Grade, and skilfully charmed the emperor until she held him in thrall. On the emperor's death, she continued her scheming to eliminate her rivals and eventually achieved such considerable power that she was in a position to have herself and her sister, Empress Ci'an declared as regents during the minority of Emperor Tongzhi, her five year-old son. (Even Ci'an was eventually disposed of, by poison it is said, in 1881.) When Tongzhi came of age, Cixi, instead of relinquishing her power, thwarted his attempts to be with his wife and encouraged him in a life of debauchery, which no doubt hastened his death at the age of 18, leaving no heir.

In flagrant defiance of succession laws, Cixi then contrived to put her infant nephew, whom she adopted, on the throne as Emperor Guangxu. She ruled in his name, 'behind a silk screen', until he reached maturity and she ostensibly retired to the Summer Palace in 1889. Nevertheless she continued to meddle in Court affairs. In 1898, in the wake of China's humiliating defeat in the Sino-Japanese War, Guangxu launched the abortive reform movement that was to cost him his freedom. He was kept in semi-captivity by Cixi, who emerged from retirement to assume supreme control of the government once more.

At the height of the chaos following the anti-foreign Boxer Rebellion, the Empress Dowager was to commit one of her most ruthless murders. The date was 15th August 1900. At the time all of Beijing was in alarm as the Allied troops approached to relieve the besieged legation quarter of foreigners. In the Forbidden City, the Empress Dowager made ready to flee to the western city of Xi'an. Donning the dark blue clothes of a peasant woman, Cixi cut her long lacquered nails and dressed her hair in Chinese style. She summoned the young emperor to prepare by torchlight for their immediate departure in three horse-drawn carts.

At the last moment, the Pearl Concubine (Zhenfei), who was the emperor's favourite, appeared before Cixi and audaciously proposed that either the emperor be allowed to stay in Beijing or that she be allowed to accompany him to the west. Like the Empress Dowager, who had been a concubine herself, this spirited young woman was not given to showing respect or submission to her superiors. She had frequently interfered with Cixi's plans by giving the emperor contrary advice. Now, it must have appeared to the Empress Dowager, the Pearl Concubine had finally over-reached herself.

According to one account, Cixi lost no time in giving orders to her trusted eunuchs, who swiftly wrapped the concubine in a carpet and carried her off, over the young emperor's objections, to the rear of the palace, where they threw her down a well. Her body was recovered a year later and temporarily buried in a field in the city's western suburbs. Later she was laid to rest in the concubines' grave, near Emperor Guangxu's mausoleum, in the Western Qing Tombs.

The well is still there, inconspicuously marked by a small Chinese plaque, in a tiny courtyard in the northeastern corner of the Imperial Palace, by the Palace of Peaceful Old Age. A few Chinese tourists are usually clustered around it, trying to figure out how the eunuchs could have forced someone down so small an opening.

The final mystery surrounding Cixi was the strange coincidence of her death with that of Emperor Guangxu. It is alleged that Cixi, adamant that the emperor should not outlive her, gave orders from her deathbed for him to be poisoned, but that is just one more sinister intrigue that will never be proved.

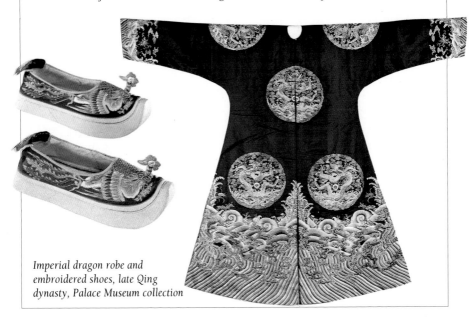

Imperial dragon robe and embroidered shoes, late Qing dynasty, Palace Museum collection

with a coin of the realm. All the profits go to the monastery.

The White Clouds Monastery is open everyday from 8am–4pm. There is a modest admission charge.

Prospect Garden (Daguanyuan)

In 1986 a new park, complete with pavilions, ponds, miniature hillocks and piped music, was opened to the public. Located in the southwest corner of the city, this pleasure ground has been built in imitation of the garden meticulously described in the great Chinese classic, *The Dream of the Red Chamber (Honglou Meng)* by Cao Xueqin. As recounted in the novel, the name 'Daguanyuan' was chosen by Imperial Concubine Yuanchun on a visitation. She wrote:

> Embracing hills and streams, with skill they wrought
> Their work at last is to perfection brought.
> Earth's fairest prospects all are here installed,
> So 'Prospect Garden' let its name be called!

From *The Story of the Stone*, translated by David Hawkes

Although somewhat lacking in authenticity, Daguanyuan is a pleasant park which draws crowds of local visitors. It recently served as the setting for a major television series based on the novel that enjoyed great success in China as well as Hong Kong and other overseas communities. Perhaps someday the series will be dubbed into English.

Western Districts

The Temple of the White Dagoba (Baitasi)

The 48-metre (150 feet)-high Yuan-dynasty dagoba, off Fuchengmennei Dajie, dominates they city's northwestern skyline. It is to the west of the White Dagoba in Beihai Park.

Even at the time of completion in 1279, under the supervision of a famous Nepalese architect, it was considered one of the gems of the Mongols' new capital. A large monastery was established here by Kublai Khan which was later destroyed, but rebuilt and renamed Miaoying Temple during the Ming dynasty. A beautiful filigree copper canopy, hung with bells, tops the dagoba.

The temple suffered damage during the Cultural Revolution and in the 1976 earthquake, but it has now been restored. The four existing halls date from the Qing and contain Yuan and Ming Buddhist statues and Tibetan *tankas*. During the restoration Buddhist scriptures and other relics dating from the Qianlong period were discovered.

THE FIVE PAGODA TEMPLE (WUTASI)

In the reign of Ming emperor Yongle (reigned 1403–24) a temple, to be named Zhenjuesi (Temple of the True Awakening), was ordered to be built on this site. It was to house a model of the famous ancient Indian Buddhist temple in Bodhgaya that was presented by an Indian monk to the Court. In 1473, in the reign of Emperor Chenghua, a building with five pagodas, based on the Bodhgaya model, was finally constructed here. Ransacked by English and French troops towards the end of the Qing, the temple never recovered its former glory. The five-pagoda building still stands, however, and its stone bas-relief carvings of figures and flowers, which are beautiful and varied, have been preserved. The Five Pagoda Temple is located one kilometre north of the Beijing Zoo in the Haidian district, off Baishiqiao Lu.

THE BIG BELL TEMPLE (DAZHONGSI)

This charming small temple one kilometre east of the Friendship Hotel on the north side of the Third Ring Road was built in 1733. In 1743 a huge bell was brought here, and the temple's name was changed to Dazhongsi. The giant bronze bell is believed to have been cast in the Ming dynasty, during the reign of Yongle, and is by this reckoning more than 550 years old. Over seven metres (nearly 23 feet) high and weighing 46 tons, it is inscribed with Buddhist scriptures in Chinese characters and is regarded as one of China's national treasures.

The bell is housed in a tower at the back of the temple, in an inner courtyard. Also displayed in the courtyard are some 30 bronze bells from various periods, showing the high degree of skill and workmanship that had been achieved. Many stone steles and statuary can be seen here, too. One can go right to the top of the Bell Tower by climbing a spiral staircase.

BEIJING ZOO (BEIJING DONGWUYUAN)

The zoo is located in the northwest part of the city. Visitors usually go straight to see the giant pandas to the left of the main entrance, but there are many other interesting animals to be seen—among them tigers from the northeast, yaks from Tibet, enormous sea-turtles from China's seas, and lesser-pandas from Sichuan.

The Beijing Zoo has an interesting and unusual history, dating back to the 17th century, when it was a garden belonging to one of the sons of Shunzhi, the first emperor of the Qing dynasty. In 1747, the Qianlong emperor had it refurbished as a park, and carried out many other major repairs on the imperial properties throughout Beijing and in the summer palaces in the western suburbs, in honour of his mother's 60th birthday.

In 1901, the Empress Dowager did another major rebuilding job, and used it to house a collection of animals given to her as a gift by a Chinese minister who had

acquired them at great cost during a trip to Germany. By the 1930s, most of them had died and were stuffed and put on display in a museum on the grounds. The zoo is open from 7.30 am to 6 pm.

FORMER RESIDENCE OF MEI LANFANG

Mei Lanfang (1894–1961) is regarded as one of the Four Great Female Impersonators in the history of the Peking Opera, an art form little understood and not widely appreciated outside of China and Chinese communities abroad. Mei's skill enabled him to perform women's roles more convincingly than any woman, so say the experts.

The courtyard house Mei lived in during his last days is open to the public as a shrine at number 9, Huguosi Jie in the western district. Mei's studio contains many of his personal possessions, and there are videotapes of the great diva's performances to watch.

But like the other 'former residences' open to the public in Beijing, Mei's home can be enjoyed for its architecture alone.

Northern Districts

WESTERN YELLOW TEMPLE (XIHUANGSI)

Located approximately two kilometres north of the Ring Road on Huangsi Lu in the Andingmenwai district, the Western Yellow Temple is one of the finest monuments of Lamaism in Beijing. It is all that remains of two temples, the Eastern and Western Yellow Temples, that were demolished in 1958 during the period of the Great Leap Forward.

During the Ming dynasty, two Buddhist temples stood in this vicinity, but both were destroyed by Li Zicheng when he invaded Beijing in 1643 and brought about the fall of that dynasty. In 1651, the first Qing emperor rebuilt the eastern temple to provide temporary accommodation for the Dalai Lama's visit to Beijing, and one year later the western temple was built to house the Dalai Lama's retinue.

As one of many Lamist temples in Beijing, this was the venue for the annual performance of the 'devil dances' that took place on the 13th and 15th days of the first lunar month in the new year. (They are still performed today in the nearby Lama Temple.) By the early 20th century, most of the buildings had fallen into disrepair.

The surviving 'marble pagoda' dates from 1781, when the Qianlong Emperor had it built to commemorate the death of a Panchen Lama who died of smallpox when he was visiting the capital. The octagonal stupa, supposedly containing the clothing of the deceased lama, is carved with scenes from the life of the Buddha. In 1990, the carvings were defaced by the foreign troops during the Boxer Uprising. But after being repaired they were defaced once again by Chinese troops.

Hall of Prayer for Good Harvests at the Temple of Heaven

The Yellow Temple bears comparison with the Five Pagoda Temple, which stands a few minutes north of the Beijing Zoo.

Shichahai: The Rear Lakes

One of the most pleasant districts of Old Beijing lies immediately north of the rear gate of Beihai Park. During much of the Qing dynasty, residence in the vicinity of the four once contiguous rear lakes was prohibited to all but the imperial clan, and the last emperor Puyi was born in a house on the eastern shores of one of these lakes that is now the property of the Ministry of Health (and next to the former residence of Song Qingling).

The willow-lined lakes were for centuries the site of a summertime night market that has been restored along the western shore of Front Lake (Qianhai), a few steps north of Di'anmen Dajie, under the name of Lotus Blossom Market (Lianhua shichang); another feature of these lakes is the luxuriant crop of lotus that drew crowds to view them before the flowers faded from the florid prime of summer to the withered desolation of autumn.

On hot nights, amateur opera singers can be heard crooning away as the lazy breezes carry their voices across the waters. In winter, a scene as if from a Breughel painting prevails with the locals taking to skates, sleds and improvised forms of transport to sail over the ice for sport.

Eastern Districts

The Lama Temple (Yonghegong)

The Lama Temple or the Palace of Harmony and Peace was built in 1694. It can be found on Dongsi Bei Dajie in the northeast of Beijing.

The prince who eventually became Emperor Yongzheng (reigned 1723–35) lived in this palace. Chinese tradition requires an emperor's former residence to be used as a temple upon his accession to the throne, so the palace was duly converted to serve a religious function.

Under the Qianlong emperor it became a centre of learning for the Yellow Hat sect of Tibetan Lamaism with considerable religious and political sway. As the residence of a 'Living Buddha' it had, at one time, a community of 1,500 Tibetan, Mongol and Chinese lamas. Today there are some 70 Mongolian lamas tending the temple.

The complex is arranged as a series of five halls and courtyards leading from a long pretty garden at the entrance. Passing **drum** and **bell towers** and two **stele pavilions** to left and right, the visitor reaches the **Hall of the Celestial Guardians** (Tianwangdian). Inside is a statue of Maitreya, the future Buddha, flanked on four sides by the Celestial Guardians of the East, South, West and North. Also revered is

CHENGDE: IMPERIAL RESORT

Chengde lies 354 kilometres (220 miles) northeast of Beijing and is the site of Jehol, or 'Warm River', the beautiful 18th-century resort of the Manchu emperors of the Qing dynasty. From 1681 the emperors used to escape the scorching Beijing summer and travel north, on a two-week journey over the Great Wall, to the cool hunting grounds of Jehol. The resort is also called Bishushanzhuang: Mountain Lodge for Avoiding Heat.

The wooded river basin in which Chengde lies is surrounded by pleated hills, punctuated at intervals by strange rock formations. Emperor Kangxi created the palace, lakes and parks to blend in with the natural beauty of the site. The palace itself is an appropriately simple building, constructed of *nanmu*, a hard aromatic wood. The audience chamber, the Modest and Responsible Hall, is connected to the other chambers by *lang*, or covered walkways, that wind around the courtyards which are themselves shaded by ancient pines.

Through the palace it is only a few minutes walk to the park and lakes. Emperor Kangxi decreed that 36 beauty spots were to be created in the park. His grandson Qianlong then doubled the number. As you wander beside the lake, there are carefully placed brightly coloured bridges which are designed to arouse your curiosity and lure you to one of the beauty spots.

Outside the palace grounds, Emperor Qianlong built eight magnificent temples, seven of which still remain. The eighth, which was built of bronze, was removed by the Japanese during the war. The first to be built was the Temple of Universal Peace (Puningsi), in 1775. This was a period in Chinese history of massive annexations, including Tibet and what is now Xinjiang. To integrate and, in some cases, to placate his new subjects, the emperor modelled the temples on their religion and culture. For this reason the Putuozongshengmiao is a copy of the Potala at Lhasa in Tibet.

Jehol lost favour with the Qing Court after the unfortunate—and ominous—accident to the Emperor Jiaqing, who was struck dead by lightning there. The summer palace and temples now form part of a public park.

Chengde can be reached in less than five hours by a daily train from Beijing Railway Station.

Suggested Itineraries

Three full days are a basic minimum for a general introduction to Beijing, but for various reasons many visitors to the city have less time. The following lists are based on a Peking pecking order that begins with the Forbidden City.

One Day Intensive
Hire a taxi for the day. Start at about 7 am with an early morning meditation at the **Monument to the People's Heroes** in the centre of Tiananmen Square. Walk through the **Working People's Cultural Palace** and get to the **Meridian Gate** (Wu-men), the main entrance of the **Forbidden City**, at around 8.30 am. Spend about four hours in the Forbidden City, following the main north road to the **Palace of Heavenly Purity** and the **Hall of Mental Cultivation**. Then head east to the **Nine Dragon Screen** and north through the various exhibitions to the **Concubine's Well** and out through the **Gate of Divine Prowess**, where your taxi should be waiting for you. Have a Peking duck lunch at either Hepingmen or at the Bianyifang at 1 pm, and then spend one and a half hours at the **Temple of Heaven**, walking from north to south. Have your driver let you off at **Liulichang** for a half hour stroll around the nearby lanes and alleys, and then drive to the **Summer Palace**, arriving there by 4.30 pm, when they stop selling tickets. Stroll around the buildings and the lake until the sun begins to set, then go out for a late dinner or dine at your hotel. This is a breathless day, but feasible. Best without jetlag.

Two Days

On day one, visit the **Temple of Heaven** in the morning, then head for the **Great Wall** where you can eat lunch. Climb the wall before or after lunch. Return to the city for a Peking duck banquet.

On day two, follow the One Day itinerary above, minus the Temple of Heaven, or add a visit to the **Lama Temple** on the way to the **Summer Palace**.

Three Days

On day one, begin with **Tiananmen Square** and the **Forbidden City** in the morning. Visit the **Temple of Heaven** and **Liulichang** in the afternoon.

On day two, go to the **Great Wall** and **Ming Tombs**, stopping for lunch along the way. Better yet, bring a picnic lunch, as the restaurants in the area can be problematical. Have dinner at a Sichuan restaurant in town.

On day three, visit the **Museum of Chinese History** in the early morning. Explore **Beihai Park** next and have lunch at either **Fangshan Restaurant** on the north shore of the island, or eat alfresco at the snack market near **Qianhai**, across the street from the north (rear) gate of Beihai Park. After lunch spend the rest of the day in the **Summer Palace**, ideally catching the sunset there, and return to the city for a late dinner.

Four Days

On day one, begin with **Tiananmen Square** and the **Forbidden City** in the morning. After a late lunch, explore the **Liulichang** and the surrounding hutongs in the afternoon, working your way back to Tiananmen Square.

On day two, go early to the **Temple of Heaven** and watch the local devotees of the martial arts attaining longevity. Then head for the Great **Wall** and **Ming Tombs**, eating lunch along the way, or better yet, bring a picnic lunch. Eat at a Sichuan restaurant for dinner.

On day three, visit the **Museum of Chinese History** in the early morning. Explore **Beihai Park** next and have lunch at either **Fangshan Restaurant** on the north shore of the island, or eat alfresco at the snack market near **Qianhai**, across the street from the north gate of Beihai Park. After lunch stroll around **Wangfujing** and visit the shops before dinner at the nearby **Donglaishun**, featuring mutton hotpots.

On day four, visit the **Lama Temple**, **Confucian Temple** and **Guozijian** in the morning. Spend the last afternoon and early evening in the **Yuanmingyuan Gardens** (one hour) and **Summer Palace** (Yiheyuan), leaving for dinner after sunset.

Five Days

Follow the four day itinerary, and on day four, add visits to the **Beijing Zoo** (to see the pandas), **Beijing Art Museum**, **Big Bell Temple**, **White Clouds Taoist Temple**, **Old Observatory**, or go out of town for a half day visit to the **Tanzhesi** or **Jietaisi** in the western suburbs.

A second alternative is to visit several of the destinations mentioned above on the afternoon of the fourth day, and save the **Summer Palace** and **Yuanmingyuan Gardens** for the afternoon of the fifth day; in the morning, visit the **Temple of the Sleeping Buddha** and the **Temple of Azure Clouds** which lie about 15 minutes by car beyond the Summer Palace. Yet another possibility on the fifth day is to make a second visit to the **Forbidden City**.

a statue of Wei Tuo, whose meritorious deeds, it is said, included the safeguarding of a bone of Buddha's.

Coming out of Tianwangdian, the visitor will come upon a large copper ding (ancient cauldron), cast in 1747.

The **Great Stele Pavilion** comes next: it contains a square stele inscribed in four languages (Han, Manchu, Mongolian and Tibetan) describing the philosophy of Lamaism.

The main hall, the **Hall of Harmony and Peace**, from which the temple takes its name, contains three statues of Buddha—past, present and future—and at their side figures of the 18 *luohan* (disciples who had vowed always to remain on earth to spread the teachings of Buddha).

To the north of the **Hall of Eternal Blessing** (Yongyoudian), is the **Hall of the Wheel of the Law** (Falundian). Its roof supports five small pavilions of Zongkapa (1417–78), who founded the Yellow Hat Sect of Tibetan Buddhism. Against the walls a collection of several hundred Tibetan scriptures is stored.

The last hall, the three-storeyed **Pavilion of Ten-thousand Fortunes** (Wanfuge) contains a unique example of Chinese carpentry—a massive statue of Maitreya. Standing over 23 metres (75 feet) high, his head reaches the third floor. The statue is supposed to have been carved out of a single white sandalwood tree, transported all the way from Tibet in the mid-18th century.

The low galleries lining both sides of some of the courtyards were originally study halls for the lamas and now contain a fine collection of Tibetan bronzes and *tanka* paintings.

The temple is open daily from 9 am to 5 pm.

The Old Observatory (Guanxiangtai)

Kublai Khan established an observatory at the southeastern corner of his city and it is still there today. Functioning as part of the more modern Beijing Observatory and Planetarium (which is right at the other end of the city, opposite the Beijing Zoo in the northwest), the Old Observatory is now a museum with a small but superb collection of Ming and Qing astronomical instruments.

Of the instruments that were made from the 15th century onwards only fifteen pieces remain, including several made by Jesuit fathers—notably Adam Schall and Ferdinand Verbiest—in the 17th century. When these missionaries came to China they proved themselves to be such skilful astronomers that they were put in charge of the observatory. (Missionaries followed in the wake of some of the first Western traders, having significant effects on Chinese attitudes to science,mathematics and technology; despite the fact that the Chinese were already advanced in these matters—the first documented eclipses were recorded in China. The most famous Jesuit was Matteo Ricci (1552–1610), who, aside from being science tutor to the emperor's

An old man plays a bamboo flute in the pavilion on the summit of Coal Hill, overlooking the Forbidden City

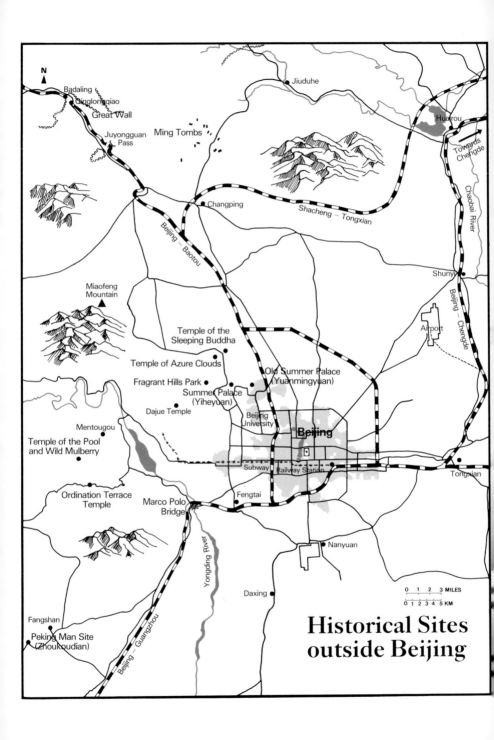

N

Jiuduhe

Badaling
Qinglongqiao
Great Wall

Juyongguan
Pass

Ming Tombs

Huairou

Towards
Chengde

Changping

Shacheng – Tongxian

Chaobai River

Shunyi

Beijing – Baotou

Miaofeng
Mountain ▲

Beijing – Chengde

Airport

Temple of the
Sleeping Buddha

Temple of Azure Clouds

Old Summer Palace
(Yuanmingyuan)

Fragrant Hills Park

Summer Palace
(Yiheyuan)

Dajue Temple

Beijing
University

Beijing

Mentougou

Temple of the Pool
and Wild Mulberry

Subway   Railway Station

Tongxian

Ordination Terrace
Temple

Fengtai

Marco Polo
Bridge

Nanyuan

Yongding River

Daxing

0 1 2 3 MILES

0 1 2 3 4 5 KM

Fangshan

Peking Man Site
(Zhoukoudian)

Beijing – Guangzhou

Historical Sites
outside Beijing

son, was also an influential preacher; he left behind hundreds of Catholic churches in the Ming dynasty.)

These instruments were taken to Germany in 1900, as spoils of war after the Allied forces had subdued the Boxer Rebellion, but were returned to China in 1919. Eight of them are displayed on the Observatory terrace here atop one of the few remaining sections of the old city wall (the other seven were moved to the Nanjing Observatory in 1931). They include three armillary spheres, a quadrant, a sextant, a celestial globe, a horizon circle and a quadrant altazimuth.

The observatory may be visited from 9 am–11.30 am and 1–5.30 pm but is closed on Mondays and Tuesdays.

The Pailous

To get to the Temple of Confucius and the Former Imperial College, one must pass at least one of the few extant street *pailous* in Beijing. But before modern transport made it necessary to reduce their numbers radically, *pailous* decorated many streets and intersections in Beijing and other cities in northern China. For example, Xidan means 'western single' and refers to a single *pailou* that once stood at the intersection of Xi Chang'an Jie and Xidan Bei Dajie, while Xisi, literally 'western four', reminds us that there were once four *pailous* at the intersection that is still referred to by that name.

Some scholars trace the origin of the *pailou* to India, where *toranas*, a gateway constructed of two columns (posts) with several decorative crossbeams (lintels), were placed at the entrances to temples. There is a striking resemblance between the stone *toranas* surrounding the large hemispherical stupa at Sanchi, and those at the Round Altar in the Temple of Heaven in Beijing. Later pailous have highly elaborate (and often ungainly) wooden superstructures with manifold roofs, always in odd numbers, and sometimes covered with glazed tiles.

In residential districts, *pailous* were erected to commemorate virtuous women or heroic men. No such *pailous* have survived in Beijing.

Pailous can be seen in the Temple of Confucius, Imperial College, Lama Temple, Beihai Park and the Summer Palace, to mention a few. The marble *pailou* at the entrance to the Ming Tombs, once painted a brilliant red and green, is regarded as one of the finest in China.

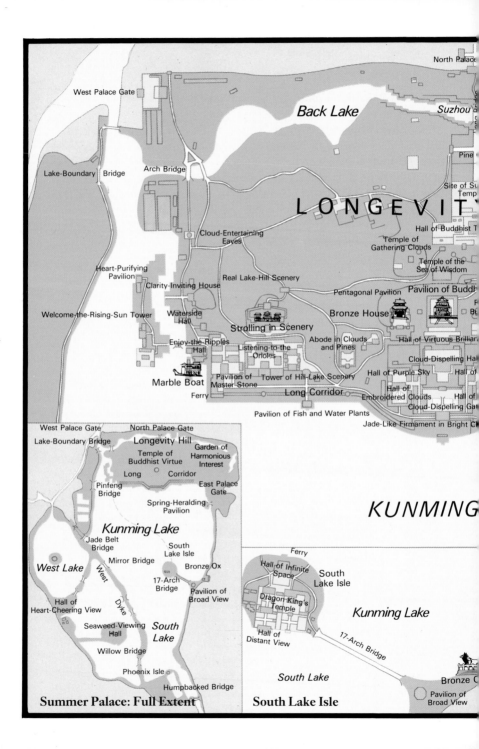

North Palace

West Palace Gate

Back Lake

Suzhou

Pine

Lake-Boundary Bridge

Arch Bridge

Site of Su
Temp

LONGEVIT

Hall of Buddhist T

Cloud-Entertaining
Eaves

Temple of
Gathering Clouds

Heart-Purifying
Pavilion

Temple of the
Sea of Wisdom

Clarity-Inviting House

Real Lake-Hill Scenery

Pentagonal Pavilion

Pavilion of Buddh

Welcome-the-Rising-Sun Tower

Waterside
Hall

Strolling in Scenery

Bronze House

P

B

Enjoy-the-Ripples
Hall

Listening-to-the
Orioles

Abode in Clouds
and Pines

Hall of Virtuous Brilliar

Cloud-Dispelling Ha

Marble Boat

Pavilion of
Master Stone

Tower of Hill-Lake Scenery

Hall of Purple Sky

Hall of

Hall of
Embroidered Clouds

Ferry

Long Corridor

Cloud-Dispelling Ga

Pavilion of Fish and Water Plants

Jade-Like Firmament in Bright C

West Palace Gate

North Palace Gate

Longevity Hill

Garden of
Harmonious
Interest

Lake-Boundary Bridge

Temple of
Buddhist Virtue

Long   Corridor

Pinfeng
Bridge

East Palace
Gate

Spring-Heralding
Pavilion

Kunming Lake

KUNMING

Jade Belt
Bridge

South
Lake Isle

Ferry

West Lake

Mirror Bridge

Bronze Ox

Hall of Infinite
Space

South
Lake Isle

17-Arch
Bridge

Pavilion of
Broad View

Dragon King's
Temple

Kunming Lake

Hall of
Heart-Cheering View

South
Lake

17-Arch Bridge

Seaweed-Viewing
Hall

Hall of
Distant View

Willow Bridge

Phoenix Isle

South Lake

Bronze O

Humpbacked Bridge

Pavilion of
Broad View

Summer Palace: Full Extent

South Lake Isle

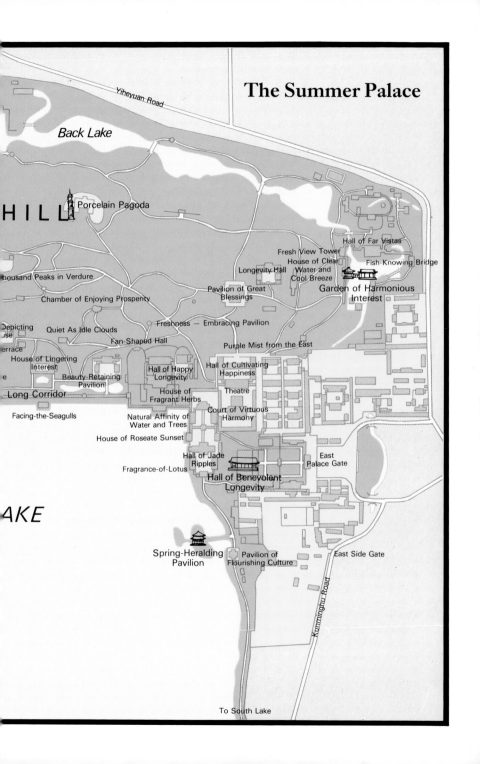

The Summer Palace

Yiheyuan Road

Back Lake

HILL

Porcelain Pagoda

Hall of Far Vistas

Fresh View Tower

House of Clear Water and Cool Breeze

Longevity Hall

Fish-Knowing Bridge

Thousand Peaks in Verdure

Pavilion of Great Blessings

Garden of Harmonious Interest

Chamber of Enjoying Prosperity

Freshness — Embracing Pavilion

Depicting use

Quiet As Idle Clouds

Fan-Shaped Hall

Purple Mist from the East

errace

House of Lingering Interest

Hall of Happy Longevity

Hall of Cultivating Happiness

e

Beauty-Retaining Pavilion

House of Fragrant Herbs

Theatre

Long Corridor

Court of Virtuous Harmony

Facing-the-Seagulls

Natural Affinity of Water and Trees

House of Roseate Sunset

Hall of Jade Ripples

East Palace Gate

Fragrance-of-Lotus

Hall of Benevolent Longevity

AKE

Spring-Heralding Pavilion

Pavilion of Flourishing Culture

East Side Gate

Kunminghu Road

To South Lake

The End of an Era

Two days after I entered the palace Tzu Hsi died, and on December 2, the "Great Ceremony of Enthronement" took place, a ceremony that I ruined with my crying.

The ceremony took place in the Hall of Supreme Harmony (Tai Ho Tien). Before it began I had to receive the obeisances of the commanders of the palace guard and ministers of the inner court in the Hall of Central Harmony (Chung Ho Tien) and the homage of the leading civilian and military officials. I found all this long and tiresome; it was moreover a very cold day, so when they carried me into the Hall of Supreme Harmony and put me up on the high and enormous throne I could bear it no longer. My father, who was kneeling below the throne and supporting me, told me not to fidget, but I struggled and cried, "I don't like it here. I want to go home. I don't like it here. I want to go home." My father grew so desperate that he was pouring with sweat. As the officials went on kotowing to me my cries grew louder and louder. My father tried to soothe me by saying, "Don't cry, don't cry; it'll soon be finished, it'll soon be finished."

When the ceremony was over the officials asked each other surreptitiously, "How could he say 'It'll soon be finished'? What does it mean, his saying he wanted to go home?" All these discussions took place in a very gloomy atmosphere as if these words had been a bad omen. Some books said that these words were prophetic as within three years the Ching Dynasty was in fact "finished" and the boy who wanted to "go home" did go home, and claimed that the officials had a presentiment of this.

Pu Yi, From Emperor to Citizen, translated by W J F Jenner

Sights Outside Beijing

The Northwest

THE SUMMER PALACE (YIHEYUAN)

In order to avoid the intense heat of the summer, the imperial court used to leave the Forbidden City and stay in a specially built resort about 11 kilometres (seven miles) northwest of Beijing. Known in the West as the Summer Palace and in China as Yiheyuan—the Garden for Cultivating Harmony—the resort encompasses Longevity Hill (Wanshoushan) and a series of palaces, pavilions, terraces and covered walks strung out along the northern shore of Kunming Lake. Indeed the Summer Palace is three-quarters covered by water and Kunming Lake, whose shape and size have been altered many times by successive landscape architects, is central to the overall design of the park. The indefatigable Emperor Qianlong, for one, reconstructed it to resemble the West Lake in Hangzhou in 1751, the year of his mother's 60th birthday (Longevity Hill was named for her).

The Old Summer Palace, known as **Yuanmingyuan** (see page 126), was ravaged by Anglo-French troops in 1860. In 1888 the Empress Dowager Cixi diverted funds allocated for improving the navy to the Summer Palace's renovation at a new site. She gave it its present name, Yiheyuan, and retired to its peaceful environs in 1889. Following further destruction in 1900, the Summer Palace was again restored at great expense.

The Summer Palace today is a delightful park, informal and less imposing than the Imperial Palace. Much has been restored and is in a fine state of preservation.

■ IMPERIAL RESIDENCES

Directly opposite the **East Palace Gate** (Donggongmen), across a large courtyard, is the **Hall of Benevolent Longevity** (Renshoudian) where Cixi and her nephew, the nominal Emperor Guangxu, gave audience to their ministers. Behind the courtyard were the private apartments of the imperial household, the **Hall of Jade Ripples** (Yulantang). This residence was made even more private when the Empress Dowager had a wall erected on its lake side. Here Guangxu was for ten years her prisoner, having flouted her authority by giving his support to an ill-fated reform movement in 1898. With him safely under guard (but officially 'chronically ill'), she emerged from 'retirement' to assume control of the government once more.

Cixi's own quarters were in the **Hall of Happy Longevity** (Leshoutang), with **Longevity Hill** behind and a pleasant lake view in front. Both sets of private apartments, hers and Guangxu's, contain contemporary Qing furniture. Another part of the compound is the **Court of Virtuous Harmony** (Deheyuan), made up of the **Hall for Cultivating Happiness** (Yiledian) and a **theatre**, built at the cost of 700,000 taels of silver to commemorate Cixi's 60th birthday. She was inordinately fond of theatricals and *tableaux vivants*, and even appeared in them herself. In this theatre a water tank had been sunk under the stage in order to provide such touches of verisimilitude as trickling streams and gushing fountains. The building, now renovated as a theatre museum, should not be missed. Attendants dressed in Qing-dynasty clothes are on hand to direct visitors to superb exhibitions of theatre costumes and stage props. A collection of Cixi's personal possessions is also on display. These include the automobile—the first imported into China—presented by Yuan Shikai, the military commander who was later President of the new Republic for a brief time; silver and gold ware; brushes, garments and perfumes. The Hall for Cultivating Happiness now displays over 200 historical artefacts, among them the four large carved screens inlaid with jade which are considered national treasures.

■ KUNMING LAKE'S NORTHERN SHORE
From the *pailou* (ceremonial arch) on the northern shore of Kunming Lake, the **Cloud-Dispelling Hall** (Paiyundian), the **Hall of Virtuous Brilliance** (Dehuidian), the **Pavilion of Buddhist Incense** (Foxiangge) and the **Temple of the Sea of Wisdom** (Zhihuihai) rise straight up the slope of Longevity Hill. Inside the Cloud-Dispelling Hall, where Cixi celebrated her birthdays, are displays of *penjing* (potted miniature landscapes) and artefacts which were almost all tributes from her ministers. The oil painting of the empress was executed by an American for Cixi's 69th birthday (*see* page 92).

■ THE LONG CORRIDOR
Following the shoreline of the lake, the Long Corridor—730 metres (2,550 feet) in length—leads from the Hall of Happy Longevity to the ferry pier beside the **Marble Boat**. All along it views of the lake mingle with pictures of birds and flowers, scenes from legends and famous landscapes that have been painted on the beams of the roofed walk (*see* picture on page 127). The Chinese like to compare the promenade with a picture gallery, and say that so beguiling is the beauty that no courting couple can emerge at the other end unbetrothed.

■ SOUTH LAKE ISLE
From beside the Marble Boat (actually made of stone), below the Summer Palace's popular lunch restaurant **Pavilion for Listening to the Orioles**, it is possible to take a ferry across the water to the **South Lake Isle** (Nanhu Dao) and the **Dragon King's Temple** (Longwangmiao). From Nanhu you can walk across the **Seventeen-Arch Bridge** (Shiqikongqiao) back to the entrance.

The Marble Boat in the Summer Palace

THE GARDEN OF PERFECTION AND BRIGHTNESS

The ruins of the old Qing Summer Palace, Yuanmingyuan, barely conjure up the former glory of the 'Garden of Gardens'. Yuanmingyuan—the garden of Perfection and Brightness—was first established by Emperor Yongzheng (reigned 1723–35), although several gardens had existed on this site since the Ming Dynasty.

From the Ming to the early Qing, garden-making gained enormous popularity and the art of taming disordered landscape and yet preserving its 'naturalness' reached the height of sophistication in the reign of Emperor Qianlong.

The northwestern suburbs of Beijing, stretching right up to the Fragrant Hills, must have appeared eminently suitable for exercising this art. The area is a large plain where terrain and natural springs provided ideal conditions for creating the private gardens and lavish resorts that came to be established there. The Fragrant Hills resort palace was one of these; the Garden of Carefree Spring (Changchunyuan) was another. In due course the whole area became almost totally the exclusive pleasure grounds of emperors and their kinsmen.

Changchunyuan was more than an imperial garden. Emperor Kangxi had a palace built so that he could administer State affairs there as well as in the Forbidden City. To the north of Changchunyuan was Yuanmingyuan, a private garden bestowed on Prince Yinzhen, Kangxi's fourth son, in 1709. On Yinzhen's accession, he embarked on a massive project to extend and transform Yuanmingyuan into a resort fit for an emperor. The Auspicious Sea (Fuhai) was excavated at that time. Water was in fact the dominant theme of the garden and extensively used by landscape artists in designing architectural groupings, scenic spots or formal views. From the time Prince Yinzhen ascended the throne as the Yongzheng Emperor, five successive rulers moved their Court to Yuanmingyuan after each New Year. Except for excursions to Chengde during the summer, they lived in Yuanmingyuan until the winter solstice.

Under Emperor Qianlong, Yuanmingyuan became even more splendid. From his inspection tours of the area around the Yangzi River, the emperor assimilated and then transplanted garden-making ideas and scenery from the south. Altogether 69 'scenes' or 'views' were created in the Summer Palace; 40 of them were recorded by Yongzheng's Court painters Shen Yuan and Tang Dai, and it is from these scrolls that historians have reconstructed a broader picture of this outstanding garden. Descriptions of it have also survived in the correspondence of the Catholic missionaries employed by the Qing Court. One of them, the Jesuit artist Giuseppe Castiglione, was commissioned by Qianlong in 1745 to design the European-style Western Mansions (Xiyanglou) that were constructed along the northern wall. It is the ruins of these extraordinary palaces that remain today.

In 1860 when Anglo-French troops captured Beijing, rampaging soldiers, on the orders of Lord Elgin, set fire to Yuanmingyuan. A young captain of the British Royal Engineers, who was later to gain fame as 'Chinese Gordon', wrote after the destruction: '[We] went out, and, after pillaging it, burned the whole place, destroying in a Vandal-like manner most valuable property which would not be replaced for four millions. We got upwards of £48 a-piece prize money before we went out here; and although I have not as much as many, I have done well.

'The people are civil, but I think the grandees hate us, as they must after what we did to the Palace. You can scarcely imagine the beauty and magnificence of the places we burnt. It made one's heart sore to burn them; in fact, these palaces were so large, and we were so pressed for time, that we could not plunder them carefully. Quantities of gold ornaments were burnt, considered as brass. It was wretchedly demoralizing work for an army. Everybody was wild for plunder.'

Thirteen years later an attempt was made to rebuild the palace to mark Empress Dowager Cixi's 40th birthday, but dwindling funds put a full-scale restoration out of the question. It was once again devastated in 1900, this time by the Allied Expeditionary Force who relieved the Siege of the Legations. Over the years the damage was compounded by local peasants scavenging for building materials.

In 1977 maintenance of the ruins of Yuanmingyuan was put in the charge of the Beijing municipal authorities, and a small museum has been set up at the site to show the scale and magnificence of the palace in its day. Despite these efforts at conservation, the area remains a wilderness with a few romantic rococo ruins for children to climb on when families picnic there. Energetic Beijing residents say that the best time to visit Yuanmingyuan is at dawn. To many other Chinese it remains a powerful symbol of imperial folly and Western aggression.

The Summer Palace is open from 7 am to 7 pm (9 pm in summer). Entrance tickets are sold up until 4.30 pm.

THE OLD SUMMER PALACE (YUANMINGYUAN)

Not far from the Yiheyuan is the site of the old Qing Summer Palace, Yuanmingyuan. Little is left of it now except some broken pillars and masonry lying about in a field. There is a museum—the Garden History Exhibition Hall—with a well-arranged display of drawings and models showing the splendour of the palace in its heyday.

The museum is part of a recent effort to turn the site into a public park, with some shrubs, trees and a few paths for the many citizens of Beijing—who can bicycle here in about half an hour—seeking respite from their urban surroundings.

In the late 1980s, a French consortium of historians and architects reconstructed the maze in concrete. For years there have been plans afoot to rebuild the entire palace as a sort of Qing-style Disneyland. But a conservative faction opposed this idea on the grounds that it was a better lesson for China and the world if this monument of Chinese splendour and foreign imperialist destruction remained in fragments rather than be turned into a commercial spectacle.

THE TEMPLE OF THE SLEEPING BUDDHA (WOFOSI)

This temple, 19 kilometres (12 miles) from the city, is reached by continuing west on the road from the Summer Palace towards the Fragrant Hills, passing Jade Spring Hill with its distinctive twin pagodas.

There is mention in the historical records of an enormous statue of the recumbent Buddha first being cast at the temple in the 14th century, but the present statue probably dates from a later period. The Buddha, in lacquered bronze, lying full length with his head supported by his right arm, is five metres (16 feet) long. Enormous shoes which have been presented to the Buddha are displayed in cases on either side. Some rare trees grow in the surrounding countryside, and a line of ancient evergreens leads up to the temple's portico.

THE TEMPLE OF AZURE CLOUDS (BIYUNSI)

A short way from the Temple of the Sleeping Buddha on the road leading to the Fragrant Hills is one of Beijing's great temples, the Temple of Azure Clouds. A temple has stood here since the Yuan Dynasty. It was restored and extended on two separate occasions by palace eunuchs Yu Jing and Wei Zhongxian, who planned to place their graves in the hill behind (they both failed in their ambition). There are many buildings here, arranged on the side of a hill, and much to see. At the top of the hill is the Diamond Throne Pagoda, an Indian-style stone temple with a

*Liu Wenjiu, one of a number of artists who occupied a village
at the Old Summer Palace in the early 1990s*

*Some of the intricate painting to be seen decorating the Long Corridor
at the Summer Palace (see page 122)*

spectacular view from its roof. It was built on the lines of the Five Pagoda Temple (see page 107) in 1792. Below is the Memorial Hall to Sun Yat-sen. After his death in 1925 the body of the founder of modern China lay in state in this temple, reposing in a crystal coffin presented by the Soviet Union. His body was moved to Nanjing in 1929 when the mausoleum there had been completed.

To one side of the Memorial Hall is the Luohan Hall, with its four inner courtyards, which was built in the mid-18th century. *Luohan* are the disciples of Buddha, and over 500 gilded wooden statues of these proselytes, each one quite distinct with an individual, and very human, personality, are crammed into this section of the temple complex.

Biyunsi, open between 8 am and 5 pm, makes for a particularly delightful excursion in the spring, when the peach and almond trees—both within the temple complex and on the surrounding hillsides—are covered in blossom.

FRAGRANT HILLS PARK (XIANGSHAN GONGYUAN)

Close to the Temple of Azure Clouds, this park is set in a belt of hills northwest of Beijing, about 40 minutes' drive away. The Western Hills, as the area is also called, has long been a favourite retreat of the emperors. In the 12th century when it was a royal hunting park, the landscape was considered so picturesque that the hills came to be designated as one of the Eight Great Scenes of Yanjing (the City of Swallows). With the addition of a resort palace in the reign of Kangxi, its attractions further increased until the park reached the peak of its splendour in the 18th century.

Roads fan out from the main east-facing gate. To the left is the Fragrant Hills Hotel, a recent construction. Many of the old beauty spots still remain, however, most notably at the northern end of the park. One can reach this part by entering through the north gate from the direction of the Temple of Azure Clouds. Crossing Spectacles Lake (Yanjinghu) one comes to the Study of Self-knowledge (Jianxinzhai), a 16th-century garden with a circular pool, enclosed by a rounded wall and promenade and shielded by clumps of trees on three sides. To the south of it are the remains of Zhaomiao, a Tibetan-style temple erected in the Qianlong period, as well as an ornamental archway and a pagoda roofed in yellow glazed tiles, with bells dangling from its eaves. There is now a cable car.

The name 'Fragrant Hills' probably derives from the two slabs of stone—shaped like incense burners—on top of the highest peak at the western extremity of the park. The wisps of mist clinging to the summit resemble puffs of scented smoke coming from the incense burners at the top. But the park is famous above all for its autumn aspect. The blaze of red on the hillsides when the leaves of the Huanglu smoke tree (sometimes referred to as maple) are turning is a sight much celebrated in poetry and painting.

The North

THE GREAT WALL (CHANGCHENG)

The Great Wall, an integral feature of the geography of North China, has captured the imagination of countless people throughout its long history.

The wall was built in a piecemeal fashion over a long period, from the fifth century BC down to the 16th century AD, as a means of defence against raids from northern nomadic tribes. When the empire was unified under Qin Shi Huangdi in 221 BC, a continuous line of fortifications was constructed by joining up the old walls.

'A wall between is a mountain' goes an old saying, and in the hearts of the Chinese, the 'Wall of Ten-thousand Li' (*Wanli Changcheng*) not only protected them from the barbaric Huns (Xiongnu). Its significance lay also in separating the familiar, safe patterns of settled agriculture, from the alien pastoral nomadic life of the steppes and deserts beyond.

Historical texts record as many as 300,000 men working for ten years on the construction of a section of the wall. Stories of the hardship suffered by these conscripted labourers have been passed down, contributing to the image of the Qin emperor as a hated tyrant. Composed partly of earth faced with brick and partly of masonry, Great Walls were built by rulers of ten dynasties and their defensive works totalled an incredible 25,000 kilometres in length. The most recently-built Great Wall, the work of all 16 Ming emperors, totalled 6,300 kilometres. Naturally, the strongest, and therefore best preserved sections, shielded the dynastic capital, Beijing.

Since the late 1950s, five parts of the wall have been restored. Visitors have traditionally been taken to the section at **Badaling**, in Nankou Pass, about 70 kilometres (44 miles) from the city, either before or after a visit to the Ming Tombs.

The road to Badaling passes through Juyongguan, or Juyong Pass, where there is a stunning white marble structure, the Cloud Platform, at the foot of a newly-reconstructed section of Great Wall. Built around 1345 during the Yuan dynasty, it originally served as the base for three pagodas which were destroyed several decades later. The platform is pierced by a hexagonal archway. The ceiling and walls are covered with wonderful carvings of the Four Heavenly Kings and the texts of Buddhist scriptures in six languages: Nepalese Sanskrit, Tibetan, Phags-pa Mongolian, Uighur, Xi Xia and Han Chinese. Earlier this century, an American traveller called it the 'language archway'.

The second most popular section of the Great Wall to have been restored is at **Mutianyu**, northwest of Beijing in Huairou county. The major advantage of visiting this section is that it is a little less crowded than that at Badaling. Before reaching the wall one has to mount some thousand steps or ride the cable car. This expanse of the wall trails off for more than a mile and one has an unobstructed view in both directions of great lengths of the defense undulating along mountain crests until they fade into the distance. Here there is a much more peaceful atmosphere and one can really get a sense of the Great Wall's history and grandeur as it spans the horizon.

Alternative sites for climbing on the Great Wall are the adjacent sections of **Jinshanling** and **Simatai**, approximately 120 kilometres (75 miles) northeast of Beijing. This is wall par excellence and is well worth a full day of your itinerary.

■ ACCESS TO THE GREAT WALL

■ BADALING
Public tourist-line bus No.6 from outside Tai Feng Lou restaurant, 300 metres west of Qianmen. Departures daily, approximately every 30 minutes from 7.00–10.00am, November–March inclusive; 6.00–10.00am, April–October. Return fare 24 *yuan*. Also, tourist-line bus No.4, from opposite Beijing Zoo on Zhanlan Lu. Times and fares as for No.6 bus. Travel time is less that two hours each way. Taxis around 400 *yuan* with driver waiting up to three hours.

■ MUTIANYU
Public tourist-line bus No.4, from outside Southern Cathedral, northeast exit of Xuanwumen subway station. From April–October, weekends only. Departures from 7.00–10.00am. Return fare 24 *yuan*. Travel time is more than two hours each way. Taxis around 500 *yuan* with the driver waiting up to three hours.

■ SIMATAI
Public tourist-line bus No.12, from outside Southern Cathedral, northeast exit of Xuanwumen subway station. From April–October, weekends and state holidays only. Departures from 6.00–8.00am. Return fare 50 *yuan*. Alternatively, a fine day's tour arranged by Jarrah Pour (tel. 67224675 ext. 203; mobile 90893286) from Jingtai Hotel, at least twice weekly in summer, 75 *yuan* return. Depart Beijing at 8.30am, spending 3–4 hours on the wall and arrive back in the city around 7.00pm. Taxis cost around 700 *yuan* with the driver waiting up to three hours.

THE MING TOMBS (MING SHISANLING)

The valley of the Ming Tombs lies about 48 kilometres (30 miles) north of Beijing. Thirteen of the 16 Ming emperors are interred here, hence the site's Chinese name, *Ming Shisanling* (The 13 Ming Tombs). The tombs were located in accordance with Chinese geomantic specifications requiring graves to be protected by high ground.

Jinshanling–Simatai Great Wall in winter

Alone on the Great Wall

Getting initial access to the Great Wall was not too problematical. Taking a long distance bus to Changping, I walked a few kilometres up to a road junction and hitchhiked southwest, then northwest beyond Hengling. Here was a convenient location to join an inner system of ramparts, well to the south of Ming's main line of the Great Wall some sixty kilometres away. Nevertheless, this was a defensive line of paramount strategy in protecting the capital and as such is built to a scale I had not before witnessed. A fearsome scramble on the broken stone-blocked ramparts and I was climbing high on the snow ridges above the glassy Gaunting Shui ku, one of Beijing's enormous reservoirs. If ever an injection of hope was needed it was now; and the sight of this solid stone dragon, its torso dotted with towers like fins and scales, was exactly that—the greatest Great Wall of China, the stupendous creation of the Ming, dipping and thrusting into the distance across multiple ridges a day's struggle away. I wanted to run fast and free.

First I had to tread slowly, climb, stretch for footholds, jump off the wall, clamber back on, chimney down, balance low for fear of the strong wind blowing me to the ground some six metres below. For the Wall is so steep, its surface rough, loose and slippery with crenellated ramparts, decaying, weather-beaten and earth-shaken. Its overgrown pavement concealed holes where rubble core had been washed away. Beacons and watch-towers rose like derelict ghost houses, for so long the providers of shelter for so many.

An awesome creation. In the afternoon sunshine its light-coloured stone contrasting with the vegetation of the slopes thinned by the approach of winter. It perched like a cardboard cut-out upon mountains, not hills, undeterred by precipices. Cold stone blocks, rectangular lime facing bricks, bound by crumbly *mortar, lay chalky white and friable at the side of the parapet, as if left by workmen just days ago. My feet were slipping on the gravel and slush, fingernails full of clay and mortar, palms grazed, knuckles scraped by thorn bush, ankles banged and bruised between boulders and rocks. My lungs gasped for breath on the climbs and teeth chattered in the bitter wind. Ice-cold inhalations stung my nostrils.*

Certainly it was a Wonder of the World, arguably the Wonder. For I was aware that the Great Wall was not merely a single view—no more than a person's life is a single day. The Great Pyramid at Cheops had been a brisk scramble amid the cries for baksheesh. Thebes and its valley of the Kings was a morning's inspection, Pompei a sultry afternoon's walk, the Grand Canyon a day's hiking. But the Great Wall was a wonder of a thousand vistas. A lifetime would be needed just to inspect every remaining rampart from the Warring States to the Qin, from Han to Ming. For when the fever-like fascination of the Great Wall takes hold of the imagination, one is drawn into studying the core millenia of China's wonderful civilisation; uncovering inventions, discovering legends, analysing the xenophobic mind, and paying respect to the labourers of countless generations who devoted their lives, somewhat reluctantly, to its construction. For beneath my feet was the world's longest cemetery. There was blood on every stone. The cannibalistic appetite of the Great Wall, perpetually in need of repair and extension, gave no dispensation from servitude to any Han generation.

William Lindesay, Alone on the Great Wall
© Hodder & Stoughton, London. 1989.

The approach is impressive. The modern road passes by a stone portico with five carved archways. This is the beginning of the imposing route known as the Spirit (or Sacred) Way. Next comes the Great Vermilion Gateway; of its three openings the central entrance was reserved for the coffins of deceased emperors, and all followers were required to dismount at this point. The whole tomb site, to which this gateway was the actual entrance, was of course surrounded by a wall, now gone.

■ THE SPIRIT WAY

The emperor's coffin would have been borne past a stele pavilion, a typical imperial structure with the floating clouds motif repeated on its supporting columns. The procession of mourners would then have filed along the Spirit Way, a funereal guard of honour of six pairs of animals and six pairs of human figures carved from large blocks of stone. The latter, all standing, are statues of scholars, administrators and warriors. The animals—lions, *xiechi* (a mythical beast), camels, elephants, unicorns, horses—are either standing or crouching. The Spirit Way ends at the Dragon and Phoenix Gate.

In its entirety, this part of the Ming Tombs dates from the 15th century. Beside the road there is now a mass of shrubs and fruit trees. Once across an arched bridge, visitors can then visit the different tombs, scattered round the valley.

■ CHANGLING

The most important tomb, appropriately, belongs to the great Yongle, the third Ming emperor, who was responsible for building so much of Beijing. He chose this site and had his burial place built on the traditional plan of a walled enclave, enclosing buildings separated by three courtyards, with the tumulus at its head. The tumulus, marked by a stele tower and traditionally referred to as the Precious Fortress (Bao-cheng), has not been excavated, but visitors may see inside the magnificent Hall of Sacrifice. This very fine structure built in 1427 is supported by 32 massive wooden pillars wrought from huge trunks of *nanmu* wood from the extreme southwest of China. The Yongle Emperor was interred in the Changling in 1424. Sixteen royal concubines were buried alive in ancillary graves following a custom that was finally discontinued during the reign of the sixth Ming emperor.

■ DINGLING

The tomb of the Wanli Emperor (reigned 1573–1620) and his two consorts is known as the Dingling. Its construction was started in 1584, when Wanli was aged 22, and took six years to complete. It was excavated in 1958, and one may now descend by a modern spiral staircase to the underground tomb behind a stele tower.

The vaulted marble palace, built deep underground so that it is cool in summer

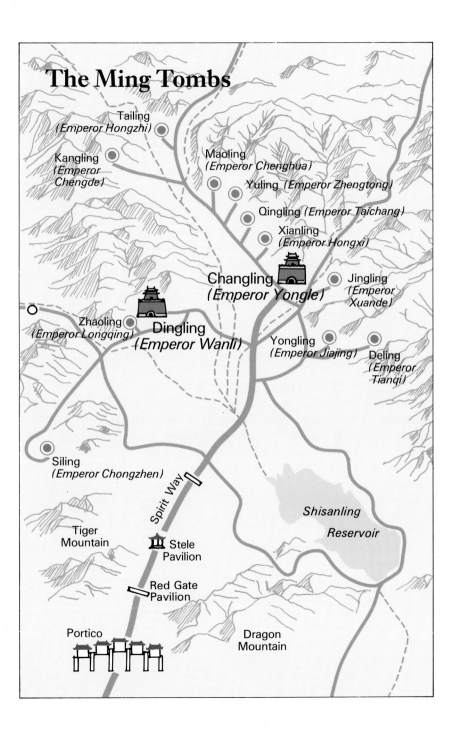

The Ming Tombs

Tailing
(Emperor Hongzhi)

Kangling
(Emperor
Chengde)

Maoling
(Emperor Chenghua)

Yuling (Emperor Zhengtong)

Qingling (Emperor Taichang)

Xianling
(Emperor Hongxi)

Changling
(Emperor Yongle)

Jingling
(Emperor
Xuande)

Zhaoling
(Emperor Longqing)

Dingling
(Emperor Wanli)

Yongling
(Emperor Jiajing)

Deling
(Emperor
Tianqi)

Siling
(Emperor Chongzhen)

Spirit Way

Shisanling
Reservoir

Tiger
Mountain

Stele
Pavilion

Red Gate
Pavilion

Portico

Dragon
Mountain

and comfortably warm in winter, consists of three burial chambers. At the entrance to the antechamber is a carved marble gateway. The floor is paved with specially made 'golden bricks' which had been fired for 130 days and dipped in tung oil before being laid. The middle chamber contains three marble thrones; in front of each of them are five drumshaped stools for holding offerings and a large glazed pot known as the Ever Bright Lamp. The lamps would have been filled with oil and lit before the tomb was sealed. The back chamber was the actual repository of the royal coffins. On being opened by the excavation team they were found to be stuffed with some 300 assorted garments. Even more lavish, countless pieces of jewellery, curios and porcelain—stowed in 26 lacquer chests—were also deposited to provide for a luxurious life in the nether world. The regalia and the treasure have all been moved to two small exhibition halls outside. They should not be missed.

Another modern addition to the valley of the Ming Tombs has recently been opened— it is a golf course laid out by Japanese investors.

The East

THE EASTERN QING TOMBS (DONGLING)

The site of the Eastern Qing Tombs is over the provincial border, in Hebei, some 121 kilometres (75 miles) east of Beijing (a journey of about four hours by car). The 15 tombs are spread over an area 34 kilometres (21 miles) wide, and built under the lee of Mount Changrui. The choice of this site as the Qing imperial burial ground is attributed to the Shunzhi Emperor, who came upon it when out hunting. He is interred here, together with the Kangxi, Qianlong, Xianfeng and Tongzhi emperors. Other tombs include those of the Empress Dowager Cixi, several less notorious empresses, concubines and royal children, as well as that of Emperor Kangxi's revered teacher.

There are some striking differences between the Ming and Qing tombs. Whereas the Ming created a single 'Spirit Way' (the approach to imperial burial grounds lined with stone animals and officials), the Qing have several shorter ones leading to tumuli which are also on a smaller scale. The Qing stone figures have their hair in the traditional Manchu plait, and while the scholar is shown wearing a string of beads of Buddhist origin, emblematic of the strong lamaistic leanings of the Manchu rulers, the Ming statues are gen-erally depicted carrying Confucian tablets. The animals too differ in style and decoration.

The tombs of the Qianlong Emperor, the Empress Ci'an and the Empress Dowager Cixi are open to the public. The underground marble vault of Qianlong is particularly impressive: every interior wall and arch is richly carved with images of the Buddha, the Celestial Guardians and with thousands of words of Buddhist scriptures in both Sanskrit and Tibetan. Ornate carving also embellishes Cixi's mausoleum, where one can see the repeated use of such imperial motifs as dragons, phoenixes and clouds. Built over a period of 30 years, the tomb was a subject of great interest to the Empress Dowager, who visited the site several times. Unfortunately both this tomb and that of the Qianlong emperor were broken into by grave robbers in the 1920s, and the fabulous treasures, buried with the view of ensuring a comfortable afterlife, have all disappeared.

Visitors may like to round off their excursion to the Dongling by calling in at the two small museums that have been established in the sacrificial halls at the tombs of the two empresses, Cixi and Ci'an. Opening times are from 9 am to 4 pm.

The Southwest

MARCO POLO BRIDGE (LUGOUQIAO)

Proceeding southwest from Guang'anmenwai for about 16 kilometres (ten miles), one reaches the Lugouqiao, celebrated not only for being Beijing's oldest surviving bridge, but also for the impression it made on Marco Polo, who saw it in 1290 (hence the bridge's Western name). He has left us with a fine description.

Marco Polo Bridge spans the Yongding River. As early as the Warring States period (475–221 BC), the site of the present bridge had been a strategically important river crossing. Initially the crossing was probably made by a wooden bridge or by pontoons. From the Jin Dynasty onwards, when the capital was at Beijing, increased traffic across the river warranted a more permanent bridge, which was completed in 1192. Constructed with careful reference to the river's flow, this solid stone structure resting on 11 arches has withstood weathering for several centuries.

The piers supporting the bridge are specially strong, being reinforced by triangular metal posts which locals used to call 'Swords for Decapitating Dragons' in the belief that evil dragons, seeing these posts, would quietly go away rather than cause mischief for river craft.

On either side of the bridge there is a parapet with 140 columns carved and surmounted with lions. Imperial steles stand at each end; one commemorates the renovation of the bridge in 1698, the other carries a four-character inscription by Emperor Qianlong, 'Bright Moon on Lugou'.

Vivid light and winter blue skies at the Eastern Qing Tombs

PEKING MAN SITE

The village of Zhoukoudian, which can be reached by train from Beijing, used to be notable for its production of lime. In 1929 it achieved worldwide fame with the discovery of the first skulls of Peking Man. The fossil remains of *Homo erectus pekinensis* have been dated to about 600,000–700,000 years ago.

The limestone caves of Zhoukoudian probably account for the location of a paleolithic settlement here. So far bones of over 40 inhabitants have been unearthed and, with the evidence of other remains, scientists have pieced together a fascinating picture of this early community.

Some of the limestone caves, on the northern slope of Dragon Bones Hills (Longgushan) to the east of Zhoukoudian station, may be visited. There is also a comprehensive museum on the evolution of man and the Zhoukoudian culture. Included in the displays are stone implements used by Peking Man and Upper Cave Man (who lived about 50,000 years ago), fossils of animals hunted by them, and evidence that

Fearsome sculpture guarding the way to the Ming Tombs

Peking Man used fire. The whereabouts of the original Peking Man fossils, lost during the Second World War while en route to the United States for safekeeping, is still shrouded in mystery. Zhoukoudian is 90 kilometres to the southwest of Beijing. It is best to go with a tour guide as very little information is available in English at the site.

Dabaotai Han Tomb

Located about 15 kilometres (ten miles) from the city limits in the Fengtai district, the Dabaotai Han-dynasty tomb is a worthwhile half-day outing. Difficult to locate on account of a lack of road signs, the best way to get there is to take a taxi (there is no public transport) to the village of Guogongzhuang and ask the way from there. Dabaotai is about four kilometres (two-and-a-half miles) directly south of the Fengtai Railway Station.

The archaeologists who excavated the tomb in 1975 are unable to determine who was buried in this spectacular underground 'wooden palace', but the choice has been narrowed down to one of two princes belonging to the Liu clan who died in approximately 50 BC.

The excellently restored tomb consists of three inner and outer coffins of wood, surrounded by a boundary wall built up of tens of thousands of square wooden beams. The wall of the tomb was further lined with a boundary wall of heaped beams, and sealed with a thick layer of plaster to keep it dry, which partially explains its excellent state of preservation. The entire tomb is 23.2 metres (80 feet) long, 18 metres (56 feet) wide and 4.7 metres (14.5 feet) deep and has been enclosed in a poorly lit building. The most extraordinary objects on view are the three lacquered chariots and 11 horses that were buried alive with them in a long narrow chamber that stands at the entrance to the tomb. A second tomb containing the remains of the queen consort was plundered and burnt in ancient times and nothing is left of it except the site.

Newly built models of the chariots are on display in a separate hall, and there is a small museum containing some of the burial objects found in the tomb, including jade carvings, miniature wooden burial figures, bronze incense burners and a bronze door decoration in the form of a grotesque beast.

The West

Western Qing Tombs (Xiling)

Like the Eastern Qing Tombs (*see* page 136), the Western Qing Tombs lie a good distance from the capital, some 125 kilometres (78 miles) southwest of the city in Yixian, Hebei Province. Four emperors—Yongzheng, Jiaqing, Daoguang and

Guangxu—are buried here, along with nine queens, 76 princes and 57 imperial concubines.

One traditional view holds that Yongzheng (reigned 1723–35), son of the great Kangxi and father of the great Qianlong, chose to be buried apart from his father because he had ascended the throne by devious means, but there is little evidence to support this. In any case, Qianlong decreed that after his own death the tombs of the emperors that came after him should be distributed alternatively between the eastern and western burial grounds. Incidentally, Puyi, the last emperor of the Qing Dynasty was cremated after his death in 1967, and his ashes were placed in the revolutionary cemetery at Babaoshan. In 1995 his casket of ashes was finally taken to Xiling for a simple burial.

The Tailing, the tomb of Yongzheng, is the largest tomb in the entire mausoleum complex. It consists of numerous gateways and buildings that were used during the various Buddhist rituals and sacrifices held in the emperor's memory.

The Muling of the Emperor Daoguang (reigned 1821–50) is small in comparison to the Tailing but is more exquisitely constructed. Soon after his ascension to the throne, Daoguang began building his tomb at the eastern burial grounds, as decreed by Qianlong. One year after its completion, however, the underground burial chamber was found to be flooded, and Daoguang, finding this inauspicious, went to the Western Tombs to select a new site for himself. Because Daoguang believed that the flooding in his first tomb had occurred because several dragons had been deprived of their homes, he lavishly decorated his second tomb with carved images of this auspicious creature.

The Chongling of Emperor Guangxu (reigned 1875–1908) was left unfinished when the Qing Dynasty fell in 1911, and was only completed four years later. Accompanying Guangxu in a tomb of her own is Zhenfei, known as the 'Pearl Concubine'. Zhenfei was forced down a well in the Imperial Palace. *(See page 104)*

The Temple of the Pool and Wild Mulberry (Tanzhesi)

Situated in the Western Hills, this Buddhist temple lies 45 kilometres (28 miles) west of Beijing. It is reached by a winding road which passes the Ordination Terrace Temple (see below) and some quite spectacular scenery, especially in the spring when the fruit trees are in blossom. One of the biggest and oldest temples in the Beijing area, Tanzhesi has been completely restored in recent years.

A temple known by various names has existed on this site for 1,600 years. Its present name is derived from the Dragon Pool nearby and from the trees, growing on the hillside, whose leaves were used to feed silkworms. The present structure, laid out on traditional lines, is typical of Ming and Qing architecture. A ceremonial arch or *pailou* (*see* page 117) frames the entrance to a compound of several halls, pavilions and courtyards: there is the **Hall of Abstinence**, the **Ordination Altar** and, at the back of it, the **Hall to Guanyin**, the Goddess of Mercy. The latter is associated with Kublai Khan's daughter, Princess Miaoyan, who entered the nunnery here in the 13th century. Her devotions were performed so assiduously, it is said, that she wore deep marks into the piece of stone on which she stood. Some of the strangely shaped trees within the temple are said to be a thousand years old.

To the right of the Hall of Abstinence is the **Flowing Cup Pavilion** (Liubeiting), where dragon-shaped channels feed spring water into the **Dragon Pool**. This water has a special quality which enables objects to float upon the surface easily. On the third day of the third month people used to gather for the 'purification of the fermented wine'; brimming wine cups were floated down the stream and only when they stopped moving was the wine drunk. Below the temple are beautiful stone stupas built over the burial sites of the temple's monks dating from the Jin, Yuan, Ming and Qing dynasties.

THE ORDINATION TERRACE TEMPLE (JIETAISI)

The temple lies in the Western Hills, 33 kilometres (22 miles) from Beijing on the road that leads to the Temple of the Pool and Wild Mulberry. There has been a temple in this mountain cleft for 1,350 years, but it was in the Liao Dynasty (916–1125) that its chief function—the ordination of Buddhist novices—was established when a monk, Fajun, founded an altar here.

The Ordination Altar, in the northeast courtyard, is of white marble and its three tiers are carved with hundreds of figures, some as tall as a metre (just over three feet). Once a year, at midnight, an initiation ceremony was conducted; the novices, having fasted all day, would endure burns from lighted incense sticks upon their tonsured heads.

As the temple was one of his favoured rest-stops, the Qing emperor Qianlong handsomely endowed it during his reign, and the present buildings date from this period of expansion and renovation. The ancient pine trees contribute to the temple's peculiar charm. One of them, which sadly no longer survives, is marked with a stone tablet to the left of the Thousand Buddha Pavilion behind the temple's main hall. In the time of Qianlong this remarkable pine was dubbed the 'Mobile Tree' on account of its ability to shake all over when any one of its branches was pulled.

TEMPLE OF THE SEA OF THE LAW (FAHAISI)

Located approximately two kilometres (one-and-a-half miles) northeast of Moshikou in the Shijingshan district, the Temple of the Sea of the Law can be visited at the same time as its neighbours, the Tanzhesi and Jietaisi.

According to an inscription in the temple, the building was completed in about 1440 by a eunuch in the Court of the Ming Zhengtong Emperor with funds he collected from various officials, lamas, monks, nuns and lay Buddhists. Its design is similar to that of other mountain temples, which are traditionally laid out on three levels.

The finest works of art in the temple are the famous frescos painted on the interior walls of the Main Hall (Daxiongbaodian), which stands on the north side of the rear-most courtyard. The paintings date back to the temple's construction, and were executed by some 15 palace painters who are named on a stone tablet found near the temple.

The frescos show groups of emperors, empresses, and religious figures engaged in Buddhist worship, as well as the objects of their worship, the bodhisattvas Guanyin (Avalokitesvara), Wenshu (Manjusri) and Samantahbadra (Puxian). Note also the painted mandalas in the three cupolas in the ceiling of this hall. These lively, colourful and wonderfully detailed examples of brush work are important monuments in the history of Chinese painting.

The Pavilion of Ten-thousand Fortunes at the Lama Temple (see page 110)

Museums

Palace Museum

Although the Imperial Palace in its entirety is regarded as a museum of architectural and artistic heritage, there are specific halls and pavilions within it—collectively known as the Palace Museum—which are used as showcases for the cornucopia of treasures in the palace. As the restoration of the Palace is constantly in progress, new areas of exhibits are opened from time to time.

Visiting hours are 8.30 am–4.30 pm with the ticket offices closing at 3.30 pm. However, the Museum of Imperial Treasures (Zhenbaoguan) closes at 4.15 pm with the ticket office closing at 3.15 pm. First enter the Imperial Palace.

The Historical Art Museum

Housed in the Hall of Preserving Harmony (Baohedian), the collection here provides a broad conspectus of Chinese cultural development. Arranged chronologically, the exhibition is in three parts. The first part deals with the period from earliest times to about 4,000 years ago, illustrated by excavated ancient painted pottery, bronzes and sculptures. The 5th to the 13th centuries—the period covered by the second section—saw the emergence of an early modern style of painting as well as major developments in the art of ivory carving, lacquerware, weaving and calligraphy. The third part of the ex-hibition shows samples of the arts during the Yuan, Ming and Qing dynasties; of particular interest is the fine porcelain that was produced in this era.

Several special exhibitions of imperial treasures are housed in the Six Eastern Palaces at the rear of the complex.

■ THE HALL OF BRONZES

This collection is shown in the Palace of Abstinence (Zhaigong), the Hall of Sincere Solemnity (Chengsudian) and the Palace of Revered Benevolence (Jingrengong), and includes examples of bronze wine goblets, tripod cooking vessels and pots from the Shang, Zhou, Spring and Autumn and Warring States periods.

■ THE HALL OF TOYS

An odd and delightful assortment of some 80 mechanical toys manufactured in China and Europe (Switzerland, France, England and Germany) in the 18th and 19th century is on display in a hall immediately inside (to the south of) the southern gate of the Imperial Garden, to the northeast of the Palace of Earthly Peace. The automatons include a songbird that sings, a conjuror who performs tricks, a smoker who exhales real smoke, and a boy waving a fan, which functioned as an early form of air-conditioning.

■ THE HALL OF CERAMICS

The Palace of Heavenly Favours (Chengqiangong) and the Palace of Eternal Harmony (Yonghegong) contains Neolithic pottery from the Shang to the Western Zhou dynasties, with examples of Longshan blackware, incised and glazed pottery from the Han Dynasty on through to the celadon ware of the Yuan, the tri-coloured glazes of the Tang and the blue and white of the Ming and Qing dynasties. Many fine examples from the famous imperial kilns of Jingdezhen can be seen.

■ THE HALL OF PAINTINGS

Scroll paintings and calligraphy are displayed in the Hall of Imperial Supremacy (Huangjidian), the Palace of Peaceful Old Age (Ningshougong) and galleries on its eastern, western and southern sides. For a few weeks each autumn, during the dry weather, the rarest examples of Chinese visual arts are brought out for public view.

■ THE MUSEUM OF IMPERIAL TREASURES

This superb hoard of ritual and everyday items used by the Qing Court is displayed in the Hall of Character Cultivation (Yangxindian) and the Palace of Happy Old Age (Leshougong). The treasures grouped together in the first hall include silver and gold tableware, jewelled knick-knacks and little Buddhist shrines. The latter, generally made of gold, include one especially made for Emperor Qianlong to preserve a strand of his mother's hair.

In the second hall, which contains the gorgeous habiliments and attire worn by emperors, empresses and concubines, there are exquisite pieces of jewellery, hair-pins and head-dresses as well as Court costumes. One of the most outstanding exhibits is Qianlong's peacock feather-trimmed robe studded with seed pearls and tiny coral beads.

The sybaritic Court amassed a vast number of ornaments and decorative pieces to adorn the palace interior. One kind of curio (which is still popular with collectors today) is the jewelled *penjing*—artificial miniature potted landscapes composed of precious stones, with leaves and petals carved out of gold, silver and jade—which are shown in the third section.

Note that although the Museum of Imperial Treasures is open 8.30 am–4.15 pm daily, the ticket office closes at 3.15 pm.

■ THE HALL OF CLOCKS AND WATCHES

A small gallery in the Hall of Ancestor Worship, located to the east of the Gate of Heavenly Purity, houses an extraordinary collection of elaborate clocks, both European and Chinese, dating from the 18th and 19th centuries.

■ EXHIBITION OF HISTORICAL RELICS FROM THE QING

Several aspects of imperial life and duties are represented by the relics here in the Palace of Heavenly Purity (Qianqinggong), for example the imperial seals for giving the stamp of royal approval to decrees issued in the emperor's name. There are also musical instruments, more ceremonial and travelling regalia plus weapons and arms.

MUSEUM OF THE CHINESE REVOLUTION AND MUSEUM OF CHINESE HISTORY

The large building which houses these two museums stands opposite the Great Hall of the People, located on the eastern side of Tiananmen Square. Both museums open from 8.30 am–3.30 pm and are closed on Mondays.

■ MUSEUM OF THE CHINESE REVOLUTION

This occupies the north (left) wing of the building. More than 3,300 exhibits, displayed on two floors, illustrate the history of the Chinese Communist Party. The collection of models, documents and materials begins with the May Fourth Movement of 1919 and moves on to the founding of the party itself, the First Revolutionary Civil War (1924–27), the Second Revolutionary War (1927–37), the Anti-Japanese War of Resistance (1937–45) and the Third Civil War (1945–49). The photographic accounts of this tumultuous period are of particular interest.

■ MUSEUM OF CHINESE HISTORY

Occupying two floors of the south (right) wing, this permanent exhibition is an extensive survey of the evolution of Chinese history and culture shown through works of art and scientific invention. Entirely refurbished and reinstalled in 1988, the Museum of Chinese History is a national showcase for great works of Chinese art, many of them unearthed in the four decades of the People's Republic. Through arrangements with provincial and municipal collections throughout the country, the museum can obtain on permanent loan any object considered to be a 'national treasure'. The result is undoubtedly the most stunning display of Chinese artistic masterpieces in the entire country, and should not be missed. Sadly, the museum does little publicity and few tourists have an opportunity to enjoy it. The most exhilarating exhibits are found in the sections that cover the period up to the Tang Dynasty, including bronzes, jades, terracotta burial figures and ceramics. And while the objects are still poorly labelled, they speak for themselves. The later dynasties are displayed on the second floor.

Safe and Sound

As for the good Government, Quietness and Ease and Cleanliness of the Gaol, I do not question but it exceeds ours in Europe. As soon as we were brought into the First Court we spy'd the Head Gaolor, who sat in great State on his Tribunal-seat; he presently ask'd for the 'mittimus' of the Criminal Judge that had sent us to him. But him we had not yet seen, (for he was still not come to himself after a great Feast he had been at the day before) so one of his Deputies sent us to Prison. Then the Gaolor began to examine us concerning our coming to China, upon what intent it was, what we liv'd upon, &c. We answer'd him with a great deal of freedom and ease, the Consequence whereof was that they put us in through another little Door which was lock'd, and had a porter at it; we went on through a Lane, and they brought us to an Idol Temple. I don't know that in the Prisons in these our Countries there is any Church of God so great, so spacious, so clean, so neat, and so much frequented by the Prisoners as that is. In all the Gaols, Dungeons and Courts of Justice throughout the Empire, they have Temples richly adorn'd, and cleanly, where the Prisoners, and such as have law-suits make their Suits; but, those Wooden and Earthen Images neither hearing nor seeing, they give no Relief to their Suppliants. At Night they turn'd us through another Lesser Door into a Court, and then convey'd us into a great Hall, quite dark and dismal, without any Window and so full of People, that there was hardly room for them to stand; this was call'd the little Prison to distinguish it from the Dungeon which was far enough from thence. Here we continued 40 days, having always Light at night and there was an Overseer who took care no Noise should be made. All Men were wonderful submissive to him, so that there was no roaring, or noise, or quarrelling, but all as hush'd as if it had been the Novice-house of a well govern'd Monastery, which we did not a little admire.

The Travels and Controversies of
Friar Domingo Navarrete, 1618–1668

Reckless Pride

"I don't understand," I said. "I thought Grandmother died when Mother was a child."
"Whatever gave you that idea?" asked my aunt.
"I don't know. I just assumed...Mother never talks about her. Why?"
"Perhaps she was too ashamed."
"What for?"
"Perhaps you should ask her."
"No, I couldn't, not now, not after all these years. Please, Auntie, you must tell me."
Only then, when I was forty-one, did I learn that once again Grandmother had defied the inviolable mores of Chinese society.
When she failed to have a son, even Grandfather, a 'modern' man who did a wicked turkey trot, could no longer flout tradition. He announced that he would be taking a second wife. Without a word, without a tear, Grandmother packed her bags and walked out of the House of Fang forever.
When I heard this, I gave Grandmother a rousing cheer. It was exactly what I would have done. My aunt shook her head at such foolishness and said, "Do not be so hasty. How can you be certain she did not regret that decision for the rest of her life?"
The idea startled me, but I refused to consider it and, shrugging a shoulder, hastened to declare, "I would not!"
"Silly one, you are an American married to an American, living in a culture and a time where husbands and wives leave one another as indifferently as the wind changes direction. But that was not true for my mother. She was a Chinese married to a Chinese in a culture and a time when marriage had little to do with love and everything to do with life. What kind of life could she have had without a husband, without her children, without a rightful place? Only one of ever-deepening sorrow."
"But she was right to leave. How could she ever again have held her head high if she'd stayed?"
"You ask the wrong question. You should be asking, how could she after she left?"

Bette Bao Lord, Legacies

BEIJING ART MUSEUM

The first major museum to open in Beijing for nearly 30 years, the Beijing Art Museum occupies the grounds of Wanshou Temple (Temple of Longevity) which for years had been occupied by the military. The museum is located immediately off Xisanhuanbeilu (the Third West Ring Road) where it crosses over the canal some 500 metres north of the Shangri-La Hotel. Hours are 9 am to 4 pm. The museum is closed on Mondays.

The Wanshou Temple dates back to 1577, when Emperor Wanli of the Ming dynasty erected it on this spot as a library for Buddhist scriptures. In front of the museum runs a canal used by the court of the Qianlong Emperor in the 17th century to travel by barge from the Forbidden City to the summer palaces in the northwestern suburbs. On the occasion of the 70th birthday of Qianlong's mother, 1,000 Buddhist monks stood on the banks of the canal as part of the birthday celebrations taking place in the temple.

Empress Dowager Cixi stayed in the now restored western section of the temple when she broke her journeys to the Summer Palace. She instigated a major rebuilding campaign in 1894. The eastern section is also scheduled for future restoration.

The museum has speciality collections of Ming and Qing textiles, Qing and Republican period paintings, Buddhist art, personal name seals, Ming and Qing ceramics, and Japanese paintings acquired from collections in the formerly Japanese-occupied areas of Manchuria. The collection was assembled in the late 1980s under the aegis of the Beijing Municipal Bureau of Cultural Relics. Opening times are from 9 am to 4 pm. Closed on Mondays.

LU XUN MUSEUM

This museum in Fuchengmennei Dajie commemorates one of China's most outstanding writers of the 20th century, Lu Xun (1881–1936), who is also noted for his considerable contribution to the liberal movement in China in the 1920s. (*See* excerpt on page 37).

The museum, which abuts Lu Xun's former Beijing residence, displays manuscripts, letters, and pages from his personal diary. Some 13,000 books from his library are also in the keeping of the museum, as well as items of clothing and other memorabilia.

The museum is open from 8.30 am–11 am and from 1.30 pm–4 pm but is closed on Mondays.

MILITARY MUSEUM OF THE CHINESE PEOPLE'S REVOLUTION

This is a permanent exhibition of 5,000 items—photographs, directives, military uniforms, weaponry including tanks and missiles and Eighth Route Army insignias, along with portraits of revolutionary heroes and martyrs—covering the Chinese revolutionary army's 29-year history between 1921 and 1949.

The museum is at 9, Fuxing Dajie and is open from 8.30 am–5 pm and closed on Mondays.

AVIATION MUSEUM

In 1989, the Chinese Air Force opened this huge display of military and civilian aircraft at Datangshan, Changping County, between Shahe and the Changping county seat, approximately 30 kilometres (19 miles) north of the city limits. After passing through Shahe on the road to Changping, make a right turn at the Baige Lu intersection, and watch for the museum on the left. The easiest way to get there is by taxi. Opening hours are 8am–4pm daily (tel. 9781054).

The 140 aeroplanes are displayed as in a used car lot. Many are parked outside in long queues, while some 50 choice specimens are housed in a long shed. Military buffs will also enjoy the mobile radar equipment and guided missiles.

Reflecting the history of aviation in China, there are specimens from the former Soviet Union, USA and Britain dating back to pre-liberation days, as well as samples of China's own fighting and passenger aircraft.

Exhibits with revolutionary associations include the 'Ilyushin 12', which used to gather samples from a mushroom cloud during a Chinese nuclear test (keep your distance); a Chinese helicopter used by Zhou Enlai during an inspection tour; a single-prop plane that buzzed Tiananmen Square during the celebration of China's first National Day (1st October 1949); a two-engine job that Chairman Mao took to Guangzhou once; and a fighter plane that saw action in the Korean War.

MUSEUM OF NATURAL HISTORY

The museum contains four halls devoted to Botany, Zoology, Paleozoology and Paleoanthropology, the latter science—the study of primitive man—being one in which China has contributed much in recent discoveries and research. It is open 8.30am–5pm (admission till 4pm only), and closed on Mondays.

THE TEMPLE OF CONFUCIUS (KONG MIAO) AND THE FORMER IMPERIAL COLLEGE (GUOZIJIAN)

Situated in Beijing's northeast quarter, close by the Lama Temple, the temple dedicated to Confucius was raised in the Yuan Dynasty and housed the ancestral tablets of Confucius and four other sages. Ceremonials and sacrifices were conducted by the prominent scholars of the day and members of the imperial court three times a year, including Confucius' birthday.

Part of the temple has been given over to the **Capital Museum**, which exhibits archaeological finds from Beijing and its environs and may be visited between 9am and 5pm except on Mondays.

Connected to the museum by a side door is the former **Imperial College** (Guozijian), first built in 1287 and substantially extended in 1784. The focal point of the former college is the square pavilion, which can be thrown open on all four sides by means of doors and shutters, called the Imperial Schoolroom. It is sited in the middle of a pool and reached by bridges. Here the emperor used to lecture on the Classics to ministers and students. On either side of the structure there used to stand 190 stone tablets engraved with 800,000 words of the Thirteen Classics, which took the calligrapher 12 years to transcribe. The tablets have been moved to a courtyard east of the main gate, Taixuemen, and the Imperial College is now the **Capital Library**.

CHINA NATIONAL LIBRARY

The National Library of China was opened in October 1987. Its total collection of more than 13 million volumes ranks it as the third largest in the world after the Library of Congress in the United States and the Bodleian Library in England. There are many rare books and manuscripts in this collection, some of which date back to the Northern Wei Dynasty (AD 458).

The library is situated on the north side of the Purple Bamboo Garden at Baishiqiao across the road from the Olympic Hotel. The surrounding area is one of the few places in Beijing where there is abundant foliage and scarce traffic or city hustle-bustle. The monolithic appearance of the library's many wings and towers is somewhat mitigated by the soft blue tint of its façade and tea-coloured tile roof which seem to help integrate the building into its surroundings.

If one calls in advance, it is possible to arrange a tour of the library. Foreigners must present their passports for inspection at the main gate . The Library is open 8am–8pm every day, but visitors are not allowed to enter on Saturdays.

CHINA NATIONAL GALLERY

One cannot help but notice the China National Gallery, a large traditional-style building at the top of Wangfujing. This edifice was constructed in 1959 and is considered one of socialist China's ten best architectural designs. It was entirely refurbished in 1991. The large central building is flanked on either side by long corridors and adjoining wings. Yellow glazed tiles, sloping roofs and upturned eaves lend this building an air of dignity and reserve. There are 14 exhibition rooms and several studios where artists can work.

This gallery holds an increasing number of interesting national and international exhibits and is a good place to discover some of the emerging trends in China's rapidly evolving art world. Many of the works exhibited can be purchased from the artist. Enquiries about how to purchase a painting can be made at the sales shop located in the west wing. The gallery is open everyday until 5pm and tickets can be purchased until 4.30pm.

Exhibitions are held from time to time at the **Nationalities Cultural Palace** (Minzu Wenhua Gong), Fuxingmennei Dajie.

The High Life

When his Majesty holds a grand and public court, those who attend it are seated in the following order. The table of the sovereign is placed on an elevation, and he takes his seat on the northern side, with his face turned towards the south; and next to him, on his left hand, sits the Empress. On his right hand are placed his sons, grandsons, and other persons connected with him by blood, upon seats somewhat lower, so that their heads are on a level with the Emperor's feet. The other princes and the nobility have their places at still lower tables; and the same rules are observed with respect to the females, the wives of the sons, grandsons, and other relatives of the Great Khan being seated on the left hand, at tables in like manner gradually lower; then follow the wives of the nobility and military officers: so that all are seated according to their respective ranks and dignities, in the places assigned to them, and to which they are entitled.

The tables are arranged in such a manner that the Great Khan, sitting on his elevated throne, can overlook the whole. It is not, however, to be understood that all who assemble on such occasions can be accommodated at tables. The greater part of the officers, and even of the nobles, on the contrary, eat, sitting upon carpets, in the halls; and on the outside stand a great multitude of persons who come from different countries, and bring with them many rare curiosities.

In the middle of the hall, where the Great Khan sits at table, there is a magnificent piece of furniture, made in the form of a square coffer, each side of which is three paces in length, exquisitely carved in figures of animals, and gilt. It is hollow within, for the purpose of receiving a capacious vase, of pure gold, calculated to hold many gallons. On each of its four sides stands a smaller vessel, containing about a hogshead, one of which is filled with mare's milk, another with that of the camel, and so of the others, according to the kinds of beverage in use. Within this buffet are also the cups or flagons belonging to his Majesty, for serving the liquors. Some of them are of beautiful gilt plate. Their size is such that, when filled with wine or other liquor, the quantity would be sufficient for eight or ten men.

Before every two persons who have seats at the tables, one of these flagons is placed, together with a kind of ladle, in the form of a cup with a handle, also of plate; to be used not only for taking the wine out of the flagon, but for lifting it to the head. This is observed as well with respect to the women as the men. The quantity and richness of the plate belonging to his Majesty is quite incredible.

At each door of the grand hall, or of whatever part the Great Khan happens to be in, stand two officers, of a gigantic figure, one on each side, with staves in their hands, for the purpose of preventing persons from touching the threshold with their feet, and obliging them to step beyond it. If by chance any one is guilty of this offence, these janitors take from him his garment, which he must redeem for money; or, when they do not take the garment, they inflict on him such number of blows as they have authority for doing. But, as strangers may be unacquainted with the prohibition, officiers are appointed to introduce and warn them.

The numerous persons who attend at the sideboard of his Majesty, and who serve him with victuals and drink, are all obliged to cover their noses and mouths with handsome veils or cloths of worked silk, in order that his victuals or his wine may not be affected by their breath. When drink is called for by him, and the page in waiting has presented it, he retires three paces and kneels down, upon which the courtiers, and all who are present, in like manner make their prostration. At the same moment all the musical instruments, of which there is a numerous band, begin to play, and continue to do so until he has ceased drinking, when all the company recover their posture. This reverential salutation is made as often as his Majesty drinks. It is unnecessary to say anything of the victuals, because it may well be imagined that their abundance is excessive.

The Travels of Marco Polo

Recommended Reading

Oxford University Press in Hong Kong has done a great deed by having made available in affordable hardback and paperback reprints of some of the classic works in English about Beijing. A good start is *Old Peking: City of the Ruler of the World* (OUP, Hong Kong), an anthology of writing on the capital by former New Zealand ambassador to Beijing, Chris Elder. Three indispensable titles that describe the city as it was from the 1920s to 1940s are the highly detailed *In Search of Old Peking* by Arlington and Lewisohn; the more prosaic and evocative *Peking* by Juliet Bredon; and the apotheosis of life in Old Peking, George Kates' *The Years That Were Fat: Peking 1933-1940* (*see* excerpt page 26). A recent historical walking tour guide to the major sites in the city is *Beijing Walks* (Henry Holt) by Don J Cohn and Zhang Jingqing.

A number of attractive coffee-table books published about the capital include the Time-Life volume *Peking*, written by David Bonavia, with excellent photographs by Peter Griffiths; Leong Ka Tai's photographic essay, *Beijing* (Times Editions, Singapore), with a text by Frank Ching; and the earlier *Peking: A Tale of Three Cities* by Nigel Cameron, with memorable photographs from the 1960s by Brian Blake (Weatherhill).

There are some books written by foreigners who have lived in Beijing in more recent years which offer particular insight into Chinese life and politics. Bernard Frolic's *Mao's People* (Harvard), Simon Leys' *Broken Images* (Allison & Busby), *Chinese Shadows* (Viking) and David Bonavia's *The Chinese* (Penguin) are highly informative and readable. Ruth Sidel gives a detailed description of the structure of life in a Beijing neighbourhood in her *Families of Fengsheng—Urban Life in China* (Penguin), while Beverley Hooper tells of student life in *Inside Peking* (MacDonald & Jane's). One of the first Western journalists to be accredited in the aftermath of the Cultural Revolution, the correspondent of *Der Spiegel* Tizano Terzani published his experiences in *The Forbidden Door* (Asia 2000 Ltd) after he was expelled from China in 1984.

Two personal accounts of the old days are David Kidd, *Peking Story: The Last Days of Old China* (Clarkson N Potter) and John Blofeld's *City of Lingering Splendour: A Frank Account of Old Peking's Exotic Pleasures* (Hutchinson) (*see* excerpt page 86). Of great historical interest is *Twilight in the Forbidden City* (Oxford reprint) by Reginald Johnston, the English tutor and tennis teacher of Puyi, the last emperor of the Qing dynasty.

Three further literary accounts in the Hong Kong Oxford reprint series are Osbert Sitwell's *Escape with Me!*, Harold Acton's *Peonies and Ponies*, and the surprisingly insightful *Superficial Journey through Tokyo and Peking*, by Peter Quennell.

Other penetrating journalistic coverage, including interesting details about life in Beijing in the 1970s and early 1980s, can be found in *China: Alive in the Bitter Sea*

(Times Books) by *New York Times* correspondent, Fox Butterfield; *China after Mao: Coming Alive* (McGraw Hill) by British diplomat, Roger Garside; *The Chinese: Portrait of a People* (Summit) by the Canadian journalist John Fraser; and *From the Center of the Earth* (Little Brown) by Richard Bernstein.

The end of the Qing dynasty is graphically portrayed in two autobiographies and a memoir—*Two Years in The Forbidden City* by Der Ling, a Manchu princess who was a lady-in-waiting to the Empress Dowager Cixi, *From Emperor to Citizen* (Beijing Foreign Languages Press) by the last emperor, Puyi, and *With the Empress Dowager of China* by Katherine A Carl (Pacific Basin Books). Marina Warner's biography of the Empress Dowager, *The Dragon Empress* (Weidenfeld & Nicolson), is particularly entertaining. The Forbidden City is described in great detail, accompanied by reproductions of contemporary paintings and copperplate etchings, in *The Architecture of the Forbidden City* (Joint Publishing), currently available only with a Chinese text.

Those interested in reading some of China's classical novels will enjoy *Dream of the Red Chamber* by the 18th-century novelist Cao Xueqin—translated as *The Story of the Stone* by David Hawkes and John Minford (5 volumes, Penguin) or as *A Dream of Red Mansions* (3 volumes, Beijing Foreign Languages Press), rendered into English by Yang Hsien-yi and Gladys Yang. A garden featured in the novel—Daguanyuan—has been recreated as a park in the southwest of Beijing (*see* page 106).

Life in pre-revolutionary China is vividly portrayed in *Rickshaw: The Novel of Luotuo Xiangzi* by Lao She (University Press of Hawaii) (*see* excerpt page 78), and *Family* by Ba Jin (Doubleday)— both well worth reading. The *Selected Stories of Lu Xun*, China's influential 20th-century writer, is translated by Yang Hsien-yi and Gladys Yang for Beijing Foreign Languages Press (*see* excerpt page 37).

Two wonderful titles that treat the customs and folkways of Old Peking are *Annual Customs and Festivals in Peking* (Hong Kong University Press), translated and annotated by Derk Bodde, and the utterly charming *The Adventures of Wu: The Life Cycle of a Peking Man* (Princeton University Press) by H Y Lowe, a Chinese journalist of the 1930s.

A contemporary poet and writer of fiction who has been hailed as a new voice in the post-Cultural Revolution literary scene is Beijing-born Zhao Zhenkai (pen-name Bei Dao), whose collection of short stories, *Waves*, has been translated by Bonnie S McDougall and Susette Ternent Cooke (The Chinese University Press, Hong Kong). *Seeds of Fire: Chinese Voices of Conscience*, edited by Geremie Barmé and John Minford, is an anthology of writings—poetry, essays and extracts from novels—representing the new 'literature of conscience'. It is published by Far Eastern Economic Review and distributed by China Guides Company in Hong Kong.

For a good picture of life in the foreign community in Beijing in the 1920s read Ann Bridge's novel *Peking Picnic* (Triad Granada). Oxford University Press's *A Photographer in Old Peking* is a beautiful volume of rare black-and-white photographs taken between 1933 and 1946, interspersed with an evocative account of people and places by the photographer Hedda Morrison. The tale of a great eccentric is told by historian Hugh Trevor-Roper in *Hermit of Peking: The Hidden Life of Sir Edmund Backhouse*, first published by MacMillan.

Hong Kong University Press has published a comprehensive book on *The Ming Tombs*, written by Anne Paludan. A much reduced version of the same book has been published by Oxford University Press in Hong Kong.

For those with a special interest in the subject, Elizabeth Halston's *Peking Opera* (Oxford University Press) is one of the best books in English. A concise paperback on the subject appeared in 1981 in Beijing—*Peking Opera and Mei Lanfang: a Guide to China's Traditional Theatre and the Arts of its Great Master* by Wu Zuguang, Huang Zuolin and Mei Shaowu (New World Press).

Mei Lanfang—Leader of the Pear Garden by A C Scott is written with much absorbing background (Hong Kong University Press). For general histories of China, a little known gem is *A Short History of the Chinese People* (Harper) by L Carrington Goodrich, which brings the reader up to the early 20th century. Slightly longer is Jacques Gernet's *A History of Chinese Civilization* (Cambridge). Modern China is prodigiously covered in Jonathan Spence's *The Search for Modern China* (W W Norton) and *The Gate of Heavenly Peace* (Penguin), and *The Rise of Modern China* by Immanuel Hsu (Oxford).

Jung Chang's *Wild Swans* (Flamingo) is a highly moving novel which documents the history of a family throughout the social upheavals of 20th-century revolutionary China. Min Anchee's *Red Azalea* (Victor Gollancez) concentrates upon the period of the Cultural Revolution, and is an extraordinary account of a young Red Guard— sent first to the countryside and then to Shanghai to be groomed to be an actress in revolutionary films—who falls in love. In addition to the growing popularity of literature from and about China, Chinese cinema is gaining far greater attention, and indeed accolades at international film festivals in the West: notably Zhang Yimou's *Raise the Red Lantern* and *Judou*, and Chen Kaige's *Farewell to my Concubine*. Incidentally, all three of these films include stunning performances by the actress Gong Li.

On His Baldness

At dawn I sighed to see my hairs fall;

At dusk I sighed to see my hairs fall.

For I dreaded the time when the last lock should go . . .

They are all gone and I do not mind at all!

I have done with that cumbrous washing and getting dry;

My tiresome comb for ever is laid aside.

Best of all, when the weather is hot and wet,

To have no top-knot weighing down on one's head!

I put aside my messy cloth wrap;

I have got rid of my dusty tasselled fringe.

In a silver jar I have stored a cold stream,

On my bald pate I trickle a ladle full.

Like one baptized with the Water of Buddha's Law,

I sit and receive this cool, cleansing joy.

Now I know why the priest who seeks Repose

Frees his heart by first shaving his head.

Po Chü-I, 772–846 AD

'Lazy Man's Song'

I could have a job, but am too lazy to choose it;
I have got land, but am too lazy to farm it.
My house leaks; I am too lazy to mend it.
My clothes are torn; I am too lazy to darn them.
I have got wine, but I am too lazy to drink;
So it's just the same as if my cup were empty.
I have got a lute, but am too lazy to play;
So it's just the same as if it had no strings.
My family tells me there is no more steamed rice;
I want to cook, but am too lazy to grind.
My friends and relatives write me long letters;
I should like to read them, but they're such a bother to open.
I have always been told that Hsi Shu-yeh
Passed his whole life in absolute idleness.
But he played his lute and sometimes worked at his forge;
So even he was not so lazy as I.

Po Chü-I, 772–846 AD

Chronology of Periods in Chinese History

Paleolithic	*c.*600,000–7000 BC
Neolithic	*c.* 7000–1600 BC
Shang	*c.*1600–1027 BC
Western Zhou	1027–771 BC
Eastern Zhou	770–256 BC
Spring and Autumn Annals	770–476 BC
Warring States	475–221 BC
Qin	221–207 BC
Western (Former) Han	206 BC–AD 8
Xin	9–24
Eastern (Later) Han	25–220
Three Kingdoms	220–265
Western Jin	265–316
Northern and Southern Dynasties	317–581
Sixteen Kingdoms	317–439
Former Zhao	304–329
Former Qin	351–383
Later Qin	384–417
Northern Wei	386–534
Weste	535–556
Northern Zhou	557–581
Sui	581–618
Tang	618–907
Five Dynasties	907–960
Liao	916–1125
Northern Song	960–1127
Southern Song	1127–1279
Jin (Jurchen)	1115–1234
Yuan (Mongol)	1279–1368
Ming	1368–1644
Qing (Manchu)	1644–1911
Republic of China	1911–1949
People's Republic of China	1949–

For a chart of the reigns of Ming and Qing emperors, see p. 76–77

A Guide to Pronouncing Chinese Names

The official system of romanization used in China, which the visitor will find on maps, road signs and city shopfronts, is known as *Pinyin*. It is now almost universally adopted by the western media.

Some visitors may initially encounter some difficulty in pronouncing romanized Chinese words. In fact many of the sounds correspond to the usual pronunciation of the letters in English. The exceptions are:

Initials

- c   is like the *ts* in 'i*ts*'
- q   is like the *ch* in '*cheese*'
- x   has no English equivalent, and can best be described as a hissing consonant that lies somewhere between *sh* and *s*. The sound was rendered as *hs* under an earlier transcription system.
- z   is like the *ds* in 'fa*ds*'
- zh   is unaspirated, and sounds like the *j* in 'jug'
- a   sounds like 'ah'
- e   is pronounced as the *o* in 'm*o*ther'
- i   is pronounced as in 'ski'(written as *yi* when not preceded by an initial consonant). However, in *ci, chi, ri, shi, zi* and *zhi*, the sound represented by the *i* final is quite different and is similar to the *ir* in 'sir', but without much stressing of the *r* sound.
- o   sounds like the *aw* in 'law'
- u   sounds like the *oo* in '*ooze*'
- ü   is pronounced as the German *ü* (written an *yu* when not preceded by an initial consonant). The last two finals are usually written simply as *e* and *u*.

Finals in Combination

When two or more finals are combined, such as in *hao, jiao* and *liu*, each letter retains its sound value as indicated in the list above, but note the following:

- ai   is like the *ie* in 'tie'
- ei   is like the *ay* in 'bay'

ian is like the *ien* in 'Vi*enn*a'

ie   similar to *ye* in 'y*et*'

ou   is like the *o* in 'c*o*de'

uai sounds like '*why*'

uan is like the *uan* in 'ig*uana*' (except when preceded by *j, q, x* and *y*; in these cases a *u* following any of these four consonants is in fact *ü* and *uan* is similar to *uen*).

ue   is like the *ue* in 'd*ue*t'

ui   sounds like '*way*'

Examples

A few Chinese names are shown below with English phonetic spelling beside them:

Beijing	Bay-jing (*jing* sounds like *ging* in 'pa*ging*')
Cixi	Tsi-shee
Guilin	Gway-lin
Hangzhou	Hahng-jo
Kangxi	Kahng-shee
Qianlong	Chien-loong
Tiantai	Tien-tie
Xi'an	Shee-ahn

An apostrophe is used to separate syllables in certain compound-character words to preclude confusion. For example, *Changan* (which can be *chang-an* or *chan-gan*) is sometimes written as *Chang'an*.

Tones

A Chinese syllable consists of not only an initial and a final or finals, but also a tone or pitch of the voice when the words are spoken. In *Pinyin* the four basic tones are marked — / \ . These marks are almost never shown in printed form except in language-learning texts.

Useful Addresses

EMBASSIES

Australia
15 Dongzhimenwai Dajie, Sanlitun
Tel. 65322331–7
澳大利亚　三里屯东直门外大街21号

Austria
5 Xiushui Nan Jie, Jianguomenwai
Tel. 65322061–2
奥地利　建国门外秀水南街5号

Belgium
6 Sanlitun Lu. Tel. 65321736–8
比利时　三里屯6号

Burma
6 Dongzhimenwai Dajie, Sanlitun
Tel. 65321425
缅甸　三里屯东直门外大街6号

Canada
10 Sanlitun Lu. Tel. 65323536
加拿大　三里屯10号

Denmark
1 Sanlitun Dongwu Jie. Tel. 65322431
丹麦　三里屯东五街1号

Finland
30 Guanghua Lu, Jianguomenwai
Tel. 65321817, 65321806
芬兰　建国门外光华路30号

France
3 Sanlitun Dongsan Jie. Tel. 65321331
法国　三里屯东三街3号

Germany
5 Dongzhimenwai Dajie, Sanlitun
Tel. 65322161
德国　三里屯东直门外大街5号

Hungary
10 Dongzhimenwai Dajie. Tel. 65321431
匈牙利　东直门外大街10号

India
1 Ritan Dong Lu, Jianguomenwai
Tel. 65321908, 65321856
印度　建国门外日坛东路1号

Israel
China World Trade Center, Room 405
1 Jianguomenwai Dajie. Tel. 65052970
以色列　建国门外大街1号国贸中心405室

Italy
2 Sanlitun Donger Jie. Tel. 65322131
意大利　三里屯东二街2号

Japan
7 Ritan Lu, Jianguomenwai. Tel. 65322361
日本　建国门外日坛路7号

Kampuchea
9 Dongzhimenwai Dajie. Tel. 65321889
柬埔寨　东直门外大街9号

Kazakstan
Sanlitun Dongliu Jie. Tel. 65326182
哈萨克斯坦　三里屯东六街

Korea
4/F China World Trade Tower,
1 Jianguomenwai Dajie
Tel. 65052608
大韩民国　建国门外大街一号国贸大厦

Laos
11 Sanlitun Dongsi Jie. Tel. 65321386
老挝　三里屯东四街11号

Malaysia
13 Dongzhimenwai Dajie, Sanlitun
Tel. 65322531
马来西亚　三里屯东直门外大街13号

Nepal
1 Sanlitun Xiliu Jie. Tel. 65321795
尼泊尔　三里屯西六街1号

Netherlands
1–15–2 Ta Yuan Office Building
Tel. 65321131
荷兰　塔园外交人员办公楼

New Zealand
1 Ritan Donger Jie, Jianguomenwai
Tel. 65322731–4
新西兰　建国门外日坛东二街1号

Norway
1 Sanlitun Dongyi Jie. Tel. 65322261–2
挪威　三里屯东一街1号

Pakistan
1 Dongzhimenwai Dajie, Sanlitun
Tel. 65322504
巴基斯坦　三里屯东直门外大街1号

Philippines
23 Xiushui Bei Jie, Jianguomenwai
Tel. 65322794
菲律宾　建国门外秀水北街23号

Poland
1 Ritan Lu, Jianguomenwai. Tel. 65321235
波兰　建国门外日坛路1号

Russian Federation
4 Dongzhimen Beizhongjie
Tel. 65322051, 65322181
俄罗斯联邦大使馆　东直门北中街4号

Singapore
4 Liangmahe Nan Lu, Sanlitun
Tel. 65323926
新加坡　三里屯亮马河南路4号

South Africa
C801 Beijing Lufthansa Centre, 50 Liangmaqiao Lu. Tel. 64651941
南非　亮马桥路50号北京燕莎中心C801

Spain
9 Sanlitun Lu. Tel. 65323629, 65321986
西班牙　三里屯路9号

Sri Lanka
3 Jianhua Lu, Jianguomenwai
Tel. 65321861–2
斯里兰卡　建国门外建华路3号

Sweden
3 Dongzhimenwai Dajie, Sanlitun
Tel. 65323331
瑞典　东直门外大街三号

Switzerland
3 Sanlitun Dongwu Jie. Tel. 65322736
瑞士　三里屯路3号

Thailand
40 Guanghua Lu, Jianguomenwai
Tel. 65321903
泰国　建国门外光华路40号

United Kingdom
11 Guanghua Lu, Jianguomenwai
Tel. 65321961–5
英国　建国门外光华路11号

USA (Consular Section)
2 Xiushui Dong Jie, Jianguomenwai
Tel. 65323831, 65321161
美国　建国门外秀水东街2号

Uzbekistan
Tayuan. Tel. 65326305
乌兹别克斯坦　塔园公寓

Vietnam
32 Guanghua Lu, Jianguomenwai
Tel. 65321155, 65321125
越南　建国门外光华路32号

AIRLINES

Air China
Airport Office. Tel. 64563604
Beijing Booking Office, 15 Xi Chang'an Jie.
Tel. 66013336 (domestic), 66016667 (international), 66017755 (information)
中国国际航空公司　首都飞机场／西长安街15号

Air France
Rm 512 , Building B, Full Link Plaza,
Dong Cheng District. Tel. 65881355
法国航空公司　东城区丰联广场B座512室

Air Koryo
Ritan Bei Lu, Jianguomenwai
Tel. 65011559
朝鲜航空公司　建国门外日坛北路

Alitalia
Rm B17, 12/F, Hanwei Plaza
(Behind Trade Centre). Tel. 65610375
意大利航空公司　汉威大厦(国贸后面)

All Nippon Airways
1/F, Development Tower,
Dong Cheng District. Tel. 65909191
全日空航空公司　东城区发展大厦一层

Austrian Airlines
Office Building S103, Kempinski Hotel,
Chaoyang District. Tel. 64622161
奥地利航空公司　朝阳区凯宾斯基饭店写字
楼S103室

British Airways
Rm 210, SCITE Tower,
22 Jianguomenwai. Tel. 65124085
英国航空公司　建国门外22号赛特大厦210
室

Canadian Airlines International
Rm 201, Office Building, Kempinski Hotel,
Chaoyang District. Tel. 64682001
加拿大国际航空公司　朝阳区凯宾斯基饭店
写字楼201室

Dragonair
A1710, Henderson Centre, Chang'an Avenue
Tel. 65182533
港龙航空公司　长安大街恒基中心A1710室

Finnair
SCITE Tower, 22 Jianguomenwai
Tel. 65127180–1, 65122288
芬兰航空公司　建国门外22号赛特大厦

Iran Air
CITIC Building, 19 Jianguomenwai
Dajie. Tel. 65124940
伊朗航空公司　建国门外大街19号国际大厦

Japan Airlines
Chang Fu Gong New Otani Hotel,
Jianguomenwai Dajie. Tel. 65130888
日本航空公司　建国门外大街长富宫饭店

Kazakstan Airlines
2nd Floor, International Hotel,
Jianguomennei Dajie. Tel. 65254719
哈萨克斯坦航空公司　建国门内大街国际饭
店二层

Korean Air
China World Trade Center,
1 Jianguomenwai Dajie. Tel. 65050088
大韩航空公司　建国门外大街1号国贸中心

LOT Polish Airlines
Chains City Hotel, 4, Gongren Tiyuchang
Dong Lu. Tel. 65007215
波兰航空公司　工人体育场东路城市宾馆

Lufthansa
S101 Lufthansa Centre Office Building
Tel. 64654488
汉莎航空公司　燕莎中心写字楼S101室

Malaysia Airlines
China World Trade Center,
1 Jianguomenwai Dajie. Tel. 65052681
马来西亚航空公司　建国门外大街国贸中心

Northwest Airlines
China World Trade Center,
1 Jianguomenwai Dajie. Tel. 65053505
西北航空公司　建国门外大街国贸中心

Pakistan International Airlines
China World Trade Center,
Jianguomenwai. Tel. 65051681–2
巴基斯坦国际航空公司　建国门外大街1号国贸中心

Qantas Airways
120B Office Building, Lufthansa Center
Tel. 64674794
澳大利亚航空公司　燕沙中心写字楼120B

SAS–Scandinavian Airlines System
14/F Henderson Centre, Chang'an Avenue
Tel. 65183738
北欧航空公司　长安大街恒基中心14层

Singapore Airlines
China World Trade Center,
1 Jianguomenwai Dajie. Tel. 65052233
新加坡航空公司　建国门外大街1号国贸中心

Swissair
SCITE Tower, 22 Jianguomenwai
Tel. 65123555, 65122288
瑞士航空公司　建国门外22号赛特大厦

Thai International
102B Lufthansa Center Office Building
Tel. 64608899
泰国国际航空公司　燕沙中心写字楼102B

United Airlines
Friendship Store, Lufthansa Center
Tel. 64631111
美国联合航空公司　燕沙中心友谊商城

Uzbekistan Airways
Rm.201, CITIC, 19 Jianguomenwai Dajie
Tel. 65002255, ext. 3212
乌兹别克斯坦航空公司　国际大厦前楼201室

AIRPORT
Beijing International Airport
Information. Tel. 64563604
北京国际机场

TAXIS
Beijing Taxi Co
Maquan, Guangqumenwai. Tel. 67712546
Bus (telephone order) 64235542
Taxi (telephone order) 67719079
北京出租汽车公司　广渠门外马圈

Capital Taxi Co
10 Yuetan Bei Jie, Xichengqu
Tel. 68527084
(English speaking dispatch) Tel. 65137461
首都出租汽车公司　西城区月坛北街10号

RAILWAY
Beijing Railway Station
Foreigners' Ticket Office. Tel. 65128968
Enquiries. Tel. 65633662
Baggage. Tel. 65256028
Customs. Tel. 65129354
北京火车站

Beijing South Station
Tel. 65635262
北京火车南站

Beijing West Station
Tel. 63216253, 63214269
北京火车西站

CAR RENTAL
Capital Automobile Leasing Co.
62 Huayan Beili, Chaoyang District
Tel. 64915259, 64915253
首汽租赁公司　朝阳区华严北里62号

CVIK Taxi Service, Car Rental
B2, Passage 4, Scitech Plaza
Tel. 65123481, 65124488
赛特出租汽车公司汽东租赁部　建国门外大街赛特饭店

TRAVEL

Beijing Blue Sky Travel Agency
7 Yabao Rd. Tel. 65004504.
Fax. 65126812
北京蓝天旅行社　雅宝路7号

Beijing Tradewinds
Room 114, International Club,
Jianguomenwai. Tel. 65025997,
65025927; fax. 65004509
北京国际四季风服务有限公司
建国门外国际俱乐部一楼114室

CITS Beijing Branch
28 Jianguomenwai Dajie
Tel. 65150515
中国国际旅行社北京分社
建国门外大街28号

CITS Head Office
103 Fuxingmennei Dajie. Tel. 66012055
中国国际旅行社总社　复兴门内103号

CTS Head Office
8 Dongjiaomin Xiang. Tel. 65129933
中国旅行社总社　东交民巷8号

CTS Main Beijing Branch
Beijing Tourism Building
28 Jianguomenwai Dajie
Tel. 65150623; fax. 65158603
中国旅行社北京分社
建国门外大街28号旅游大厦

CYTS (China Youth Travel Service)
23 Dongjiaomin Xiang. Tel. 65127770
中国青年旅行社总社　东交民巷23号

BANKING REPRESENTATIVE OFFICES

American Express
China World Trade Center,
1, Jianguomenwai Dajie. Tel. 65052838
美国运通银行　建国门外大街1号国贸中心

Bank of America
2722–3 China World Trade Center,
1 Jianguomenwai Dajie. Tel. 65053508
美国美洲银行　建国门外大街1号国贸中心

Bank of China (Head Office)
410 Fuchengmenwai Dajie. Tel. 66016688
中国银行总行　阜成门外大街410号

Bank of China (Beijing Branch)
19 Donganmen Dajie. Tel. 65199114
中国银行北京分行　雅宝路8号

Bank of Tokyo
1701 China World Trade Center,
1 Jianguomenwai Dajie. Tel. 65055346
东京银行　建国门外大街国贸中心1701室

Barclay's Bank
1211 SCITE Tower, 22 Jianguomenwai Dajie.
Tel. 65122288, ext. 1211
英国巴克莱银行
建国门外大街22号赛特大厦1211室

Citibank
16/F Guanghua Chang'an Tower, Chang'an
Avenue. Tel. 65102933
花旗银行北京分行　光华长安大厦16层

**First National Bank of Chicago (Beijing
Branch).** Tel. 65002255
芝加哥第一国民银行北京分行　国际大厦16层

Hongkong and Shanghai Bank
COFCO Plaza, Chang'an Avenue
Tel. 65260669
香港上海汇丰银行　中粮广场大厦

Royal Bank of Canada
China World Trade Center,
1 Jianguomenwai Dajie. Tel. 65054205
加拿大皇家银行　建国门外大街1号国贸中心

Standard Chartered Bank
14/F Swissôtel, Hong Kong - Macau Centre
标准渣打(麦加利)银行　港澳中心14层

THEATRES AND CINEMAS
Beijing Concert Hall
Bei Xinhua Jie. Tel. 66055812
北京音乐厅　北新华街

Beijing Hu Guang Guildhall
Hufangqiao, Xuanwu District
Tel. 63518284
北京湖广会馆古戏楼　虎坊桥3号

Capital Theatre
22 Wangfujing Dajie. Tel. 65249847
首都剧场　王府井大街22号

Chang'an Grand Theatre
7 Jianguomennei Dajie
Tel. 65101309
长安大戏院　建国门外大街7号

Chaoyang Theatre
36 Dongsanhuan Bei Lu, Hujialou
Tel. 65072421
朝阳剧场　呼家楼东三环北路36号

China Children's Art Theatre
64 Donganmen Dajie. Tel. 65134121
中国儿童艺术剧院　东安门大街64号

Chinese Opera Theatre
Xishan Bei Lu, Haidianqu
Tel. 68419381
中国剧院　海淀区西三环北路

China Opera and Dance Institute
2 Nanhua Dong Jie, Hufang Lu
Tel. 63036058
中国歌剧舞剧院　虎坊南华东街2号

Liyuan Theatre
Qianmen Hotel, 175 Yongan Lu
Tel. 63016688, ext. 8860
梨园剧场　前门饭店

Sanwei Bookstore (Tea House)
Xidan, opposite Minzu Hotel. Tel. 66013204
三味书屋茶馆　西单（民族饭店对面）

Zhengyici Theatre
220 Xiheyan Dajie, Xuanwu District
Tel. 63036233
正乙祠戏楼　宣武门西河沿大街

SPORTS FACILITIES
Beijing Gymnasium
4 Tiyuguan Lu, Chongwenmenwai
Tel. 67027381 ext. 502, 67016995
北京体育馆　崇文门外体育馆路4号

Beijing Worker's Gymnasium
Gongren Tiyuchang Bei Lu. Tel. 65022961
北京工人体育馆　工人体育场北路

Beijing Worker's Stadium
Gongren Tiyuchang Bei Lu. Tel. 65025505
北京工人体育场　工人体育场北路

Capital Gymnasium
Baishiqiao. Tel. 68322255
首都体育馆　白石桥

POST AND TELECOMMUNICATIONS
Beijing Main PTT (Post, Telephone and Telecommunications) Bureau
Dianbao Dalou, Fuxingmennei Dajie
Tel. 66034900, 66034426, 66036292
北京邮电局　复兴门内大街电报大楼

Beijing Telecommunications Bureau
131 Xidan Dajie. Tel. 66037700
北京电信局　西单大街131号

Beijing Telegraph Office
11 Xichang'an Jie. Tel. 66014834, 66034900
北京电报局　西长安街11号

Beijing Courier Service Corp.
Zhengyilu. Tel. 65127566
北京邮政速递公司　正义路

Beijing Foreign Transport Co.
6 Beisanhuan Dong Lu
Tel. 64671741
北京对外运输公司　北三环东路6号

Bell South China Inc.
Rm S123, Lufthansa Center. Tel. 64651685.
Fax. 64651686
南贝尔中国有限公司
北京燕莎中心办公楼S123室

DHL Sinotrans Ltd
Zuojiazhuang Tel. 64662211
Xisanhuan Rd. Tel. 68472211
中外运—教豪国际航空有限公司
朝阳区左家庄

FedEx
3/F, Gaolan Tower (East Lufthansa
Center). Tel. 64685566
联邦快递 高澜大厦三层(燕莎中心东面)

**International Post and
Telecommunications Office**
Jianguomen Bei Dajie. Tel. 65128120
国际邮电信业务组 建国门北大街

Sanlitun PTT
1–3–11 Sanlitun Bei. Tel. 65321085
三里屯邮电信业务 三里屯1-3-11

HOSPITALS & EMERGENCY CENTRES

AEA International
Building C, BITIC Leasing Center,
1 North Rd, Xin Fu San Cun. Tel. 64629100
(24-hour service); toll free: 8008100180;
fax. 64629111
亚洲国际紧急救援中心 幸福三村北街1号
北信租赁中心C座

Beijing Emergency Centre
Qianmen Xi Dajie. Tel. 120, 66014433
北京市急救中心 前门西大街

Capital Hospital
Dongdan, Dongcheng District
Tel. 65253731
首都医院 东单

Friendship Hospital (Youyi Yi Yuan)
Tianqiao. Tel. 63014411
友谊医院 天桥

Hong Kong International Medical Clinic
Swissôtel Hong Kong-Macau Center
Tel. 65012288–2346 (24-hour service)
北京香港国际医务诊所
港澳中心瑞士酒店

Peking Union Medical College Hospital
Emergency (foreigners' section)
Dongdan, Dongcheng District
Tel. 65296114
北京协和医院 东城区东单

Sino-German Policlinic Zhong De Zhen Suo
(privately run 24-hour ambulance service,
performs minor surgery)
B1, Landmark Tower, 8 Dong Sanhuan Lu
Tel. 65011983, 65016688, ext. 20903
中德诊所 东三环8号亮马大厦

Sino-Japanese Friendship Hospital
North end of Heping Jie, Chaoyang District
Tel. 64221122
中日友好医院 朝阳区和平北街

MISCELLANEOUS

**Beijing Municipal Public Security
Bureau** (foreigners' section)
85 Beichizi Jie. Tel. 65253102, 65255486
北京公安局外事科 北池子街85号

Beijing International Convention Center
8 Beichen Dong Lu. Tel. 64910246
北京国际会议中心 北辰东路8号

Exhibition Hall at China World Trade Center
1 Jianguomenwai Dajie. Tel. 65053832
中国国贸中心展览馆 建国门外大街1号

China International Exhibition Centre
6 Beisanhuan Xi Lu, Chaoyang District
Tel. 64664433
中国国际展览馆中心
朝阳北三环西路6号

Practical Information

Hotels

Over the past decade there has been a rapid surge of hotel construction in Beijing in an attempt to keep pace with demand from the fast-increasing number of visitors who flock to the capital. Beijing's hotels offer the visitor quite a choice of quality and price, ranging from leading international chain properties, down to utilitarian hostelries where you may stay, dormitory-style, for about 50 *yuan*. Quality of management covers an equally broad spectrum. In some hotels you will find polite, well-intentioned (possibly well-trained) English-speaking staff; in others, management still pays little attention to cleanliness, maintenance, or charm.

Beijing Municipality lists over 200 hotels in the city which accept overseas guests. In practice some of these are not keen to have foreigners stay there. The reasons for this include problems with language, inflexible meal times, unreliable hot water supply etc. Others could only be recommended as a last resort when every-where else in the city is full.

Most of Beijing's top hotels are mostly financed from overseas and run by foreign management groups. With overseas staff from Hong Kong in top managerial positions, these joint-venture hotels are aiming at international-standard service and facilities—and they charge international prices for them.

The new joint-venture hotels have the great advantage of a workable confirmed booking system—always a major difficulty for non-group travellers in China. As a rule, it is difficult to get confirmed bookings for Beijing's Chinese-run hotels, even though more travel agencies, including CITS, can now arrange bookings for a select few. Attempts by individuals to get bookings confirmed by letter or telex still tend to go unanswered.

In peak months (March through to November), rooms in the capital have been very hard to come by. Although the shortage should ease as more hotels open up over the next few years, it is still advisable for travellers who want a good hotel to book it as far in advance as possible.

Some of Beijing's older hotels, run by the municipality, have been inspired by standards set by new hotels, and have made visible efforts to improve—though none seem entirely able to throw off the quirks of hotel management Chinese-style.

Chinese-run hotels typically have private bathroom, telephone, heating, and sometimes air-conditioning. Boiled drinking water is placed in each room. There are outlets for electric razors, the supply being 220 volts. There are TV sets in the public lounges and in rooms. Room service is patchy, but one can usually get beer and soft drinks until late at night by approaching the floor-attendants who look after most services. There are small shops, bank, postal and telegraph facilities in the hotel foyers. Chinese and Western food is available, and private dinner parties and banquets can be arranged. Standard meal charges will be in the range of 50 *yuan* per day, exclusive of drinks and special dishes. A range of imported foreign wines and spirits, Coca-Cola, cigarettes and films can be bought at special stalls in most big hotels and Friendship Stores. Some hotels also stock overseas newspapers and magazines.

In many Chinese hotels, the attendants have an surprising habit of opening the door one has carefully locked. Try not to get annoyed—they are confident that no one is going to interfere with one's possessions. But be prepared for attendants walking into your room with barely a knock, and even dusting around while you are trying to change. Do bear in mind that thefts may occur in budget hotels.

The following list of hotels gives an approximate range of rates for rooms and suites in 1999, to be used as a basis for comparison, rather than an accurate picture of current prices many of which are discounted from 15 to 50 per cent. Only special facilities (beyond TV, bank, post office, hairdresser, tourist shops) have been mentioned. **Note that most hotels in Beijing now add a 15 per cent service charge to the room rate**.

Readers will understand that in the selection of hotels and restaurants a great deal of subjectivity is inevitably involved. In a rapidly developing city like Beijing, not only do addresses and telephone numbers change, but also management—including, in the case of restaurants, fine chefs, and in the case of hotels, outstanding general managers! The following pages include places that we or our friends have enjoyed visiting or eating at. Corrections and suggestions from guidebook users are most welcome, so please write to **Odyssey Publications Ltd, 1004 Kowloon Centre, 29–43 Ashley Road, Tsim Sha Tsui, Kowloon, Hong Kong. Fax: (852)2565 8004; e-mail: odyssey@asiaonline.net**

SUPERIOR HOTELS

Beijing International Club Hotel

21 Jianguomenwai Dajie. Tel. 64606688; fax. 64603299

北京国际俱乐部饭店　建国门外大街21号

One of Starwood Sheraton's 53 Luxury Collection properties worldwide. Consists of a 287-room hotel, luxury office building and international athletic club of apartments and sports facilities. The complex is in the grounds of the historic Beijing International Club, established in 1911.

The Great Wall Sheraton Hotel Beijing

10 Dongsanhuan Beilu, Chaoyang. Tel. 65905566; fax. 65905938, 65905398;
e-mail: business@greatwall.linexcel.com.cn

长城饭店　朝阳区东三环北路10号

1,007 rooms, US$280–2,700 + 15% service charge. Executive floor, 24-hour business centre, nightclub, Clark Hatch health club, indoor/outdoor swimming pool, tennis, billiards, theatre (max. 900), ballroom (max. 1,800), conference and banquet (max. 1,000). Very convenient, plush interior; joint-venture hotel located near Sanlitun embassy district. Shuttle service to city centre.

China World Hotel

1 Jianguomenwai Dajie. Tel. 65052266; fax. 65053164, 65050828;
e-mail: cwhbc@public3.bta.net.cn

中国大饭店　建国门外大街1号

745 rooms, US$265–2,400 + 15% service charge. Health club, gym, sauna, swimming pool, nightclub/disco, supermarket, conference and banquet facilities (max. 2,000). Jewel in the crown of the Shangri-La hotels in China. Part of a huge new complex that includes the Traders Hotel and the China World Trade Center, thus offering every conceivable service.

Grand Hotel Beijing

35 Dong Chang'an Jie. Tel. 65137788; fax. 65130048–50; e-mail: grand@ht.rol.cn.net
http://www.grandhotelbeijing.com

北京贵宾楼饭店　东长安街35号

218 rooms and suites, US$300–2,500 + 15% service charge. Business centre, health club. Westernmost wing of the Beijing Hotel, but independently managed. Large atrium, grand style decor with a palatial Chinese Emperor's suite available, fine location, intimate comfort. Palace View Bar on top floor gives fine view of Forbidden City at sunset.

Jianguo Hotel

5 Jianguomenwai Dajie. Tel. 65002233; fax. 65002871

建国饭店　建国门外大街5号

575 rooms, US$120–209 + 15% service charge. Business centre, indoor swimming pool, delicatessen. Within walking distance of Beijing's diplomatic quarter, pleasant atmosphere; joint-venture hotel. Favoured by long time visitors. Fine lobby and popular Charlie's Bar.

Beijing Hilton

1 Dongfang Lu, Chaoyang District. Tel. 64662288; fax. 64653052;
e-mail: Hiltonbj@public3.bta.net.cn
北京希尔顿酒店　朝阳区东三环北路东方路一号
365 rooms and suites, US$250–1,900. Three executive floors with private lounge and
three non-smoking floors. Conveniently located close to Sanlitun diplomatic, business
and shopping districts with immediate access to airport and exhibition centre.

Holiday Inn Crowne Plaza

48 Wangfujing Dajie. Tel. 65133388; fax. 65132513; e-mail: hicpb@public3.bta.net.cn
国际艺苑皇冠假日饭店　王府井大街48号
380 rooms, from US$200–600 + 15% service charge. The third Holiday Inn in
Beijing, this well-located hotel features an art gallery and an art salon where there
are regular performances of popular and classical music.

Kempinski Hotel, Beijing Lufthansa Center

50 Liangmaqiao Lu, Chaoyang District. Tel. 64653388; fax. 64653366;
e-mail: regushbc@public.east.cn.net
北京燕莎中心，凯宾斯基饭店　朝阳区亮马桥路50号
540 rooms. US$280–2,400 + 15% service charge. 13 restaurants, bar, business and
health centres, pool, tennis, squash, Beijing City Club, disco, 6 function rooms (max
850). Excellent Sunday brunches.

The Palace Hotel

8 Goldfish Lane, Wangfujing. Tel. 65128899; fax. 6512905; e-mail: tph@peninsula.com
王府饭店　王府井金鱼胡同8号
575 rooms, US$280–3,500 + 15% service charge. Business centre, indoor swimming
pool, health club, disco, billiards, delicatessen, Western, Chinese and Japanese
restaurants, conference (max. 550) and banquet (max. 400) facilities. Stunning luxury
hotel in fine location. Managed by the Peninsula Group of Hong Kong.

Shangri-La Hotel

29 Zizhuyuan Lu. Tel. 68412211; fax. 68418002/3/4; e-mail: slbbc2@ht.rol.cn.net
香格里拉饭店　紫竹院路29号
786 rooms, US$230–1,300 + 15% service charge. Business centre, health club, indoor
swimming pool, music room, ballroom and function rooms (max 750). Elegant,
comfortable; a joint-venture hotel. Shuttle service to the city centre. The Horizon
Floor executive rooms here are some of the nicest in the city.

Swissôtel, Hong Kong-Macau Centre
Gongren Tiyuchang Beilu, Chaoyang District. Tel. 65012288; fax. 65012501;
e-mail: swissotel@homeway.com.cn
北京港澳中心，瑞士酒店　朝阳区北大街工人体育场北路
500 rooms, US$220–500 + 15% service charge. Health club, indoor swimming pool,
tennis courts, office and residential tower, convention and meeting facilities (banquet
max. 400). First hotel in Asia with full facilities for the handicapped.

Beijing Hotel
33 Dong Chang'an Jie. Tel. 65137766; fax. 65137842;
e-mail: business@chinabeijinghotel.com.cn
北京饭店　东长安街33号
871 rooms, US$160–680 +15% service charge. Business centre, conference and
banqueting hall (max. 1,000), Beijing's oldest (1900) and best-known hotel. Centrally
located near Tiananmen Square. This hotel has developed some character with its age.

Chang Fu Gong New Otani Hotel
Jianguomenwai Dajie. Tel. 65125555; fax. 65125346; e-mail: chfgbc@ccnet.cn.net
长富宫饭店　建国门外大街
512 rooms, US$180–650 + 15% service charge. Grand ballroom, Japanese restaurant,
health club, indoor swimming pool, tennis courts, sauna, banquet and conference
facilities (max. 700). Under Japanese management. Located near the Friendship
Store in the embassy district.

Jing Guang New World Hotel
Hu Jia Lou, Chaoyang District. Tel. 65978888; fax. 65973333;
e-mail: jghef@ht.rol.cn.net
京广新世界饭店　朝阳区呼家楼
492 rooms, US$190–1,200 + 15% service charge. Medical centre, taxi fleet, supermarket,
disco, Chaozhou restaurant, Food Street. In a commercial and residential skyscraper
somewhat outside the city centre.

LUXURY HOTELS
Radisson SAS Hotel Beijing
6A Beisanhuan Donglu, Chaoyang District. Tel. 64663388; fax. 64653186;
e-mail: gb_{ny98@public.gb.com.cn
北京皇家大饭店　朝阳区北三环东路甲6号
347 rooms, US$180–350 + 15% service charge. The hotel is located next to the China

International Exhibition Center, which holds around 30 major exhibitions each year. Includes three restaurants, a bar and banquet facilities for up to 400 people. The Health Club provides heated swimming pool, Finnish sauna, gym, tennis and squash courts, and solarium.

Beijing Airport Mövenpick Radisson Hotel
Xiao Tianzhi Village, Shunyi County. Tel. 64565588; fax. 64561234;
e-mail: bjmphtc@public.bta.net.cn
北京国都大饭店　首都机场南小天竺路
420 rooms, US$135–255 + 15% service charge. Includes a 24-hour business centre, outdoor tennis courts, indoor swimming pool, gym, pub. Five minutes from the airport but 40 minutes from town. Excellent food services, including arguably the best ice-cream in China.

Beijing International Hotel
9 Jianguomennei Dajie. Tel. 65126688; fax. 65129972; e-mail: bih@ht.rol.cn.net
北京国际饭店　建国门内大街9号
1,049 rooms and suites, US$165–1,200 + 15% service charge. Business centre, health club, tennis courts, indoor/outdoor swimming pool, bowling centre, billiards, games room, shopping arcade. A massive structure built by the China International Travel Service. A five-minute taxi ride to Tiananmen Square and set nearby the Beijing railway station.

Holiday Inn Lido Beijing
Jichang Lu, Jiangtai Lu. Tel. 64376688; fax. 64376237; e-mail: lido@ht.rol.cn.net
北京丽都假日酒店　机场路
1,000 rooms, US$170–800 + 15% service charge. Health club, bowling centre, indoor swimming pool, billiards, TV games, supermarket, delicatessen, disco. Very remote location, but close to the airport; offers the widest range of facilities including a sports club. Shuttle service to city centre.

Harbour Plaza Beijing (Beijing Hai Yi Jiu Dian)
8 Jiang Tai West Rd, Chaoyang District. Tel. 64362288; fax. 64361818;
e-mail: plaza@public.fhnet.cn.net
北京海逸酒店　朝阳区将台西路8号
429 rooms. US$140 + 15% service charge.

Tianlun Dynasty Hotel

50 Wangfujing Dajie. Tel. 65138888; fax. 65137866; e-mail: tianlun@public.bta.net.cn
北京天伦王朝饭店　王府井大街50号

408 rooms, Rmb1,080–4,000 + 15% service charge. Business centre, bowling alley, tennis and squash courts, disco, rooftop garden, Vietnamese restaurant, conference and banquet facilities (max. 600). Opened 1991. Luxury hotel featuring the largest atrium in East Asia. Excellent downtown location.

Capital Hotel

3 Qianmen Dong Dajie. Tel. 65129988; fax. 65120309
首都大酒店　前门东大街3号

326 rooms, Rmb1,500–16,700 + 15% service charge. Business centre, Chinese, Japanese and Italian restaurants, coffee shop, bar, shopping arcade, swimming pool, tennis courts, bowling alley, billiards, sauna, gym, conference and banquet facilities (max. 400). Centrally located in a busy section of town. Owned by the State Council.

Fragrant Hills (Xiangshan Hotel)

Xiangshan. Tel. 62591166; fax. 62591762
香山饭店　香山

288 rooms, Rmb670–1,350. Health club, outdoor swimming pool, tennis courts, gardens. Designed by I M Pei; located in Fragrant Hills Park. Suffering from neglect; very remote.

Friendship Hotel

3 Baishiqiao Lu. Tel. 68498888; fax. 68498866
友谊宾馆　白石桥路3号

1,500 rooms, Rmb830–12,000 + 15% service charge. Outdoor swimming pool, gym, theatre, tennis courts. Originally built to house Russian advisors during the 1950s, it is a massive complex of many buildings. Pleasant atmosphere. Shuttle service to city centre.

Jinglun (Beijing-Toronto)

Jianguomenwai Dajie. Tel. 65002266; fax. 65002022
京伦　建国门外大街

695 rooms, US$180–260 + 15% service charge. Business centre, ballroom (max. 400). Within walking distance of major business centres, very efficient service. Joint venture hotel.

Traders Hotel

1 Jianguomenwai Dajie. Tel. 65052277; fax. 65050818, 65050828;
e-mail: thbc@public3.net.cn
国贸饭店（国贸中心）　建国门外大街1号
298 rooms, US$160–450 + 15% service charge. Access to China World Hotel facilities.
Younger sibling of the China World Hotel. A modest, well-run hotel favoured by
business people.

Gloria Plaza Hotel

2 Jianguomennan Dajie. Tel. 65158855; fax. 65158533;
e-mail: GPHBC@public.bta.net.cn
凯莱酒店　建国门外大街1号
430 rooms, US$120–1,200 + 15% service charge. Business centre, indoor swimming
pool, sauna, gym, Lawyers Club (pub, library, offices), conference and banquet
facilities (max. 350). Located near the Friendship Store in the embassy district.
Well-run upmarket hotel under Hong Kong ownership and management.

Landmark Hotel

8 Beisanhuan Lu. Tel. 65906688; fax. 65906513
亮马饭店（亮马公寓）　北三环路8号
500 rooms, Rmb850–1,870 + 15% service charge. Medical clinic, baby-sitting, drug
store, indoor swimming pool, sauna, tennis and squash courts, health club, conference
and banquet facilities. Opened 1990. Residential and commercial complex close to
the Sheraton Great Wall near the diplomatic quarter. Joint venture with Singapore,
run by Beijing Travel and Tourism Corporation.

Xiyuan Hotel

Erligou. Tel. 68313388; fax. 68314577; e-mail: xyhotel@public3.bta.net.cn
西苑饭店　二里沟
750 rooms, Rmb1,400–9,500. Health club, indoor swimming pool, business centre.
Good facilities but somewhat inadequate service. Located near Erligou, Negotiations
Building and Beijing Zoo.

Xin Da Du Hotel

21 Chegongzhuang Lu. Tel. 68319988; fax. 68338507
新大都饭店　西城区车公庄路21号
400 rooms, Rmb1,400–2,600. Business centre, bowling alley. Beautifully renovated
tourist hotel run by Beijing Municipality. Located in a residential area near the
Beijing Zoo.

Zhaolong Hotel
2 Gongren Tiyuchang Bei Lu, Chaoyang. Tel. 65972299; fax. 65972288
兆龙饭店　朝阳区工人体育场北路2号
270 rooms, Rmb1,290–8,850 + 15% service charge. Theatre (max. 200), banquet (max. 300), health club, indoor/outdoor swimming pool. This hotel was a gift to China from Hong Kong shipping magnate Y K Pao. Located near Jianguomenwai business area.

STANDARD HOTELS
Dragon Spring Hotel
Shuichi Bei Lu, Mentougou. Tel. 69843362; fax. 69844377
龙泉宾馆　门头沟水池北路
235 rooms and suites, Rmb480–880 + 15% service charge. Conference (max. 500) and banqueting (max. 180) facilities, indoor pool, tennis courts, health club, billiard room, secretarial services. Traditional Chinese architecture; pleasant atmosphere. A joint-venture hotel, very remotely located near the Fragrant Hills. Boasts of having the best ice-cream in Beijing. Shuttle service into central Beijing.

Holiday Inn Downtown
98 Beilishi Lu. Tel. 68338822; fax. 68340896; e-mail: downtown@public.east.cn.net
北京金都假日饭店　西城区北礼士路98号
347 rooms, US$80–500 + 15% service charge. Swimming pool, health club, Indian restaurant. Opened in 1990. Economical, unpretentious hotel in a non-tourist neighbourhood.

Olympic Hotel
52 Baishiqiao Lu. Tel. 62176688; fax. 62174104
奥林匹克饭店　海淀区白石桥路52号(首都体育馆北面)
338 rooms, US$105–300 + 15% service charge. Business centre, shop, Cantonese and French restaurants, two bars, 24-hour coffee shop, hair salon, Chinese medical centre, conference facilities (max. 300), shuttle service to city centre. Hotel is located in pleasant surroundings near Purple Bamboo Park and Capital Gymnasium. A joint venture hotel; attractive, cheery.

Exhibition Centre Hotel
135 Xizhimenwai Dajie. Tel. 68316633; fax. 68327450
北京展览馆宾馆　西直门外大街135号
250 rooms, Rmb800–1,200. Health club, American bar. Friendly, upbeat, well-managed joint venture, near Beijing Zoo in the grounds of the exhibition centre.

Huadu
8 Xinyuan Nan Lu. Tel. 65971166; fax. 65971615
华都饭店　新源南路8号
522 rooms, Rmb715–990 + 10% service charge. Ballroom and conference facilities (max. 500). Built and run by CTS. Few taxis and no buses make it an inconvenient place to stay.

Jin Lang Hotel
75 Chongnei Dajie. Tel. 65132288; fax. 65136809
北京金朗大酒店　东城区崇内大街75号
408 rooms, Rmb830–1,600 + 15% service charge. French brasserie, health club, business centre, conference and banquet facilities (max. 110). Convenient downtown location near Beijing railway station and historical neighbourhoods.

Minzu
51 Fuxingmennei Dajie. Tel. 66014466; fax. 66014849
民族饭店　复兴门内大街51号
615 rooms, Rmb723–1,800 + 10% service charge. Conference and banquet facilities (max. 400), gym, billiards, recently renovated. Located to the west of Tiananmen Square near Xidan Street, an important shopping area.

City Hotel
4 Gongren Tiyuchang Dong Lu. Tel. 65007799; fax. 65008228
城市宾馆　工人体育场东路4号
85 rooms, 135 studios and suites, US$75–100 + 10% service charge. Business centre, nursery, karaoke, health club. Not to be confused with Jing Guang New World Hotel, this is a modest hotel near the Sanlitun diplomatic district.

Qianmen
1 Yongan Lu. Tel. 63016688; fax. 63013883
前门饭店　永安路1号
460 rooms, Rmb705–1,250. Located in an interesting old section of Beijing near Liulichang. Service is adequate. Nightly Beijing opera performances are given in the Liyuan (Pear Garden) Theatre.

Jinjiang Asia Hotel
8 Xinzhong Xijie, Gongti Bei Lu. Tel. 65007788; fax. 65008001
北京亚洲锦江大酒店　工体北路新中西街8号
298 rooms and suites, Rmb1,030–1,400 + 15% service charge. Health club, Chinese, Mediterranean and Korean restaurants. Opened 1990.

Taiwan Hotel
5 Goldfish Lane, Wangfujing. Tel. 65136688; fax. 65136896
台湾饭店　王府井北金鱼胡同5号
268 rooms, US$120–210 + 15% service charge. Business centre, health club. Well located near Wangfujing. Inexpensive tourist hotel that offers concessions to groups from Taiwan.

Xinqiao
2 Dongjiaomin Xiang, Chongwenmen. Tel. 65133366; fax. 65125126
新桥饭店　崇文门东交民巷2号
320 rooms, Rmb660–1,200. Conference and banquet facilities (max. 300), health club, *boulangerie*. Located in old Legation Quarter near city centre. Renovated in 1991.

Yanjing
2 Fuxingmenwai Dajie. Tel. 68536688; fax. 68526200
燕京宾馆　复兴门外大街2号
507 rooms, Rmb560–1,100. Ballroom (max. 150), banquet facilities (max. 300), indoor swimming pool. Mainly used by tourist groups.

Bamboo Garden Hotel
24 Xiaoshiqiao Hutong, Jiugulou Dajie. Tel. 64032229; fax. 64012633
竹园宾馆　旧鼓楼大街小石桥胡同24号
40 rooms, Rmb830–1,200. Picturesque setting with covered walkways and gardens. The hotel is the former residence of Kang Sheng, head of the Public Security Bureau during the Cultural Revolution. Difficult to get reservations.

Tiantan Hotel
1 Tiyuguan Lu, Chongwen District. Tel. 67112277; fax. 67116833
天坛饭店　崇文区体育馆路1号
200 rooms, Rmb842–1,680.

Qiaoyuan
Youanmenwai, Dongbinhe Lu. Tel. 63038861; fax. 63184709
侨园饭店　右安门外东宾河路
200 rooms, Rmb308–1,080. A pleasant hotel.

BUDGET HOTELS

Beijing Jing Tai Hotel

65 Yongwai, Jingtaixili. Tel. 67224675; fax. 67212476

北京景泰宾馆　北京永外景泰西里65号

Rmb130–160.

Beiwei

13 Xijing Lu. Tel. 63012266; fax. 63011366

北纬饭店　北纬路13号

226 rooms, Rmb240–342. Adequate facilities, friendly service. Located near Qianmen shopping district.

Cherry Blossom Hotel

17 Huixin Dongjie, Hepingli. Tel. 64934455; fax. 64918628

樱花宾馆　和平里惠新东街17号

192 rooms, Rmb280–600 + 10% service charge.

Hadamen Hotel

2A Chongwenmenwai Dajie. Tel. 67112244; fax. 67116865

哈德门饭店　崇文门外大街2号

210 rooms, Rmb400–450. Business centre, Bianyifang Peking Roast Duck Restaurant. Near the Beijing railway station, this is a conveniently located basic hotel.

Huguosi Hotel

Huguosi Jie, Western District. Tel. 66181113; fax. 66180142

护国寺宾馆　西城区护国寺街

80 rooms, Rmb280–540. Coffee shop, Chinese restaurants. Located in the heart of the old city on a bustling street.

Jimen Hotel

1 Xueyuan Lu. Tel. 62016701; fax. 62015355

蓟门饭店　海淀区学院路1号

200 rooms, Rmb232–392. Chinese restaurant, bar. A spartan building with adequate facilities and service. It is rather isolated in the northwest of Beijing but convenient for Beijing University, Qinghua University and Beijing Languages Institute.

Overseas Chinese Hotel (Huaqiao Fandian)
5 Santiao Beixinqiao. Tel. 64016688; fax. 64012386
华侨饭店　北新桥三条5号
175 rooms, Rmb420–1,700 + 10% service charge. Near the Lama temple in north of city, transportation is difficult to arrange.

Tiantan Tiyu Binguan (Sportsmen's Inn)
10 Tiyuguan Lu. Tel. 67113388; fax. 67115388
天坛体育宾馆　体育馆路10号
100 rooms, Rmb388–448. Few buses or taxis; good facilities, pleasant staff.

Wanshou
12A Wanshou Lu. Tel. 68214433; fax. 68216290
万寿宾馆　万寿路12A号
80 rooms, Rmb360–580. Adequate facilities, interesting neighbourhood.

Youhao Binguan
7 Houyuanensi, Jiaodaokou. Tel. 64031114; fax. 64014603
友好宾馆　交道口后园恩寺7号
50 rooms, Rmb310–500. Charming atmosphere—former residence of Chiang Kai-shek. Reputed to have the best Japanese restaurant in Beijing.

Ziyu
5 Huayuancun, Xisanhuan Bei Lu. Tel. 68411188; fax. 68411355
紫玉饭店　西三环北路花园村5号
125 rooms, Rmb350–1,800.

Restaurant Selection

Most Chinese restaurants outside China serve Cantonese, Sichuan or Shanghai food. The typical food of Beijing is rather different. Rice is not grown in north China as abundantly as in the south and the staple cereal is wheat. Steamed bread, dumplings and many kinds of noodles form the basis of any Beijing meal. The most commonly eaten vegetables are those of a northern climate—carrots, spinach, turnips, onions, scallions and large white cabbages.

Beijing has adopted and modified various northern cooking techniques—particularly for barbecueing or boiling mutton—which are not a special feature of its cuisine. But the capital's most celebrated dish, famous far beyond the borders of China, is 'Peking duck'.

White-feathered Beijing ducks are raised in the outskirts of the city. One such farm, near Landianchang alongside the Jingmi Irrigation Canal that flows out of Kunming Lake, can be visited on the way to the Summer Palace. For the last two weeks of their life, the ducks are force fed a rich diet of grain and beans. When they reach the kitchen, boiling water is poured over the bird, which is then hung for several hours to dry. The duck is basted with syrup, and air is pumped into it to separate the skin from the layer of fat underneath, so ensuring that the skin is crisped while the bird cooks on a spit. The skin, which is the delicacy, is eaten with small pancakes, scallions and a thick, salty bean sauce. After slices of meat have been eaten, the rest of the bird is often used to make stock for soup which is served at the end of the meal.

The other famous dish of Beijing is the *shuanyangrou*, usually known in English as Mongolian hotpot. More suitable for winter than summer, cooking is done at the table in boiling stock contained in a charcoal-burning metal pot with a chimney. The diners themselves plunge finely sliced mutton into the stock, then vegetables, bean-curd, and vermicelli.

Beijing has a long-established tradition of possessing excellent restaurants which offer the best of China's many regional cuisines. This reputation is still well justified, and first-class restaurants serve food from Sichuan, Shanxi, Shandong, Qinghai, Canton and Shanghai.

Most foreigners travelling in groups drink Chinese beer or sweet Chinese-produced soft drinks. Chinese wines are mostly quite sweet, although dry grape wines, both red and white, are increasingly popular in places where foreigners eat. There are some excellent rice wines, such as Shaoxing. The highly potent Chinese spirit Maotai, made from sorghum, is good for any flagging social occasion and is a great stimulus to speechmaking, but it is an acquired taste. Imported alcohol is widely available in restaurants, as is draught beer. Some Chinese wines produced by joint-venture wineries are quite palatable, especially Dragon Seal and Great Wall wines for between 25 and 50 *yuan* per bottle.

Most of the restaurants listed below are used to preparing set banquets for visitors, served in private rooms. But while a private room may be preferable for a special occasion or for large groups, the adventurous diner going out alone, or in a small group, should not be deterred from asking to eat in the same part of the restaurant as the local Chinese.

The quantity of food served at a banquet can sometimes be overwhelming—there may be as many as 15 courses. One way to avoid this is, when booking the meal, to stipulate only five or six courses and a low price per head. Banquet prices in Beijing generally range from 50–250 *yuan* a head, depending on the restaurant. Restaurants tend to close very early in Beijing. It is almost always necessary to book in advance. Hotel staff are usually very willing to help you book a table.

For more adventurous dining one can stroll through the Dengshikou intersection of Wangfujing and Jinyu Hutong where each evening private vendors set up stalls and offer a wide range of specialities from their various provinces. Here one can spend an evening sampling regional dishes and browsing through the nightmarket which takes over the streets.

Another excellent outdoor snacks market with a fine view of the Rear Lakes is the **Lotus Blossom Market** at Shichahai, which begins across the street from the north entrance to Beihai Park and extends along the shore of the lake for several hundred metres. It is open for lunch and dinner, and features a variety of Beijing and other regional snacks: dumplings, steamed buns, pancakes, shashlik, almond pudding, stewed lungs etc.

A **tourist snack market** has been set up in the grounds of a former Qing dynasty garden immediately to the east of the Peace Hotel and across the street from the Palace Hotel. Some 50 of Beijing's leading restaurants and hotels operate their own snack stands, selling everything from Japanese sushi and Chinese fried noodles to fresh donuts, chocolate brownies and spaghetti. This has all the makings of an international buffet, and the high standards of sanitation and low prices make it an ideal place for an informal dinner. Open nightly from 5pm to 9pm and for lunch as well on Sunday. Nominal admission charge.

A novel dining experience can be had at one of the many restaurants in Beijing's **underground city**. In the late 1960s, a huge underground network of tunnels and shelters was built as protection from nuclear attack. Now these shelters have been transformed into shops, restaurants and hotels. One entrance at 192 Xidan Jie, just north of Chang'an Jie, leads to a small section of the underground city where several small restaurants are located, the best known of which is the Dongtian (Cave Heaven) restaurant.

In recent years, dozens of privately or cooperatively run restaurants have opened in every corner of the city. Some occupy old residences, others are carved out of unused factory space, but most of them provide excellent food for surprisingly low prices. Four major areas to look for these restaurants are Qianmen and Dazhalan (Dashalar); the block behind the Beijing Hotel; and in the Dongdan and Dongsi shopping areas. Perhaps the best way to judge a restaurant is whether or not it is crowded.

Virtually all international-standard hotels have top-quality Chinese restaurants. Although perhaps not as exciting as dining out in a local restaurant, these hotels offer some of the best Chinese food in the city, with polished service to match. They are particularly safe bets for the visitors staying for just a short while or those with sensitive stomachs. For Cantonese food (prepared under the professional eye of Hong Kong chefs), you could try the **Four Seasons** at the Jianguo Hotel (tel. 65002233) which serves a particularly good *dim sum* (11.30am–2pm); the Grand Hotel's **Rong Yuan** Sichuan restaurant (tel. 65137788); the **Fan** at the Great Wall Sheraton Hotel (tel. 65005566); the **Spring Garden** at the Holiday Inn Lido (tel. 65006688); the refined **Shang Palace** at the Shangri-La Hotel (tel. 68312211) and the **Chinese Brasserie** at the Radisson SAS Hotel (tel. 64663388).

Recent additions to the roster of luxurious hotel restaurants are **Fortune Garden** Cantonese restaurant and the **Palace Restaurant** serving Sichuan food at the Palace Hotel (tel. 65128899) and the **Summer Palace** restaurant at the **China World Hotel** (tel. 65052266). For Shanghai food, try the **Shanghai Restaurant** in the Kunlun Hotel (tel. 65003388).

Beijing
Beijing Duck Restaurants (Beijing Kaoya Dian) 北京烤鸭店
A Beijing duck banquet may consist of far more than just the serving of the crisp skin and meat of the tender bird, accompanied by pancakes, sesame buns, scallions and thick brown fermented sauce. Cold duck dishes—which may include meat in aspic, shredded webs, and sliced liver—are usually served first, followed by fried duck heart, liver and gizzard, and the delicious duck soup which comes at the very end of the meal.

Most visitors to Beijing want to try the famous duck dinner and, as a result, the branches of the official Beijing Duck Restaurant tend to turn out rather routine meals. Opinions vary on the best place to go to sample Beijing duck, but many would favour the small restaurant off Wangfujing, known locally as the 'Sick Duck' because of its proximity to the Capital Hospital. Other branches are the 'Small Duck', the 'Old Duck' and the 'Big Duck' (a four-storey modern building that can seat about 2,000 people at one time).

'Sick Duck' (Wangfujing Kaoya Dian)
13 Shuaifuyuan. Tel. 65253310
王府井烤鸭店　师府园13号
'Small Duck' (Pianyifang Kaoya Dian)
2 Chongwenmenwai Dajie. Tel. 67120505
便宜坊烤鸭店　崇文门外大街2号
'Old Duck' (Qianmen Kaoya Dian)
32 Qianmen Dajie. Tel. 65112418
前门烤鸭店　前门大街32号
'Big Duck' (Heping Kaoya Dian)
14 Building Qianmen Xidajie. Tel. 63018833
和平烤鸭店　前门西大街14号楼
'Jinsong Duck' (Jinsong Quanjude Kaoya Dian)
Tel. 67711211, 67712197
劲松烤鸭店

Imperial Cuisine
Fangshan
Beihai Park. Tel. 64011889
仿膳饭庄　北海公园
This prestigious restaurant, opened in 1925, uses recipes from the 19th-century imperial court. Banquets are highly elaborate and expensive—a meal including delicacies such as shark's fin and bird's nest soup might cost over 200 *yuan* per head. Some Westerners find the food over-rich and indigestible. But with a magnificent setting, this must surely rank as one of the most splendid restaurants in China.

Li Jia Cai (Li Family Restaurant)
11 Yangfang Hutong, Denei Dajie. Tel. 66180107
厉家菜餐厅　德内大街羊坊胡同11号
Founded by Li Li, winner of a national CCTV banquet contest. Her great grandfather was a chef in the Qing court. A homely restaurant serving court cuisine and other Beijing dishes. Make phone bookings.

Pavilion for Listening to the Orioles (Tingliguan)
Yiheyuan. Tel. 62581955
听鹂馆　颐和园
In attractive rooms round a courtyard in the heart of the Summer Palace, this lunch restaurant is very popular with Western visitors. The food is an eclectic mixture of different Chinese styles, all of the dishes appealing to foreigners. Try the deep fried steamed bread and fresh fish from the Summer Palace's Kunming Lake.

Other Restaurants
Clay Saucepan (Shaguoju)
60 Xisi Nan Dajie. Tel. 66021126
沙锅居　西四南大街60号
This is the oldest restaurant in Beijing, claiming a history which goes back some 300 years. Perhaps the best known all-pork restaurant in Asia, it is said to have originated as a shop selling off pigs that the emperor had sacrificed for a good harvest. An all-pork banquet can be ordered in advance, or it is possible to try just a few of the famous dishes, such as deep fried pork liver or fried pork ribs, along with various soups and vegetable dishes.

Ritan Park Restaurant
Ritan Park. Tel. 65005939, 65005883
日坛公园饭店　日坛公园
This little restaurant in the southwest corner of the Temple of the Sun Park is located in a delightful courtyard beside a small pond complete with arching bridges and pavilions. It is possible to eat outside when the weather permits. It is particularly popular for its very good *jiaozi*—steamed dumplings.

Tan Family Cuisine (Tan Jia Cai)
1. Tan Palace. 188 Xizhimennei Dajie. Tel. 66183162
谭家菜餐厅　西直门外大街188号
2. Yunlaitang Restaurant. Beijing Hotel. 33 Dong Chang'an Jie. Tel. 65137766
谭家菜餐厅　北京饭店东长安街33号
A sub-school of Beijing cooking founded in the 19th century that features seafood. It is named after a Cantonese official who lived in Beijing and hired the best chefs in the capital to cook for him. The entire repertoire consists of approximately 100 dishes developed in their kitchens. Tan cuisine is a combination of both northern and southern styles.

CANTONESE

Beijing Orient Restaurant

Zhengyang Market, Qianmenxi Dajie. Tel. 63016688

北京东方明珠酒家　前门西大街正阳市场4号楼

One of the best Cantonese restaurants in the city, the Beijing Orient is pure Hong Kong.

Chaozhoufang Restaurant

Exhibition Centre Hotel, 135 Xizhimen Jie. Tel. 68316633, ext. 7025

潮州舫餐厅　西直门街135号（北京展览馆宾馆内）

Chaozhou is in Guangdong Province yet its cuisine is quite distinct from typical Cantonese-style cooking, using less sugar and a unique blend of spices and aromatics. The origin of Chaozhou cooking is not certain but one story claims that the style evolved after a minister of the Ming court was banished to this region for poor conduct. The minister, unsatisfied with the local culinary fare, set about instructing cooks on how to enhance certain flavours, and he passed his time experimenting with many local ingredients. The result was a dramatically new cuisine.

Dasanyuan

50 Jingshan Xi Jie. Tel. 64103920

大三元　景山西街50号

Outside the joint venture hotels, this is one of the few authentic Cantonese restaurants in Beijing, but it is quite pricey. Meat and vegetables are brought in daily from Guangdong province to supply the restaurant with its many specialities, which include roast suckling pig, dog meat, seafood, chicken cooked in tea, turtle meat and special seasonal dishes such as 'battle between the dragon and the tiger'—cat meat with three kinds of snake—and crab and giant salamander.

Fortune Garden

Palace Hotel, Wangfujing. Tel. 65128899, ext. 7405

越秀厅　王府井（王府饭店内）

Maintains the high standards associated with the Peninsula Hotel in Hong Kong.

Jingguang Food Street

4th Floor, Jing Guang Centre, Hu Jia Lou, Chaoyang District.
Tel. 65108888, ext. 2534

京广中心食街　朝阳区京广中心

Hong Kong Food City
18 Dong'anmen Dajie, Wangfujing. Tel. 65136688
香港美食城　王府井东安门大街18号
Perhaps the most popular upmarket Cantonese restaurant in Beijing, the joint venture Hongkong Food City offers a wide selection of fresh and live seafood prepared by chefs from Hong Kong. Branches have been opened in Huangzhuang, Haidian and on Dong Sanhuan Beilu in the Chaoyang district.

Renren Restaurant
18 Qianmen Dong Dajie. Tel. 65112042, 65113408
人人大酒楼　前门东大街18号
This large four-storey, joint venture restaurant features Cantonese food and does lively business. With each successive floor, the dishes become increasingly exotic and expensive. The restaurant's specialities include many standard Cantonese dishes such as suckling pig braised in barbecue sauce, shark's fin and dog. Although the decor is heavily ornate with large red columns and glass-fringed light fixtures, the atmosphere is casual and friendly.

Tsui Heng Village Restaurant
Shopping Arcade, Overseas Chinese Village, Jianguomenwai. Tel. 65158833
翠亨村茶寮　建国门外华侨新村
A joint venture with the Hong Kong Mirimar catering group, the Tsui Heng Village is one of the finest Cantonese restaurants in Beijing, with a large dining area and numerous private rooms for luxurious banquets. Prices equivalent to upscale Hong Kong restaurants.

MONGOLIAN
Donglaishun
198 Wangfujing, at the north entrance of Dongfeng Market. Tel.65253562
东来顺饭店　王府井198号
This is an excellent place to try Mongolian hotpot in unpretentious surroundings with pleasant service. Highly popular with the people of Beijing, this restaurant is always busy. The lamb *shashlik*—chunks of lamb rolled in sesame seed and barbecued—is specially good, and for the more adventurous, there are other Mongolian specialities to try such as braised camel's hump or camel tendons.

Kaorouji
14 Shishaqianhai Yan. Tel. 64012170
北京烤肉季　前海东沿14号
This small and sometimes expensive restaurant specializing in Mongolian barbecued
lamb is sought out by discriminating visitors. Situated just north of Beihai Park in
the Rear Lakes district, the restaurant has a balcony which looks out over an
interesting neighbourhood.

MOSLEM
Afanti
2 Houguaibang Hutong, Dongcheng District. Tel. 6525 1071
阿凡提餐厅　东城区后拐棒胡同2号
Cafe-bar atmosphere with short interludes of ethnic music and dancing. Variety of
Xinjiang dishes from a bilingual menu are tasty but not as authentic—or reasonable
—as better fare in the spit-and-sawdust eateries of Xinjiang Village. Try *kao yang rou
tui* (roast mutton leg) or a whole roast lamb for about US$100. Finish with *baisi
baishu* (caramel dipped sweet potato). Drink sweet and fortified wines or Tsingtao
beer. Lively but smoky.

Hongbinlou
82 Xi Chang'an Jie. Tel. 66038460
鸿宾楼　西长安街82号
This long-established Moslem restaurant, serving no pork, has been open for nearly
a century, and continues to specialize in some of Beijing's favourite dishes—Beijing
duck, Mongolian hotpot, and pieces of lamb barbecued on skewers—but its wide
menu includes many other famous dishes well worth trying, such as sliced sautéed
eel, and chicken breasts in red sauce.

Xinjiang Village (Weigongcun)
Off Baishiqiao
新疆村(魏公村)
Dubbed 'Uyghurville' by its foreign patrons, this street lined with small restaurants
brings the unique taste of China's far-flung westernmost region, Xinjiang, right to
the capital's heart. The **Tian Shan** and **Afanti** are outstandingly good. Order *da pan
ji*, or 'big plate of chicken': a casserole of chicken on the bone with potato, peppers and
noodles in a thick tomato-spicy sauce. Good with *nan* bread. Another gem, a classic
Uyghur high day and holiday dish, is *poluo* in their own language, or *zhua fan* in
Chinese: rice with carrots and beef. For a quick lunch, a plate of *laghman*, thick

noodles with plenty of chunky vegetables, is satisfying. All to be washed down with black tea.

REVOLUTIONARY

Mao became a cult figure once again after 1989 when former red guards, by then in their late thirties, craved for the nostalgia and character-building years spent together being re-educated by the peasantry in the Great Northeastern Wilderness of Heilongjiang and elsewhere. Restaurants opened up to cater for their tastes and provide ground for networking, and while you can *chi ku*, eat bitter, under portraits of Mao just like in the good-bad old days, there are also wholesome dishes on the menu. But to taste the revolution try *da cha zi zhou*, cornmeal gruel and *ji ji cai*, a wild vegetable stuffed into steamed buns. Restaurants serving Hunan dishes, from Mao's home province, provide feasts for lovers of hot and spicy food. The Chairman believed that eating hot food produced good revolutionaries. His favourites were *hong shao rou*, red boiled beef, and *chao jian jiao*, stir-fried red chillies!

Heitudi Restaurant (Black Earth)
9 Hepingli Dongdajie, Chaoyang District. Tel. 64271415
黑土地餐厅　朝阳区和平里东大街9号
Serving *Dongbei Cai*—food from the northeastern provinces.

Shaoshan Maojia Restaurant
4 Hepingli Zhongjie. Tel. 64219340
韶山毛家饭店　和平里中街4号
Pictures of Mao adorn the wall and an altar to his memory has been set up.

Sunflower Village (Xiang Yang Tun) Restaurant
15 Wanquanhe Road, Haidian District
Tel. 62562967, 62614715
向阳屯餐厅　海淀区万泉河路15号
Simple and reasonably-priced food amid atmospheric surroundings of Maoist flavour.

Yuebin Restaurant
Dongsi, opposite China Art Gallery
悦宾餐厅　东四(中国美术馆对面)
The owner was Mao's private chef. After Mao died, he started his own business, serving tasty, wholesome and very reasonably priced dishes in an atmospheric room.

SHANDONG
Confucius Restaurant
3 Liulichang Xi Jie. Tel. 63014824
孔膳堂饭店　琉璃厂西街3号
Crowded restaurant featuring the cuisine of Confucius' native place and banquets as prepared in the hereditary mansion of the Kong family (Confucius was surnamed Kong). Located in Liulichang. Try the deep fried scorpion!

Cuihualou
60 Wangfujing. Tel. 65134970
萃华楼　王府井60号
A popular and long established restaurant serving Shandong-style food. Among its specialities is 'peak flower rice'—crispy-rice over which is poured, in front of you at the table, a sweet and sour prawn sauce, so that it hisses and pops and must be eaten quickly before the rice turns soggy.

Duyichu
36 Qianmen Dajie. Tel. 67021555
都一处烧麦馆　前门大街36号
Centuries old institution that serves famous *shaomai* steamed dumpling and Shandong cuisine.

Garden of the Horn of Plenty (Fengzeyuan)
Liujiayao, Yongdingmenwai. Tel. 67611336
丰泽园饭庄　永定门外刘家湾
One of Beijing's most famous eating houses, the Fengzeyuan is celebrated for its Shandong food. The cuisine of this coastal province south of Beijing includes some excellent fish dishes. Particularly well known here are the sea cucumber, soup with cuttle-fish eggs, and braised fish with a rich brown sauce. The restaurant enjoys a high reputation, and banquets here are invariably good.

Tongheju
3 Xisi Nan Dajie. Tel. 66185700
同和居　西四南大街3号
A Shandong-style restaurant with private dining rooms off a small courtyard in the northwestern part of the city. Seafood specialities include sea cucumber, 'squirrel fish' in sweet sauce, jumbo prawns in various styles, and crab and eel in season. Steamed white bread rolls are popular here and their dessert is famous throughout Beijing—'three no sticks'—an elusively flavoured but delicious custard, made from

egg yolks and cornflour with an extraordinary texture—whence its name comes—
'won't stick to your plate, won't stick to your chopsticks and won't stick to your
palate'.

SHANGHAI

Laozhengxing
46 Qianmen Dajie. Tel. 65112145
老正兴饭庄　前门大街46号
Named after a famous restaurant in Shanghai, Laozhengxing features authentic
Shanghai cuisine with an emphasis on seafood.

SHANXI

Jinyang
241 Zhushikou Xi Dajie. Tel. 63031669
晋阳饭庄　珠市口西大街241号
This interesting restaurant in the southern section of the city was the residence of Ji
Xiaolan (1724–1805), a scholar official of the Qing dynasty. The finest rooms in the
house now serve as impressive dining rooms. The kitchens specialize in the cuisine
of Shanxi, one of the earliest centres of Chinese civilization. This is the perfect setting to try the delicious crisp duck of the province—to some Western palates preferable to the rich Beijing duck.

SICHUAN

Gongwangfu Sichuan Restaurant
Liuyin Jie. Tel. 66156925
恭王府四川饭店　柳荫街(北海后门)
This elegant restaurant in attractive traditional old buildings with dining rooms
arranged round a series of courtyards has moved from Rongxian Hutong to Liuyin
Jie and been replaced by the China Club owned by a Hong Kong tycoon. But the
food still has a good reputation in Beijing for the hot spicy cuisine of this large southwestern province. All of the many specialities here are worth trying. The smoked
duck, spiced beancurd, and braised egg-plant are specially recommended. Some of
the finer dishes are not spicy.

Palace Restaurant
The Palace Hotel, Wangfujing, Jiajinglou. Tel. 65128899, ext.7900
嘉陵楼　王府井金鱼胡同王府饭店
Spectacular food in sumptuous surroundings. Authentic ingredients and Sichuanese
chefs, with excellent service.

Rong Yuan
Grand Hotel, 35 Dong Chang'an Jie. Tel. 65137788
荣苑　北京贵宾楼饭店东长安街33号
Teahouse style restaurant located in a luxury hotel.

Shenxian Dou Hua Village
Ritan Park (southwest entrance). Tel. 65005939
神仙豆花村　日坛公园（西南方入口）
Popular outdoor/indoor restaurant in the embassy district. Make a meal of the varied snack menu. Pleasant garden-like atmosphere.

Sichuan Dou Hua Restaurant
Guanggumenwai. Tel. 67712672
四川豆花饭庄　广渠门外
This three-storey restaurant has a rather original character; in the upstairs dining rooms, women in traditional Sichuan costumes serve you while men in black tunics steadily refill your teacup. All of this takes place in charmingly decorated private dining rooms. The menu offers all of Sichuan's best known dishes such as hot peanut chicken, spicy *doufu*, and noodles in *dandan* sauce. For the unacquainted, this restaurant is a wonderful introduction to authentic Sichuan cooking.

Yuen Tai
Great Wall Sheraton Hotel, 10 Dongsanhuan Beilu. Tel. 65905566, ext. 2162
长城饭店云台餐厅　朝阳区东环北路
Enjoy Sichuan cuisine at its best amidst splendid surroundings.

Suzhou
Songhelou
10 Taijichang Jie. Tel. 65241815
松鹤楼菜馆　台基厂大街10号
The original Songhelou was in Suzhou, where it specialized in the delicate, tender, slightly sweet cuisine of the city, which was particularly favoured by the Emperor Qianlong. Recommended in the Beijing restaurant are dishes typical of the Suzhou area—squirrel-shaped mandarin fish, beggar's chicken, turtle with white sauce, Tai Lake greens soup, and winter mushrooms with bamboo shoots. Songhelou's banquet rooms are modelled on the original Suzhou restaurant.

VEGETARIAN
Gongdelin
158 Qianmennan Dajie. Tel. 65112542
功德林素菜馆　前门南大街158号
The original Gongdelin is in Shanghai. Atmosphere here is somewhat more refined than at the Beijing Vegetarian Restaurant but menu is similar.

ASIAN
Indian
Omar Khayyam
Asia Pacific Building, 8 Yabao Lu, Chaoyang District.
奥马克亚姆　朝阳区雅宝路8号　亚太大厦内

Shamiana Indian Restaurant
Holiday Inn Downtown, 98 Beilishi Lu. Tel. 68322288, ext.7107
香味廊　西城区北礼士路98号　北京金都假日饭店内

Japanese
Fuji House
155 Beiheyan Lu, Dongcheng District. Tel. 65265057
富士屋　东城区北河沿路155号

Ge Peng Bai Yun
Youhao Hotel, 7 Houyuansi, Jiaodaokou. Tel. 64031114, ext. 3264
割烹白云　交道口后圆恩寺7号　友好宾馆内

Sukura
Chang Fu Gong New Otani Hotel, Jianguomenwai Dajie. Tel. 65125555, ext. 1226
樱花餐厅　建国门外大街长富宫饭店

Korean
Bobea Won
Beijing International Hotel, 9 Jianguomennei Dajie. Tel. 65129844
宝杯苑　建国门内大街9号　北京国际饭店

Meigetsukan Restaurant
Jing Guang New World Hotel, Hujialou, Chaoyang District. Tel. 65012032
京广明月餐厅　朝阳区呼家楼　京广新世界饭店

Mu Dan Feng
Hualong Jie Food Street, Nanheyan Lu. Tel. 65125133
牡丹峰餐厅　华龙街（北京饭店后）

Thai
Borom Piman Thai Restaurant
Holiday Inn Lido Beijing, Jichang Lu. Tel. 64376688, ext. 2899
泰国厅餐　将台路　北京丽都假日饭店

Red Basil
South of Sanyuan Bridge, Beisanhuan Dong Lu. Tel. 64602342
三元桥　北三环东路
Fine Thai style dining.

Siam Plaza
COFCO Plaza, 8 Jianguomennei Dajie. Tel. 65263903
暹逻宫　建国门内大街　中粮广场

WESTERN
Beijing's foreign-managed hotels, with European chefs heading the kitchen staff, have greatly improved the standard of Western cooking in the capital. Ten years ago, it was almost impossible to find acceptable Western food. Although none of Beijing's Western restaurants can match Hong Kong's best, the foreign-managed hotels have good European restaurants, with pleasant service, and a palatable, although not extensive wine list. (Wine prices are very high, largely because of hefty import duties.) For many foreign visitors to China, dining in a softly-lit leisurely atmosphere makes a welcome change from the austere and hurried mood of many Chinese restaurants. Because so many of the ingredients still have to be imported, as well as the staff to prepare them, you should expect to pay a lot for a European meal.

But cheap meals can be had at **McDonald's**, **Kentucky Fried Chicken** and **Pizza Hut** which continue to open stores galore throughout the capitals. A little more upscale are **Kenny Rogers Roasters** with outlets in Haidian and Chegongzhuang, and **T.G.I. Friday's** on the east Third Ring Road. Continuing with value for money, go for lunch buffets in various hotel coffeeshops, or best of all, Sunday brunches, most spectacularly at the Kempinski, Radisson SAS, Great Wall Sheraton and Hilton.

The **Moscow Restaurant** (tel. 68316677, ext. 4331) at the Beijing Exhibition Center alongside the zoo is still a favourite, and an historical reminiscence from the 1950s. Now it has competition for the custom of many Russian traders in Beijing from the **Elephant** (tel. 65024031) located near the Yabalu clothing market where large Russians can be seen carrying large bags full of Chinese clothing.

Most American and continental food outlets are basically cafes or bars offering food a grade or two up from fast food. For classier fare the hotels are about the only option: most superior hotels have several options. Dining in the Grand Hotel's **Red Wall Cafe** (tel. 65137788) comes with a splendid view of Chang'an Avenue, while the same hotel's **Old Pekin Grill** is a rare treat. **Justines** at the Jianguo Hotel (tel: 65002233), the **Laxen Oxen** at the Radisson SAS (tel. 64663388) and the **Bavarian Bierstube** at the Palace will rarely disappoint.

Pasta lovers should look no further than the **Metro Cafe**, 6 Gongrentiyuchang Xilu (tel. 65917828).

American
Frank's Place
Gongti Dong Lu, Chaoyang District. Tel. 65072617
万龙酒吧　朝阳区工体东路

Hard Rock Cafe
Landmark Arcade, West Wing, 8 Dongsanhuan Bei Lu, Chaoyang District. Tel. 65016688, ext. 2571
硬石餐厅　朝阳区东三环北路8号　亮马大厦

San Francisco Brewing Co.
West Wing, Asia Jinjiang Hotel. Tel. 65007788, ext. 7156
旧金山啤酒屋　北京亚洲锦江大酒店

T.G.I. Friday's
Huapeng Mansion, 19 Dongsanhuan Bei Lu, Chaoyang District. Tel. 65951380
星期五　朝阳区东三环北路19号

Continental
Justine's
Jianguo Hotel, Jianguomenwai Dajie. Tel. 65002233, ext. 8039
建国西餐厅　建国门外大街　建国饭店

Hof Brauhaus
15 Dongsanhuan Beilu, Chaoyang District. Tel. 65914598
豪夫门啤酒坊　朝阳区东三环北路15号

Maxim's
2 Chongwenmen Xi Dajie. Tel. 65121992
马克西姆 崇文门西大街2号

Szenario Restaurant
Swissôtel Beijing Hong Kong-Macau Centre, Dongsishitiao. Tel. 65012288, ext. 2271
风景城餐厅 东四十条 瑞士酒店北京港澳中心

Russian
Moscow Restaurant
Beijing Exhibition Centre, 135 Xizhimenwai Dajie, Xicheng District. Tel. 68354454
莫斯科餐厅 西城区西直门外大街135号 北京展览中心

Scandinavian
Laxen Oxen
Radisson SAS Hotel, 6A Beisanhuan Donglu, Chaoyang District. Tel. 64663388, ext. 3430
北欧扒房 北三环东路 北京皇家大饭店

Fast Food
Kenny Rogers Roasters
Sichuan Tower, Fuchengmen, Xicheng District. Tel. 68350610
罗杰斯烤鸡 西城区阜城门四川大厦
Xuhai Tower, Zhongguancun, Haidan District. Tel. 62535491
海淀区中关村旭海大厦

Kentucky Fried Chicken
肯德基家乡鸡
More than one dozen in Beijing.

McDonald's
麦当劳
More than 50 in Beijing.

Pizza Hut
必胜客
More than half a dozen in Beijing.

Index

for Helen
I hope you enjoy it!
Fr. Julian
10/13/07

Love-Ability

Love-Ability

Becoming Lovable by Caring for Yourself and Others

Madeline Pecora Nugent
Julian Stead, o.s.b.

NEW CITY PRESS
Hyde Park, NY

Dedication

This book is dedicated to all unhappy
people. We recommend that they read it
slowly and try to put into practice
what they read as they go along.
That way, they may be happier by far
by the time they finish the book.

Published in the United States by New City Press
202 Cardinal Rd., Hyde Park, NY 12538
www.newcitypress.com
©2007 Madeline Pecora Nugent and Julian Stead, O.S.B.

Cover design by Durva Correia

Library of Congress Cataloging-in-Publication Data:

Nugent, Madeline Pecora.
  Love-ability : becoming lovable by caring for yourself and others /
Madeline Pecora Nugent and Julian Stead.
     p. cm.
  Includes bibliographical references.
  ISBN 978-1-56548-268-5 (alk. paper)
  1. Love--Religious aspects--Christianity. 2. Compassion--Religious
aspects--Christianity. 3. Caring--Religious aspects--Christianity.
4. Personality--Religious aspects--Christianity. I. Stead, Julian. II. Title.

BV4639 .N65 2007
241' .4--dc22   2007010969

Printed in the United States of America

Contents

Preface

So you want to be loved? Everyone does! To be loved is every human's greatest need. What is the proof? In the nineteenth century and through about 1920, nearly 100 percent of babies abandoned to institutions died, not from lack of food or sanitation, but from lack of love.[1] James L. Halliday, a psychiatrist who studied psychosocial issues in medicine, concluded that "infants deprived of their accustomed maternal body contact may develop a profound depression with lack of appetite, wasting, and even marasmus [wasting away] leading to death."[2] Doctors realized that babies need to be loved, that is, held, cuddled, caressed, and carried. When institutional procedures began to include loving and cuddling, as well as bathing, feeding, and changing, the abandoned infants began to thrive. A malnourished baby who is loved will fight harder to live than a well-fed but neglected infant. Older people also fight harder to live if they know they are loved. A gentle touch is vital to a dying person because it conveys love.[3] Love is the food of your soul. You need love to thrive.

Where is love found? Not on a grocery shelf or in a catalog! Love cannot be earned, bought, or created. It just emanates naturally from another person's heart. Are there ways to encourage love? Oh, yes, but they begin not with the other person, but with you.

No one can be compelled to love you. People will not love you because you are witty, beautiful, talented, wealthy, intelligent, or stylish. For that matter, they will not love you because you are a bore, ugly, clumsy, poor, stupid, or sloppy either. But they can love you if you are witty or a bore, if you are beautiful or ugly, if you are talented or clumsy, wealthy or poor, intelligent or stupid, stylish or sloppy. Love has nothing to do with those traits. Love has to do with being loving. Just like chickens come from chickens and apples come from apples, so love comes from love. If you want to be loved, you have to love. Those who love others find that others love them. What could be more simple?

But love is not that easy. It is great to be loved. It is like sitting down to a sumptuous dinner and enjoying every bite. But loving, like preparing the dinner, takes work. It can be messy and time-consuming. And sometimes it does not get the praise that it deserves. Who ever thanks enough the chef who has spent hours preparing a terrific meal? Does the chef stop cooking because the diners are not appreciative? Not at all. He or she loves cooking. In the same way, those who "love to love" keep on loving even if nobody thanks them.

To be loved, learn how to love. You learn how to sew or to play the violin by practicing. Similarly, you learn to love by practicing loving. Learning to sew or to play the violin can be difficult. Learning to love may not be easy either, especially if you have never been taught. But just as every person has some innate sense of how to make a straight seam or how to tell a pleasant sound from a screech, so every person is born with an innate sense of how to love. That is because God, who is love (see 1 Jn 4:8),[4] made every person in his* own image. Love created each person as a lovable being capable of loving. Knowing how to love comes naturally.

Consider newborns. They exude love. Even anencephalic infants, who are missing most of their brains, lie peacefully and gently in their parents' arms. They are giving and receiving love. Every human being is born loving. Unfortunately, some people have forgotten how to love because others have rejected, ridiculed, or scorned their love through abuse, neglect, or other evil tactics. The longer evil continues, the more people forget how to love. Only others loving them can help them again learn how to love others. But it will be a long journey back.

Maybe you do not have many friends, or many close friends, or one, very special friend. Perhaps you feel invisible or neglected. You might be convinced that no one could ever love you. Or maybe you just want to be loved more or in a fuller or more proper way. On the other hand, you might feel confident that others love you, but you want to become a more loving person yourself. Whatever your reason for choosing this book, these pages will help you become more lovable and, therefore, more joyful. "A joyful heart," wrote Mother Teresa of Calcutta, "is the normal result of a heart burning with love."[5]

---

* God is inclusive regarding gender. Scripture (Gn 1:26–28) states that God made male and female, "in the image of God he created them." In other words, man and woman taken together give a clearer image of God's attributes than either sex considered singly. In determining which pronoun, if any, to apply to God in this book, the authors felt that using the pronoun "it" is unacceptable in addressing the Divine Person who God is, while using no pronoun tends to imply that God is impersonal. Therefore, this book, following traditional usage, uses the masculine pronoun for God.

1
God?

In 1998, "God billboards" appeared in south Florida. An anonymous donor paid for the billboards in an effort to prompt people to think about God. The idea spread across the United States and "God billboards" are still flourishing. Some of the sayings on them are:

Tell the kids I love them. — God

That "Love Thy Neighbor" thing ... I meant it. — God

I love you and you and you and you and ... — God

Who is God? What is God? Does God exist? Does God care? How are these questions relevant to a book about love? Do the "God billboards" hold some clues?

A myriad of books and articles have been written about the existence of God. The world has seen about as many religions as societies and cultures. For much of history, people took the existence of God for granted. Today a good many people are not sure about it. Maybe you are one of them. Or maybe you believe in God but deduce that, with all the different religions in the world today, you cannot possibly know the truth about God.

It is beyond the scope of this book to provide extensive arguments on the existence of God or to delve into proofs that the God revealed by Jesus Christ is the God who is. But this book is much richer if read with a belief in God's existence. You can become more lovable without believing in God. But you will become the most lovable if you do believe. In fact, those who believe in and know God can love most perfectly because, as John the Evangelist reveals, "God is love" (1 Jn 4:8).

Does God exist? Errors in loving might prompt this question. "No one should be surprised at the difficulty of faith," Dietrich Bonhoeffer notes, "if there is some part of his life where he is consciously resisting or disobeying the commandments of Jesus.... The man who disobeys cannot believe, for only he who obeys can believe."[1] What did Jesus command?

" 'You shall love the Lord your God with all your heart, and with all your soul, and with all your mind.' This is the greatest and first commandment. And a second is like it: 'You shall love your neighbor as yourself' " (Mt 22:37–39). If you are unsure about God's existence, then of course you cannot obey this commandment of Jesus. You cannot love what you do not know nor, as Bonhoeffer would say, can you love others properly, completely, or selflessly if you do not love God first of all.

Why not explore the question of God's existence? Consider this book as part of your research! Bonhoeffer implies that, when you learn to love properly, you will naturally find God.

The Ultimate Lover

People hold many different ideas about God. Sigmund Freud taught that your idea of God comes, in large part, from the way your parents, particularly your father, treated you. If you had an absentee father, you tend to think of God as aloof and distant. If dad was abusive, you might imagine God to be stern, exacting, and unpredictable, always looking for something to punish and some way to do it. An inconsistent and unreliable daddy will leave you feeling that you cannot trust God because he will let you down. A dad who loved, listened to problems, and tried to help, however, helps you see God as trustworthy and approachable.

Who is the real God? Benedict XVI writes, "God is the absolute and ultimate source of all being; but this universal principle of creation — the *Logos*, primordial reason — is at the same time a lover with all the passion of a true love."[2]

Love preceded and is primordial to human existence. Human beings are born with the capacity to love. That is, infants will respond positively to caresses and hugs and, as they physically develop, will give the same to others. Infants who are not loved do not thrive. You are born with a need to be loved.

All mammals seem to have some capacity to love. If baby mammals are taken from their parents, they whine and cry. Their parents whine as well and will search for their missing youngsters. After a few days, animals seem to adjust to their losses. Humans, on the other hand, can and do remember loved ones. This is why people put flowers on graves and post memorial notices to newspapers, even many years after the death of a loved one. Scripture records, "God created humankind in his image, in the image of God he created them" (Gn 1:27). Since people are born craving and giving love, does God, who made people in his image, also crave and give love? What other conclusion is there? Human love, like human beings, is finite and often imperfect, but God's love must correspond to his divinity and immortality, that is, his love must be infinite and perfect. Possessing such love, God has to be the Ultimate Lover.

God and You

If God exists, what does he have to do with you?

Everything!

God is an omnipotent Being, infinitely superior in every way. He created your eternal, unconquerable spirit, often called your soul. Because of this, you are able to know, love, and serve God through your body. In perfected form, your body and soul will live with God, with love, forever.

Jesus is the Son of God who came to reveal who God is. History records the existence of Jesus Christ. It also records his crucifixion and death as well as the spread of Christianity and its subsequent persecution. The gospels, written by Jesus' followers, recount that, following Christ's death, his disciples went into hiding for fear of being killed themselves. Yet these same timid followers later claimed that Jesus was alive, that they had seen him and eaten with him, and that he had told them to spread God's message of love to the world. None of them revoked this story. None of them received money, power, or prestige because of it. On the contrary, every one of them was persecuted, hunted, and maligned. Of Jesus' eleven apostles alive at the time of his crucifixion, ten were killed in later years and the eleventh exiled, precisely because they insisted on preaching the resurrection.

The behavior of Christ's followers, and their transformation from cowards to evangelists, is evidence that they had experienced a dead Christ who had been raised as he had predicted. Experiencing the resurrection proved to them that Christ was who he claimed to be, and they were ready then to endure anything for him, even their deaths, which he had also predicted.

John, one of Christ's apostles, wrote not only a Gospel but also three letters and a book of Revelations to the Christians of his time. In these writings, John states that "God is Love." John told his followers: "Beloved, let us love one another, because love is from God; everyone who loves is born of God and knows God. Whoever does not love does not know God, for God is love" (1 Jn 4:7–8). Benedict XVI titled his first encyclical *Deus Caritas Est,* that is, *God is Love.*

God's Greatest Acts of Love

The humble ways in which God gave himself reveal his love. He, who is Lord of heaven and earth, relinquished his glory to assume weak human flesh. He abandoned heaven's riches to be born into poverty. Leaving behind the adoration of angels, God came to earth to face rejection and ridicule from human beings. The All-Perfect One walked among, touched, preached to, healed, and fed the imperfect. The All-Powerful One allowed himself to be captured, tortured, and crucified. Having risen from the dead, he returned to his heavenly Father, yet, every moment, God's Spirit is still present. He answers prayers and grants spiritual gifts that guide you through life, whether or not you believe in him. "The consciousness that, in Christ, God has given himself for us, even unto death, must inspire us to live no longer for ourselves but for him, and, with him, for others."[3] God's compassion and humility were made flesh in Christ. As Christ gave himself without reservation, so God calls you to that same level of sacrifice.

Every believer is to become "bread broken for the life of the world," wrote John Paul II in his October 2005 "Message for World Mission Sunday." "Let us always be open to the voice of the Spirit and to the needs of humanity." Everywhere, humanity cries out in need. Being loving means recognizing and attending to those needs. John Paul II had great hopes that "every Christian community [will] respond with fraternal solicitude to some of the many forms of poverty present in our world, because by mutual love and ... by our concern for those in need we will be recognized as true followers of Christ." The Pope saw love as "always a mutual relationship between persons,"[4] whether those persons are human, divine, or one of each!

The Pope noted that any one community, indeed, any one person, can respond to only some of the many needs. As "bread broken" for others, you, figuratively speaking, "feed" one person at a time. Being loving means loving the person right in front of you, right now, and meeting his or her needs as best you can. Christ is the model, noted John Paul II, "who offers himself under the sacramental sign of his love for all mankind, ... a project of solidarity for all of humanity ... which gives eternal life (cf. Jn 6:33) and opens the human heart to a great hope.... Jesus alone can satisfy humanity's hunger for love and thirst for justice."[5]

Loving the person in the here and now models Christ. You unite with the person you are "feeding," thus creating a solidarity with all other people. This is only possible if God is working through you. No one can satisfy even one person's "hunger for love," but God, present through you, can. Because you are made in the image and likeness of God (see Gn 1:26–27), you do not create love. Any love you feel is a participation in God's love. You love because God, who is Love, put his Spirit, which is love, into you. Plants withering with drought will revive if watered, but the hose does not create the water; it merely channels it. Love, coming from God, channels through you to others. "Since God has first loved us (cf. 1 Jn 4:10), love is now no longer a mere 'command'; it is the response to the gift of love with which God draws near to us."[6]

Suffering and Love

How can God be loving when he allows innocent people to be hurt, little children to suffer, and families to be demolished through death and disaster? Is not a God who permits those things more of a sadist than a savior? It is beyond the scope of this book to discuss the nature of and reasons for suffering. Refer, instead, to John Paul II's Apostolic Letter *Salvifici Doloris* (*On the Christian Meaning of Human Suffering*). In his thorough discussion of suffering, John Paul II makes this point: "The sufferings of Christ created the good of the world's Redemption. This good in itself is inexhaustible and infinite.... Insofar as man becomes a sharer in Christ's sufferings — in any part of the world and at any time in history — to that extent *he in his own way completes* the suffering through which Christ accomplished the Redemption of the world.... Yes, it seems to be part *of the very essence of Christ's redemptive suffering* that this suffering requires to be unceasingly completed" (Section 24).

In other words, suffering brings about good because it completes the suffering by which Christ redeemed the world and opened heaven to all humans. Heaven is the place of all peace, all justice, all love — in other words, of all goodness. Through suffering — Christ's and everyone else's united to his — the Great Lover combines both justice and mercy, perfecting and purifying you as he brings you into total union with himself. "Suffering is, in itself, an experience of evil. But Christ has made suffering the firmest base of the definitive good, namely the good of eternal salvation.... And slowly but effectively, Christ leads suffering man into this world, into this kingdom of the Father, in a certain sense through the very heart of his suffering" (*Salvifici Doloris*, Section 26).

Studying suffering reveals a great truth. Even though loving acts often involve a sense of satisfaction or fulfillment, they always involve sacrifice. In some way, love always brings death to self while giving life to the other. Christ reveals this completely by his death for your salvation, but self-sacrifice is also evident in some form in everyone else who ever loved. The truth that "God is Love" reveals the truth that God is self-emptying. He pours himself constantly into the other, that is, into you and every other person. God, an eternal wellspring of love, can always give more of himself. Paul wrote to the Corinthians, "And now faith, hope, and love abide, these three; and the greatest of these is love" (1 Cor 13:13). Love is the greatest since, in heaven, you will no longer need faith because you will know. You will no longer need hope because you will have attained what you had awaited. But you will love forever, because you will be united with God, and God is Love.

2
What Is Love?

Everybody craves it, but nobody can get too much of it. What is it?

Love

Love seems to have more definitions than there are poets, thinkers, and lovers. Books of quotes devote numerous pages to love. Internet sites define love in countless ways. Every person seems to have a favorite way of explaining love. Fulgence of Ruspe calls love "the stairway that would enable all Christians to climb to heaven."[1] Thérèse of Lisieux calls love "the vocation that includes all others."[2] Augustine of Hippo says that "Love [is that which] alone distinguishes between the children of God and the children of the Devil."[3] Margaret of Cortona calls love "the way of salvation."[4] In the musical *Fiddler on the Roof*, Golde defines love as years of cooking for, cleaning up after, and living with her husband Tevye. John Paul II deems love "a communion of persons" (General Audience, 23 July 1980). Although these definitions seem dissimilar, they are really several ways of saying what Benedict XVI articulated: "Love is not merely a sentiment.... It ... engages the whole man.... Love is never 'finished' and complete; throughout life, it changes and matures."[5]

In other words, love is a process. It begins with the Divine Lover, progresses with his grace, and ultimately has him as its goal. It is, indeed, the stairway climbed, the vocation lived, the way followed to salvation, the relationship that blossoms, and the quality that divides good from evil. Hubert van Zeller put it this way: "If you live Christ's life you love with Christ's love. His life is all love; his spirit is all love. It is not so much that his love 'rubs off' on us but that it actually animates us and 'informs' our every activity. We ... love with his love ... we cannot

15

fashion charity as we can fashion a rose garden or an omelette. The most we can do is direct it from him within us to him outside us."[6]

A simpler way of explaining this is to say that Love is maximum movement toward the Good.

Good is that which perfects. Things that perfect you are going to make you more like God who is perfect, who is "all good." Jesus instructed, "Be perfect, therefore, as your heavenly Father is perfect" (Mt 5:48). Loving perfects you. More than feeling, love is an action, in fact many actions, one after the other, that move both the lover and the beloved toward the Good. Perfect love is recognizable, not in receiving, but in self-giving. Victor Hugo put it this way, "What a grand thing, to be loved! What a grander thing still, to love!"[7]

Everybody wants to be loved. Love is so important that, as Sir James M. Barrie is often quoted, "If you have it [love], you don't need to have anything else. If you don't have it, it doesn't matter much what else you do have." King Richard III might have given his kingdom for a horse, but most people would give just about anything to be loved. Many of people's ills come from their futile attempts to buy or create love. The Song of Songs (8:7) puts it beautifully: "If one offered for love all the wealth of one's house, it would be utterly scorned." Love is not found in and through passion, possessions, prestige, power, or persons. Love springs up when one person recognizes the good in another. This can be spontaneous or willed. You feel a touch of love when you automatically smile at a newborn in the park. You can will to love when you pray for your enemies, something you can do only because you realize that they, too, are made in God's image. In the Biblical account of creation, "God saw that it was good" (Gn 1:12). When human beings were created as the pinnacle of all formed beings, "God saw everything that he had made, and indeed, it was very good" (Gn 1:31). Love creates good and loves his creation because it is good. Love is a natural consequence of the Good.

Real and Fake Loves

Love fosters unity. Therefore, anything that divides people, even though some may call it "love," is not love but sin. Evil often masquerades as love. A husband who becomes jealous if his wife attracts another man's attention is not displaying his love for his wife. Rather, jealousy reveals the husband's possessiveness. Similarly, romantic fantasy that imagines the beloved to be other than who he or she is, cannot be love.

Instead, it is a denial of the other's uniqueness. Unreasonable doubt about someone's love means that you mistrust the other person, not that you love him or her. Misjudging a beloved's motives indicates an unwillingness to discuss them or to believe what the beloved says. Wallowing in loneliness when a beloved is absent means that you have made someone else responsible for your happiness. What an unreasonable burden to put on someone! Resenting a lover's attention to anyone other than yourself signifies a desire to shackle that person to you alone. Love shackles no one; it frees. Over-dramatizing love signals insecurity in the relationship. Lovers do not have to prove their love. They know it exists.

Some people have been so wounded that they have forgotten how to love, or perhaps have repressed their knowledge of it. Lovelessness may lie hidden in the soul unconsciously, or half-consciously. Hans Urs von Balthasar in *Heart of the World* deemed this void "the gaping hollow which man no longer notices because he himself is hollow."[8] Those who cannot or will not love are like unused goblets. They never fulfill their function. Goblets are to be filled with beverages, and human souls ought to filled with love.

Love generally involves an emotion called "affection." Is affection loving? That depends on the object of the affection. Saint Augustine wrote, "After all, what is it in any one of us that prompts action, if not some kind of love? Show me even the basest love that does not prove itself in action. Shameful deeds, adulteries, villainies, murders, all kinds of lust — aren't they all the work of some sort of love?"[9] What an intriguing question! Obviously strong affection can masquerade as love. But it is not love if the affection is directed toward what is evil or what can cause evil. Recall the earlier definition of love — love is maximum movement toward the Good. If evil is drawing you, no matter how much you insist that you "love" to get drunk, get high, or get laid, you are not experiencing love. You are experiencing a stampeding lust that focuses on yourself rather than on the other. Augustine elaborates, "Love as much as you like, but take care what you love. Love of God and love of your neighbor are called charity; but love of the world, this passing world, is called greed or lust. Lust must be reined in, charity spurred on."[10]

Consider how people use the word "love." Everybody cannot be talking about the same thing. People love poodles, banana splits, sunrises, spouses, a special teacher, their new snow blower, a walk by the sea, Spanish class, their mothers, their nation, looking twenty-five, a part of the country, getting A's, wearing dangly earrings, polkas, roses, diamonds, country music, and Jesus. Certainly all of these, and an infinite number of other things people "love," are not all in the same category of importance, fondness, or function. Classic scholars recognized all the different people, things, and characteristics that you "love" and came up with four different words to designate four different "loves." The words are eros, philia, storge, and agape.

Eros is basic, romantic, sexual love, what you might call "Hollywood" love, so prevalent in novels, on movie and television screens, and in internet chat rooms and online dating sites. Benedict XVI defined this love as "That love between man and woman which is neither planned nor willed, but somehow imposes itself upon human beings."[11]

Philia is love between friends, a bond against the world that makes you and your friend share each other's joy and pain.

Storge is love of family and nation, the tenderness a mother shows her child, the loyalty that draws a family together during travail, and the patriotism that makes a person rally around a country's flag.

Agape is love that seeks out the best for others, the quality that Jesus enumerated when he admonished you to "love your neighbor as yourself" (Mt 22:39).

This list suggests that most of the world's "loves" fall into the category of eros, with philia and storge existing a bit less frequently, and agape being the rarest of all. The irony is that all people who love anything are ultimately pursuing their God-given claim to happiness, but are they all chasing the right hare? Happiness is elusive. To arrive within sight of happiness, follow love's lead. Eros, philia, and storge point in the right direction, but only agape can bring you to the goal.

Agape is a sincere love precisely because it is not always a fuzzy, pleasurable emotion. Love means acting in the best interests of the one loved. Ironically, that might make you unloved. Jesus' treatment of the moneychangers in the temple was neither soft nor tender, but he loved those men (see Jn 2:14–17). Parents who love their children discipline them. Benedict the monk wrote about tough love in his Rule, in the chapter "On the Good Zeal which Monks Ought to Have." "[N]o one following what he considers useful for himself, but rather what benefits another" will make the community into a loving one.

Why does God consider love so vital? Because "God wants nothing more ardently than to join us together in unity," noted John Chrysostom in his commentary on the Sermon on the Mount.[12] Love unites; lack of love divides. Christ forbids not only injury to another but even calling a neighbor "you fool" or a lot of other worse names (see Mt 5:22). Such epitaphs rob a person of dignity and create animosity, that diabolical energy Christ came to destroy. Agape love gives others what they need to become holier people, even if it is not what they want. Even if one person becomes unhappy, love's ultimate goal is unity. It seeks to bring both parties into one accord with their sights set on him who is Love.

Ultimately love is a spontaneous or willed quality that moves you toward union with God and with his image in other people. Love is the reason for your creation, the purpose of your life, and your final goal. Benedict XVI calls love your "destiny."[13]

3
How to Love

Everyone wants to be loved. Generally, if you are loving, others will love you. Therefore, how do you become loving? This chapter will cover the general principles. The remainder of the book will delve into specifics.

First, ask God for the grace to be loving. Fulton Sheen wrote, "God never refuses grace to those who honestly ask for it.... All you need do is to voice these two petitions: Dear Lord, illumine my intellect to see the Truth, and give me the strength to follow it. It is a prayer that is *always* answered."[1] Love requires knowledge and awareness as well as courage to act. God's grace will supply these.

Scripture enumerates the qualities you ought to have in order to be loving: "Love is patient; love is kind; love is not envious or boastful or arrogant or rude. It does not insist on its own way; it is not irritable or resentful; it does not rejoice in wrongdoing, but rejoices in the truth. It bears all things, believes all things, hopes all things, endures all things" (1 Cor 13:4–7).

This passage does not only describe love. In it, Paul the Apostle also describes a perfect friend. Substitute the words "my friend" for "love" and "he" or "she" for "it" and you will see. To become lovable, you actually want to become the perfect friend. That is a lofty goal. You can spend a lifetime perfecting one quality of friendship.

"Without friends, no one would choose to live, even if he had all other goods," Aristotle believed.[2] Everyone desires the intimacy of friendship, but, since Adam's fall, most are afraid of it. Clothing keeps bodies private, but most people cloak their thoughts, too. Souls are bared to a select few, if to anyone. Are you afraid that something that you might say, do, or forget could damage or destroy some or all of your friendships? If so, those whom you call "friends" are really "very close acquaintances." A true friend meets the criteria that Paul attributed to love.

"Very few modern people think friendship a love ... at all," wrote C. S. Lewis. "To the Ancients, friendship seemed the happiest and most fully human of all loves."[3] Aristotle and Cicero classified it among the virtues, and so did the medieval Aelred of Rievaulx. In *On Christian Friendship*, he wrote "No medicine is more valuable, none more efficacious, none better suited to the cure of all our temporal ills than a friend to whom we may turn for consolation in time of trouble — and with whom we may share our happiness in time of joy."[4]

Friendship naturally involves love and intimacy. The truest friendships are those in which both parties can be themselves. Neither friend worries about putting on a good front for the other because each is secure in the other's affection. You may have many acquaintances, but a true friend is rare. In your quest to become more loving, you are really striving to be a better friend or to have one. If you want to have a good friend, you have to be a good friend. Being a good friend begins with love.

Love One Another

When a lawyer asked Jesus, "Teacher, which commandment in the law is the greatest?" Jesus gave one of the cleverest replies in history. "He said to him, 'You shall love the Lord your God with all your heart, and with all your soul, and with all your mind.' This is the greatest and first commandment. And a second is like it: 'You shall love your neighbor as yourself.' On these two commandments hang all the law and the prophets" (Mt 22:35–40).

Obviously, Jesus wants everyone to love God and neighbor without reservation. Jesus is not only talking to me. He is talking to you, too. In other words, I am your neighbor and you are mine. Being lovable is good for you because others will love you more, and you will like that. But it is good for me, too, because your being lovable makes it easier for me to love you. Becoming more lovable is good for everyone!

Jesus was unambiguous regarding love. "I give you a new commandment, that you love one another. Just as I have loved you, you also should love one another. By this everyone will know that you are my disciples, if you have love for one another" (Jn 13:34–35).

To understand what love means, to know how to love, is vital if you want to live as Christ taught. Love of others should be the distinctive mark of Christians, yet even those who are not Christian want to be loving. In other words, you want to love others and want others to love you.

It might be frightening to hear, "Just as I have loved you, you also should love one another." Jesus called this a "commandment." In his great

discourse on love, he elaborates, "No one has greater love than this, to lay
down one's life for one's friends" (Jn 15:13). Some people would say that
he demanded an even greater depth of love when he admonished, "Love
your enemies, do good to those who hate you, bless those who curse
you, pray for those who abuse you. If anyone strikes you on the cheek,
offer the other also; and from anyone who takes away your coat do not
withhold even your shirt. Give to everyone who begs from you; and if
anyone takes away your goods, do not ask for them again" (Lk 6:27–30).
What kind of love is this? The kind of sacrificial, self-emptying love that
brought Jesus to a cross to die for us. "But God proves his love for us in
that while we still were sinners Christ died for us" (Rom 5:8). Benedict
XVI noted, "Love can be 'commanded' because it has first been given."[5]

Jesus asks you to give up your life, not only for your friends but also
for your enemies. He is asking your enemies to give up their lives, too,
for you. Such mutual self-sacrifice equals perfect love. "Love is the only
force capable of transforming an enemy into a friend," Martin Luther
King. Jr., thought. He considered love to be "the most durable power in
the world."[6] Genuine love usually generates an immediate reward. As
you relinquish your wants to help others, you are making yourself more
lovable. Others become more willing to renounce their desires to help
you. Love becomes an ever-expanding circle, moving from you to others
to God and back again.

No Guarantees

Being the most lovable person in the world cannot guarantee that
everyone is going to love you. Consider Jesus Christ. He was Love
enfleshed, yet many people hated and despised him in his own day and
many others feel the same animosity toward him now.

Even though being lovable cannot guarantee that everyone will love
you, many people will. This book will share numerous ways to become
more lovable. Nevertheless, it is impractical to take one idea, practice
it for a day or a week, and then take another idea and practice it for
the same length of time. Being lovable is somewhat like an orchestra
piece. Consider Rimsky-Korsakov's symphonic suite *Scheherazade*. If
a conductor rehearses the string section of *Scheherazade* on Monday,
the woodwinds on Tuesday, the brass on Wednesday, and the percussion
on Thursday, all of them would be *Scheherazade*, but at the same time,
none of them would be what Rimsky-Korsakov had in mind when he

composed the piece. Only when the full orchestra plays harmoniously together is the audience delighted with the rendition of *Scheherazade*. In the same way, all lovable traits must be present simultaneously in anyone who aims to be lovable. Therefore, read the book to learn where you need practice. Tend well those loving areas that are already flourishing and cultivate those that are a bit barren. If you are lacking certain amiable traits, follow this book's advice to nurture them. With time, practice, prayer, and the grace of God, you can become more lovable.

Love is often associated with feelings. Feelings leave you vulnerable to being hurt if someone rejects or ignores your love or if the beloved dies or leaves. Is it better not to love so as to never be hurt? *Emmie** *loved her pets very deeply, only to have one die after the other, whether from accident, age, or illness. Finally she decided not to love any more because, if she did not love, she would not be hurt when a pet died. As Emmie matured, she began to doubt the wisdom of such an attitude. In college, she accepted the truth that Alfred, Lord Tennyson wrote in "In Memoriam": "It is better to have loved and lost than never to have loved at all." Not to love meant not to live. Even though Emmie had learned that loving can cause pain, she decided to love again.*

Caring

Despite all this talk about love, you may still be unsure what it is all about, especially if you have never been loved yourself. You will consider how you have been raised as being "normal," until exposed to other ideas. If you did not know many loving people in your formative years, you may be unsure about how to love.

When Jesus talked about love, he was not talking about sex or about a hunger or longing for certain material things. He did not mean what the gentleman meant when he said, "I love everybody. It's just certain individuals whom I can't stand." English does not have a word for what Christ really meant by love. Several years ago, boys at Portsmouth Abbey School in Portsmouth, Rhode Island (USA) chose the word "care" as being the closest word to what Christ meant by "love," translated into the Greek as "agape."

Caring for others means caring about them and about their feelings. It means getting inside the skin of every person you meet and trying to walk

---

* Examples in this book are real but names and some identifying information have been changed to protect the privacy of the individuals.

around in it mentally. Caring means following the Golden Rule of doing unto others what you would like them to do to you. That idea came from Jesus. "In everything do to others as you would have them do to you; for this is the law and the prophets" (Mt 7:12).

You can probably understand caring. If you saw someone who was hurt, how would you care for that person? How would you want to be treated if you were in need? If you notice an injustice, what do you think ought to be done? Your answers reveal your insights into caring. Caring is certainly very close to loving. God cares for you. You ought to care, too, about God, about others, about your world, and about yourself.

Loving Yourself

Ask, "Do I love myself?" Jesus commands, "[L]ove your neighbor as yourself" (Mt 22:39). How can you love your neighbor if you do not love yourself? Obviously the journey toward loving others begins with you loving you.

Suppose that you harbor only hate for yourself. How can you learn to love yourself? Remember that love is a self-emptying, a suffering. To begin to love yourself may involve some pain. Remember what love is — the maximum movement toward the Good. To begin to love yourself, you begin by seeking the good for yourself. If you abuse yourself in any way (cutting, getting drunk, taking drugs, sleeping around, denigrating yourself, breaking up your relationships, quitting jobs, cheating, or lying, for example), you acknowledge that these behaviors harm you. You also admit that they might make you comfortable because they reinforce your comfortable negative self-image (Nobody likes me. I'm unreliable. I'm a drunk. I'm worthless. What's the use? Who cares? Or whatever else you tell yourself).

Doing good for yourself means caring for your body and your spirit. Would you, by caring about another, advise him or her to do what you do to yourself? If not, then it is time to treat yourself with love. You can care for yourself and grow toward a healthy self-love. Lighten your load, if circumstances and the boss allow. Release yourself from bad habits such as feeling guilty over past mistakes. Set aside any resentments. Turn off your inner, fault-finding critic. Calm yourself in the face of worries. Pray for yourself. Try meditation. Take the exercise you need.

Breaking patterns of behavior always involves suffering. So anticipate suffering while you change. Once you have broken the pattern of negativity, you can create a new pattern of hope which will bring you much freedom and joy.

Why should you treat yourself with love? Because, no matter what you have done or what has been done to you, God considers you lovable. To God, you are not what you have done. You are God's child. Although your actions might be quite unlovable, you never are. God made you in his image, and God is Love.

"No one can see the kingdom of God without being born from above," Jesus said (Jn 3:3). Jesus was not referring only to baptism. He also meant that you need to accept your origin as God's good and innocent creation. Try this exercise. Relax. Mentally go back in time. Imagine yourself as a newborn baby. You are pure, good, and lovable. Since your birth, all negative events in your life have thrown a layer of dirty rags over your spirit. That baggage drags you down, makes you feel like rubbish, and smothers you. Shove that weight aside and probe below for that pure and innocent newborn. Once you rediscover yourself, treat yourself the way you would treat that baby. That puts you on the way to loving yourself!

Loving Others

Once you love yourself, you can begin to love others. The word here is "love," not understand. When you cannot understand — and that is frequently the case — allow God to judge another's motives. He knows the heart and will of your neighbor. He understands rationalizations. You do not, so play the game of life honorably and permit God to be its umpire.

Suppose you are not merely indifferent toward someone. Instead, every thought of that person provokes hatred, bitterness, or animosity. Some people hate, or are tempted to, people of a certain political party, or all parties, or of an ethnic group, a certain religion, or the media. Some people are tempted even to hate God, because they are afraid that he is out to get them, to send them to hell, or to spoil their fun. They do not understand that God is Love and that all he does is for their good.

If you recognize hatred in yourself, pray for the person, group, or place you loathe. Ask God to send his grace to the one you despise. Pray for your enemies and for anyone who might hate you. Pray once. Pray twice. Pray every day, a few times a day, and make prayer for your enemies into a habit. Praying for those whom you hate and those who hate you can lead to perfect love.

By now, it should be obvious that sometimes love begins by willing it. Praying for your enemies, or even for those whom you generally ignore, is an active and practical way to love them. You have to pray for everyone else, too, including those unknown to you personally. This book will suggest many ways to become more lovable. Every one of these ought to begin, proceed, and end with prayer. Prayer is the spice that must season all loving actions, because prayer is communication with God who is Love. At a wedding feast at Cana, Jesus' mother communicated to Our Lord, "They have no wine." Then she said to the waiters, "Do whatever he tells you." The waiters obeyed Jesus' instructions, and the wine was miraculously replenished (Jn 2:1–11). When you communicate with God through prayer, God's Spirit directs you toward loving acts and grants you the grace to perform them. To try to act in loving ways without prayer is like trying to make a pie without a pan. The crust and filling are not going to hold together very well without the pan to provide the form.

Love of Humanity

Essentially, love is good will or benevolence toward fellow human beings, an active, practical desire for the well-being and happiness of others. When you love, you lose no opportunity to help another in any way that you can.

Akin to benevolence and good will is philanthropy, which means the love of humankind in general. Maximus the Confessor wrote, "He that loves God leads an angelic life on earth … always thinking good of *every* man.… If you hate some, and some you neither love nor hate, while others you love but only moderately and others again you greatly love, learn from this inequality that you are far from perfect charity which supposes that you love every man equally."[7]

"What is wrong with loving friends or family more than other people?" you may ask. Maximus is not saying that it is wrong to feel intense love for those you know best. Such a love is purely natural and comes from God. But he is saying that a supernatural love for everyone must be based on the simple fact that everyone is a child of God.

Loving all equally might seem quite impossible, but Jesus is merely calling you to imitate himself. He, after all, died for the good, the bad, and the indifferent. As Maximus explains, "Therefore too our Lord and God Jesus Christ, manifesting his charity for us, suffered for the whole of mankind and granted equally to all the hope of resurrection, though each individual makes himself fit either for glory or for punishment.... He who is perfect in love and has attained the summit of detachment knows no difference between 'mine' and 'thine,' between faithful and unfaithful, between slave and freeman, or indeed between male and female. Having risen above the tyranny of the passions ... he considers all equally and is disposed equally towards all. For in him there is neither Greek nor Jew, neither male nor female, but everything and in all things Christ."[8] In simpler terms, love binds all people together equally.

An internet site devoted to religious tolerance explains that nearly all religions share belief in the Golden Rule and urge their followers to treat others decently. The site also mentions that, "In our opinion, the greatest failure of organized religion is its historical inability to convince their followers that the *Ethic of Reciprocity* applies to all humans, including those of other religions, the other gender, other races, other sexual orientations, etc. Only when this is accomplished will religiously-related oppression, mass murder and genocide cease."[9]

The point is well taken. Why should people take any religion seriously if its adherents do not follow its basic tenets about loving others and treating them with respect? You cannot change the world, but you can certainly help change your little nook in it. Begin by changing yourself. Then others who see you will begin to change, too.

Random Acts of Kindness

It has been well documented that people who observe a kind act will often perform a similar act. Those who observe another driver yielding the right of way at an intersection will themselves go on to yield the right of way. Those who hold the door open for others, instead of letting it slam in their faces, inspire those who see it to hold the door for someone else. Goodness is like a rock tossed into a placid lake. The ripples of a good action expand outward even though the rock has no knowledge of them nor control over them.

You can toss rocks of good deeds into the pond of life and create a ripple effect of good that works its way back to those on the shore. A popular bumper sticker reads, "Practice random acts of kindness." The Random Acts of Kindness Foundation, Inc. has been created to encourage people to care about others. The Foundation's website displays this quote from George Alliston, "How beautiful a day can be when kindness touches it."[10]

The love Jesus spoke about certainly includes kindness. But it also goes beyond kindness. You are probably kind to those who are kind to you, whether they are strangers or acquaintances. But Jesus asks you to love others as he loves you. Such a love does not depend on another's attributes. You are to lavish this inclusive love on another person, no matter how unpleasant he or she can be. The popular quote, "The measure of love is to love without measure" is a corruption of a quote by Bernard of Clairvaux, cited by Thomas Aquinas in the *Summa Theologica*: "Bernard says that 'God is the cause of our loving God; the measure is to love Him without measure'" (Question 16, Article 6, Objection 3). To love God without measure means, in Jesus' words, to love your neighbor as yourself. In other words, you treat your neighbor the way you would want to be treated. You have returned to the Golden Rule.

Therefore, the answer to the question "How do I love?" is "How do I want to be loved?" How do I want others to treat me, no matter how extravagant and unimaginable it may be? Is it possible for me to treat others that way? If so, how may I do it? The popular "What Would Jesus Do?" fad, which involved bracelets, bookmarks, and necklaces sporting the acronym WWJD, induced people to evaluate their actions by measuring them against Christ's behavior. How does Jesus view others? How would he treat them? If you want to be loving, and hence, lovable, you ought to treat them in the same way.

4
Compassion

Jesus told a parable about a Jewish man who had been beaten by robbers and left to die on the road. Two religious leaders passed by, but a man from Samaria, a country hostile to Israel, stopped and tended the victim. The good Samaritan brought the wounded man to an inn, asked the innkeeper to care for him, and instructed him to charge the expenses to the Samaritan's account. Jesus then asked his listeners, "Which of these three, do you think, was a neighbor to the man who fell into the hands of the robbers?" The answer that Jesus commended was, "The one who showed him mercy" (see Lk 10:30–37).

Compassionate (merciful) people notice that others are hurting and try to help them. Compassion begins with consciousness of another's pain. Luke discloses that all three men in Jesus' parable saw the robbers' victim and knew that he was gravely wounded. The two religious leaders crossed the road to avoid helping. The Samaritan would not pass by a needy person. He would help even an enemy. In Jesus' parable, he did just that.

Many people carry wounds which are not as obvious as those of the robbers' victim. How good are you at recognizing these? Here are some ways to heighten your awareness.

Look at People

Looking at people to see if they may need help might seem obvious, but for some people this is difficult. When you go anywhere, are you looking at people around you or are you looking at the ground or gazing into space? Some of us, such as those with Asperger's Syndrome, are uncomfortable looking at others. Whether you have Asperger's or whether you are generally self-absorbed, you must start looking at people if you want to help them. You can become loving only if you are aware of others.

To develop "people attentiveness" skills, take a small notepad and go someplace where you will see many people. This might be a store, beach, airport, library, sporting event, or mall. Find a place to sit down and take out the notepad. Now look at the people who walk past, pick one of them at random, and record on the notepad one special characteristic about that person. Then pick out another person and repeat the exercise. Do not talk to anyone. Just observe. Keep at this for a half hour, but do not repeat any trait. For example, if you write that one person is "tall," you cannot use that trait for anyone else. After a few minutes, you are going to find yourself running out of obvious traits so you will have to look more closely. After recording many subtle traits, you will find yourself scrutinizing people to find something different about them. Look at their hands, faces, clothing, gait. Listen to their voices. Follow their gaze. Note how they interact with one another. At the end of the thirty minutes you will be much more perceptive.

Go back a second day for part two of this exercise. Return to the same spot with the same notepad. Begin to watch people but, instead of describing the peoples' traits, try to ascertain their emotions. Who seems to be at peace? Who is frustrated? Upset? Angry? Bored? In a hurry? Lackadaisical? Pick one person at random and record the emotional state of that person on the notepad. Then pick another person and repeat the exercise. At first, many will seem indifferent but look closely. Study people's faces, especially the eyes and mouth. Observe their gait and pace. What are they doing with their hands? You will get better at discerning emotional states if you spend thirty minutes trying to discern them. Write at least ten different emotional states on your notepad.

During these exercises, if anyone seems to need help or a kind word, by all means temporarily abandon the exercise and minister to the needy person. You can always resume your exercise, but you cannot always regain a chance to show love.

Do Little Things for Others

Doing little things for others often involves creativity. Once you adopt the habit, you will notice many little ways to make life more pleasant for others. If you live with someone else, take ten minutes to walk through your dwelling, noting all the simple things you could do to make your place more comfortable for your housemate(s). If you live alone, go to a place that you frequent and spend ten minutes there on the same exercise.

Straighten a towel. Refill a salt shaker. Sweep the floor. Empty a waste can. Sharpen a pencil. Straighten a pile of paper. Take clothes out of the dryer. Fold clothes. Wipe up a spill. Wash a window. Dust a computer. Put a cheery note on someone's desk. Slide a chair back under a table. Pick up trash. Bring in a newspaper. Take someone a cup of coffee. *Francis of Assisi had his own way of being loving. He used to pick up earthworms crawling across the roads and put them in the grass where they would not be trampled.*[1]

Expect no thanks for these little favors. People may not even notice that you have done them. But you will know that you have been loving. That is reward enough.

Visit Shut-Ins and the Ill

Mother Teresa of Calcutta noticed that many people in a large, beautifully furnished nursing home were all gazing toward the door. When she asked why, she was told that the elderly patients were always anticipating visitors, but few people ever came.[2] You do not have to know the patients in a nursing home or hospital in order to visit them. Begin to visit, and you will get to know the patients. Everyone has an innate desire to be spoken to, listened to, and touched. Visiting those who cannot visit others is a good way to show love.

Shut-ins, especially those who live alone, often are lonely. Take a shut-in a meal or offer to shop for groceries. Bring a cake to celebrate a birthday or a filled stocking on Christmas. Ask the person if you could tape-record some personal experiences or stories for family and friends. Ask if the individual would like you to write a letter while he or she dictates it. Pick a bouquet of flowers and provide the vase. Compassionate actions like these tell the shut-in, "You are cared for." Not even medicine can make a person feel as good.

Pray for and with Others

"More things are wrought by prayer than this world dreams of," wrote Alfred, Lord Tennyson.[3] Paul the Apostle advises you to "pray without ceasing" (1 Thes 5:17). Prayer is not twisting God's arm to do what you wish. It is communicating with God about your needs and those of others and asking him to work his perfect will in their lives and yours. God has the perfect plan.

You might wonder how you can "pray without ceasing" when you may not remember to pray at all. The following story from the life of Thomas Jonathan Jackson (who earned the nickname "Stonewall" as a Civil War general) is helpful. *When Jackson was a professor at the Virginia Military Institute, a friend discussed with him the difficulty of the Bible's injunction to pray without ceasing. Jackson replied that obedience to the precept is simple, and gave examples. "Whenever I drop a letter into the box at the post office I send a petition along with it for God's blessing upon its mission and upon the person to whom it is sent.... When I go to the classroom, and wait for the arrangement of the cadets in their places, that is my time to intercede with God for them. And so of every familiar act of the day." "But don't you often forget them — coming so frequently?" asked his friend. "No," he answered, "I have made the practice habitual to me; and I can no more forget it than forget to drink when I am thirsty. The habit has become as delightful as regular."*[4]

Throughout the day, Jackson prayed spontaneously to God. You might also come together with others to pray at specific times. Most communities have at least one prayer group that meets regularly. Meeting with its members will reveal many needs. Record the prayer requests in a notebook and pray daily for them. When a prayer is answered, thank God and then cross it off the list.

You can also find prayer lines and prayer lists on the internet. Consider being part of a telephone prayer chain that calls others with prayer requests.

Be courageous enough to pray with a person. This is almost always an impromptu event. You might be sharing with someone, either in person, on the phone, or online, and you learn about a need. In addition to promising your prayers, go a step beyond. Pray with the person right then and there. Some people are comfortable with this and others are not. If you are uncomfortable, pray a familiar prayer, such as the Our Father, with the person. In time, you may feel led to offer a spontaneous prayer.

Volunteer without Being Asked

Two kinds of people seem to exist in the world — those who wait to be asked and those who volunteer. Unless they are unable to assist, those who sit back and watch while others are hard at work are generally either lazy, inattentive, insecure about offering help, or self-absorbed. Volunteering your help is a loving thing to do. You do not have to be on committees to volunteer. You can do it anyplace. If you are at someone's house, volunteer to help with dinner or the dishes. At work, volunteer to carpool. If a task is being discussed, volunteer to do it.

Beware of two unloving hazards. First, do not insist on helping if the other person says, "No, thanks. I have everything under control." People who respond this way want things done a certain way, or else they dislike overseeing someone else. They are much happier being left alone to work as they wish. Lovingly respond to their refusal of your help. Say, "All right. Just ask if you need help."

Secondly, do not volunteer to do something that you cannot do well. If someone's car breaks down, volunteer to help fix it if you know what to do. Otherwise, volunteer to call a mechanic.

Anticipate Needs and Fill Them

How wonderful when someone anticipates your needs and helps without being asked! *Lenny pays attention to the gas gauge in his wife's car. When the tank is getting low, he takes the car and fills the tank, all without being asked.* Anticipating needs and then satisfying them makes life run along more smoothly. How might you anticipate needs? Pay attention to the toilet paper roll and put out a new one when the other is getting low. If someone has to go for a physical, offer to drive. Ask your daughter if she would like you to buy a playpen to keep at your house so that she will not have to bring hers along when she comes for a visit with your grandbaby.

Jump In with Assistance

As you learn to keep your mental antennas up, you will start noticing ways to help others. *Justin passed two young men trying to push a stalled car off the roadway, so he stopped and helped push, too. The three of them managed to get the vehicle out of traffic's way. Marilyn dropped her rosary while she was in line to receive the Eucharist. Les, who was behind her, immediately stooped down to pick it up for her. Sue noticed a frail, elderly woman looking at the top grocery store shelf. "Would you like me to get something down for you?" Sue asked.*

Sometimes you might be afraid to assist, thinking that you might be rebuffed. Why be upset if you are? Think instead of the person who needed help that you did not offer to give. Maybe you never noticed.

Perhaps you wanted to mind your own business. Might you have feared rejection? Had you helped that person, you could have lightened his or her day. When you consider only how you feel or how you might be treated, you are being self-absorbed. When you consider others' needs, you are being lovable.

Overlook Faults

Each person has faults. Of course, some faults irritate more than others do. The problem may be with the faults, but it might also be with you. It is easier to overlook the faults of someone for whom you feel sympathy or love. You may even find such a person's faults humorous or amusing. Students often mimic teachers behind their backs, rather accurately portraying their instructors' idiosyncrasies and verbal quips. Often this mimicry is playful because the students like their teachers. Students who dislike certain teachers generally castigate rather than mimic them.

You will probably find it difficult to overlook the faults of someone you dislike. Ask yourself, "Does that person's existence annoy me, or am I only bothered when he talks with his mouth full? Do I think it looks gross when he chews his spinach, or do I have trouble understanding his diction?"

Sometimes you might focus on faults more than you should. You can learn to overlook faults if you see the person in spite of those faults. When Mother Teresa of Calcutta said she was seeing Jesus in "the poorest of the poor," she was not necessarily referring only to lepers. "Who are the poorest of the poor? They are the unwanted, the unloved, the ignored, the hungry, the naked, the homeless, the leper, and the alcoholic in our midst. To be able to see and love Jesus in the poor, you must be one with Christ through a life of deep prayer."[5] Someone who consistently displays an annoying fault is the "leper." No one likes to be with people whose faults make others uncomfortable, especially if those faults violate society's norms. You certainly can try to correct people who may not know that they are offending, but if you do not succeed, then what? Mother Teresa says to begin with prayer. Often you can follow prayer with simple actions.

Create Something Positive from the Negative

If you cannot correct someone's faults, try to create something positive from them. Doing so will take some reflection and planning.

For example, if someone chats excessively on the phone when you have a lot of work to do, keep a list of work that you can do while you talk. This might be stamping envelopes, sweeping the floor, mending, or straightening the tool bench. *Lou-Ann prepares dinner every day while chatting with her long-winded friend Noella.*

Instead of gawking at the lips of a person who is talking while chewing, why not look at his eyes instead? *Esther did this and fell in love with Doug. They have five children today and Doug finally learned not to talk while chewing — at least most of the time!*

If a person has a nasty habit of verbally crucifying just about everyone, take all her vinegar and sweeten it with positive comments. *Whenever her high school friends got catty about someone, Melissa would interject a "she was always nice to me" comment and deflate the negativity.*

Toleration

Sometimes you may find it difficult to create anything positive from another person's faults. If the person cannot or will not change, the only loving response may be toleration. Saint Thomas More put human faults into proper perspective. "Would to God that we were all of the mind to think that no man is as bad as ourselves! For that would be the way to mend both them and ourselves. But as it is now, they blame us, and we blame them, though both sides are actually worthy of blame, and both are more ready to find others' faults than they are to correct their own."[6]

Sometimes whole communities can exercise the virtue of toleration. *Butch, a homeless man with poor personal hygiene, attended Mass every Sunday. Among his many quirks, he insisted that nuns wear habits. He decided to teach a lesson to those in the parish, who dressed in secular garb. In his convoluted reasoning, he decided to use his body odor as a weapon. He would position himself at one end of the nuns' pew. They would try to stay in place, but Butch's overpowering scent would force them to inch down the pew. He would wait a few moments and then slide closer until the nuns, one by one, had quietly moved away. Having banished all of them, Butch would stand up, turn to face the congregation, and bow. Neither the pastor, the nuns, nor anyone else could convince him to cease this routine; so rather than keep him away from the sacraments, the parish tolerated his eccentricity.*

Adjustment

Sometimes a person has a behavior pattern, human quirk, or personality trait that resists change. If this is difficult to tolerate, perhaps you can make a loving adjustment. Think creatively. Sometimes a small change can make a big difference. *Because Polly found herself constantly scolding her three children for "borrowing" scissors, tape, and paper from her office-in-the-home, Polly bought a lock for her office and a pair of scissors and roll of tape for each child. That made everyone happier.* Sometimes more drastic measures will help. *Sister Mary Rose McGeady tells the story of Michael, who was thrown out of his house because he snored too loudly. He found his way to Covenant House, a New York City home for runaway and homeless teens. When his snoring bothered residents there, Sister Mary Rose gave him his own room. Suddenly he could sleep all night through without anyone awakening him. He soon obtained a job and was talking about applying to college.*[7]

Confronting Evil

Toleration never extends to tolerating evil. When facing evil, you must take a moral stand for the good. That is the only compassionate response.

Frequently those who sin the most believe that they sin the least or not at all. Once a person, or a society, begins to consider sinful practices legitimate, every action could become a matter of choice. When nearly all choices are thought to be moral, then only two things can possibly be wrong — judging another person's choice to be wrong and forcing someone to accept an unwanted choice. "When a man is shamelessly and notoriously wicked, then, the more freely he commits every kind of evil, the more he thinks it lawful, and in imagining it lawful, he is thereby immersed in it all the more." Gregory the Great (Admonition 32) could have applied these words to societies as well as to individuals. Consider modern attitudes toward sexuality and human life. Never could Gregory have imagined a world in which abortion and sexual license are deemed human rights. Within a decade after abortion was legalized in the

United States in 1973, Francis Schaeffer and Dr. C. Everett Koop wrote a book called *Whatever Happened to the Human Race?* In it they detailed what they described as a domino effect. Legalizing abortion would lead, they said, to euthanasia and infanticide. Why? Because society has adopted a "humanist world-view." "Within this world-view there is no room for believing that a human being has any final distinct value above that of an animal or of nonliving matter. People are merely a different arrangement of molecules."[8] Benedict XVI takes this idea even further. "Today there is a remarkable hatred among people for their own real greatness. Man sees himself as the enemy of life, of the balance of creation, as the great disturber of the peace of nature (which would be better off if he did not exist), as the creature that went wrong."[9] This attitude rejects the traditional Christian view of humanity revealed in Genesis, namely that all people are made "in the image of God" (Gn 1:27). "Even though man is strictly bound to the visible world, the biblical narrative does not speak of his likeness to the rest of creatures, but only to God.... The Creator seems to halt before calling him into existence, as if he were pondering within himself to make a decision: 'Let us make man in our image, after our likeness ... ' (Gn 1:26)."[10]

Once people no longer see the divine image in one another, then individuals begin to make decisions that once belonged to God alone. Human life becomes expendable; what used to be called "killing" becomes a "loving choice." Today not only are women aborting unborn children as a matter of choice, but parents and partners often pressure women into abortions, and physicians do the same if diagnostic prenatal tests reveal disabilities in the unborn child. In some countries, infants who are born with severe disabilities are being killed to "prevent their suffering." In the United States, nearly everyone has heard of the forced starvation of the severely disabled Terri Schiavo, but worldwide many terminally ill or severely disabled people meet similar deaths. Nations and states are legalizing assisted suicide. Researchers are creating human embryos and using their stem cells to treat diseases in more mature humans. They are also experimenting with human and animal hybrid clones. How near in the future might be the soldier and worker clones of fantasy and science fiction novels, those strong but dull-witted humans cloned to perform the dirty work for their societies? Already in the United States a nine-year-old girl who has a severe mental disability has been sterilized and given hormones to keep her a child, the reason being that she would be "easier to manage."[11]

Artificial birth control has separated intercourse from procreation. This division naturally leads to society accepting and legalizing extramarital sex, whether with someone of the same or opposite gender. Since many marriages are intentionally infertile, why not legalize same-sex-marriages? In some same-sex unions, the couple has adopted a child or one of the pair has been artificially inseminated and borne a child. The only difference between these unions and heterosexual marriages is that both partners share the same gender.

If morality cannot be legislated, why try? Why ban intercourse between animals and humans? Between adults and children? Polyandry? Polygamy? There are proposals to legalize all of these. Why not? When evils are called choices, will any choices be considered evil? What might Gregory the Great say if he could see contemporary society? "I warned you. You have not only hit rock bottom in the history of human morals; you are falling through it." Faced with so much evil, how can you be loving? You must live the truth, witness to it, and work to eliminate the wrong. You must not vote to legalize evil nor vote for those who would do so. If the only choice of candidates is between one who would restrict the evil without eliminating it and the other who would set no limits, you have a moral obligation to vote for the candidate who would curtail the injustice. Work for moral laws and moral political candidates. Speak to pastors and other religious leaders and ask them to preach on moral values. Use ethically sound ways of family planning. Model marital fidelity to the community. Words and deeds, whether writing to newspapers or sharing views with neighbors and acquaintances, can persuade people to choose the good. Sometimes this means actually assisting them. *Estella and her husband Skipp were pro-life. When Lori needed a place to stay to avoid her family's pressure to abort her unborn baby, the pro-lifer couple invited her to use their spare bedroom. Lori lived with the family until her baby was born and placed for adoption.*

Be Sympathetic

Being sympathetic means understanding, or trying to understand, the weaknesses of others, whether they are infirmities of the soul, mind, or body. Being sympathetic also means understanding what makes others happy, or angry, or frustrated, or any of a host of emotions. Sympathy deals with emotions more than with situations. Chiara Lubich defined sympathy this way: "When others cry, we ought to weep with them, too.

If they laugh, enjoy it with them. This way the cross is split up and borne on several shoulders, and the joy gets multiplied and shared in many hearts."[12] In a commentary on Matthew 4:10, she wrote, "We need to fill our hearts with love for God and to love our neighbors by sharing in their worries, sufferings, problems, and joys."[13]

You might not know exactly how others feel, or why, but you can identify with and accept their emotions without trying to "fix" or "improve" them. How do you know when to "fix" things and when to offer sympathy? Are you able to "make it better"? If not, then at least be sympathetic. You cannot bring someone back from the dead, for example. Saying, "He is in a better place," may not be as helpful as you might like to think. Perhaps you could practice "emphatic listening." By emphatically listening to the grieving party, you hear what the person says and then repeat it a bit differently, to show that you understand. Say to the sorrowing survivor, "You must miss him very much" or "I can see how deeply you loved her."

Sympathy can pave the way for advice, but evaluate the situation before offering suggestions. Sometimes counsel needs to wait until a person is in the right frame of mind to receive it. Explaining things from the boss' point of view may be unwise when an employee is angry. First reveal your empathy by saying, "You seem to have focused on some injustices" or "If I had been addressed like that, I would be mad, too." After the employee's anger subsides, offer some insights into why the boss' reaction could have been justified.

Sometimes, sympathy smoothes the way for help. Suppose that someone is getting frustrated in performing a task. Saying "Here. Let me do it," might only bring resentment and an angry, "Do you think I'm stupid?" First offer a little sympathy by saying, "That is really getting to you, isn't it?" Then allow the frustrated person to talk. When and if he or she seems receptive to assistance, ask, "Do you want some help?" *Rachel was friends with Bridget and her husband Paul, who worked out of town. When Bridget complained that Paul was returning to his place of employment on Sunday afternoon rather than early Monday morning, Rachel listened while Bridget voiced her opinion that her husband ought to spend more time at home with the family. Only after Bridget spoke for over an hour did Rachel feel that she could offer some suggestions regarding activities Paul might do with the family while he was home so that Bridget could accept his leaving early. Then she offered to sit down with both Bridget and Paul to help them work out a plan that would satisfy them both.*

5
Honesty

Lying and cheating are sure ways of losing others' trust, but some people do not realize that they are lying or cheating. Is telling someone that she looks nice, when you really think that she looks hideous, a big lie or a little one? Instead of trying to figure it out, refrain from lying! If someone asks how he looks, make an honest but tactful comment. "That is the most interesting hat I have ever seen" encompasses many different reactions. Suppose that your boss uses your summer home for a vacation. Is it cheating to claim the rent as a business expense on your tax return? Rather than trying to decide, ask a tax expert. An honest person is free from deception in thoughts, words, and deeds. Honesty is loving because you are being truthful with yourself and with others.

Masks

Some people care only that other people think well of them. So they "do evil secretly and good openly." In Admonition 36 of Pastoral Care (Chapter III), Gregory the Great unmasks this terrible deception. At the end of time, "the sentence of Heaven ... penetrates even to what is hidden ... for everlasting requital." Certainly God will reward good deeds and punish evil ones. God does not overlook secret evil; he knows about it and so does the evil-doer. Evil pulls one away from God whether or not it is widely known.

To deserve the love of others, be honest and try to make your public and private behavior, your thoughts and words, conform. How will you know that friends are true if what they like are the masks that you wear? Would these friends still like you if you revealed who you really are?

If you hide behind a mask, ask yourself why. Perhaps, when you were a youngster, you wanted to appear to be good. Therefore, you did and said just what your parents and other authority figures wanted. Now that you are older, you continue this immature behavior. Saying what others want to hear makes everyone think highly of you. But do they know the real you? Your secret thoughts and wishes reveal your true self which, according to Gregory the Great, God alone knows. Moreover, putting on a good front, without the interior conversion to match it, can lead to extremely unloving results. *Julian the Apostate was only a child when in 353 the Emperor Constantius, son of Constantine the Great, assumed control of the Roman Empire. Then six years old, Julian witnessed the murder of his father, brother, and other family members by the guards of the imperial palace, a crime that Julian attributed to Constantius. Always presenting himself as an exemplary Christian, Constantius proceeded to enact laws against the heathens while apparently filling his own pockets with gold purloined from pagan temples. Infuriated by such hypocrisy, Julian outwardly avowed Christianity while interiorly he deplored it. When he became emperor, Julian decided to restore paganism to the Roman Empire. Imitating Constantius by wearing a mask of holiness, Julian proceeded to persecute and martyr Christians.*[1]

Be Honest with Yourself

How does being honest relate to love? First of all, if you are dishonest with yourself, you may either love or hate a distorted image of who you actually are. A fantasy is not the real you.

How can you be honest with yourself? Find a block of time when you can be alone, alert, and undisturbed. Depending on your situation, you may need someone to mind your children, your pets, or your elderly or ill parents while you do this exercise. Take a sheet of paper, or a blank document on your computer, and begin to write who you really are. Start with the basics. "I am a female who is forty years old. I am married. I have two children and a loving husband," and so on. Once you exhaust the facts, you will naturally begin to record deeper insights regarding how you feel and respond. "I love soft music and get really angry when someone is mean to a pet. I am easily frustrated especially if someone does not explain things clearly and then expects me to do what they have asked." Keep writing, not bothering to edit anything. Write on until you can think of nothing more. Then wait five minutes. If no new thought about you comes in those five minutes, consider the writing part of this exercise done. Do not edit anything. Read over what you have written and say, "This is who I am." If you believe in God, ask him to help you love the real you. If you do not have faith, then say to yourself, "From now on, I am going to treat myself with love." Then try to do that. If this exercise stirs up troubling or dangerous ideas, seek the help of a professional counselor. Some disturbing ideas include a desire to harm yourself or others, a compulsion to destroy property, or a revelation of an addiction or life-threatening behavior.

Keep your essay. From time to time, you may realize that you are trying to deceive yourself. For example, you may be trying to convince yourself that you want to do something when, deep inside, you are saying, "No way." Or you may be telling yourself that you do not care about someone when you cannot get him or her out of your mind. If you find yourself deceiving yourself, read the essay again and say, "This is who I am."

Doing this exercise will probably reveal several unpleasant characteristics in yourself. Expect this. Work to change them into likable traits. A year from now, repeat this exercise and write down again who you really are. If you have made changes, your essay will change, too.

You can only be honest in deeds and words if you are honest in thought first. Why? Because you speak and act upon your thoughts. For example, if you keep telling yourself that you are kind when you are actually cruel, you will come to think that cruelty is kindness. People who say, "The kindest thing I could do for him was give him a piece of my mind" probably view themselves dishonestly. Cruelty cannot be kindness any more than darkness can be light. In the same way, middle management bosses who put a few coins in the church collection basket and consider themselves generous are deceiving themselves. If your neighbor were treating you the way you treat others, how would you feel? How would you respond? What opinion would you have of your neighbor? Do your words and actions correspond to your self-image or is it time to re-evaluate the real you?

Be Yourself

Being honest with yourself leads to being honest with others. Would you rather deal with a deceptive person or an honest one? Sharing your real self with others is evidence of your respect for them. Gregory the Great (Admonition 12) compares a dishonest person to a hedgehog. When lifted, a hedgehog tucks its head and legs and curls into a tight ball. All you see are its spines. Gregory compares the animal's head to the beginning of crime and the feet to the steps through which evil, either in deed or in pretense, is committed. The curled up hedgehog conceals its body parts just like the insincere person, caught in a lie, makes excuses for what he did until "every vestige of the evil is concealed" and "by strange pleas a proof is offered that evil was not even initiated" (Admonition 12). Deceptive words confuse the person who discovered the subterfuge, as the evil-doer's convoluted explanations minimize, conceal, or justify evil. *In his book* People of the Lie *psychiatrist Dr. M. Scott Peck shares the story of Billie, who underwent six years of therapy before she could understand that her mother's manipulative words and actions were not evidence of concern and love but merely techniques to keep Billie home in order to assuage Mom's loneliness. One more year of therapy helped her realize that Mom's control of Billie's life was precisely the pattern that she had adopted to control the men in her own life.*[2]

Oh, what tangled webs we weave when first we practice to deceive! How right Sir Walter Scott was when he wrote that! Mark Twain masterfully described duplicity in his character Huckleberry Finn, who tried to navigate between his good heart and his malformed conscience. Huck discovered that a first lie led to subsequent, more outlandish tales as he attempted to conceal the truth. Gregory the Great (Admonition 12) calls duplicity "burdensome." "For in the fear of discovery they ever try to defend themselves even dishonorably, and are ever agitated with fear and apprehension.... When a man is forced to defend his deceit, his heart is wearied with the toilsome labor of doing so." One lie leads to another until the liar muddles a detail and is caught in a contradiction.

According to Gregory, an all-good God cannot cooperate with evil. Therefore, God does not communicate with the deceitful (Admonition 12). Liars may consider their lying prudent, but they have severed themselves from God, the source of all prudence. Scripture says, "a holy and disciplined spirit will flee from deceit ... for wisdom is a kindly spirit" (Ws 1:5–6). Becoming lovable requires communicating with God, the Great Lover. Honesty prepares for recognition of the inner promptings of God's Spirit.

Moderating Honesty with Charity

Beware carrying honesty to extremes, not by being "too honest" but by saying too much. Gregory the Great (Admonition 12) notes that "The sincere are to be commended for their intention of never saying anything false, but they should be warned that they should know how to withhold

the truth on occasions. For, just as falsehood always harms him who utters it, so the hearing of the truth has sometimes done harm. Wherefore, the Lord, tempering speech with silence in the presence of His disciples, says: 'I have yet many things to say to you, but you cannot bear them now.' "
Second-grader Marla resisted her mother's suggestions. One day while dressing for school, Marla decided to use the dog's leash as a belt for her skirt. Although Mom noticed, she wanted to avert a power struggle. She knew that a negative comment about the leash would make Marla insist that she had made a stylish choice. Suspecting that classmates and teachers, whose opinion Marla valued, would likely enlighten her, her mother said nothing. Who knows if anyone at school said anything, but she never wore a leash again.

How will you know when to withhold something from the listener? Ask if the person needs to know. If so, speak up. If not, ask yourself if speaking will do more harm than good. If it will, refrain. For example, if someone visiting your school asks where the cafeteria is, point it out. If asked, "Is the food good?" instead of replying, "I can't stand it," why not say instead, "You can try it yourself. Lunch is served at noon."

Confronting Capital Sins

You might be able to overlook someone's habit of always using the word "like" or another person's wimpy handshake, but how should you respond if someone wants you to accept a capital sin? Often sinners do not consider their behavior wrong. But you know better. Anything that hurts another, unless the hurt is intended to bring healing (such as an operation for cancer or heart disease) is a sin. Sometimes people say, "I am not hurting anyone." But that may be untrue. Sin always hurts the sinner and generally others as well.

Should sinful behavior be accepted as if it were good? You might think so because repudiation might provoke an angry outburst. Acquiescing to sin, however, is unloving. Commending what is right may not motivate the sinner to change, but at least you will have a clear conscience. Keeping your conscience clear is a loving way to treat yourself. *Edwina's college roommate Julia asked her to room with a friend so that Julia's fiancé could share the room for the night. "He won't use your bed," Julia winsomely explained. Not wanting to cause discord, Edwina at first agreed but then had second thoughts. She had seen Julia's birth control pills so it took little imagination to picture what would be going on in Julia's bed. So*

Edwina spoke up, "I'm sorry, but I cannot leave the room when I am not planning on being away. You do what you want with your lifestyle, but I believe that premarital sex is wrong. If I left, I would be an accomplice to what goes on here, and I am not comfortable with that." Julia was civil. "I thought you would say that," she remarked. Then she proceeded to explain that she had made plans to switch rooms permanently so that Julia would be living with a girlfriend of similar mind. The girlfriend's current roommate, a Maryknoll nun, would be living with Edwina. The nun turned out to be a far more congenial roommate.

Condemning Julia or snubbing her would be unloving. Edwina kept the doors of communication open even though Julia exhibited no change in attitude. Nevertheless, both avoided additional sins of anger, bitterness, and resentment by the way they handled their disagreement.

Occasionally a "big" sinner will repent. In that case, the one who has not sinned needs to remember that "It often comes about that the life of one burning with love after having sinned is more pleasing to God than a life of innocence that grows languid in its sense of security. Wherefore, it is said by the voice of the Judge: Many sins are forgiven her because she hath loved much" (Gregory the Great, Admonition 29). Humility helps keep things in perspective. Those who have not sinned ought to "dread all the more anxiously headlong ruin" because they might sin, too. No one should be so cocksure as to think that he or she cannot or will not sin.

Correction

Gregory the Great calls those who will not accept reproof "insolent" (Admonition 9). "The insolent, greatly relying on themselves, scorn reproofs from all others ... [they] esteem everything they do to be singularly excellent." To correct the insolent, Gregory advises, "show them that what they believe they have done well has really been ill-done." Sometimes this does not work. *A college professor received terrible reviews from his students. They said that he was a nice man but a poor teacher. Ray blamed the negative reviews on the students' not doing their homework or studying for tests. A few colleagues gave him advice about teaching. He told them that he was trying, but maintained that the primary problem lay with the class. He did not change his teaching style significantly and after continued poor reviews, his main courses were taken from him and given to another.*

Sometimes you must give a more radical correction. Gregory points out that, when Paul saw the Corinthians being prideful about having a particular teacher over another (Paul, Apollo, Cephas, or Christ), he pointed out to them the crime of incest in their midst, "as if he said in so many words, 'Why in your insolence do you say you are of this one and of that one, seeing that by your dissolute lawlessness you show that you are of none of them?' " (Admonition 9).

If someone calls attention to something that you have done wrong, try not to get defensive. Listen to the correction and evaluate it. Possibly you were in the wrong.

You might realize on your own that you have erred. Are you concerned about others' reaction if you admit your mistake? Consider this: what are you more willing to forgive — sins that others admit, sins that they will not admit, or sins that they try to cover up or justify? Admitting wrongdoing does not indicate weakness. On the contrary, only those of strong character can acknowledge wrongdoing. If you have made a mistake, admit it, repent of it, make up for it, and get on with your life. People will respect you for your honesty. *Mildred thought that she had paid in advance for a book that she wanted to order. When she never received it, she telephoned the store, which had no record of her order. When the manager asked Mildred the title, she could remember only that it was a spiritual self-help book. He suggested some titles and sent her two. After receiving them, she realized that she had not paid in advance after all. She phoned the bookstore, apologized for her mistake, and said that she was going to send a check for the two books as she liked them very much.*

Mildred's mistake was small, but suppose that your sin is great. Perhaps something has been troubling you for years. Perhaps only you and God know about this secret sin. Seek a counselor or member of the clergy and discuss your guilty feelings. God looks on you with love. You need not fear him if you repent. Gregory the Great (Admonition 30) reminds you that "The Lord would not with loving-kindness confront the sinner's gaze with sins to be lamented, if He had wished only to punish them severely." Scripture tells you that if you are sorry the Lord is kind and merciful. The key word here is "if." Gregory notes that you ought to be appropriately sorry for your offenses, not comparing them with those of other people and eschewing a false security that you can "repent later on." The time to repent is now. Hans Urs von Balthasar marvels that "No one can ... explain how it is that God no longer sees my guilt in me, but only in his beloved Son, who bears it for me; or how God sees this guilt transformed through the suffering of love and loves me because I am the one for whom his Son has suffered in love. But the way God, the lover, sees us is in fact the way we *are* in reality — for God, this is the absolute and irrevocable truth."[3]

Ask God to bring something good out of any evil that you have done. He will find a way because all things are possible with God. *When she was in college, Winnie had an abortion. Almost immediately she regretted her choice. After years of spiraling downward emotionally and spiritually, she found the organization Women Exploited by Abortion and experienced spiritual healing. Then Sheila, a pro-life pregnancy counselor, asked Winnie to share her experiences with Corinne, another woman trying to deal with grief over an early abortion. Winnie wrote to her, "God did not will my abortion. It was my choice and it was evil. But God has used my experience to help other women who have had abortions. He cannot change evil into good, but he can bring good out of evil. Ask him to bring something good out of your abortion. I will pray for you."*

Make Restitution

Once you have acknowledged your wrongdoing, in love you are bound to make restitution. In 1970, the popular movie *Love Story* proclaimed falsely that "Love means never having to say you're sorry."[4] On the contrary, love often demands saying you are sorry. You cannot repair damage by ignoring it. If you have offended or insulted someone, apologize. If you have lost, stolen, or broken something, replace it or pay for it. Whether your misdeed happened recently or years ago, you can find a way to make restitution. *Decades earlier while in college, businessmen had hired Lester to go into the homes of sharecroppers who could not pay their bills and to destroy their belongings. As he approached old age, he wished to make restitution but could not locate the families whose homes he had entered and ruined. They had moved away. To make restitution, he paid for a new school to educate the children of the poor in that area and set up local people in businesses of their own.*

Judge Yourself Fairly

Love harms no one. Rather, love does good to all. On the other hand, sin harms you as well as others. You must evaluate your sins fairly. Were they as bad as you think they were, or perhaps even worse?

Are your thoughts sinful? Gregory (Admonition 30) advises you to determine whether your thoughts come spontaneously. Temptation, Gregory notes, is not sin. "Sometimes, however, the mind is so engulfed in temptation, that it offers no resistance at all, but deliberately consents to what thrills it with delight; and if external opportunity offered, it would at once execute in effect its inward wishes." In this case, "the sin is not only one in thought, but one of deed also" because you would commit the deed if you could.

According to Gregory, sin progresses through three stages: "the suggestion of it, the pleasure experienced, and the consent." When judging yourself, remember that the mind's suggestion of sin is not sin. Suppose you take pleasure in and encourage sinful thoughts. Then you have sinned because you commit sinful acts mentally. Jesus referred to mental compliance with sin when he said that a person could commit adultery in the heart (see Mt 5:28). If you try to commit a sin, or verbally suggest it to another, then you have also sinned because sinful thoughts are leading to sinful actions.

Since sinful thoughts can lead to sinful actions, you ought to repudiate and avoid them. If you harbor a sinful thought, take heart. Gregory notes that "Often the merciful God absolves sins of thought the more readily, in that He does not allow them to issue in deed." In other words, thank God that you avoided sin even though you thought of it.

Fight Dejection

Feeling dejected impedes lovable qualities. Dejection leads to depression, which makes others uncomfortable. When someone feels rejected or worthless, you feel helpless. You want to make dejected people feel better, but nothing you say or do seems to raise them from their slump. Gregory the Great (Admonition 9) calls these people fainthearted. "[T]he fainthearted, too conscious of their weakness, commonly fall into despondency.... The fainthearted think what they do is extremely despicable, and, therefore, their spirit is broken in dejection."

Gregory advises admonishing dejected people by first referring to "some of their good points" before discussing the bad. As an example, he refers to the Apostle Paul who, in his first letter to the Thessalonians, "first praised them for those things in which they displayed courage, and afterwards ... strengthened them in that matter wherein they were weak." Specifically he extolled their faith and charity before admonishing them for being afraid that the end of the world was imminent. Dale Carnegie advises this same tactic in his classic *How to Win Friends and Influence People.*[5] Preface a correction with a compliment. Remember that a little bit of sugar makes the medicine go down.

When feeling dejected, consider your good points. Nobody is all bad. A refrigerator magnet based on a popular song of the 1990s proclaimed, "I know I'm special 'cos God don't make no junk.' "[6] Although the grammar is wrong, the meaning is correct! God does not make junk. Scripture proclaims, "I am fearfully and wonderfully made" (Ps 139:14). That applies to you! To combat dejection, take five minutes and write down all the good things that you have done for others. All the times that you shared meals, drove others various places, sent cards, visited shut-ins, phoned friends, paid compliments, turned in your best work, petted dogs, babysat, gave donations, volunteered, prayed, assisted, advised, comforted, taught, attended funerals, and so on. Even if you are able to write more, stop after five minutes and read your list. You have many lovable qualities. Thank God for them and go on to develop others.

Be Genuine

To be loved, you do not have to be perfect but you do have to be genuine. Genuine people are happy being themselves. "I yam what I yam and that's all that I yam," the cartoon character Popeye the Sailor Man sang.[7] Popeye was glad to be who he was.

Being genuine encompasses the desire to improve. Is your desire genuine, or are you trying to fool yourself or others? Some people cry crocodile tears. They bewail their sins and bad points but do nothing to correct them. Gregory the Great drives home a good point. "[People who] confess their evil deeds but do not avoid them must weigh betimes what they will say to excuse themselves when confronted with judgment" (Admonition 33). Those who do not believe in God do not worry about God's judgment, but no one can avoid the judgment of others. Are you patient with those who claim that they will change their ways but never do? How patient will others be with you, if you do the same?

If you sincerely desire to improve, you can probably find someone to help you. Ask someone close to you (a spouse, your child, or a friend) to tell you your bad points. Request that the person be blunt and accurate. Solicit your confidant's help in changing. Then accept advice and correction.

Addictions

Those who suffer from addictions harm themselves and others by their excessive use of anything that interferes with a normal, well-balanced life. You can be addicted to drugs, drink, sex, work, shopping, computer games, gambling, chocolate, exercise, or any number of other things. No matter how much "fun" or how "important" these activities seem, such addictions can be extremely unloving.

Ask yourself the following questions. Am I irritable if I cannot engage in a certain behavior? Do I spend much time on this activity while neglecting my loved ones? Have I lost money or peace of mind by engaging in this pastime?

You must conquer what has conquered you. Admit your addiction and seek treatment. First, contact any social service agency. Anonymously tell the intake clerk your problem. Ask where to get help. Write down the information and contact those individuals until you find someone who can assist you. The loving way to deal with addictions is to eliminate them.

Do Not Pretend to Agree When You Disagree

Many times you are in no position to influence decisions. You have to accept what others decide. But sometimes you can offer input. Whether or not you say anything may have much to do with your personality.

Some people dislike conflict. For others, expressing a differing opinion makes them uncomfortable. So they agree with every opinion and proposed course of action even if they disapprove.

Do you think that avoiding disagreement is loving? Think again. Not voicing dissent allows others to define a course of action that subconsciously you will resist. Sooner or later, others will sense that you are not as supportive as they thought you would be. They will wonder what you are really thinking. *Wanting to be a loving dad, Mark*

accompanied his children and his wife Denise on every outing that she
planned. On these excursions, however, he felt irritable and impatient.
Denise sensed that he did not want to go, even though he kept protesting
that it was OK. She realized that she could not make him enjoy something
that he disliked, so she told him to stay home even though he continued
to insist that he would go along. Eventually Mark admitted that he never
liked outings. His feet hurt with so much walking. He really wanted to
stay home and nap. Denise told him to do that, so he did. From then on,
the rest of the family had more pleasant outings.

Spare others the mental game of trying to figure out your real feelings. If you disagree, say so politely and continue the discussion civilly. You and the other parties will come to a decision that everyone can tolerate.

Speak and Desist

Share your opinion clearly and thoroughly. Then be quiet. Badgering, bullying, and prolonging the discussion demean your listeners. Do you think that they did not understand what you said the first time? Are you trying to wear down others by repeating your thoughts? Are you trying to keep them from expressing opinions? Good communication is a two-way street. Both parties must allow each other to speak.

Speech, the chief means of communication, is a great gift, but the tongue must be used well. St. James' admonition is classic. "Anyone who makes no mistakes in speaking is perfect, able to keep the whole body in check with a bridle" (Jas 3:2). Conscious of the risk of abuse through speech, the sage abbot Benedict quoted Psalm 38 (39) in Chapter 6 of his Rule: "I said, 'I will guard my ways that I may not sin with my tongue; I will keep a muzzle on my mouth.' "

The key words here are "sin" and "guard." Few people can keep silent. Families would soon separate if their members did not communicate. Some offices keep speech to a minimum and communicate by email and written notes, but certain people cannot stand the silence. Occasionally religious communities give outsiders the impression that they dislike each other by never speaking. How can a collective become a "community" without communicating? Silence is good, but it can be overdone. Some things need to be discussed. How do you do it? How much should you say? Freedom of speech is a spiritual gift, and the First Amendment to the United States Constitution allows it! Nevertheless, giving speech free rein will likely make you unpopular. *Jane Wyman divorced Ronald Reagan because he talked too much about the Screen Actors' Union and political issues that did not matter to her.*[8]

Do you talk too much or too long? How will you know? Try this "Brevity Practice." Imagine the details of these scenarios:

- ❧ Your car motor explodes and you barely escape with your life.

- ❧ You are madly in love with someone who has the most beautiful eyes you have ever seen.

- ❧ You have a job interview tomorrow for the job of your dreams.

In the privacy of your room, practice talking about each of these scenarios. First share about each one in thirty seconds or less. Then reduce your sharing to twenty seconds, and then to ten. What have you learned about brevity?

When sharing, check your watch! Generally you ought to make a point in thirty seconds or less. If you must advance a detailed argument, allow no more than sixty to ninety seconds. Keeping to a time limit will help you become more concise. Give the other person a chance to respond. Instead of thinking about your rebuttal, listen to what is being said. Even if people disagree, a discussion can be loving.

Limit Talking about Yourself

Most people are more interested in themselves than they are in you. If you must use yourself as an example, or if you want to share a personal story, keep to the sixty-to-ninety-second rule. Unless you are speaking to your therapist, your listener is not being paid to hear you talk about yourself.

Unless you have pre-arranged a time to meet with someone to discuss your concerns, a long conversation is probably unloving. Lengthy discussions force the listener to choose between being polite to you and being attentive to others. Do not edge someone into this position. *As a volunteer for a political action agency, Sarita coordinated a massive telephone campaign. Cedric, one of the solicitors, considered Sarita a good listener and used to keep her on the phone for close to an hour. The calls began to impede Sarita's time with her young children. She tried to limit Cedric's sharing but could not. He would remark, "Sure you can get back to the kids, but let me say this one thing." Realizing that Cedric ended the conversation only when he wanted to, Sarita was forced to say, "Thanks for sharing, Cedric, but I have to go now." Then she would hang up.*

Always Give Your Best

God gave his best in Christ. Following his example, the best you can do is give yourself. "Put your best foot forward" is time-tested advice. Unfortunately some people believe that saying does not apply to them. They try to slip by with the minimum. *Every semester, college students ask Jack, their professor, "What do I have to do to get a C?" Students who aim just to pass a course might fall short and fail.*

The 4–H motto "To Make the Best Better" applies not only to youth in 4–H clubs.[9] Always do your best and then try to improve it. "Raising the bar" stretches your capacities and helps you to become all you can be. If you always do your best, you can do no more, so take satisfaction in the results.

Give an Honest Day's Work

Jack's students are not the only ones who try to slip by with the minimum. Employees often do the same. They may gloat about "having the boss fooled" into thinking that they are always busy. Companies pay their employees for certain qualities and quantities of work. Why should they pay slackers? Meeting work obligations is wise as well as loving. Slackers may find themselves looking at want ads.

Likewise, bosses ought to expect no more than an honest day's work from their employees. *In a scenario reminiscent of the Jews making bricks in Egypt, Zoe had her hours and salary cut but was expected to maintain a similar level of work. Zoe's boss Mrs. Tucker, a faith-filled Christian woman, happened to be going through tough times financially. While she may have thought it prudent to cut Zoe's salary but not her workload, the decision was unloving. To be loving, she ought to have consulted Zoe to determine what she could produce in the shorter hours.*

Do Not Use People

A popular saying goes, "Use things, not people." Pope John Paul II felt that the opposite of loving people was using them.[10] Some routinely use others to gain advantage. *Glenda flatters her boss in order to get a good recommendation, but, behind his back, she castigates him. Jay flatters Judy to obtain sexual favors; she consents because she wants him to marry her. Gustave, a weak student, befriends Emil, a strong one, in hopes of Emil's help in getting better grades. Valerie cooks her husband's favorite meal when she wants to borrow the car. Tim compliments his wife before asking her to do an errand.* Sooner or later, people realize that they have been manipulated. How stupid and foolish they feel then! And how angry with the persons who used them! If you want people to love you, be courteous, kind, and friendly, but avoid ulterior motives.

Measure your thoughts, words, and deeds against the yardstick of honesty. Honesty is not simply the best policy. It is the only policy if you want to be loving. Anything less than honesty is dishonesty. Nobody feels loving toward a dishonest person, not even another dishonest person. Build love on trust, and build trust on truth.

6
Promises

God made the first promise — that Adam and Eve would live forever in the Garden of Eden as long as they did not eat the fruit of one of its trees. The serpent implied that God was deceitful and that they would not die if they ate the fruit; instead, they would become like God. Although Adam and Eve broke their promise to God and sampled the apple, God kept his. He banished Adam and Eve from the Garden, decreed for them a life of hard toil, and made sure that they would not live forever (see Gn 3). Then he made another promise. He would send a Redeemer so that Adam, Eve, and their descendents (us) would not suffer eternal death but instead could inherit eternal life upon returning to him wholeheartedly (see Jl 2:12).

A promise says, "I will do as I say." Adding "cross my heart and hope to die" does not make a promise any more binding. All promises are to be kept. Therefore, if you want to lose friends and alienate people, try breaking your promises and contracts. Then you will destroy not only other people's plans but also their confidence in you.

The *Catechism of the Catholic Church* (2410) says "Promises must be kept and contracts strictly observed to the extent that the commitments made in them are morally just." Good point! Unjust contracts and promises ought to be broken, and fast! Contracting with a gangster to murder an enemy is not the only kind of unjust contract. Charging more than is fair or signing on for more time than you are able to give is unjust, too. Justice, the *Catechism* says, "is the moral virtue that consists in the constant and firm will to give their due to God and neighbor" (1807).

Evaluate your contracts and promises. If you discover that they are unjust, admit and correct the wrong. *Gert was tired of telling eight-year-old Harold to put his outerwear into the closet. "The next time I find your clothes all over the house, I am going to throw them into the garage," she promised. But Harold did not reform. Instead, he was perfectly content to retrieve his clothes from the unheated garage. One winter day the weather turned bitterly cold. When Harold had to dress for school, he found that his snow-encrusted clothing was stiff with ice. Recognizing the folly of her promise, Gert thawed Harold's clothes in the clothes dryer. While driving him to school, she made a new promise. "If I find your clothes lying around the house, I will dry them if they are wet, but then I am going to hide them. If you want them back, you will have to do an errand." Harold decided that his regular errands were sufficient. Soon he was putting away his clothes.*

Avoiding Hasty Promises

Probably you have heard the advice "Never make a promise that you cannot keep." Yet many people not only make promises that they cannot keep; they make promises that they never intended to keep. Sometimes they reason, "I will make her happy if I promise that." Or "I can get what I want if I promise to give him what he wants." Promises that you never intended to keep are really lies. Lying is so evil that God forbids it: "You shall not bear false witness against your neighbor" (Ex 20:16).

Sometimes people intend to keep their promises before they have evaluated them. Jesus advised scrutinizing a course of action before undertaking it (cf. Lk 14:28, 31). His advice also applies to making promises. Do you tend to promise things impulsively? If so, make this short saying part of your vocabulary: "Let me think about that." Here is some practice:

"Would you be chairperson of the bazaar committee?" "Let me think about that."

"Can we go to the zoo tomorrow, Mommy?" "Let me think about that."

"Would you marry me?" "Let me think about that."

Saying "Let me think about that" gives you time to "think about that" and decide whether or not you really can do what someone asks. If you can do it, great. If you cannot, then gently decline. Memorize and use these few words: "I am sorry, but I cannot."

"I have thought about chairing the bazaar committee. I am sorry, but I cannot."

"I have considered going to the zoo tomorrow. I am sorry, but I cannot."

"I have prayed about marrying you. I am sorry, but I cannot."

Clarifying a Promise

Different people can interpret the same promise differently. To avoid hurt and confusion, be sure that all parties understand the promise in the same way. Having the other person repeat the promise will clarify the matter. Here is an example.

"So now, are we both on the same wavelength? What are our plans?"

"You said you would meet me for lunch in the lunchroom tomorrow."

"Not exactly. I said I would try to meet you. I have a morning meeting that might extend through the lunch hour. But I will definitely meet you in the lunchroom if the meeting concludes on time."

"Oh, thanks for clarifying that! I thought that our lunch date was a definite."

"It is a definite if I am free. Save me a seat and I hope I can make it. If not, let's plan on another day."

Breaking a promise brings hurt and disappointment. Keep your promises. If you cannot keep them, do not make them.

Completing the Good You Have Begun

When people profess to live a religious rule of life, the Church representative receiving their pledge or vow says to them, "May God who has begun this good work in you bring it to fulfillment."[1] In your dealings with others, you will begin good things with every intention of completing them. If you later get discouraged and think of quitting, recall Gregory the Great's reminder that, when you do not accomplish what you proposed to do, you might "shatter to pieces" what you had begun. "For if that which evidently must be done is not advanced with assiduous application, even what had been done well deteriorates" (Admonition 35). This is easy to understand if you have ever begun a project but never completed it. The partly knitted afghan and the never-completed woodworking project collect dust and eventually will be discarded. All the preparations for the dinner dance fundraiser were for nothing if the dance was cancelled.

In the spiritual life, faltering leads to backsliding. "In this world, the human soul is like a ship going up stream: it is not allowed to stay still in one place, because it will drop away to the lower reaches unless it strives to gain the upper ... it might have been more tolerable for them not to start in the way of rectitude, than to turn back after having begun" (Admonition 35). Gregory is hypothesizing that God may be more merciful toward those who never start on the path of spiritual improvement than he is toward those who begin but who fall back into previous sinful behaviors. Those who never begin have not yet reached the conversion needed to change, while those who have converted, but who then return to former lifestyles, are more culpable because they have rejected what they have come to know is good.

Gregory refers to Scripture. "I wish that you were cold or hot, but because you are lukewarm, and neither hot nor cold, I will begin to vomit you out of my mouth" (Rv 3:15). He explains, "A person is hot who both undertakes and completes good enterprises. He is cold who does not even begin anything" (Admonition 35). The person who is trying to better his life is in transition from cold to hot and so is lukewarm. If he remains lukewarm without striving for conversion, he is going to grow cold. *Bill converted to the Catholic faith and immediately began a prayer group that he faithfully conducted for many months. As time went on, Bill thought that the prayer gathering was taking too much of his time and so he stopped promoting the meetings. The group soon disbanded and Bill, although he remained a Catholic, slipped back into his worldly concerns.*

Spiritual Sluggishness

Peggy Noonan notes that spiritual sluggishness traps some people. "I think about things more than I do them; I ponder what seems their goodness more than I perform them…. But a thought alone isn't quite enough."[2] Indeed, if good thoughts are to take you anywhere, you must turn them into good deeds. *For many years Henrietta considered joining a Third Order whose members were living a spiritual rule of life in their homes. She even contacted the group but never came to a meeting.*

Do you think that any of this book's ideas have merit? Have you tried any of them? If not, you might be a victim of spiritual sluggishness. Since you want to become more lovable, you have to begin to act in loving ways. Merely thinking about what to do is going to neither change you nor help anyone else.

Obedience

Modern people tend to think that obedience is meant for servants or dogs. They want to be independent people answerable only to themselves, but even the most self-willed person can recognize the folly in that attitude. Everyone obeys bodily needs for sleep and food. Most have to obey others, too, such as doctors, bosses, and police. Obeying other people frequently brings a benefit. When a wife calls her husband to dinner, he benefits from coming so that he can eat.

Sometimes obeying someone else, however, benefits only others. Obeying anyway, as long as it causes no harm, lets obedience reflect love. In Chapter Five of his Rule, the abbot Benedict cites Jesus as an example of obedience. At the Sea of Galilee, Jesus told the crowd, "I have come down from heaven, not to do my own will, but the will of him who sent me" (Jn 6:38). Every human has profited from Christ's obedience, but it cost him his life.

Benedict notes that "The first degree of humility is obedience without delay." Obedience should be "done without hesitation, delay, lukewarmness, grumbling or complaint because the obedience which is rendered to superiors is rendered to God." Your boss may not look divine to you, but if you obey him promptly, you will acquire merit with God. You might also earn a promotion!

Everyone loves prompt obedience. Just imagine how you would feel if you told your daughter to pick up her toys and she said, "OK" and then immediately did it! Adults can practice loving obedience by coming promptly when called, answering instantly when addressed, and hurrying to answer the telephone or doorbell. Imagine the type of home that has a tired-sounding voice relaying this message on the phone's answering machine. "Hello. You have reached the Smith residence where everyone waits for someone else to answer the phone. Please leave a message and someone might call you back if they feel like it."

If you are not used to obeying promptly, you will have to develop the habit. Once you do, you will be more lovable.

Benedict adds that obedience should be offered with a "cheerful" heart and not with "ill will" or "murmuring." *Every time one of their cars needed repair, Ashley drove her husband Frank to the garage. However, she always complained about having to interrupt her schedule. One cold, rainy day, when one of their cars was at the garage for repairs, Ashley heard Frank go outdoors. She knew that he never wore a raincoat unless she made him, so she went out to call him in to get one. "Where are you going in this pouring rain?" she called. "The car is fixed, and I am going to get it," he said. "I can drive you," she offered. "You are always so busy. I can walk," he responded. Ashley knew that Frank was being sincere. He did not like imposing on anyone, and he had, he thought, discovered a way not to impose on her. She was struck with remorse that her complaining would make him walk in a downpour rather than ask her to stop what she was doing and drive him. She insisted that he let her take him to the garage, and he agreed. After that Ashley no longer complained when Frank asked her to drive him anywhere.*

Loyalty

Loyalty, sometimes called devotion, constitutes another facet of love. Husbands and wives ought to be loyal to each other and to their children. People in the military or the civil service ought to be loyal to their nations. Leaders ought to be loyal to their followers. Instead of promising a specific action, loyal persons promise themselves not just for a day but often forever. Loyal people are not fair-weather friends; they remain loyal even when the spiritual, social, and emotional climate grows foul. You may have heard the saying, "When troubles come, you know who your real friends are." Loyal soldiers hold fast in the thick of battle, and loyal friends stick with their buddies in difficult times. Needy friends need friends to be present to them, to support and encourage them, and to help. To have a friend, be one.

The opposite of loyalty is betrayal. One of humanity's most treacherous evils, betrayal violates the trust of one friend in another. "It is not enemies who taunt me — I could bear that; it is not adversaries who deal insolently with me — I could hide from them. But it is you, my equal, my companion, my familiar friend, with whom I kept pleasant company; we walked in the house of God with the throng" (Ps 55:13–15). Betrayal besmirches history, Scripture, and mythology. *Delilah betrayed her lover Samson to the Philistines. Brutus turned on his trusting emperor Julius Caesar. Macbeth murdered his guest King Duncan. Jason begot children with Medea, then rejected her in favor of a king's daughter. Jesus' apostle Judas led the Jewish guard to Christ. The crowds who acclaimed Jesus on Palm Sunday clamored for his crucifixion. Peter, the head of Christ's apostles, denied knowing him. When Jesus hung on the cross on Golgotha, only a few loyal followers stood by him — his mother, his beloved apostle John, Mary Magdalene, and a few other women.*

"Our love for our friend must be subordinate to our love for our Lord; and He may, perhaps, test our loyalty,"[3] M. Eugene Boylan noted. Suppose that someone you know does something wrong. Loyalty to God and to your ethical system obliges you to confront the person about the misdeed and perhaps to inform the proper authorities. On the other hand, righteousness declares that you remain loyal to a friend who has been wrongly accused even if that means that you may also be attacked. *Vicky and Herb had a close business relationship for several years. However, Herb's spouse Wanda never liked it and eventually became so jealous that she broke up not only the relationship but also the business. Through months of false accusations of adultery, Vicky's husband Bret remained staunchly loyal to his wife, weathering the vitriol that Wanda continued to throw his way.*

Negligence

Negligence does not mean overlooking faults. Rather it means neglecting to do what is right. You would be irritated if visitors put their coffee mugs on your polished end table or waxed hardwood floor instead of on the coasters. Your boss will be annoyed if, after working late, you leave all the lights glowing when you leave. People expect others to pay attention to details and to fulfill their duty.

You are also being neglectful if you do not communicate information to those who need it. Teachers neglect their duty if they do not tell parents that their children are in danger of failing. Theater and play managers would not only be neglectful but, in case of fire, could also be sued if they had not pointed out the exits to the audience. *Brother Martin, a member of the Brothers and Sisters of Perpetual Consideration (BSPC), and Brother Roderick, a member of the Little Disciples of Saint Obscurity (LDSO), worked at a religious house which served both religious orders. When Sister Maryellen, BSPC, and some young girls asked to use the house for two weeks of discernment, Brother Martin scheduled them. However, he neglected to write this on the calendar and also forgot to mention the two-week stay to Brother Roderick, even when Roderick said that he had made arrangements for his superior Father Gerald, LDSO, to stay at the house when he flew in from overseas. As a result, when Father Gerald arrived, he found Sister Maryellen and the girls already occupying the house, leaving him no place to stay. Father Gerald concluded that the Brothers and Sisters of Perpetual Consideration were exactly what he suspected, a sect which extols consideration without practicing it.*

If you neglect to tell someone necessary information, how are they to learn it? You cannot assume that "they will find out when they have to." You can avoid ill will by sharing necessary information in advance. For example, you may have to tell a friend that the man she is dating frequents the local pub until closing. If you say nothing, the woman may unwittingly marry an alcoholic. She may still marry him no matter what you share, but at least she has been told of his problem.

Obligations

Commitments incur obligation. If you have ever been "stood up" for a date, you can understand the disappointment and confusion that people feel when others renege on their agreements, often without explanation or apology. What plans did you suddenly have to change? Did you still want to date the person? Ignoring commitments drives away friends.

Who knows whether a religious vocation was lost when a retreat house reneged on its commitment regarding a discernment weekend? *By some strange oversight, Gentle Voice Retreat Center had scheduled a vocation discernment weekend for girls as overlapping part of a week's discernment for men. When the men arrived, they were told that the teens would be arriving the next day and that the men would have to leave. Father Alfred refused to take his young men elsewhere, so what did Gentle Voice Retreat Center do? Its staff did not put forth extra effort to find an alternate location for the girls, but phoned the nuns and told them that they would have to cancel the reservations of the six teens. Who knows what negative effect that cancellation had on the girls, their vocations, and their families?*

To ensure that you meet commitments, keep a calendar. Write your commitments on it. If you have many, buy a date book — or, if that is too small, a notebook — and date each page. Fill your calendar in with obligations, appointments, and chores. Cross off the items as you complete them. Keep the calendar in one spot! Read through your obligations each day. *Tillie, chairperson of a giant yard sale to raise money for a pro-life crisis pregnancy center, had planned a final meeting before the big event and twice reminded the committee members about it. Then she herself neglected to look at her calendar and forgot. When Tillie remembered the meeting, it was already over!*

Unfortunately politicians' behavior often leads voters to expect that public figures will lie, will break their commitments, and will not keep their word. If only those who kept their promises won elections, the nation might be better off politically. Not keeping one's word is bad business, too. Breaking one's word not only hurts the customer, but it also undermines the business which can lose its clients' trust. *Boondocks Bonny Motel lost more than one customer when it cancelled a conference. Reginald, the founder and chairman of The Society of Chaucerian Language, had booked the motel for the society's annual meeting. About thirty scholars, some from overseas, were expected. Only four or five days before the date, the motel granted its kitchen staff a few days of vacation. Never thinking to hire a caterer, Boondocks cancelled the conference. Embarrassed at this sudden turn of events, Reginald had to inform the invited members that the meeting would be held in his home. Several of the scholars were so disgruntled by what they considered to be Reginald's poor management that they refused to meet again in his country. Moreover, in scholarly circles, Boondocks Bonny Motel gained a reputation for unreliability, which certainly hurt its business.*

Punctuality

Being punctual is a way of keeping your word. Do you like to be kept waiting for a late arrival? If not, then you can understand that others do not appreciate waiting for you. Be on time or a minute or two early. Being too early can also be impolite. The other person may not be ready for you. Early arrivals frequently surprise people who are getting dressed, putting on makeup, or straightening the house. *Henry would rather be ten minutes early than thirty seconds late. So he allows himself plenty of time to get someplace. When he has to meet someone at his or her home, he realizes that it can be unnerving for the other person if he arrives too early. So Henry waits in his car until one minute before he is due to arrive.*

Keeping your word is a simple matter of the Golden Rule: "Do unto others as you want them to do unto you." Generally people know this, but they do not always do it. When you fulfill your obligations, your promises and deeds correspond perfectly.

7

Good
Sportsmanship

Good sportsmanship means behaving in a civil, charitable way when in competition with others. Competition does not have to be on a basketball court or in a chess tournament. People compete for jobs, attention, promotions, recognition, and even mates. Whether you win, lose, or do not even qualify, you still have many chances to show good sportsmanship. Good sportsmanship recognizes the dignity and worth of others. "Love does no wrong to a neighbor; therefore, love is the fulfilling of the law," wrote the Apostle Paul (Rm 13:10). Good sportsmanship does good to others.

Become a Good Loser

In life, more people lose than win. Consider how few win the lottery or bingo. Although many apply, only a few win scholarships or are hired for jobs. Often you have no direct dealings with those who best you, but you do deal with yourself and others. Your charity, or lack of it, toward the winner will influence how beloved you become to others.

Everyone loves a cheerful giver, but everyone loves a cheerful loser, too. What possible benefit could you realize by complaining, judging, or looking for sour grapes? Instead, wish the winners well and trust that they deserve the victory. *Since they presented dairy foods demonstrations in 4–H public speaking contests, Linda and Lea often competed with Debbie and Diane. Both teams gave excellent presentations and would most often place first and second. The four young ladies got to be friends with one another, each team congratulating the other for a job well done,*

64

no matter which team placed first. More than once they enjoyed a good laugh when, in one competition, Linda and Lea placed ahead of Debbie and Diane, but, in the next event with the exact same presentations, the order was reversed.

Be a Good Winner

Wnners ought not gloat. Charitable persons do not rejoice at their brother's fall. Moral theologians call such an attitude "gaudium de malo," that is, joy in evil or licking one's lips over another's defeat or downfall, particularly of someone whom you envy. Gloating is an insidious temptation. Certainly winners should rejoice, but exulting over an opponent's loss offends all charity. Instead of sneering, shake hands with the loser or offer a hug of consolation. Tell the person how well he or she played and offer good wishes for the next competition.

Accept Correction

Everyone receives many corrections in life — everyone is imperfect. Accept some corrections and dismiss others. How you accept correction indicates how loving you are. Most admire people who accept it. And most dislike those who think that they are always right. *Bernice thinks that many people make mistakes, but not her. At different times of her life, she found fault with teachers, classmates, parents, siblings, doctors, and bosses. The only one who never seemed to be at fault was Bernice. She complains that she is the product of her alcoholic father and neglectful mother and of illnesses that sap her mental and physical strength. Her doctors misdiagnose her, no one understands her, her friends evade her, and her bosses are unsympathetic. She cannot retain a job so she demands money from her relatives, who give it to her. Those who have tried to correct her are met with a litany of all her woes, and the correction goes unheeded because, of course, it is unfounded. Bernice laments the fact that she is approaching forty but has never had a serious boyfriend.*
Because you may be sensitive or prideful, you may have to learn how to accept correction. First, do not dismiss it or laugh about it as if it were unimportant. Do not disregard it in an attempt to prove that you were right. Do not let it devastate you, either. Reject the idea that the other person considers you worthless, inept, or stupid. And do not consider

yourself dimwitted. Think of yourself as a student in the School of Wisdom. Like all students in that school, you will be corrected at times. Remember your elementary school days. When you were in second grade and mispronounced a word, your teacher corrected you. You might have felt embarrassed, but you soon got over it. Correction as an adult might be embarrassing, too, but life goes on.

When you are corrected, assume that the person who corrected you was sincere and immediately offer your thanks. Thanking the person does not mean that you agree. Simply say, "Thanks for that suggestion. I appreciate your telling me." Then evaluate the admonition. You might want to consult others, too. Were you wrong? Do you need to change? If so, how can you improve?

Elevate Others above Yourself

Charitable people do not muddy others' reputations or maliciously plot against them. Rather they congratulate others for jobs well done and strive to make others look good. *Pearl, the executive director of a nonprofit organization, often receives praise for the quality of her work. She returns every compliment by referring to others who also worked on the project so that they, and not she, receive the credit.*

Charitable people not only are willing to make others look better; they also are willing to help them to be better. To prefer the last place and to help another achieve the first reveals the true nature of love. Become more lovable by helping others to be their best. *An author of several published books, Jacqueline frequently critiques, without charge, books and articles written by rookie authors. She considers this payback for a favor from a college professor when Jacqueline was a college freshman. A published author himself, that professor took the time to read Jacqueline's amateur writing and to give her suggestions on style and content.*

Jealousy and Envy

Occasionally you may want something that someone else has. That could be a good name, a top grade, a special friend, a great job, or a beautiful face. There is nothing wrong with wanting. Envy rears its ugly head when you wish ill to or think ill of the person who has what you want. You grumble because someone is more successful, more respected, more winsome, or more loved than you are. Or you undermine their achievement with petty comments intended to belittle the one whom you envy. In *Othello*, Shakespeare characterized jealousy as a green-eyed monster, a cat that toys with its food before killing it. In addition to being the color of a cat's eyes, green also characterizes illness and signifies growth. Certainly the sick emotion of jealousy, if not restrained, will grow into a monster-like passion that destroys not only the jealous person's peace of mind but also his or her life. How many times have you read about a jealous lover killing a rival?

If you recognize jealousy in yourself, battle it in a loving way. Pray for the prosperity of the individual whom you envy. Ask the Lord to consider your every jealous or bitter thought as a prayer for your rival. Pray that God will bless that person above yourself and will grant him or her even more of the trait that you envy. *Ingrid was wounded by a couple whom she had considered to be her friends. Business that used to come her way now went to them, and she felt anger and jealousy toward the prosperous twosome. With her feelings paralyzing her, Ingrid began to pray, "Lord, let my every bitter thought about them become a prayer for them. Grow their business above my own and make them capable proprietors. Prosper them more every time I think ill of them." Whenever Ingrid felt jealous, she prayed this sort of prayer and, after many months, she actually was wishing them well.*

Forgive and Pardon

Eleanor considered her husband James, a dedicated physician, to be a saint. Many people agreed with her. One evening she came into the living room and, for the first time in their fifty years of marriage, saw him crying. He had written to Attorney Gruff, who managed James' estate, which at the time was the object of family disputes. James had offered to help in any way he could to resolve these disagreements. In his reply, Gruff told James to "go to hell." Even ten years after James had died, Eleanor refused to forgive Gruff.

Was Eleanor justified in her attitude? Not if she wanted to become more lovable. Bearing a grudge hurts the one who bears it and others who know about it. *Brother and sister, Eric and Clarissa had no idea how their feud made life more difficult for their other siblings. Although their different personalities often clashed, they were fairly good friends until Clarissa refused to attend Eric's wedding when he married outside their church. For years the two did not speak to one another. Finally,*

Eric had enough. He approached Clarissa and the two reconciled. This eased things for the entire family which, up until that time, had to be careful not to invite both to the same family gathering.

For some people, forgiving hurts presents no problem because they embrace the Stoic ideal of freedom from passions. Since stoics claim to feel no hurt, they have nothing to heal. But stoics do not feel love, either. If you want to become lovable, you must feel love and many other emotions as well. You must learn to channel those feelings in loving ways toward God and others.

Grudges thrive on bitterness. Those who harbor them are never as happy as they would be if they forgave. Jesus valued forgiveness so highly that, when asked for instructions on how to pray, he said to begin by forgiving enemies (those who have hurt you) so that God will forgive you. Here are the exact words: "And forgive us our debts [sins] as we also have forgiven our debtors [those who have sinned against us]" (Mt 6:12).

A charitable person does not harbor grudges and resentment, but banishes all memory of injuries. God will punish you severely, Jesus said, "if you do not forgive your brother or sister from your heart" (Mt 18:35). Jesus loved others more than you ever could. Yet he was hurt by others in more ways than can be imagined. Nevertheless, he forgave everything by dying for those who abused him. He invites you to measure your forgiveness by the yardstick of his example. *Father Benedict Groeschel tells the story of Father George Wong, a Chinese Jesuit imprisoned for fifteen years and forced to work on a labor farm for another fifteen years, all because of his faith. Father Wong remained loyal to his faith and attributes his survival to God. He could have been angry and bitter, but instead was gentle and forgiving.*[1]

The biggest injuries require the most profound forgiveness. Forgiving someone for eating the chocolate cookie that you were saving for yourself is much easier than forgiving a drunk driver for killing your teenager. When someone is inexcusably and irreparably hurt, forgiveness can be almost impossible. Forgiveness can come only with God's grace. If you ask for that grace, God will grant it. *As a child, Andrea had been abused by her mother. After a profound religious experience, Andrea chose to release the anger, bitterness, and resentment that had been consuming her spiritually for years. Without feeling forgiving in the least, she chose to pray for and to forgive her mother. In time, Andrea realized that she really had forgiven. Today she visits her elderly mother several times a week and*

*does her grocery shopping, drives her to appointments, and takes her on
outings. A few years ago, Andrea discovered that her husband was having
an affair. Distraught and angry, Andrea again decided to forgive. Rather
than eject Kirk from the house, she moved into another bedroom so that
both parents would be home for their teenaged children. The children are
now out of the house and Andrea has her own apartment, but she and
Kirk remain such good friends that Kirk came to her for consolation and
support when his mistress jilted him.*

National, ethnic, or family grudges lay "collective guilt" on those
who belong to a group that has done others wrong. Grudges against
peoples, families, or nations can hurt those who personally had nothing
to do with the injury, but more often they hurt the opinionist. *An African-
American, Adam did not trust Caucasians, so he avoided socializing
with them until his college basketball teammate Luigi succeeded in
befriending him and in introducing him to several Caucasian buddies.
Felix, who is from Massachusetts, will not associate with Southerners
because of their role in the Civil War, nor will he attend courses or
lectures given by a professor with a Southern accent.*

Such grudges should not be dismissed, nor should they be overlooked.
Try to heal them. Begin by mingling with those whom you resent.
Suppose that you are a Jew whose memory of the Holocaust makes it
impossible for you to be around those of German descent. To conquer this
attitude, you must do what you are avoiding. Take a two-week vacation to
Germany, volunteer to work on a German festival in your community, or
find people with German last names in the local nursing home and visit
them. You will discover that Germans are people just like you. Heal your
grudges instead of allowing them to enslave you. Then you will release
anger, smile more easily, and quench any smoldering desire for revenge.

If you are harboring animosity toward someone, how do you begin to
forgive? *Christopher News Note #409* offers these suggestions:

> Recognize that a problem exists
> Acknowledge the pain that you feel — or caused
> Ask for help, guidance, another opinion
> Do one small, concrete thing to create change
> Make amends if appropriate
> Remember that you always have choices
> Pray for strength, courage, healing
> [we would add: understanding]

Share what you have learned with others
Do not give up hope or extinguish it in others
Forgive yourself. Forgive others.

In addition to the suggestions on this list, pray daily for those who have harmed you. In that way, you bring good out of evil, defeating the devil's purpose and turning a temptation into a blessing. Just as you are one of God's children, so is each person who hurt you. That makes you siblings! God the Father cares about all his children. Praying for another person proves that you, too, want to care about him or her.

In addition to praying, choose to forgive your enemy. You may not feel forgiving. That feeling may come much later. *Motivational speaker Charlie Osburn tells how he could not bring himself to forgive the next door neighbor who for two years had abused two of Charlie's children. Spiraling downward into alcoholism, hatred, and bitterness, for nearly ten years Charlie lived with an unforgiving heart. Then, through the counsel of his friend Father James Smith, he finally realized that he had to forgive his neighbor. One day as he got out of his car, Charlie saw the abuser getting out of his. Inspired, Charlie walked over and embraced him, saying, "I forgive you." Charlie meant what he said. His forgiveness had a profound effect on the abuser, who after many years returned to the sacraments.*[2]

Releasing grudges and resentments leaves more time and energy because you are not constantly replaying the hurt. You see those you used to hate in a new light. Anger is changed into compassion for those you have forgiven.

8
Thoughtfulness

Thoughtfulness, which is one way to care, makes life easier for others. However, benevolence requires balance. Doing too much for people can be suffocating, not thoughtful. *Frail, elderly Margaret lived alone and tried to care for her house. When her daughter-in-law Alice came to clean, Margaret said she was able to do it herself, although Alice could see that the place needed attention. Finally, instead of offering to clean the whole house, Alice offered to scrub the kitchen floor and to have one of her children vacuum the carpeting. Margaret accepted this help. She needed the dignity of being considered able to care for herself, at least in part.*

Kindness, whether in words or deeds, is thoughtfulness in action. But it begins in the mind. When you think kindly of others, kind words and deeds follow. *Dennis lived with his parents his entire life. When they died in their nineties, he was close to seventy. Members of his church, knowing that this shy bachelor had little experience in cooking, sent him meals to heat up in the oven or microwave.*

Kindness is a type of altruism that involves alertness and sensitivity to the feelings and needs of others. It is coupled with a desire never to cause unnecessary pain, but to be a source of happiness and of help. Whoever needs assistance is a neighbor, even if he or she lives on the other side of the planet. *When Anastasia developed breast cancer, her family was dismayed, not only because of the cancer but because no hospital in her country possessed state-of-the-art technology to treat her condition. However, Anastasia had developed a regular email correspondence with the Morgan family. They invited her to their country to live in their home for many months while receiving treatment at one of the best hospitals in the world. After months of surgery and chemotherapy, Anastasia returned home, cancer-free.*

Listen

Communication is a two-way street, but some people seem to consider it a one-way alley. They answer a question before the other has finished asking it. Or they will not listen at all. Do they believe that others could not possibly share something unique, relevant, or interesting? Some love to talk without giving others a chance to share. Others prefer the solitude of the newspaper or their computer screen if they cannot monopolize the conversation.

Cardinal Giovanni Mercati, reputed to be a great scholar, took as his motto, "Semper paratus doceri" — "always ready to be taught," or "open to instruction."[1] No wonder he had such a reputation! People will comment on your conversational skill, not if you actually converse, but if you listen to them while they are talking.

Have you ever noticed that you remember nearly everything that someone you love says? Listening means not just hearing sounds but understanding and feeling empathy with the speaker. If you are not a good listener, you can become one. The next time that you engage in conversation, do more than nod or utter one-word acknowledgements. Respond to speakers without telling them that they are right or wrong. Instead, share comments that indicate what you understand. Such interaction generally draws others into sharing more. Once you understand another person, you may be able to offer an opinion. Move a conversation along by rephrasing a person's comments and adding a question. Here is a sample dialog:

Other: I was never so scared in my life.

You: Sounds like you were really terrified. What happened?

Other: We were in the car on the way home from shopping and this huge truck came barreling out of a side street right for us.

You: Sounds like you thought you were going to be hit.

Other: Yes! And he almost did hit us. He came so close that I could have touched the cab with my hand. I was never so scared in my life!

You: That was close. Did he stop at all?

Other: He kept going. What a jerk! Here he almost kills us and zips on by like we were nothing.

You: Imagine not even stopping when he almost hits you. Did you call the police?

Begin a Conversation

Occasionally you might be at a social gathering where you hardly know anyone. Instead of feeling awkward and focusing on yourself, do the loving thing and think about the others around you. Those quietly standing alone probably do not have a partner either. Walk over and begin a conversation!

"Who, me?" you may be saying. Yes, you. Striking up a conversation makes the other person feel comfortable and noticed. Everybody wants to be recognized, and talking to someone makes that happen. Sometimes beginning a conversation with a wallflower can lead to a friendship. So how do you do it?

Do not "accidentally" spill your martini on someone's shoes! Use a question or a remark to open conversation. Introduce yourself and extend your hand while saying, "Hi, I am _____. And you are?" Use the person's name in your next remark. "Nice tie you have there, Bert." Follow this up with a comment. "Are you a race car fan?" would be a reasonable question if Bert's tie portrays demolition derbies. If car racing interests Bert, you could spend an entire evening listening to him share his opinions and experiences. However, the person to whom you introduce yourself may appear bland and not talkative. How do you react if the other person answers every question with "Yes," "No," or "I don't know"? Phrase all your questions so that they cannot be answered yes or no. Instead of, "Is that pastry tasty?" ask, "I have not seen that pastry. What does it taste like? Where in the buffet did you find it?" If the person continues to speak in monosyllables, you might elicit more sharing if you share about yourself. "I tend to go for spicy pastries myself. How about you?" It is impolite at gatherings to spend the whole evening with one person, so look for other loners with whom to try out your conversational skills. If you persevere, you will find someone who will share a conversation.

Walk in Another's Moccasins

Try to determine the interests, immediate goals, and backgrounds of the new people you meet. If you do not try to understand others' needs, you might make a mistake when you try to be loving. *Cynthia and her parents were touring a college to which they thought she might apply. Visiting the science department, they were greeted by Professor Hampton, who was in charge of the laboratories. He was glad to tell them all about his department, and did it politely, he thought; however it took the family two hours to get away. Cynthia did not appreciate having little time left for the rest of the tour. Professor Hampton would have done well had he taken the time to put himself into Cynthia's place. Then he would have known that she wanted to tour the entire campus, not just his department. He would have given a brief tour and then sent her and her parents to the next professor.*

Phone Calls

Consider the other person's needs when planning a phone call. When is a good time to call? What may be a good time for you may be a poor time for someone else. In what time zone does the other person live? How many hours is the time ahead or behind yours? Does the other sleep late or go to bed early? What are the family's mealtimes or the usual mealtimes in that country? In the United States, most people are awake by 9 a.m. and getting ready for bed after 9 p.m. Mealtimes generally fall around noon and 6 p.m. In other countries, this is not the case. In Jamaica, for example, businesses routinely open at 7:30 a.m., close down for a few hours around noon for the siesta, and reopen from later in the afternoon until well into the evening. In some countries people eat their meals quickly, but in others they may take several hours. Besides these variations, individuals have different routines which correspond to their personal body clocks and work schedules. *Sophia awoke at 3:30 a.m., ate lunch at 11 a.m., dinner at 4 p.m., and was in bed before 7:30 p.m. Phoning Sophia at 5:30 a.m. before she went for her morning walk was a good time to reach her. However, the ringing phone would wake up her still-sleeping husband.*

Help with Advice

People generally do not appreciate unsolicited advice. If you keep in mind the other person's needs and motivations you will be able to offer appropriate suggestions, help, or encouragement. Begin by asking others for their advice. They will be flattered that you consulted them and generally will be more receptive to listening to your recommendations. *For example, Tomasina thought that her friend Josephine cooked with too much fat. To help her cook in a healthier manner, Tomasina might first ask what cookbooks or recipes Josephine uses. Then Tomasina could study the recipes and refer to specific ones in making suggestions. She might begin by saying, "Do you know that doctors have determined that excessive fat is not good for you? They say to reduce the fat in many recipes or substitute something healthier." Then she could suggest reducing the ¾ cup of butter in a pound cake recipe to ½ cup of margarine or browning stew meat in olive oil instead of in bacon grease.*

Not everyone will ask for counsel. Some of those who do are not really looking for advice. They just want someone to listen to their woes. On the other hand, some of those who struggle in silence would like you to volunteer your input or help. How will you know the difference? Proceed cautiously. Ask, "Would you like some help?" If the response is, "No. I know what to do. I am just complaining," smile and say, "OK. Just thought I would ask." If the individual would like to hear what you have to say, share your thoughts respectfully. Never belittle anyone by using phrases such as, "It is simple" or "That is so obvious." Such casual remarks make a person feel stupid for not having thought of the solution. Instead say, "Things like this can stymie a person. Have you thought of trying this?" Then share your idea. Sharing this way advances your ideas while respecting the other person.

Keep Secrets

Everyone needs to communicate. Friendships blossom between individuals who share ideals, hopes, and experiences. But people do not have the right to know everything about each other. Even best friends harbor secrets. And so it should be. Do not share hurtful things unless a greater good can come from knowing. *If, years before any of them were wed, Marci had sexual relations with the man whom her best friend Grace eventually married, it may not be in Grace's best interest to know. Marci can keep Grace as a close friend, even while keeping this secret.*

Similarly, unless doing so would be immoral, respect the wishes of someone who shares a secret and asks that you not tell. For example, it would be wrong not to alert the police to a neighbor engaged in filming child pornography, but it would be right to keep the secret of another neighbor's battle with and victory over addiction.

You might initiate a secret yourself if you wish to do a good deed without embarrassing someone. *Nicholas of Bari secretly tossed through*

the window of a poor man's house enough money for a dowry for his three
daughters, so that they could marry rather than be sold into prostitution.
This kind bishop has been forever immortalized as Good Saint Nick or
Santa Claus.[2]

Be Careful with Jokes

Most people like others who have a good sense of humor. Telling
jokes could make you more likable because everyone enjoys a good
laugh. But tell appropriate jokes. Pick jokes that do not stereotype or
belittle any race, nation, or character trait. Look over books or internet
sites to find "clean" jokes that do not inadvertently offend someone.
Keep a notebook of jokes and memorize them. Practice in front of a
mirror with a tape recorder. When you feel comfortable, share an
appropriate joke at an appropriate moment, and watch the number of
your friends increase.

Smile

Some people are afraid to smile. Others are "uptight" or have a natural
glare or frown that could make friendships difficult. *Pastor Brogan*
mentioned to his friend Rabbi Grau that he could not understand why
others were always glaring at him. The Rabbi replied, "Because you
look like you are always glaring at them." Even though he was a very
gentle soul, the pastor did not realize how severe he looked. He needed to
practice softening his naturally harsh expression.
A smile encourages others. Smiling is the cheapest and one of the
easiest ways to become lovable. If you find smiling difficult, practice!
Look at yourself in a mirror. Try different smiles. See which looks good
on you. Then practice in public. Smile at appropriate times when talking
and when listening. In time, you will smile spontaneously.

Encourage

Encouraging others will certainly make you more lovable. But be
genuine. Do not encourage someone to do something beyond his or her
strength. Do not tell a teen who thinks that he is going to become a multi-
million-dollar rock star in six months, "I bet you will" if you think that he

is being impractical. On the other hand, do not blurt out, "That will never happen." Instead ask, "Are you practicing?" Or, if you do mean it, "You have a lot of talent. I hope you go far." Comments like these encourage the teen to work toward the goal without implying that he might attain it within an unrealistic time frame.

Life's inevitable disappointments and setbacks teach lessons and build strengths. Sometimes people do not understand that they can turn troubles into triumphs. They need encouragement. Do you know someone who could offer advice? Are you aware of sources of helpful information? Can you research the problem or work toward a solution? Offer whatever help you can give. Sometimes troubled persons respond if you listen to and pray for and with them. Prayer and a receptive ear are priceless gifts.

Go Beyond What Is Required

Being thoughtful means doing more than the minimum. Jesus referred to this when he said, "If anyone forces you to go one mile, go also the second mile. Give to everyone who begs from you, and do not refuse anyone who wants to borrow from you" (Mt 5:41–42). *Brother Juniper, one of Saint Francis' first friars, mastered going beyond what is required. He had so much pity and compassion for the poor that when he saw anyone badly clothed or bare, he would immediately rip off his sleeve or cowl or some piece of his habit and give it to the poor man. And so the guardian ordered him under obedience not to give all or part of his habit to anyone. A few days later it happened that he met a poor man who was almost naked and who begged Brother Juniper for the love of God to give him something. Juniper said to him compassionately: "My dear man. I have nothing to give you except my habit — and my superior has told me under obedience not to give it or part of it to anyone. But if you pull it off my back, I certainly will not prevent you." The beggar immediately pulled the habit off, inside out, and went off, leaving the generous brother naked.*[3] If you open your spiritual eyes, you will see many ways in which you can do more than is required. The following examples might raise your awareness. If you have the talent, use calligraphy even if only legible printing is required. Bring your garden produce to a neighbor. Invite someone to go ahead of you in the grocery line. Doing more than the minimum will give you great satisfaction.

Remember Special Days

Keep a calendar to record loved ones' special days. Palm Pilots and electronic calendars will even remind you. If you are not technically savvy, a perpetual calendar will do. On a spiral-bound or Rolodex calendar with one day per page, record on the appropriate date the occasion (birthday, anniversary, or other occasion) to be acknowledged. Keep the calendar from year to year and remember to look at it! For each special day, send a card or make a phone call. Such simple gestures show love.

Think Before You Speak

Are you too quick to speak? James advises you in his Epistle to be "slow to speak" (Jas 1:19). Counting to ten before you reply works well whether or not you may reply in anger. A hasty comment can be unloving because you might say something you could regret. Or you might answer incorrectly or promise what you cannot deliver. Develop the "pregnant pause." Before blurting out something, wait. As advised earlier, a simple, "Let me think about that," allows time to formulate an appropriate response.

Be Tidy

Two environments make many people uncomfortable. A squeaky clean and impeccably organized one makes people uncomfortable because it gives the impression that it is strictly for display. Even sitting seems out of place. Sometimes it is! *Ms. Gifford, a second grade teacher, drove to pick up a friend for a school meeting. Ms. Hanson was not ready so Ms. Gifford sat in a rocking chair in the pristine living room to wait. Ms. Hanson's mother came in and cautioned, "No rocking! You might bump and scratch the wall!" Taken aback by the comment, the teacher felt suddenly reduced to the age of the children she taught — seven.*

The second uncomfortable environment is messy, dirty, and disorganized. Guests wonder if the place is sanitary or safe. Disorder makes guests feel confused and uncomfortable. *Jenny's friend Bea has one dog, three cats, and a house piled with stuff and dirty dishes. When Jenny visits, Bea has to clear a space on the table to put down a cup of coffee. Jenny always comes away from Bea's house feeling vaguely ill.*

If you are not naturally tidy, strive to improve when visiting others.

Hang up your coat in your friend's closet or drape it over a chair. After a meal, put your dishes into the sink. Before you leave, replace any items you may have moved, including your kitchen chair.

Tidiness also means putting things away in your own home. Disorder causes frustration. How much time is wasted and how many arguments sparked when a family member cannot find something? Maintaining a tidy house shows loving concern for all who live there. It does not mean being compulsive. If you have a place for everything and you try to keep things in place, however, everyone in your family can find things more easily. Nevertheless, do not expect a messy house to remain tidy once you straighten it. Permanent changes require educating the people who live there. If everyone works together, a house can become neater. Here are some tips:

- Giving away or throwing away whatever you can will leave fewer things to keep straightened.

- Use cabinets and closets and close the doors.

- Recycle newspapers more than a week old.

- Put trash into waste cans immediately.

- Put dirty dishes and cups into the sink or dishwasher. Wash dishes daily.

- In every room keep a broom and dustpan or a carpet sweeper. Use them every other day.

- Dust weekly.

- Cover piles of stuff with a pretty blanket.

- Get a headset for the phone and clean up while making or receiving calls.

- Allow family members who leave their own bedrooms messy the freedom to live as they wish, but close their doors.

"Cleanliness is next to godliness" because God is Love, and being clean and tidy is certainly loving.

Pick Up Trash

Caring people do not toss trash into a street or parking lot, but you can do better than merely using the waste receptacle. Pick up somebody else's trash. Not only do you show respect for the environment, but you also assist employees whose job is to clean up while transforming a messy scene into a pleasant one. *When Karin takes her daily walk, she carries the plastic bag from her morning paper. She fills it with roadside trash and, when she gets home, separates the garbage from the recyclables. Unlike other streets in the neighborhood, Karin's street is clean.*

Keep a garbage bag in your car for wrappers and when you park, pick up other nearby trash and empty it all into a receptacle. If there is none, take the trash home to discard. The more you look for trash to pick up, the more you will find.

Be Kind for Kindness' Sake

A Buddhist maxim states, "If you light a lamp for somebody, it will also brighten your path."[4] Kindness brings its own rewards. Being kind to others in the hopes that you will be able to control them, however, is manipulative and deceitful. Such a charade cannot continue for long because no matter how kind you are you cannot possess people or make them do what you want. Everyone has personal freedom.

On the other hand, you can return kindness shown to you. *Elissa's mom was a big help in getting her business up and running. Mom designed the website, helped write advertising, and referred friends. Although Elissa was watching her pennies, she thanked her mom by treating her to a movie.*

Kindness will help others love us, but the intensity of that love cannot be predetermined. Kindness can lead to a broken heart if you become emotionally involved with the person you are trying to help. *Miss Alma, the protagonist of Tennessee Williams' play* Summer and Smoke, *is altruistic. When her high school sweetheart John comes back to town after finishing medical school, she tries to help him, as she has helped so many other people. She wants to cure him of his drinking, but she also desperately wants to marry him. She does cure him, but his falling in love with her protégée Nellie leaves Alma emotionally unstrung.*

Expecting repayment for a thoughtful act may lead to disappointment. Do good things simply to do them, not because the recipient will reciprocate. Jesus advised doing good for which you cannot be thanked. As an example, he suggested inviting poor people and beggars to a wedding feast because they cannot bring expensive gifts nor can they extend an invitation in return. In cases like this, God repays charity with wondrous heavenly rewards (see Lk 14:12–14). *Philip Yancey mentions a bride-to-be whose story appeared in the* Boston Globe *in 1990 and who could have used Jesus' story as a basis for her own banquet. Although ten years earlier this woman had lived in a homeless shelter, she had found a well-paying job. After she booked the reception at the Hyatt Hotel in downtown Boston, signed a contract and gave a non-refundable deposit, the groom-to-be changed his mind. Once she recovered from her disappointment and anger, she decided to proceed with the banquet by inviting those who could never repay her. She sent invitations to all the homeless shelters and rescue missions in the city. The poor and down-trodden, bag ladies and addicts, came in droves to enjoy an unforgettable evening of food, drink, and dance.*[5]

Thoughtfulness in Families

It often is easier to be thoughtful to strangers and friends than to those in your own family. After all, strangers and friends are often grateful for your kindness while family members may take it for granted. One family's teens had developed the habit of saying, "If you don't want to drive us to events, help us with homework, or pick up after us, why did you have kids?" They saw no reason to be grateful for what they considered parental duty.

Spouses need to cultivate thoughtfulness toward one another. Some have become so accustomed to each other that "familiarity breeds contempt" seems written about them. Gregory the Great (Admonition 28) advises spouses to "study to please their consorts without offence to their Maker ... and not fail to desire the things that are God's." Spouses must love one another, but above all God, recognizing that both loves exist simultaneously. God is probably not pleased if a wife snaps at a husband who interrupts her prayers with a question.

Gregory goes on, "The married are to be admonished to bear with mutual patience the things in which they sometimes displease each other, and to assist each other to salvation by mutual encouragement.... They are also to consider not so much what each has to endure from the other, as what the other is made to endure." In other words, you might be putting up with your spouse's idiosyncrasies, but your spouse is putting up with yours, too. The song that ends *The Fantastiks* recalls, in the winter of life, the blossoming of love that took place much earlier. "Deep in December it's nice to remember / The fire of September that made us mellow."[6] Spouses should remember the fire of their earlier love and treat each other now the way they would have treated each other then, when love was new.

Married Love

Gregory (Admonition 28) discusses something not much talked about these days. "The married must bear in mind that they are united in wedlock for the purpose of procreation." Indeed, this has to be true. Why does the marital act exist if not for procreation? Of the many ways to show love, only intercourse leads to new life. It goes without saying, perhaps, that Catholics are obliged to follow the Church's teachings on sexuality. Only a married husband and wife may legitimately have sexual relations. Everyone else can show their love in non-sexual ways.

Thoughtfulness in marriage means respecting the most intimate of unions for what God intended it to be. Spouses must be open to new life, be their child healthy or sickly. Therefore the Catholic Church permits only natural family planning, which is effective if used properly. Spouses may refrain from sexual union to avoid conception only for valid reasons and in complete concern and love for the other. If they conceive, intentionally or otherwise, parents must accept the child even if the family faces great difficulties and even if the baby has a serious or even a fatal condition. If they cannot raise a child parents must choose adoption or foster care rather than abortion or early termination of pregnancy, both of which cause the baby's death.[7] The same fabric of love interweaves respect for marriage, for spouses, for spousal union, and for all children conceived. *Hannah and Emery had not been trying to get pregnant, but it happened. They welcomed this, their eighth baby. Prenatal testing, however, indicated that unborn Greta had a lethal form of dwarfism. Their faith in God and in one another supported them during the pregnancy as they researched every possible treatment to help Greta if she survived. After her birth, she lived for eighteen minutes. Faith and love transported Emery and Hannah through the loss to healing.*

Pace Yourself

Married couples with children spend a great deal of time exercising the Spiritual and Corporal Works of Mercy* in their own families. Those without children or who are single may have more time to exercise the Spiritual and Corporal Works of Mercy with others. No matter how you show love to other people, remember to exercise love toward yourself, too. Whether you are married or not, trying to do too much for too many leads to burnout. Then you will be doing nothing for anyone. Jesus told us, "You always have the poor with you" (Mk 14:7). No matter how many people you help, you could always find more. No one can help everyone.

Who should be helped, and how much? First, pray. Ask God to show you how to minister, and then do your best, take care of yourself, relax, sleep. You will be most thoughtful of others if you do not run yourself into the ground. *Becky, a busy mom and grandmother, frequently is asked to help with numerous causes. She always responds, "Let me pray about that, see what word God gives me from Scripture, and then get back to you."*

The stress of being too busy can cause abruptness with others. An aphorism states, "If the devil can't make you bad, he'll make you busy."[8] Snapping at others because of pressure to do more than is possible, in less than the time available, is a consequence of failing to pace yourself.

Doing too much causes another problem. It reduces your time with God. When activity must be cut back, prayer seems to be the first to go. *One day a harried bishop came to visit the saintly Curé d'Ars. The*

---

* The **Spiritual Works of Mercy** are:
Instruct the ignorant
Advise the doubtful
Correct sinners
Be patient with those in error or who do wrong
Forgive offenses
Comfort the afflicted
Pray for the living and the dead

The **Corporal Works of Mercy** are:
Feed the hungry
Give drink to the thirsty
Clothe the naked
Shelter the homeless
Visit the sick and imprisoned
Ransom the captive
Bury the dead

bishop complained that he was too busy to complete all his work. The Curé advised him, "If you are busy, you need to pray an hour a day." Taken aback, the bishop replied, "But you do not understand. I am so busy that I do not have time to pray." The Curé calmly answered, "My dear bishop, if you are that busy, you need to pray two hours a day."[9] What did the Curé mean? The more you have to do, the more you need to seek God. Prayer is not something to fit into your leisure. It is the first thing to do!

American social activist Dorothy Day offered this advice to harried people: If you cannot meet your standards, "lower your standards."[10] She did not mean "do shoddy work." She meant, "Evaluate your life style. Are you expecting too much from other people? Are you trying to achieve unrealistic goals? Are you doing tasks that are unnecessary or too complex? How can you simplify your life or, if you are in a position of authority, the lives of those for whom you are responsible?" *Lorraine took Dorothy Day's words to heart. Preoccupied with raising five children, Lorraine concluded that the additional chores of preparing for Christmas were causing her too much stress. So, instead of baking several kinds of homemade cookies, she prepared cakes from store-bought mixes and frostings. Instead of decorating a large, real tree, she purchased a small artificial one that she could store each year with the decorations on it. Instead of writing out Christmas cards, she typed the addresses so that they could be printed on self-adhesive labels, and she wrote and photocopied a Christmas letter.*

If you are not sure how to begin to simplify your life, pray about what to do first. Ask God for the courage to make changes that will bring peace and help you be more loving to others. Being loving does not require doing everything. Far better to act with love than with anxiety. *Sue Monk Kidd "wanted to be supermom, superwife, successful career woman, church pillar, community helper and fulfilled person, all at once.... I was defining my life around those Herculean expectations."*[11] *The possibility of heart disease forced Sue to re-evaluate her lifestyle. Through prayer and courage to change, she gradually discovered that God could love her for who she was, not for what she did.*

Thoughtfulness begins by asking God for the virtue. The grace of the Holy Spirit will let you become more attentive to others' needs as well as to your own. Working to make life more comfortable for everyone certainly shows love.

9
Courtesy

Respect for others and attention to their needs naturally leads to courtesy. Courteous people extend their respect and attention to everyone. Medieval knights valued courtesy highly. *Francis of Assisi, who once aspired to knighthood, insisted that his friars be courteous. One winter evening, Francis and a companion visited the castle of a rich and powerful nobleman, who embraced the friars, washed their muddy feet, and kissed them. Then he lit a great fire, prepared a sumptuous feast, and served it himself. After the meal, he offered to pay for anything that the friars needed. Concerning this man's actions, Francis commented, "Courtesy is one of the qualities of God, who courteously gives His sun and His rain and everything to the just and to the unjust. And courtesy is sister to charity. It extinguishes hatred and keeps love alive." Francis felt that the nobleman would make a good friar and prayed that God grant the man the vocation. In time, he did enter Francis' Order.*[1]

The Courtesy of a Reply

Invitations to parties, weddings, and other events often request "the courtesy of a reply." Thinking "I do not have to respond if I cannot attend," is false reasoning. The host cannot read your mind. *Georgia and Derek mailed their wedding invitations and had included a "Please respond" card with a choice of entrées for the dinner. They also enclosed a stamped, addressed envelope. Two days before the caterer had to know how many of each entrée to prepare, Georgia and Derek had to spend hours on the phone, calling people who had not responded.*

It is also a courtesy to respond to phone calls and emails. Do not assume that the person will know that you received the message. *Edward had emailed his flight information to his dad. When he had not received a response by the day before he was to fly home for his college break, he had to re-send the information and ask if his dad would pick him up at the airport. His dad responded, "Oh, I did get that information a few weeks ago." But he had not emailed Edward about it. In a similar incident, Lily never returned a message on her answering machine. Her friend Hazel had to call again to ask her if she could come to dinner as planned. "Oh, sure," Lily said. Hazel replied, "I wanted to double check because sometimes you are not feeling well but do not phone to cancel."*

Write down the details of phone messages and give them to the person for whom they were intended. Do not delete the message from the machine until that person has responded. *Because her toddler was whining, Melinda was distracted when she retrieved a phone message. After scribbling down the information, she deleted the message, which was intended for her husband Steve, and gave him the information when he came home from work. Steve, however, did not recognize the name of the caller and, when he returned the call, no one at that number seemed to understand why he was calling.*

Take down the call-back information carefully, if a call is for someone else. Double check with the caller to be sure that you have recorded it correctly. It takes very little time to say, "Your name is Sally Smith and your number is 123–456–7890. Correct?"

Manners

In some places, a selfish individualism has replaced a sense of love and caring for one's neighbor. Thinking only of self causes table manners to deteriorate. Why? Because manners deal with the treatment of others. If you love others, good manners follow naturally. *The apostolic brief which numbered Germaine Cousin among the Blessed of the Catholic Church describes her as "A simple maiden, humble, and of lowly birth, but so greatly enlightened by the gifts of divine wisdom and understanding, and so remarkable for her transcendent virtues, that she shone like a star not only in her native France but throughout the Catholic Church."[2] Daughter of an agricultural laborer, Germaine suffered from birth with ill health and physical disability. Her mother died while Germaine was still an infant, her stepfather showed her no love, and her stepmother treated Germaine worse than the sheep which Germaine was sent to tend. Abused physically and verbally, Germaine was given scraps to eat and had to sleep in the stable or the open field. Nevertheless, Germaine shared her pittance with those poorer than she and also taught the village urchins about God. Her good manners and virtues came, not from her upbringing, but from her love of God and neighbor.*[3]

External Manners

Because rules of conduct vary from one society to another, good manners in one place may be poor manners in another. To avoid offending others, find out what constitutes good manners in the social setting where you find yourself.

Books on etiquette, even those written for children, offer valuable suggestions for someone who may never have been taught good manners or who may have grown lax regarding them. For example, in North America holding the door for the people behind you, waiting patiently in line, talking in a moderate tone on the telephone, and picking up after a dog all reveal good manners.

Good manners also can be developed by mingling with those who use them. At a formal social event observe the other guests. Not everyone at such functions will display good manners, but find those who do. Look for people who walk gracefully, chat quietly with others, and seem more interested in listening than in talking or eating.

Table Manners

At everyday meals, good manners — or a lack of them — stand out. Some are relatively trivial. Does it really matter which fork to use when eating salad? Others, which involve how to treat others, matter a great deal. Benedict the monk, a master of how to live in community, sees human society in terms of a healthy body whose every organ, bone, and muscle must fulfill its proper function in communion with the rest. Think of a soccer team. At every moment of the game, each player — striker, sweeper, goalkeeper — must do a prescribed part if the team is to succeed.

In Benedict's community, and in families and other social groups, meals provide a time for fellowship, for being together as teammates, so to speak. Benedict was firm in fostering community at meals. At the signal for a meal or for prayer, each monk was to hasten to his own place. If late, he was to take a place, visible to all, that the abbot had set apart. The monk could receive the spiritual nourishment of prayer and the physical nourishment of food, but not among the others. Separation from the community was considered a punishment.

Why? In Benedict's day, the community was a great good. Today, people tend to be individualistic. They eat when they want, where they want, and what they want. Benedict did not permit this. His monks were to eat what was served, only at the time it was served, and with the others. These rules foster good manners.[4] When each member of a family or a community eats and drinks separately, the sense of being part of a group that cares about each other fades. Sharing a meal is sharing of self. Emotionally healthy families plan at least one daily meal at which all the members are present.

At meals, be aware of others. That requires good manners, such as:

- Come to table promptly when called or at the proper time.

- Respectfully listen to or participate in mealtime prayer.

- Pass the food in the direction everyone agrees to.

- Say "please" and "thank you."

- Give others a chance to talk.

- Swallow before you speak.

- Indicate that you are listening by nodding or making a brief comment.

- Refrain from arguments.

- Remain at table until most or all are done eating.

- Use a napkin.

- Refrain from using a telephone or PDA while at table.

- Take small portions of food until all are served.

- Use silverware appropriately.

- Eat what is served without complaint.

- Eat moderately, neither overeating nor fasting.

- Be aware of hygiene. For example:

- • Do not a dip a cracker or vegetable that you have already bitten into a serving bowl.
- • Excuse yourself from the table to wash your hands if you have blown your nose or sneezed into a handkerchief.
- • Serve yourself with the utensils from the common bowls, not your own.
- • Do not return any of your food to the serving plate.

    ∞ Lift the food to your mouth; do not shovel it in.

    ∞ Do not touch moist food with your fingers.

    ∞ Decline food you prefer not to eat with a polite "No, thank you."

    ∞ Compliment the cook.

    ∞ Wipe your mouth with your napkin.

    ∞ Rest used silverware on a plate or napkin, not on the table.

    ∞ When finished, excuse yourself before leaving.

    ∞ Unless at a banquet or restaurant, carry dirty dishes to the sink.

Such simple rules make mealtime an opportunity to be loving.

Treat All as Equals

God made every human being equal. Each person — without regard to age, race, creed, sex, intelligence, education, income, place of residence, or social standing — deserves respect. Disrespecting others for any reason is the opposite of loving them. The image of God, God's presence in each person, is the basis of equality. Mother Teresa of Calcutta trained her nuns to see the Lord Jesus in the poorest of the poor. Because each sister looked for Christ's image, she was able to treat each person, whether the most wretched beggar or a diplomat, with dignity.

Parents, police officers, and public authorities deserve particular respect and obedience. Disagreement with them — or with anyone else, for that matter — never justifies insolence. If you disagree with someone, you must not imply you are in any way superior. Respect all individuals, regardless of their opinions, because they are made in God's image. *Pope John Paul II met and embraced the Communist mayor of Rome even though the philosophy and policies of the two men were worlds apart.*[5]

Treat Each One as Special

List twenty acquaintances; for each, write down a positive unique trait. Each person is one of a kind.

When treated as a unique creation, a person notices. Your attentiveness is a great compliment and a testimony to his or her worth. People naturally love those who pay attention to them. *Quinn has the knack of making everyone feel equally important. During a conversation, he looks directly at you and holds your gaze. He leans slightly forward in his chair, attentive to your words. He allows you to talk and acknowledges what you say with interest. Quinn treats you as special because he believes you really are.*

Having good manners means treating each person as equal to yourself, special in a good way, and worthy of respect. Manners make the social environment more inviting and friendly. Striving to create a pleasant environment for others shows love, and they will reciprocate your love and respect.

Internal Attitudes

Good manners also include your opinion of others. Strive to transcend prejudices. If you asume the best about other people and situations, you allow them to be all they can be. People and events often live up to or surpass expectations. *When invited to a party, Heidi assumes that she is going to have fun. Even if she attends alone, she assumes that she will meet people with whom she can chat. She assumes that the food will be good and the entertainment entertaining. Heidi has never been disappointed!*

Do Not Jump to Conclusions

Some people tend foolishly to make judgments or to act based on partial information. Those who jump to conclusions are not only impolite; they are often mistaken. Allow others to explain or demonstrate what they mean. Phrase your comments to show your understanding, but always allow others to explain fully. *Harriet aggravates her husband Mike by jumping to the conclusion that he is coming to ask her something if he happens to walk near her workroom. When she calls out, "What now?" Mike often replies abruptly, "I'm only walking past."*

Check Assumptions

Ascertaining that assumptions are valid before acting on them avoids much aggravation. Although an event was held at a certain time in the past, this year the planning committee may have made some changes. The friend you last saw six years ago might have divorced and remarried. When you make dinner plans, arrange ahead whether to meet at the restaurant or at your house. Always check your assumptions. *Because his older sister Betty's recent death from cancer depressed him, Mort was resting when the doorbell rang. He assumed that the caller was a member of a religious sect that had been evangelizing door to door in the neighborhood. In no mood to talk when he was grieving, Mort was not about to answer, but glanced out to see that the person was carrying flowers. Bolting out of his easy chair, he ran to the door and called back the florist. The sympathy bouquet filled three vases and brightened his day.*

Always assume the best about others, and about their words and actions. Sharon Ellison's book *Don't Be So Defensive!* details how many take offense by jumping to conclusions. *Emily felt hurt for weeks because she assumed that Rita had snubbed her. One day, meeting Rita by chance in the grocery store, she asked, "Are you mad at me?" Startled, Rita replied, "No! Why would you think I was?" "Because last month when you were shopping at The Friendly Five and Dime, you didn't even say hello to me." Rita remembered that shopping trip. Distracted by her two active toddlers, she barely had time to get what she needed before having to leave the store. She had not even noticed Emily.*

Keep Moods to Yourself

Moods affect everyone. If you feel depressed, cry or complain in a private place or with a confidant. Try not to spill your mood onto everyone around you. No one takes pleasure in the company of someone who is grumpy, complaining, or mean. Keep your moods, particularly the grim ones, to yourself. *When Jessica gets into one of her monthly moods, what she had patience with one day will upset her the next. Family members have learned to avoid her when she gets in these moods, lest she take out her frustration and pain on them. Others who know her less well believe that she has a bad attitude. Sadly, she has only one friend who, out of pity, puts up with her.*

No one deserves to be treated like garbage. If you cannot hide a bad mood, admit it. Say, "I apologize for being cranky. I cannot seem to shake this bad mood. I hope I will not snap, but, if I do, please forgive me." Or you might make a joke about it, at your own expense. "I apologize, but I seem to be a grizzly bear today. Grrrr!" Then try to keep to yourself until the anger goes away.

10
Putting Others First

Putting others first means putting self last. Not second or third, because if you are any place but last, then someone else remains behind you. Only the humble can put others ahead of themselves. Humility means realizing, as Father Frank Pavone says, "There is a God and he is not me."[1] Humble persons realize their own true value and the value of others, too. Everyone has equal worth, so out of love and respect for others put them ahead, hoping genuinely that good might come to them first. Putting others first imitates Christ who, as Lord of all, became a humble man and died for us. If that is not putting himself last, what is?

Selfless Service

Putting others first implies dedicated, ungrudging, selfless service that does not ask, "What is in it for me?" Christ singled out as the truly great in his Church those who put others first. One day his disciples were arguing about who was the greatest among them. Calling the twelve apostles to him, the Lord said, "Whoever wants to be first must be last of all and servant of all." To drive home the lesson, he placed a little child into their midst. "Whoever welcomes one such child in my name welcomes me, and whoever welcomes me welcomes not me but the one who sent me" (Mk 9:33–37). Jesus did this to teach that Christians must center their lives around God, who makes himself present even in the least powerful. Jesus reminded the apostles of this selfless service when, on the night before he died, he performed a lowly servant's job of washing the feet of each apostle (Jn 13:1–17). When you serve even the humblest human being for God's sake, you are serving God.

Love requires self-sacrifice or, better, "selfless sacrifice." Focusing on self and self-sacrifice produces a self-absorbed martyr complex. Selfless

93

love focuses on the other. Columba Marmion wrote, "True sanctity manifests itself by charity and the entire gift of self."[2] The gift of self without reserve leaves no more self. You become self-less.

Opposite to selfless sacrifice stand selfish ambition and cowardice. Both focus not on other people, but on me, myself, and I. The selfishly ambitious serve others only to get advancement or recognition. Like the ambitious, cowards also serve no one but themselves. Fearing that they will endanger themselves if they help others, they do nothing. *A genuine desire to help others leads Ralph to serve in one of New York City's many soup kitchens. Darlene does so to ingratiate herself with the soup kitchen manager, whom she hopes will provide her a good job reference. Penny refuses to serve because she fears that someone may pick her pocket or mug her. Only Ralph is acting out of love. Darlene serves out of selfish ambition, and Penny refuses because of cowardice.*

Communicating with the Non-Communicative

To show love by putting others first, put yourself into their shoes and minister to others the way they would desire. This can be difficult when trying to serve a recluse. People who do not want to communicate, who live behind closed doors, who are loners, act as if they really want to be left alone. And they probably do. Respect their wishes. These people may resist friendship due to terrible past hurts. Rather than risk being hurt or taken advantage of again, they withdraw.

Keeping apart from other humans, however, is unnatural. God made each person in his image, and God is a Trinity of Love. The Three Persons in God are in loving and continual communion with one another. Each human soul, made in God's image, also longs for communion. Fear has made loners suppress this need. Only a love that gently and patiently overcomes fear allows the loner to regain trust. Ultimately loners may develop community with only one other person, if they develop trust at all.

Do you know a loner? Are you willing to try to be his or her trusted friend? Gently, patiently, persistently, pebble by pebble, work to break down the barriers to trust. *In* To Kill a Mockingbird, *Boo Radley's parents made him a loner. Jem and Scout tried to "make him come out" with their pranks. He began to feel comfortable with them and bit by bit reached out to them, even though he never let them see him. They never realized*

that Boo perceived their self-centered bravado as genuine interest in him.
As a result, he became their guardian and lifesaver and finally presented
himself to them.

How does one communicate with a loner? Avoid pranks such as those
that Jem and Scout played on Boo! Instead, try initiating communication
by sharing necessary information and by showing genuine concern. It
may be necessary to tell a loner something important (her mother is
dying of cancer, for example), or to check up on him (does he have
enough to eat?).

With a recluse, communicate by letter or email rather than face-to-face
or by phone. With a letter, enclose a self-addressed, stamped postcard
with a check-off box. "Please check. ___ I got your note that my mom is
sick." Or "Please check _____ I am doing all right or _____I could use
something. It is _____ (please write what you need. I will get
it and drop it off at your door)." Use this technique to send the loner a
compliment or to share information about the neighborhood. "I wanted
to tell you that your daffodils are fabulous this year," or "I thought you
might like to know that the town will repave the street next week." Keep
the communication short and very, very infrequent. Communication
more than a few times a year may make a loner feel threatened. Do
not expect the ice to break any time soon. Only after several years may
a thaw come about. Even if that never happens, show interest in the
recluse not because of yourself, but for his or her own sake. Loners need
to know that someone cares.

Generally loners do not attend public events. Sometimes, however,
they have to attend a funeral, wedding, or other function where they
might appear uncomfortable and keep to themselves. Engage loners
in conversation using techniques that generally work with shy people:
speak a few words, try to sense if a loner needs assistance (if so, offer
it), and then move on to another person. The loner will recall, however,
that someone took an interest and showed love.

Making the Shy Comfortable

Some painfully shy people have difficulty even looking anyone in
the eye. They walk with their gaze cast down and rarely greet anyone
unless greeted first. In gatherings they tend to keep to themselves; in
discussions, they say nothing. Some shy people simply do not know

how to interact. Others are cautious. Before they risk sharing, they want to become familiar with other people and new situations. Many have been hurt emotionally and have withdrawn to avoid additional pain. If you are shy, consider the many valuable tips on overcoming shyness in this book.

How do you deal with a painfully shy person? Because many have such a low self-image, look for kind and loving ways to interact with them. For example, pay a compliment. Ask for advice. Invite them to participate in an activity. Tell an appropriate, tasteful but corny joke, then laugh at yourself for being so silly. At a fish fry you might ask, "What kind of money do fishermen make?" Answer: "Net profits."

By paying attention, you indicate to shy persons their importance and worth. Over time, small acts of love will make them comfortable, not only with you but also with others. *Celene, a brilliant young woman, has an IQ at the genius level. As a child, she so outstripped her peers that, unable to compete with her intellectual prowess, they chose to defend their own self-esteem by making fun of her thick glasses. As a result, she retreated into painful shyness and developed a poor self image. In college, she met shy, brilliant Garrett, who accepted her for who she was. As their relationship developed into love, Garrett took her to meet his parents. At first she clung to Garrett and said little. Over time, however, Celene realized that Garrett's family was being kind to her. They accepted her even though she held social and political views that differed from theirs. Now she feels comfortable staying in one room while Garrett stays in another, each discussing different topics with different members of the family.*

If You Are a Loner

If you are a loner who wants to become lovable, you must reach out to others. This requires courage and trust. You might not be able to do it alone. Do you know someone who could help you to become more sociable? How about a member of your church? A long-time acquaintance? Someone who has many friends? Someone who has been friendly to you? If you are a person of faith, pray, "Lord, who could help me?"

You may ask, "How will I know if the person who comes to mind will want to help me?" You can know only by asking. That can be frightening because your request for help could be rejected. Consider this. If you meet rejection, have you lost any ground? If that person agrees to help you, however, what might you gain? Why not keep asking people to help you become more sociable until you find one who agrees?

Tell your confidant the truth. "I have been a loner for a long time. I really want to reach out to others, but even thinking about it scares me. How do I do it? Would you try to help me to get started?" If the person agrees, follow the advice, if you can. If you have difficulty, tell your confidant. Ask for other suggestions. Evaluate the results. Because each person has a different style of communication, each will suggest different techniques to help you come out of your shell. If you really want to make more friends, you will find someone to help you.

Acquiring Humility

Maybe you consider yourself humble and try to act that way. Are you really? Are you impatient? Self-righteous? Long-winded? Do you overreact? Are you haughty? A know-it-all? A wise guy? An egotist? Are you aggressive? If you want to put others first (a trait that will help you become more lovable), you must learn how to put yourself last, something everyone needs to practice. Change begins, says Gregory the Great (Admonition 35) by "demolishing those things" that have you in their evil grasp. Only when you recognize that your current behavior is unloving will you wish to change. As Gregory notes, "The people whom Peter persuaded 'to do penance and be baptized' (Acts 2:37), for their own good, had first to realize their fall and destruction. When the bright light from Heaven burst on Saul, he did not hear at once what he ought to do, but what he had done wrongly." Self-centered attitudes not only alienate people, but they also prevent union with God. God is Love, and love directs itself to the other. Examine any attitudes that lead you to focus your thoughts on yourself. Here are some insightful questions and some solutions:

- ❧ Deep down inside, do you think that you have no real faults? To address this problem, talk to the person who knows you best. Ask him or her to tell you your faults, one at a time. Write them down and read the list a few times. Francis of Assisi used to do this with great profit.[3] You might not see your faults, but others do.

- ❧ Do you let others know that you have the right answer or solution? It requires fortitude to bite your tongue and allow someone else to answer. You will need willpower to permit other ideas to prevail. Consider this: If you want someone else's ideas to take precedence over yours, then, if your idea is disregarded, you have gotten your wish, haven't you?

  ❧ Do you know more than most other people? You might betray your boredom with conversations you consider to be inane. Challenge a know-it-all attitude by mingling with people who know things that you do not know. Attend a Chemical Society meeting, take a course in quilt-making, or sign up for a seminar on schizophrenia. Find an activity which requires skills or knowledge that you lack. You will soon learn your limits. How humbling, yet enlightening! You will begin to develop tolerance for others whom you may have considered less intelligent.

  ❧ Do you have a high social standing or impressive possessions? Stand naked in front of a mirror and look at yourself. That naked person is you. Nothing but your naked body is going to accompany your naked soul when you die. Then what good can your social standing or possessions do you?

  ❧ Do you have exceptionally good looks? Emphasize your appearance less, but not so much that you jeopardize your job or embarrass your family. No need to resemble a bag lady or a hobo! On what do you pride yourself? Changing that will make you less haughty. Use simpler makeup. Arrange your hair more simply. Wear simpler clothing. You may discover that people may have felt intimidated by your physical appearance. *Jeannine told Roberta about her anger when, while commenting on its beauty, one of her friends had touched her long and luxurious hair. "Nobody touches my hair," she exclaimed. Roberta remarked that she used to take pride in her hair, too, but she cut it into a shorter style so that she would not have to take so many pains about her appearance.*

  ❧ Do you think you know more than your pastor? Do you really know more, or do you just think so? Have you researched the tenets of your faith to see if you believe what your church teaches? Or is your "knowledge" merely opinion? If you actually do know more, how do you inform others? Do you work for real change, or do you merely stir up dissent? Talk is cheap. Change takes work. No religion extols pride. The Bible exhorts humility. Your tone of voice and manner of delivery ought to be consistent with your belief. Do you preach your own ideas or God's? If God's, do you respect your listeners as much as God does? Do you seek your own glory, or God's? Badgering, belittling, or lording it over others makes enemies, not friends. Such behaviors also lead people to dig in their heels and resist suggestions. Instead of guiding people into the faith, you may be driving them from it. Present your ideas gently.

- Do you take pride in good works? List good works that you could do but do not. A quick look will provide a useful lesson in humility.

- Do you expect people to serve or help you? Do you get annoyed when you are ignored? Read and then reread Matthew 20:28 ("The Son of Man came not to be served but to serve, and to give his life as a ransom for many.") and Philippians 2:8 ("He humbled himself and became obedient to the point of death — even death on a cross.").

- Do your words and demeanor belittle others? Pay attention to what you say. If you catch yourself belittling someone, apologize and turn the negative comment back on yourself. "How can you be so stupid? Oh, sorry! Stupid me for saying that! I had no right to say that to you." Change demeanors that make others feel small. If you are particular about how things are done and tend to stand over others when they are completing a task, purposely walk away. If you have a certain flourish, gait, or stance that proclaims, "I am really something," then practice other ways of presenting yourself by observing yourself in a mirror. Soon you will feel more comfortable speaking and acting with more humility.

If you consider yourself superior in any way, remind yourself that evil elevates itself, but goodness lowers itself. Satan, a creature, wished to appear superior even to God so he fell from heaven. In his wounded pride, satan attempts to drag humanity with him into the abyss. In direct contrast to satan's pride, God's humility brought about humanity's redemption. In the person of Jesus, God-made-man died to rescue people from the abyss. Humble souls rise to the likeness of God while haughty ones sink to the level of the rebel angels. Superiority lowers; humility elevates. Work and pray to eliminate any attitude of superiority, and you will find yourself more lovable. This prayer may help:

> Deliver me, O Jesus,
> From the desire of being loved,
> From the desire of being extolled,
> From the desire of being honored,
> From the desire of being praised,
> From the desire of being preferred,
> From the desire of being consulted,
> From the desire of being approved,
> From the desire of being popular,
> From the fear of being humiliated,
> From the fear of being despised,
> From the fear of suffering rebukes,
> From the fear of being calumniated,
> From the fear of being forgotten,
> From the fear of being wronged,
> From the fear of being ridiculed,
> From the fear of being suspected,
> Deliver me, O Jesus.[4]

Correcting Others

Taciturn people refuse to talk when they ought to speak up. Gregory the Great (Admonition 15) succinctly notes that "They often bridle the tongue beyond moderation, and as a result suffer in the heart a more grievous loquacity." In other words, all the anger and correction held within seethes in their minds. Gregory deems their silence "violent and indiscreet." Not wishing to appear to be "fault-finders ... their mind is sometimes puffed up in pride and it scorns as weaklings those whom it hears speaking.... The man represses the tongue, but lifts up his mind, and without any regard to his own bad qualities, he accuses others within his own heart." If this admonition hits close to home, Gregory advises becoming aware of such inner dialog because God judges thoughts as well as words.

In important matters, keeping silent might cause worse feelings than speaking up. Gregory (Admonition 15) adds, "For they are to be admonished that if they love their neighbors as themselves, they should most certainly not fail to speak up when they have reason to reprehend them. Indeed, those who observe evil in their neighbor and yet hold their tongue, withhold the use of salves, as it were, from wounds which they see, and thereby become the cause of death" because they refused "to cure the poison when they could." How can you learn what to say and when to say it? "The tongue, then, must be prudently curbed, but not completely tied up.... The Prophet considers this matter well when he says: *Set a watch, O Lord, before my mouth, and a door round about my lips.* He does not ask that a wall be set before his mouth, but a door, which, you see, can be opened and closed."

Thinking that you have no right to correct anyone else is false humility. Everyone has a moral obligation to confront wrongdoing. If no one corrected others, chaos and evil would choke the world.

The opposite however — talking too much — is also a fault. Do you offer correction by making example of others through gossip or slanderous stories? Are you trying to improve people, or wearing them down through the sheer weight of your words?

Parents must not overdo instruction or exaggerate consequences. Children ignore what they perceive as nagging or improbability. Constant criticism about the disorder of a boy's bedroom, with the additional suggestion that the mess might be breeding germs, probably will not motivate Joey to clean up. Better to put Joey in charge of his room. Then keep the door closed. When he wants to bring home a special friend, he may clean up without his parent's urging.

Correct others without appearing self-righteous. Begin with praise. Gregory (Admonition 18) presents this suggestion: "We should introduce either some good qualities which they possess, or at least mention some such qualities that could be present, though they actually may not be; and then only should the evil in them that displeases us be cut away, when the good points which are pleasing to them have in advance rendered their mind well-disposed to listen to us." Gregory does not suggest lying. "Mention some qualities that could be present, though they actually may not be," means saying something like "You might be a very disciplined person about some things," even if only disorganization is apparent. Some things cannot be seen; perhaps that person's medicine cabinet is the model of order.

People accept correction if they do not feel threatened. It is loving to correct others gently because harshness can cause emotional harm. Gregory (Admonition 18) suggests "beg[ging] their amendment as a favor to us rather than to themselves." *While journeying in the desert, to deter his brother-in-law Hobab from mingling with Gentiles Moses told him, "Come with us and be our guide, because you know the best places to camp." Gregory explains that "Ignorance of the way did not trouble Moses ... who was guided outwardly by the pillar [of God] going before him ... but he asked the other to lead the way that he might himself lead him to life." Hobab went along with Moses because he thought that he was guiding the one who was correcting him* (see Nm 10:29–32).

Offer correction by presenting a parallel case. Let the person draw his or her own conclusion. "Then, when they give a right judgment on what apparently is another's case, they are to be taken to task regarding their own guilt by a suitable procedure," Gregory advises (Admonition 3). *King David had many wives but lusted after one more. When his commander Uriah was at war, David called for and slept with Uriah's wife Bathsheba. When Bathsheba became pregnant, David tried to induce Uriah to sleep with his wife so that the officer would think that the baby was his. When this trickery failed, David suborned Uriah's murder, while making it appear accidental. He then married Bathsheba, thinking that he had concealed his adultery. Nathan the Prophet, however, enlightened by the Holy Spirit, knew full well David's deadly sins. In order to get David to face them and repent, he sought the king's legal judgment. A poor man, Nathan said, had one little ewe lamb that used to sleep with him and follow him wherever he went. A rich man wanted to give a feast for a visitor and so, instead of taking a lamb from his vast herds, he took the poor man's lamb and killed it. Nathan asked David what should be done. King David was furious. "As the Lord lives, the man who has done this deserves to die!" he declared, at which point Nathan said, "You are the man." The story brought David to repentance* (see 2 Sm 11–12).

Some people do not realize that their behavior is making them terribly unhappy. Suggesting that their lifestyle might be causing their woes may cause them to reject your perception as old-fashioned, reactionary, or judgmental. Gregory the Great (Admonition 14) advocates the use of gentle admonitions. "Frequently sick people who cannot be cured by a strong potion of drugs, have been restored to their former state of health by tepid water; and some wounds that cannot be cured by incisions, are healed by fomentations with oil." "Walk softly but carry a big stick" applies here — a gentle approach, but a powerful message. *In a panic, Sharon phoned a crisis pregnancy center. She had been sleeping with different men and using illegal drugs with some of them, so she was unsure when she became pregnant or by whom. Although the test proved negative, Ms. Ames, the counselor, suggested that Sharon visit a physician who could examine her for venereal disease. On the thirty-minute drive to the doctor, Ms. Ames asked Sharon if she was happy with her lifestyle. "No," Sharon confided, "but what else can I do?" She really wanted to hold down a job, complete her high school education, and have a steady boyfriend. Ms. Ames suggested that Sharon begin by going to Narcotics Anonymous to help her eliminate the drug habit, which was ruining her health as well as preventing her from holding a job or succeeding in school. Ms. Ames also suggested that real satisfaction would come through waiting for a "special someone," not through a series of one-night stands, and then there would be no worry about pregnancy or venereal disease. Sharon listened politely and promised to think about making some lifestyle changes.*

When offering correction take care not to gloat over your own virtue. Love "does not rejoice in wrongdoing" (1 Cor 13:6). Rather, love mourns the wrong in others and seeks, by advice, encouragement, action, and prayer, to turn wrong into right.

Sexuality

Putting the other first finds its purest expression in the sexual relationship. Are you being loving in your sexual relationship? Do you want to be? The sexual union, and the intimate acts that lead up to it, ought to express a deeper love, one that respects, trusts, and enriches the other person. Because humans are made in God's image, they crave intimacy. On a human level, physical union fulfills that need most profoundly. Because people are created male and female, it is obvious that the Lord intended this union, for from it comes new life. Christopher West explains that "We discover in the mystery of human sexuality man's basic hunger for the God who is Love. As John Paul so eloquently states, 'Man cannot live without love.' "[5]

The sexes would never battle if each person put the other first. Then the sex act would proceed only with the full consent of each partner and only with the full acceptance of its consequences. Are you willing, for good reasons, to forgo sexual intimacy? Or are you ready to engage in sexual activities at a particular time? Do you discuss your feelings when one of you wants to initiate sexual activity? If not, how can your lover be sure that you are comfortable at that time with sexual advances?

Become more lovable in your sexual relationship by being totally honest with your beloved. Say what pleases you and what does not. Do not say yes when you mean no. Ask your partner to be honest with you. Treat the other as he or she wishes. One couple at Marriage Encounter suggested that each spouse indicate their readiness by putting a silk rose into a vase in the bedroom. Only when the vase held two roses would either partner initiate sexual activity.

Explain Your Faults

Everyone has faults. Only our Lord Jesus and his mother were perfect. Other people's faults may annoy you, but you have faults, too. Sometimes you might shock yourself — as well as those you are with — by doing something out of character. Then you ought to explain your shortcomings so that others do not conclude that they may have caused the regrettable action. *While organizing readers for a prayer service, Beverly asked Cleo if she would be willing to read. Cleo could have said, "No," but she knew that such an answer might make Beverly feel uncomfortable for having asked. So Cleo explained. "Oh, I would love to, but I just cannot do it. I get so scared standing up in front of a crowd. I know that seems silly, but I just could not read in front of others." Beverly laughed and commented, "We will have to get you doing something in a smaller group first!"*

Self-Denial

Putting others first might require self-denial, which takes many forms. *Doris and Madge were attending a potluck dinner together. At the dessert table, both reached for the remaining piece of blueberry pie. "You take it," Doris said. "I like chocolate cake, too, and will have that." "Thanks," Madge said. "Blueberry is my favorite." Little did Madge realize that it was Doris' favorite too.*

Brice asked Eugene to drive him to the garage to pick up his car, because Brice's wife was home with a sick child. Eugene did the favor, never telling Brice how busy he was that day.

Leona was trying to complete a project when her friend Sherrie unexpectedly came to visit. Leona could tell that she wanted to talk and invited her in to tea. Sherrie was comforted by the visit and Leona completed her project the next day.

Avoid Complaining

No one likes everything. Griping about what you cannot change makes an unpleasant situation worse and tends to drive people away. Some people seem to complain about everything. Whining might make them feel better, but it does not make them lovable. *Yvette had complained all her life. She was always ill, she complained, and no one visited her often enough or treated her with enough compassion. Now in a nursing home, she has few visitors other than her son and his family. Most of Yvette's friends and relatives have never seen her smile or heard her laugh.*

Are you a chronic complainer? If so, you may have grown up with one or both parents who were complainers. In your family, perhaps only complainers received attention. In the adult world, constant complaining can label you. Once people think that nothing ever meets your approval, they will stop consulting you or trying to help. Instead of getting attention, you will be ignored. If you must gripe, do it in your head and be done with it.

Be Accepting

People are going to be the way they are, not the way you think they ought to be. So love them the way they come while trying to help them become better. Even if they cannot or will not improve, keep on loving. Recognize the difference between accepting people and accepting their behavior. Drug dealers deserve love because they are made in God's image, even if it is difficult to discern that image. But drug dealing cannot be accepted. Even though evil must be condemned, the persons committing the evil still deserve respect because God created them. *In her life Gloria tried to follow the Ten Commandments. In college, she met Barry and his partner Calvin. She maintained a friendship with these two students, chatting with them, sitting with them at meals, and*

*laughing at their silly antics, but, when the subject came up, she did
not hide her views on homosexual activity in light of church teaching.
Barry and Calvin understood that Gloria liked them, even though she
disapproved of their sexual activity. After all, they disagreed with her
views, too. Thus, accepting one another while acknowledging their
different views, the three were able to remain friends.*

Take No Offense

To be loving, cultivate a thick skin. Being willing to take the last
place already prepares you to take no offense. Being offended means
being prideful. How can someone offend you if you know that you are
imperfect? You will thank someone who points out your bad points and
ask for help to improve. *Florence and Ian worked together. He did not
always agree with her decisions or actions, and used to tell her so.
She would listen and take his advice if she agreed. If she disagreed,
she would explain why. Ian was amazed at Florence's ability to take
correction without taking offense.*

Someone misunderstanding your good points, or telling an off-color
joke, or making sexist or racist remarks in your presence might offend
you. Putting yourself into the other person's shoes lets you feel pity
rather than disgust or anger. Pray for the person who committed these
social blunders, who sadly has failed to become all that God desires. In
addition to prayer, offer a gentle correction.

Putting others first is a challenge, but those who act with love can do
it. All people are sons and daughters of God, equal in his eyes, so why
should you, and not others, be first? Jesus divested himself of power and
glory to take the lowest human place, being born in a stable. Try to take
a lower place than you deserve. Allow others to be first. Permit others to
achieve recognition above your own, go ahead of you in line, choose the
first places at the dinner table, the first foods at a buffet, or the first items
at a sale. Accept others without judging them. Listen to suggestions
when you think that you have all the answers. Doing these things and
more say, "I respect you." Respecting others is a way of showing love.

11
Respect

Respect means considering someone worthy of esteem, honor, or high regard. Those who want to become more lovable need to respect all human beings because God created them. Even though a person's actions may be reprehensible, that person still deserves the respect owed someone in whom the image of God dwells. Respecting others' lives means not ending those lives prematurely through abortion, infanticide, euthanasia, capital punishment, murder, or any other means unless in self-defense. Respect means doing everything possible to prevent someone else from taking another's life. It means defending others against an unjust aggressor, abandoning all stereotypes including racism and sexism, and abjuring violence, favoritism, abuse, bullying, gossip, and similar evils that harm, manipulate, or deceive others.

Some bitter and critical people seem to have ungrateful hearts. Those who harbor a negative attitude need an expert spiritual physician, such as a compassionate member of the clergy or a psychologist, to achieve victory over this personality trait. A negative attitude habituates the mind to rash judgments, to gossip, and to slander. Thomas à Kempis noted that "We should have much peace if we would not busy ourselves with the sayings and doings of others."[1]

Some people indulge in rash judgments for the sheer intellectual delight of being an amateur psychiatrist. If they frequently guess correctly, they can become confident in their ability and find it difficult to stop. Such a tendency requires the help of a competent psychologist. By and large, people are ten times as good as they appear, and deserve a chance to prove it.

All people are interconnected. The link with others in the human family demands respect. Martin Luther King, Jr., commenting on Christ's parable about the man who was a fool (Lk 12:16–21), noted that "The rich man was a fool because he failed to realize his dependence on others.

His soliloquy contains approximately sixty words, yet 'I' and 'my' occur twelve times. He has said 'I' and 'my' so often that he had lost the capacity to say 'we' and 'our....' He talked as though he could plough the fields and build the barns alone. He failed to realize that he was an heir of a vast treasury of ideas and labor to which both the living and the dead had contributed."[2] Such egotism, egoism, and self-absorption still plague the world.

Do you disregard others? Here are some ways to find out:

- Do you stereotype people according to race, social standing, education, nationality, place of residence, or any other factor?

- Do you think that abortion is sometimes justified?

- Do you think that euthanasia deserves a place in medical treatment?

- Do you shun certain neighborhoods strictly because people of a certain ethnic or racial background live there?

- Do you dislike foreigners?

- Do you listen to or spread gossip?

- Do you justify brutality toward your spouse, children, or anyone else because you believe that you have a duty to "keep them in line"?

- Do you lie?

- Do you make fun of certain individuals or categories of people?

Anyone who agrees with any of these statements has a problem with respecting others. How can disrespect be changed into respect? Begin by desiring to change. As difficult and limiting as this is, try to imagine why God made each one of the persons whom you disrespect. What does God think of each person? Would he want anyone to be used, abused, shunned, killed, demeaned, or stereotyped? All of these actions hurt others physically, emotionally, or both.

Would God approve of telling secrets about others or spreading unflattering information about someone, even if it is true? Such behaviors harm others by robbing them of their good reputation. If people do not need to know the dirt on someone, why tell them? *Oliver and his brother Gabe were at odds. One day Oliver confided to his friend Pascal that Gabe, a member of the church choir, was engaged in an extramarital affair. Pascal, who had not known this, suddenly lost his respect for Gabe, who had seemed to be a holy man.*

God does not laugh when his sons and daughters are mocked. Does God think that human quirks deserve ridicule? Or does he love people despite their foibles and work to correct the serious, harmful traits? Belittling others or making fun of them reduces them to objects and ignores their dignity. Making fun of others in their presence is especially evil. *Byron, born with both arms missing from the elbows down, was abandoned at birth and raised in an orphanage. He remembers bitterly how the children ridiculed his missing limbs. Even though he grew up in a loving adoptive home, memories of those first painful years remain. He still finds it difficult to reveal his disability to people until he gets to know them well.*

To know how to treat others in ways that God would approve, reread Chapter One of this book. God is Love, and Love is self-sacrificing. Is your love self-sacrificing? Will you help others even if doing so makes your life less convenient? Love never harms another. Does what you consider to be loving harm anyone? *Gretchen and her husband Peter were told that Geoffrey, their unborn baby, had anencephaly, that is, was developing without a brain. Geoffrey would certainly not live long. Their doctor gave Gretchen and Peter a booklet which described "induction of labor" to "end the pregnancy early" as a "loving" choice. The couple realized that their doctor was urging them to abort their child. They thought, "How can ending Geoffrey's life be loving? God made our son so he knows about the anencephaly. Our job is to parent Geoffrey until God calls him home." They continued the pregnancy, gave birth to Geoffrey at the normal time, and loved him intensely for the six days that he survived.*

To determine whether what you consider to be loving actually respects others, measure your actions and attitudes against the advice in this chapter. Does your "respect meter" need adjustment?

Be Merciful

Certainly physicians and nurses should be merciful, but mercy involves more than bandaging physical wounds. The first step toward being merciful is to avoid causing unnecessary hurt.

"Be merciful, just as your Father is merciful," said Christ. "Do not judge, and you will not be judged; do not condemn, and you will not be condemned. Forgive, and you will be forgiven; give, and it will be given to you. A good measure, pressed down, shaken together, running over, will be put into your lap; for the measure you give will be the measure you get back" (Lk 6:36–38). *According to her nephew, Miss Letitia Pope, an American lady who had lived most of her ninety years in Florence, had never been heard to say anything negative about another person.*[3] *She was a merciful woman.*

In dealing with others, especially with those in your immediate family, recall that only the greatest saints were on their best behavior all the time. To expect perfection in others is to expect the impossible. Nonetheless, no matter what their behavior, all people deserve respect, that is, compassion and forgiveness. Respect for others will tend to draw out the best in them, just as disrespect will tend to draw out their worst. Even children tend to fulfill expectations, be they good expectations or poor ones. *McKenzie was only four years old, but she lived up to what her grandmother thought of her. Three generations of family were living in one house, grandparents Helen and Harry on the first floor and their daughter Paulette, her husband Patrick, and grandchildren McKenzie and Mavis on the second floor. One day Paulette came into Helen and Harry's apartment and asked for crayons and paper so that McKenzie and Mavis could color. Helen found the items, and Paulette started back to her own apartment. McKenzie pouted, however, because she wanted to stay at Grandma Helen's. Helen was trying to meet a work deadline and did not have time to spend with McKenzie so she said, "You take the crayons to your place and make some pretty pictures. When you are done, bring them back to me so I can put them on our refrigerator." The little girl willingly went upstairs to do what her grandmother expected of her.*

Possessiveness and Control

Possessiveness mixes love with demonic pride, transforming it into an attempt to control. People say that they "have" a friend or a spouse or children, but people are not possessed the way vehicles or houses are. Possessive people, however, believe that they "own" those whom they "love." Little do they know that pride, greed, a selfish desire to control, or perhaps a combination of all of these has distorted and corrupted their "love." Possessiveness disparages the dignity of the beloved. Genuine love does not control. It frees.

"Love is the child of freedom, never that of domination," wrote Erich Fromm in *The Art of Loving*.[4] Love is a fragile butterfly. Holding it tightly crushes and kills it. Only when allowed the freedom to come and go is love genuine. *Francie believed that it was her vocation to make other people happy. Well-educated in the humanities, she had a strong sense of social justice, but her noble motives always worked to her own advantage as long as others allowed her control. Widowed in middle age, Francie returned to her hometown where she met Radstock, whom wartime circumstances had separated from his family and his wife Sylvia. Because he became infatuated with intellectual, altruistic Francie, she was able to control him under the guise of loving him and wanting to make him happy. First, she made him relinquish his former friends unless they happened to be her friends as well. Then she drew him away from his in-laws, all of whom disapproved of the apparently adulterous or bigamous relationship. Saying that she was dedicated to her late husband and did not want to remarry, however, Francie managed to keep their relationship purely platonic. Nevertheless, she was so possessive that she would not permit Radstock to meet Sylvia when Sylvia was able to return home at the end of the war. Francie caused him to be alienated from his siblings and in-laws. Not content with having Radstock to herself, Francie also took control of his teenage son Joshua. First she withdrew Joshua from school, saying that it would be good for him to earn his living and to live on his own. Then she broke up Joshua's relationship with one girl in favor of another whom she preferred. When that relationship did not work out, Joshua ran away. Radstock's obsession with Francie kept him from challenging her. Convinced that she loved him, he happily spent all his time with her. He had become her psychological prisoner.* No person should possess another as Francie possessed Radstock. No loving relationship demands that one person abandon everyone except those whom the beloved approves.

Sometimes parents can become possessive of their children. Other times teachers and other "youth ministers" might try to exercise too much control, especially on teens. Such control inhibits growing or grown children from making their own decisions. Loving children, or anyone else, requires trusting them to make their own choices, as long as those choices are not unethical. Every mature person has the right, within ethical boundaries, to manage his or her life. No one wants others to suffer the pain of poor choices. Refusing to allow them control of their own lives, however, keeps them in social infancy. Whether intentional or not, such control fosters a far worse outcome of rebellion and alienation. *Faye and Roland had two sons, but one died in childhood. They tried to completely control their remaining child, Chandler. When Chandler graduated from high school, Roland was determined that he become a doctor, even though Chandler was not enamored of that profession. After graduating from medical school, Chandler was miserable in medical practice. Finally he realized that he had to follow a career that he wanted and not one his parents wanted for him. Although Roland and Faye felt emotionally betrayed when Chandler left his medical practice to become a salesman, they eventually accepted his decision because otherwise they would have alienated him completely.*

Take time to evaluate the tendency to possessiveness. What freedoms ought you allow others? Are you comfortable with this? If not, do you fear that the other person will leave you? Forget you? Do things differently? Yes, all these things might happen. You respect others, however, only when you allow them the freedom to be themselves. Little children could be hurt because they do not recognize danger, but you ought to begin to relinquish control when they begin to reason and think. Show others love by allowing them the freedom to experience life, to make decisions, and to learn from their successes and mistakes. Controlling others may seem to simplify their lives, but it may actually make their lives more complicated. *Sebastian managed a ranch that raised prime cattle. When the owner was about to retire, he hoped to sell the herd to Sebastian, who wanted to buy them. Knowing how hard his son was working, Sebastian's father Colin refused to loan him the money, saying that he needed an easier, five-day-a-week job. Two years after someone else had bought the ranch and cattle, Sebastian had saved up enough money from his nine-to-five job to buy his own ranch and begin a new herd. Colin regretted not loaning him the money, because Sebastian would need years to breed a herd that matched the quality of the one he could have bought.*

Being a Good Example

You might not want to be noticed or praised for the good that you do. Humility however, cannot excuse being "guilty of withholding edification" if good actions that others could have imitated are concealed. Christ said, "Let your light shine before others, so that they may see your good works and give glory to your Father in heaven" (Mt 5:16). Giving good example can inspire others to perform similar actions and can help them to praise God's goodness they see in you. *Ivonne and Carey work tirelessly for a volunteer organization that assists the poor. While they do not broadcast what they do, they make themselves available for help and referral. Others who witness their caring are inspired to help the poor, too.*

Gregory the Great (Admonition 36) mentions something that might be mistaken as a loving act. "Those who do good in secret, yet allow themselves to be thought ill of openly ... are to be admonished that while they keep themselves alive thanks to the good they perform, they must not use themselves to slay others by the example of their evil repute." It is a mistake, Gregory is saying, to think that you are fostering humility by allowing others to think ill of you while you secretly do good. "If they themselves take a wholesome drink, they should not pour out a draught of poison for minds that are watching." Giving others the false impression that you are sinning provides bad example and can lead them to sin. As Gregory says, "Those who carelessly allow evil to be attributed to them, do not, indeed, commit evil personally, yet in the persons of those who imitate them they do commit a multiple sin."

What is the proper response to a false accusation? Speak and show the truth gently, then let matters go. The truth will prevail in time. *Cora and Crosby had a close working partnership, which led Crosby's wife Lisa to accuse the pair of adultery. This had never happened; the relationship, although close, was never sexual. In fact, both Cora and Crosby were committed to their own marriages. Lisa's accusation led Crosby to admit having an affair with Cora although he privately told her husband Burnett that nothing had happened. Lisa then badgered Cora, trying to make her acknowledge the affair, but Cora refused. She knew that no affair had taken place. Through counseling Crosby and Lisa tried to rectify a marriage that her false accusation had devastated, but weathering the ordeal together in trust and honesty strengthened Cora and Burnett's relationship.*

Say "Thank You"

Two little words go far in showing respect to others. How many times a day can you say "Thank you" and for how many things? Beginning tomorrow morning, make a point of saying "Thank you" every time you can. When someone gives you a paper, say "Thank you." When you receive a phone call, say "Thank you for calling." When your spouse serves you dinner, say "Thank you for cooking dinner." When your child greets you when you come home from work, say, "Thank you for saying hi!" Thanking people honors what they do for you, respects them as persons, and is one of the simplest ways to show love.

12
Be Observant

Those who are observant can discover ways to make most situations more pleasant. You can go beyond opening the car door for someone and displaying good manners. Occasionally, unusual ways to show love present themselves. *At her bookstore, Larissa often has seen customers handling their credit card receipts carelessly, not realizing that someone who finds a dropped receipt could use the card number fraudulently. So whenever anyone makes a credit card purchase in her store, she carefully cuts the credit card number from the receipt, tears it into little pieces, and tosses the scraps into a waste can. She then hands the customer the receipt.*

People who are natural observers notice the smallest details. *Two-year-old Nicole noticed her grandmother resting. With a dry face cloth, Nicole began to stroke Grandma's arm as if to comfort and soothe her.* Others remain oblivious. Even everyday details escape them. *After twenty-five years of living in the same house, Farrell still did not know the color of his bedroom walls. His wife Nina, on the other hand, was quick to notice that someone had been in her office because the door to one of the cabinets had been left slightly ajar.*

Powers of observation can be learned. In any situation, ask yourself:

- What is going on here?
- Do people seem comfortable?
- Who needs help?
- How can I help?

Before offering, ask if help is wanted. You may have misunderstood the situation. *Irene has two lower-limb prostheses. On icy sidewalks, she appreciates a steady hand. When the sidewalks are clear, she needs no assistance although her unique gait might make some people think she does. She does not like it when told, "Here. Let me help you." She prefers to be asked, "Would you like some help?"*

Looking for the Lovable in the Unlikable

Although it may seem unrealistic, every person can be loved. Some people have co-workers who never fail to insult or call others obscene names. How can someone like that be loved?

Start with your own thoughts. If you have already convinced yourself that such a person cannot be loved, your inability to love becomes a self-fulfilling prophecy. You cannot control another's free will, but you can control your own. To reform others, begin with yourself.

In Chapter Three, you learned a technique to help you to love yourself. Now use it to foster love for the unlikable. Imagine disagreeable persons as newborn infants. Can you find something to love in each of them? What might have happened to those babies to make them into the people you know? Each person is the product of his or her past, just as you are of yours. Each may have suffered unimaginable hurts and abuse. Who knows what wounds people carry? Perhaps something you said or did, or failed to say or do, inadvertently opened an old sore. Pray for disagreeable people. Praying may supply enough light to discover lovable qualities in the unlovable.

When others direct abusive language toward you, try lowering yourself to using the same language toward them, pretending to be angry, but following up with a grin. They might actually be pleased. Perhaps they wanted to provoke you, to see if you were too weak to get angry. Some people confuse meekness with weakness; until you defend yourself, they will not respect you. In other cases, if you keep silent the taunts may stop because some individuals enjoy getting a rise out of the people they ridicule. Moreover, never underestimate the power of humor; it may be able to break the ice, or even thaw it. When others are laughing at you, it might do good to laugh with them. You can never be sure what will work, but you can try. If you fail, what have you lost? But if you succeed, you might turn enemies into friends.

Seek the Good

Understating an obvious truth, John Paul II wrote that "It is difficult to deny that in the realm of human experience one also finds good and evil, truth and beauty, and God."[1] What one person considers good another might consider evil, and vice versa. What some believe to be truth may actually be a lie. Where one sees beauty, another may see only ugliness. Do ultimate realities exist?

Yes, indeed. God is the Truth, the Good, and the Beautiful. The Truth must be known, the Good must be chosen, and the Beautiful must be loved. What individuals choose, think, or consider are merely personal preferences. But in God, what is really true, good, and beautiful can be understood because God is the ultimate measure of those qualities.

Beauty can relieve depression and reaffirm that it is good to be alive. All of creation is beautiful and good because God does not create ugliness or evil. God's most beautiful creation is the human being, not only because of outward appearance but also because of the perfection that can exist within the human soul. Being made in the likeness of God, every human being becomes more beautiful as he or she approaches that likeness. Try to see the good in each person. In some people it may be difficult to find, but good lies dormant in even the most disagreeable person's soul or he or she would not exist.

Seek goodness, truth, and beauty in the man or woman you may choose as a spouse. The most physically beautiful person may not make the best friend or partner. A prudent choice in love demands that emotion be ratified by good will and good judgment. Beauty stirs the heart, but intellect and will must have the final say. A wise love will discover hidden beauty. *Although others disparaged her appearance, Samuel Johnson referred to his wife as a "pretty creature."*[2]

If you search for goodness, truth, and beauty, you will find them. The Psalmist, who begs God to "show me your face," was praying to comprehend truth, goodness, and beauty as expressions of the Divine. Nature's magnificence reflects God's grandeur. Certainly other human beings, made in God's image and likeness, ought to move your heart to praise and bless the Creator. Recognizing truth, goodness, and beauty in other people should foster love in your heart for them. Lovable actions will follow.

To discover goodness, truth, and beauty in other people, try this exercise. Fold a paper in half and then in half again to make four sections. Title the first column "Enemy," the second "Truth," the third "Goodness," and the fourth "Beauty." Draw five horizontal lines across each section. Under "Enemy," write the names of five people you consider your enemies or, if you have none, five people whom you dislike. These should be people whom you know personally from regular, face-to-face contact. Now, as you seek to complete each of the other three sections, ask God for help in understanding how each of the five reveals truth, goodness, and beauty. Write down what comes to you in the appropriate section. Take your time. Many days may pass until the Lord reveals something positive. If you cannot come up with any traits, ask others who know these people to help you. When you have finished, study what you have written. Pray for the persons whose names you recorded. Seek out an opportunity to meet each of them; when you do, look for those qualities of truth, beauty, and goodness. Thank God for letting you discover these characteristics. Ask God to show you how to use encouraging words and actions to reinforce those qualities in these enemies of yours.

Observe Yourself

Do you consider yourself rich or poor? You cannot pick "middle class" in this exercise. Rich or poor? Which are you?

If you said "poor," you need to encourage yourself. Do you realize that God considers you precious? Gregory the Great (Admonition 3) reminds you that God values the poor when he says, "I have chosen thee in the furnace of poverty" (Is 48:10). A furnace might seem a negative image, but in this context it is not. Metal workers use a furnace to refine precious metals. Intense heat consumes the imperfections, leaving behind pure gold or silver. A poverty of possessions or of spirit will consume worldly attachments and pride, leaving only a pure and humble servant of God, more precious than gold.

If you said "rich," beware taking pride in who you are or what you have. Riches are uncertain and can be lost in an instant. Witness what happened when Wall Street crashed in 1929 or when fire devastates a mansion. Consider how Ronald Reagan, handsome actor and president of the United States, lost both his looks and his mind to age and Alzheimer's. Gregory (Admonition 3) cautions, "[You] certainly cannot retain the wealth" that you have.

On the other hand, Gregory notes how a poor person can be proud and a rich person humble. Attitude determines poverty or wealth, because

God created each person to be his child who will live forever with him
in the perfection of eternal life. What needs to be strengthened, changed,
or eliminated to reach that goal? This exercise may lead to an answer:
On one sheet of paper write "poor," and on another "rich." Pray about
your traits, inclinations, desires, and achievements. On the "poor" sheet,
write what makes you less than you could be. On the "rich" sheet, write
what brings you closer to becoming the person God wants you to be.
Each week, focus on one item. Do all that you can to improve your good
qualities or to eliminate your bad ones. Whether you begin this exercise
"rich" or "poor," it will help you grow.

Face Your Fears

To become more lovable, recognize your fears and phobias. Some
things may be unnerving: snakes, spiders, mice, worms, heights, close
spaces. Unexpectedly confronting objects or situations like these may
make you react impulsively, and the possibility of such panic could make
others avoid you. Would you want to travel with someone who is afraid
to go outdoors after a rainstorm because earthworms might be crawling
on the sidewalk?

Deal with phobias by small degrees. Visit a zoo's snake exhibit. Look
at spiders and worms in a book. Go to a pet shop to see the white mice.
Take an elevator to the second floor and look down. Walk into a closet
and close the door. Then do more. Hold a snake, a worm, or a mouse. Go
up to the fifth floor. Crawl through a tunnel. Fears cramp your horizons.
The authors of this book live on a ten-mile-long island where some
residents are so fearful of crossing bridges that they have never been to
the mainland. What bridges are you afraid to cross? What experiences
have you missed because of your fears?

Perhaps you fear suffering, God, ridicule, rejection, exploitation. Such
fears can be confronted only through a deeper love for and trust in God.
"Perfect love casts out fear" (1 Jn 4:18). "For you did not receive a spirit
of slavery to fall back into fear, but you have received a spirit of adoption.
When we cry 'Abba! Father!' it is that very Spirit bearing witness with
our spirit that we are children of God" (Rom 8:15–16). Gregory the Great
(Admonition 14) offers this reminder: "The mind, therefore, that is under
the slavery of fear, does not know the grace of liberty." Uncontrolled
fear can ruin your life. *Regina's visible birth defect left her so afraid of
rejection that she kept her distance from everyone and had few friends.*

She attributed her loneliness to fear of exploitation: "You can't trust anyone."

Discovering what frightens you is not always easy. Fear may lie hidden until it surfaces unexpectedly. Label an envelope "My Fears." On a sheet of paper list all your fears. Each night pray for the strength to deal with them in emotionally healthy ways. When you discover a new fear, add it to the list and add it to your prayers. When you realize that God's grace has enabled you to conquer a specific fear, cross it off. In time, by the grace of God, most of these fears will become manageable or even disappear.

Fear of Damnation

Some people who have strong faith fear eternal punishment. Fearing damnation makes perfect sense, but becoming lovable requires progress beyond that fear. Love God because he is good, not because he might punish evil acts. Gregory (Admonition 14) notes a subtle truth that people who fear hell may not want to admit. "The man who acts well from fear of the evil of torments, wishes that what he fears did not exist, so that he might boldly commit sin." In other words, such a person would sin if damnation were not the consequence. Does this apply to you?

If you succumb to temptation frequently, write at the top of a sheet of paper the sin that entices you. Below it, list in one column the positive consequences of this sin and in another the negative. When you cannot think of anything more, ponder what you have written. Consider not the length of each column but the seriousness of each consequence. Does this sin do anything to help others? How does it hurt them? What unforeseen harm might it cause? Avoid anything that harms others or yourself, unless that harm will help them in the long run (performing a root canal might hurt the patient at the time, but will provide years of pain-free chewing). This exercise can help you avoid a particular action not because God will punish you, but because it is not loving.

Spread God's Message

"If any of you put a stumbling-block before one of these little ones who believe in me, it would be better for you if a great millstone were fastened around your neck and you were drowned in the depth of the sea" (Mt 18:6). Spiritually harming another person alienates you from God's favor, just as benefiting another endears you to the Lord. The twelve were the first but not the last apostles. God gives every person, including you, the vocation to be an apostle. You can fulfill that vocation by praying for others, but God wants more. He wants your speech and actions to proclaim Christ's love. You may have little opportunity to bring that message to the rich and powerful, so bring it to the "little ones." Nothing will have real and lasting value unless Christ comes with it, or unless it leads others to Christ. You are to be a missionary!

Being lovable requires spreading God's message. No excuses. The excuse of being not good enough, learned enough, eloquent enough, or brave enough is, Gregory the Great says, "excessive humility" (Admonition 26). Those who have funds but refuse to give them to "indigent neighbors" are "abettors of distress." Even worse, Gregory claims, is "withholding the word of preaching from sinning brethren," because doing so is "hiding the medicine of life from souls that are dying.... If a famine were wasting away the people, and these same people kept their corn hidden away, they would undoubtedly be the authors of death. Consequently, let them consider what punishment is to be meted out to those who do not minister the bread of grace which they themselves have received, when souls are perishing from hunger for the Word."

Most will never preach from a pulpit or write articles or books about faith. Some may catechize young people or adults, but many do not have this ministry. How is it, then, that every Christian can communicate Christ's message? Francis of Assisi had the right idea. In his Earlier Rule, he writes that, following the regulations of the Church, those who preach may do so only with proper permission, but "All the brothers, however, should preach by their deeds."[3] Lives of love bear witness to God. By putting into practice the suggestions in this book, you will be spreading God's love.

It has been said, "You may be the only Bible that some people will ever read." Proclaim your faith by wearing a visible sign of it. T-shirts that proclaim your belief in God are not the only way to become a walking billboard. For Christians, a simple cross or crucifix lapel pin, necklace, or brooch says in a quiet way, "I believe in Jesus." The Confraternity of Penitents, who live a Rule of Life in their own homes as lay people, requires that Catholic members and non-Catholic associates alike wear a cross or crucifix as a visible sign of their belief in Christ.[4] How fitting that the motto of this association is love of God and love of neighbor![5]

Other faiths have other visible symbols of belief. *Wearing a Star of David necklace, Golda attended a National Day of Prayer rally. Happy to display her Jewish faith, Golda believes that people of all faiths must pray together for their country.*

Gregory (Admonition 26) assures you that those who spread the message of Christ receive "the fullness of interior increase" and become "increasingly inebriated with the draught of multiplied grace." God gives you the grace to spread his message. The more you spread it, the more grace you receive to continue being his missionary. Teachers obtain many graces when they spread God's word. God grants grace to all his followers in the communications industry, for they bear a responsibility to transmit valuable information, to correct error, and to eliminate prejudice. God gives you a measure of his grace because you teach and communicate by word and example. *Clement thought of a good way to spread God's message. He had a print shop create business cards that read "God Loves You. Pass it on!" He puts one of these into the envelope while paying his bills and hands one to employees when paying tolls or buying gasoline.*

In Admonition 26 Gregory emphasizes the need to know a subject before speaking about it. "Our Redeemer himself ... did not wish to become a teacher of men on earth before his thirtieth year.... At twelve years of age Jesus is recorded as sitting in the midst of the doctors not teaching but asking questions." Knowledge comes with age and experience, but different people are capable at different times in their lives. *About 1246, twelve-year-old Rose of Viterbo became a street preacher, exhorting her town to rally to the Pope's side.[6] More recently, because of his knowledge and insight, eighteen-year-old Rusty was appointed to the governing council of an international religious organization.*

Assume that you know your faith and that you wish to share it. Do not lecture or badger people with polemics. Proceed slowly. Note verbal and bodily cues. Are your listeners receptive? Ask for feedback. "What do you think?" Listen not only to words but also to tone of voice. If you sense that someone does not understand, is tuning you out, or is growing hostile, end the discussion. Say, "Those are my thoughts. Thanks for hearing me out," then change the subject. Gregory (Admonition 26) likens continuing such a discussion, during which a person is hardening against the information, to constructing a building when "the frame has not been sufficiently strengthened, and heavy timbers are placed on it." The result, Gregory reminds us, "is not a dwelling but a ruin." Continuing to badger in the face of opposition or indifference is to destroy faith, not to build it.

13
Self-Respect

Becoming more lovable requires you to respect yourself. Imagine someone whom you respect. How does that person act, think, or speak? Can you use that person as your model?

Respect all people because God made them. Also, however, recognize human respect, which is not automatically due to someone but must be earned. God's image, tarnished as it may be, must be respected in Adolf Hitler, but his atrocities cost him human respect.

Humanly, others deserve respect for many reasons — their power, achievements, beauty, holiness, intellect, authority, and so on. Even if you feel few or none of these qualities in yourself, still you deserve respect because God respects you. Evaluate yourself, not by human standards, but by God's. *God directed the prophet Samuel to go to Jesse and to anoint one of his sons as king of Israel. Samuel thought Eliab, the eldest son, must be God's chosen one, but the Lord told him, "Do not look on his appearance or on the height of his stature, because I have rejected him; for the Lord does not see as mortals see; they look on the outward appearance, but the Lord looks on the heart." Samuel scrutinized each son in turn until he finally asked Jesse to bring in the youngest from tending the sheep. Then the Lord said, "Rise and anoint him; for this is the one." The one God chose was David, who loved the Lord intensely even though he was but a youth* (see 1 Sm 16:1–13).

Inordinate self-respect can cause you to put yourself ahead of everyone else. That form of pride is obnoxious to God and everyone else, too. But self-hate can be a form of pride, too, because it may spring from a thwarted desire to be the greatest or to have more than others. Perhaps you hate yourself because you do not measure up. Not measuring up would not bother you if you were not prideful. In fact, you are a unique creation of the Almighty. Others cannot be compared with you, nor you

with them. Care for who you are. And care for others, too. If you harm
or despise others or yourself, you lose favor with God.

God is looking at your heart. If your desire to become more lovable
is sincere, you can be certain that God approves. After all, if you want to
become lovable, you really want to become more like God who is Love.
Would you respect someone who aimed toward that goal? No matter
how others may stereotype or disrespect you, evaluate your self-worth
by God's standards. Whoever you were in the past has disappeared. You
are the "you" of the present moment. To continue allowing disrespect and
disapproval to undercut you is to cheapen yourself in your own eyes. Why
permit negativity to control your life? Your parents' love or rejection, the
friends you had or did not have, the things you did or avoided doing, the
thoughts you entertained or dismissed, the studies in which you excelled
and those you failed — all of these influence who you are today, but
none of them defines your value. You are priceless. Jesus bought your
salvation with his life. Since he respected you, foster that same respect
for yourself.

Making Changes

Sometimes small faults seem unimportant. You might even justify
them. You may tell yourself that you are not, after all, a great sinner. You
may see yourself as "pretty good." However, you owe it to yourself to try
to eliminate your defects. Without them, you can relate better to others.
Gregory (Admonition 34) advises those who err frequently in small ways
that little sins, frequently committed, are like raindrops one after the
other which, taken together, cause floods. By falling away little by little,
one falls completely because each little sin slowly weakens resistance
to sin. Failing to control your temper might harm someone eventually.
Entertaining sexual fantasies about adultery can lead to actual infidelity.
Spreading gossip destroys reputations. Missing Mass one Sunday makes
it easier to miss the next. And so it goes.

Warfare against your frailty takes vigilance. Resistance can be tiring.
Yet you grow in strength and grace as you persist. Beware thinking
that you have achieved perfection. Those who think this way might be
"actually seeking to spread for themselves the odor of a holy reputation"
(Admonition 34). That desire lets pride enter.

Be realistic. What can you change about yourself? To find out, cut
paper into strips. On each write one thing about yourself that you dislike.

Keep cutting and writing until you cannot think of another unlikable trait. Then make two envelopes. Label one "Things I Can Change" and the other "Things I Cannot Change." Reread the strips of paper and ask God to let you know if you can change each trait. If you cannot, put it into the "Cannot Change" envelope. If you can change, write on the back how you might do so; then put that slip into the "Can Change" envelope. Work on changing what you can change and pray to accept the things you cannot change. Pray to accept yourself, too.

Do not let success in conquering small sins lead to overconfidence, a condition dangerously close to complacency, the precursor to falling into grave sin. Remember that God's grace, not human power, keeps you from succumbing to temptation. Overconfident individuals who overestimate their resistance to sin might knowingly walk right into temptation. *Denton worked hard at conquering his faults. On a cruise, he watched an X-rated movie because he did not want his buddies to think he was a prude. At the time he was certain that he could withstand its harm, but even years later, his mind occasionally replays the lurid scenes he thought he could resist.*

Do Not Boast

Use your talents as God intended when he gave them to you. Concealing them indicates either false humility or laziness. Jesus said, "[L]et your light shine before others, so that they may see your good works and give glory to your Father in heaven" (Mt 5:16). Your talents and skills can improve your corner of the world. If someone praises you for a job well done, turn the praise to God by saying, "Thank God that he gave me these talents, and thank him that he gave you yours!"

Use your talents without boasting. Bragging will not make others respect you nor help you respect yourself. Those with real self-respect have no need to tell others how wonderful they are. Even those who are religious can have a problem with boasting. Telling others how much you give to your church is not going to inspire them to give more.

Among those less religious, boasting can consist of recounting misdeeds with a certain sense of pride. Gregory the Great (Admonition 32) notes that these types "offend more by their mouth than by deed" because their tales of evil spread the sin to more people than their actual deeds influenced. Gregory says, "If they fail to eradicate their own evil, they should at least dread the sowing of it, and be content with their individual damnation....

If they are not afraid of being wicked, they should at least be ashamed of being seen for what they are." Gregory notes that sin concealed is often sin avoided because people are ashamed of being caught in it. Years ago, men and women tried to keep their sexual liaisons secret. Now newspaper birth announcements often do not identify the parents as being married. Although many no longer acknowledge the sin of fornication, popular opinion does not define morality as God sees it.

Sometimes those who used to be involved in evil have a conversion, yet still boast about past evil actions. Boasting differs from giving a testimony. People who testify to their conversion express regret for past transgressions. The boastful do not truly convert, but continue to brag about past exploits rather than renouncing them. *Alex, who had a profound conversion, used to delight in telling others that he had broken all Ten Commandments except the fifth (Thou shalt not kill). He seemed to want others to know that he had risen from the depths of depravity to the heights of devotion. Had his devotion been more humble, Alex would have kept the depravity to himself.*

Purity

People who are pure respect themselves. Cultivate the virtue of purity by:

- Refraining from telling, reading, or listening to jokes that deal with sexual, sexist, racial, or ethnic humor.

- Dressing modestly. Father John of the Trinity, a Carmelite hermit, describes modest clothing as that which "is meant to conceal rather than reveal."[1] Evaluate your wardrobe in light of that description.

- Avoiding pornography in any form. There is no such thing as "light" porn. Any word or image that exploits the human body in any way or which portrays a person as a sex object is pornographic.

- Avoiding sexual self-stimulation.

- Engaging in foreplay and intercourse only with one's spouse.

- Refusing to dwell on impure thoughts.

    ~   Recognizing impurity in others as degrading to their dignity as persons.

    John the Evangelist tells us, "Beloved, we are God's children now; what we will be has not yet been revealed. What we do know is this: when he is revealed, we will be like him, for we will see him as he is. And all who have this hope in him purify themselves, just as he is pure" (1 Jn 3:2–3). Becoming lovable means being pure because being lovable means being like God, who is pure.

    Have you been impure in the past? Take heart! You can be "re-virginized"! *Until his conversion, Augustine of Hippo had lived an impure life, even fathering a child out of wedlock.*[2] Live purity in the present moment. Begin now!

Take Care of Your Body

    If you respect yourself, you will care for your body. Your body houses your soul, and, at the resurrection, both will appear before the Lord. Eat wisely. Dress warmly. Take vitamins. Exercise. Do whatever is needed to keep healthy. The physically healthy can concentrate more readily on spiritual health because their bodies do not distract them with other concerns. *Sister Mary Regina swims several times weekly. Brother Caleb cooks organically grown foods and uses herbal remedies for his fellow friars. Father Justus takes a long, daily walk, picking up trash as he goes.* Each of these people is close to God spiritually. If those who have embraced a religious vocation keep physically fit, certainly those in the secular world can do it.

    Taking care of your body demonstrates love for others. Use deodorants and mouthwashes. Drink more water and less coffee. Comb your hair. Keep your hair and beard trimmed. Bathe regularly and thoroughly. Launder and press your clothes. If you need help with personal hygiene, ask for it. *Mae always cared for herself impeccably but as she entered her eighties, her sense of smell decreased. Her son Joel and his wife Holly noticed that Mae wore the same clothes day after day. They suspected that she was not bathing thoroughly but were embarrassed to talk to her about it until a friend from church commented on her odor. Then they told her. She had lost strength in her arms and legs and so could not launder her clothes, climb into the tub, or scrub herself as she used to do. Joel and Holly persuaded her to change her clothing daily, to allow*

Holly to do her laundry, and to permit a nurse to help her weekly with her personal needs.

If you suspect that your personal hygiene needs improving, do what you need to do. If you know someone who could use some instruction in the area of personal cleanliness, do the person a favor and tactfully speak up. Personal unpleasantness can ruin friendships and employment. *Pierce's bosses praised his work but did not renew his contract, saying he "did not fit in." After he found another position, his friend Allen confided to him that perhaps his personal hygiene had cost him the job. Allen suggested that he keep his beard and hair trimmed, press his clothes, shower and apply deodorant daily before going to work. Pierce took the advice. He had a successful year, his contract was renewed, and he earned a promotion.*

Those who use perfume or cologne may become insensitive to the aroma. Use scents moderately because some people have allergies to them. *Every Sunday, Gil sat at least five pews away from Phyllis, whose perfume gave him headaches.*

Some smokers try to mask the odor of tobacco smoke with perfume or after-shave. Doing so only makes the problem worse. If you smoke, launder your clothing frequently. Take a shower and wash your hair daily. Even second-hand smoke causes lung disease and cancer, so, if you cannot quit, at least smoke outdoors so as not to put others' health at risk.

Drunkenness is an age-old problem. "Do not get drunk with wine, for that is debauchery," St. Paul admonished the Ephesians (Eph 5:18). He told the Romans, "let us live honorably, as in the day, not in reveling and drunkenness" (Rom 13:13). Not without reason, the Islamic law forbids any use of alcohol. Jesus drank wine, however, changing water into wine at the marriage feast of Cana (see Jn 2). Moderate use of alcoholic beverages can be healthy and socially acceptable. In some cultures it constitutes the norm. But drinking too much causes physical harm and destroys families, while drunk driving endangers the lives of others. Often those who imbibe too much do not realize that they are being immoderate. Ask a trustworthy friend to tell you whether you drink to excess. If the answer is "yes," attend an Alcoholics Anonymous meeting and ask a few questions to see if your friend might be correct. If you need to change, AA can help you.

It goes without saying that illegal drugs or overuse of prescription or over-the-counter medicine can cause bodily harm or death. Discuss with a physician the drugs that you use, and use only what your doctor prescribes. If these drugs do not seem to be helping you, consult your doctor. If you feel that your condition is worsening but your doctor seems unconcerned, consult another. An incorrect prescription can cause harm. *Masie had been having back problems for some time, so her doctor advised her to take aspirin. She did so regularly. When the pain increased her doctor told her to increase the dosage as needed. As the pain grew, Masie took more and more aspirin. One day she fainted and her husband rushed her to the hospital. Her severe pain had not been from her back. Rather, the aspirin had caused an ulcer, allowing stomach fluids to enter her abdominal cavity. Three weeks after being rushed to the hospital, Masie died.*

Take Care of Your Spirit

A healthy soul does not simply avoid sin, but strives to improve. Spiritual improvement is closely linked to emotional health. Here are some suggestions for fostering emotional health:

- Do not belittle yourself in word or deed. You need not brag about who you are, but do not discredit what God's grace has done in you. Give him the glory for anything good that you say or do.

- Accept compliments graciously. When someone says, "What a nice shirt you are wearing!" do not say, "Oh, it has a stain right here. See." Instead say, "Thanks."

- Accept only those responsibilities that you can meet. No one can do even 1/100th of the good that needs doing. Do what you can, do it well, and be satisfied.

- Spend time on healthy hobbies. Others may not enjoy what you do, but they can have their own pastimes. By doing enjoyable things, you rejuvenate yourself to tackle your duties.

- Relax. Even God took time off from work! The Lord asks that the Sabbath be a day of rest and relaxation. Do you observe it that way? If not, begin this week. Relaxation will allow you to return more gladly to work.

  ☙   Relax in your own way and help others to relax in theirs. What you may find relaxing may be work for someone else. *After a mentally taxing work week, Kyle visited Anthony. They spent the morning fishing and chatting, then Kyle decided to prune Anthony's raspberry patch. Anthony considered gardening to be work but went along with Kyle's idea as a gesture of friendship.*

  ☙   Find a friend who will accept you as God accepts you — for who you are. Everyone needs this sort of acceptance. *Fifty-five-year-old Rickie befriended Lonnie, who is almost thirty years younger. People who find it difficult to understand the friendship because of their age difference do not realize that Rickie and Lonnie think alike and accept each other's quirky personalities and styles. Sometimes these two musicians annoy one another, but they always apologize and rebuild the friendship because each one likes the other for who he is.*

Self-respect comes from accepting who you are, correcting your faults, strengthening your gifts, and loving yourself. You cannot be what anyone else is. Others are better at being themselves than you could ever be at being them. On the other hand, no one else can be who you are, let alone who you are meant to be or to become. Work toward becoming everything that God created you to be. Then self-respect will follow naturally.

14
Good Stewardship

Entrepreneurs hire stewards to manage their goods. You are God's steward because you are to care for his creation. God "pays" well because good stewards serve the Lord joyfully in this life while earning perpetual union with him in the hereafter. If you do not believe in God, you still ought to consider yourself a steward of the world you use but do not own. The world belongs to all creation.

Talents

You have talents and abilities which can help others. Using them wisely is loving. You cannot do everything, but you can do something. Your talents can help make the world happier.

To recognize your talents ask yourself, "What can I do better than someone else?" You might think, "Nothing," but that is not true. Every person, even a baby born with a fatal condition, has talents. *Trevor was born with Potter's Syndrome, a fatal kidney abnormality. In the few hours that he lived after his birth, Trevor gave, received, and elicited love from his parents, siblings, and health care professionals. If only more people had Trevor's talent!*

Discover your talents by keeping a diary. Write down what you do — shop, pray, clean, work, garden, read, knit, converse, play a sport, hunt, fish, build, and so on. At the end of a week, read what you have written. Look for patterns. What do you do frequently? What are you good at doing? These indicate your talents. How do they benefit others? In answering this question, think creatively. You might believe that enjoying crime novels benefits no one, but trying to solve crimes (even fictional ones) makes you a more interesting person. It also helps you to see things in original ways. That ability could be useful some day. Ask yourself, "How do my talents help me to be more loving toward God and my neighbor?" The answer may surprise you!

Those who have more talents than they can find time to employ must select and use well as many as they can. Others neglect talents that they could use. Your unused talents might be the very ones that could help others. *When Nancy retired from her forty-hour-a-week job, she learned knitting so that she could make outfits for the new babies of needy mothers at a local crisis pregnancy center.*

Money

Money can be a snare. Most people want more money than they have, even if they have millions, and may use their funds selfishly. Popular wisdom says that money can buy happiness, but it cannot — it can only purchase things. Of course, the real poverty of too little money can cause people to suffer.

Remember that "Nothing that is God's is obtainable by money."[1] Money is not going to buy you virtue, fortitude, or love. The American cowboy humorist Will Rogers is said to have repeated the aphorism, "Money's like manure. It's no good unless you spread it around."[2] To spread it, you need to have it. Not every way to obtain money is loving, nor is every way to spend it!

Obviously, it is unloving to mug a pedestrian and steal his wallet. But it is equally unloving to cheat on your taxes, purposely give a low estimate when you know that something will cost more, or overcharge. It is also unloving to run up unnecessary debt, to live above your means, or to squander money on frivolities. *Vivian loved collectibles and gambling. She amassed such a credit card debt that her husband had to file for bankruptcy.*

Learn to manage money. Write down how much you have and then how much you spend according to categories (food, clothing, utilities, gifts, correspondence, rent, mortgage, taxes, personal items, travel expenses, recreation, tuition, charity, and so on). Which expenditures are necessary? Which can be reduced or eliminated? Where can you find savings? Are you spending money in loving ways?

Do not become a miser. Splurge a bit, even on yourself. People need a little fun, or they are no fun to be around. Everyone needs vacations and holidays. Spending to brighten your life a bit will make you happier, and a happier you will brighten your acquaintances, too. Invite some friends to the movies, to dinner, or on a vacation, perhaps at your own expense, and enjoy the time together.

Almsgiving

Giving to the poor (almsgiving) is a traditional way to show love. Jesus said to keep almsgiving secret. Broadcasting your generosity will gain only the praise of others. But if you give secretly, without expecting public acclaim, "your Father who sees in secret will reward you" (Mt 6:4). Modern life provides many opportunities for secret almsgiving. Mail a check or use a credit card to donate to charity, and neither friends nor strangers will know unless you tell them.

Giving alms brings great rewards, but withholding them incurs severe judgment. Jesus told a parable about those who helped the hungry, thirsty, naked, homeless, prisoners, and those who refused to help. Those who serve their neighbors in what Mother Teresa of Calcutta called "the distressing disguise of the poor" serve Jesus. Those who do not, ignore Jesus. Jesus is also the Lord who rewards or punishes, based on how a person treats "the least" (see Mt 25: 31–46). Gregory (Admonition 21) says this about those who ignore the needs of others: "They are not told that they committed robberies or some other violent deeds, and yet they are consigned to the everlasting flames of hell." If refusing to give alms is the same as robbing others of their goods, what judgment will you face?

Most do not plan to rob a neighbor's house. Nevertheless, they are not guiltless. Holding back what could be given means "walk[ing] about amidst the carnage" of your neighbors (Gregory the Great, Admonition 22). Those who are stingy "almost daily destroy as many persons as are dying in poverty" because they have the means to help but refuse to give it. Basil the Great wrote, "The bread you store up belongs to the hungry; the cloak that lies in your chest belongs to the naked; the gold you have hidden in the ground belongs to the poor."[3] Francis of Assisi told his friars, "It would be considered a theft on our part if we did not give to someone in greater need than we are."[4]

"For when we administer necessities to the needy … we pay a debt of justice, rather than do a work of mercy," Gregory continues. "[I]t surely is a matter of justice that they who receive what is bestowed by the Lord of all, should use it for the common good." Jesus alluded to stingy wealth in the parable of the rich man who feasted at his table but who gave not even a scrap to the beggar at his gate. When the rich man died, although he had done no positive evil, he was sent to hell (see Lk 16:19–31). Not sharing surplus wealth is the same as robbing others of what is theirs. Even those who do not have much are still obliged to give alms to the even less fortunate. *Mother Teresa frequently told the following story. "One evening a gentleman came to our house and told me, 'There is a Hindu family with eight children, and they have not eaten for a long time. Do something for them.' I took some rice, and I went straightaway. I could see in the children's faces terrible hunger. And yet when the mother took the rice she divided it in two portions and went out. When she came back I asked her, 'Where did you go? What did you do?' She gave me one answer only: 'They are hungry also.' She had next-door neighbors, a Muslim family, and she knew they were hungry."*[5]

Giving alms, however, must be done morally. "Obviously, it is one thing to show mercy for sins committed, another to sin in order to be able to show mercy" (Gregory the Great, Admonition 22). Despite his best intentions, Robin Hood committed a moral evil by robbing the rich to give to the poor. His "merry men" would have done better to imitate Francis of Assisi's merry friars who begged from the rich the food and goods they then shared with the poor.

Some will offer to God the loot they steal from the poor. This is a prime offense against charity. "Like one who kills a son before his father's eyes is the person who offers a sacrifice from the property of the poor" (Sir 34:20). Slumlords who collect rent from the poor cannot expiate their guilt by paying for the construction of a new suburban church, temple, or mosque.

Gregory the Great (Admonition 21) warns against disdaining those who receive alms. Those who give are no better than those who receive. Almsgivers must "acknowledge that they have been appointed by the heavenly Lord to be the dispensers of temporal means, and display their humility the more … when they consider that they are appointed for the service of others … fear should hold them down."

You are a steward of what the Creator has given. Your money and your goods do not belong to you. They belong to God who gave you the talents and means to succeed. Even hard work reveals more the generosity of God than of yourself. Had God created you differently or allowed you to be raised differently, you might not be able to work so hard. So when you give alms, be generous and wise, never expecting thanks or praise and not begrudging the gift or taking pride in having given it.

Some people want to give only "worthy" people alms. *Agnes attends church services and prayer meetings regularly, but she refuses to give to the AIDS foundation because most of those suffering from AIDS are homosexuals. By contributing to health care for homosexuals, Agnes believes that she is approving behaviors condemned by her church.* Gregory the Great (Admonition 21) demolishes such false religiosity. "He, however, who gives his bread to an indigent sinner, not because he is a sinner, but because he is a human being, actually nourishes a righteous beggar, not a sinner, for he loves in him not his sin but his nature." Of course, you may not have money enough to donate to every cause, but prejudice must not influence the causes you choose.

Some people may give alms in hopes of making restitution for past sins. This worthy motive is not without danger. Righteousness cannot be bought. It is wrong to sin, thinking that you can later repent and be forgiven. Nor can you sin, thinking that you can make up for the evil later by giving alms. Of such a person, Gregory (Admonition 21) says, "To God he gives his possessions, but himself to the Devil." God may be merciful, but he is not a fool.

Use and share all goods and possessions lovingly. Getting rich for the sake of having more is neither moral nor loving. Such a choice focuses on self to the detriment of others whom that wealth could help. Jesus reminded us, "For what will it profit them to gain the whole world and forfeit their life?" (Mk 8:36) He told a parable about a rich man who had such a bountiful harvest that he planned to build bigger barns to store it all. Then he intended to "relax, eat, drink, be merry" for many years. "But God said to him, 'You fool! This very night your life is being demanded of you. And the things you have prepared, whose will they be?' So it is with those who store up treasures for themselves but are not rich towards God" (Lk 12:16–21). Generosity benefits those who receive, but also those who give. *Joseph Matose is an artist whose work is becoming more widely recognized. Joe tithes, that is he gives away 10 percent, of all his earnings. He also gives away numerous prints and cards featuring his artwork. In addition, he donates paintings to various charities. While he does not have a classy advertising campaign, his work has found a wider and wider market. Joe attributes his success to God's grace.*[6]

What are some unique ways to give alms? Slip a coin into someone else's expired parking meter. On a toll road, pay your toll as well as that for the car behind you. Skip snacks and give the money to your favorite charity. *Every day, Wendy took an extra sandwich for a homeless man who frequented the sidewalk outside her office.*

Dealing with Success

Your talents come from God, who deserves more credit than you. Success proves your stewardship of God-given gifts. Give God praise and thanks. Basking in success makes a person grow lazy and forget that this world is not a permanent dwelling place. A team may win the championship one year, but may well lose it the next. The goals you achieve someone else will challenge or surpass. A new house will grow old and need repair. The transitory things of this world are reminders of the love that God, the great Giver, lavishes. Therefore, while doing good to others, refer all good back to God.

Dealing with Evil

Sometimes God seems to give not good, but evil. First, God, who is all-good, cannot give evil. He may, however, withhold good or permit evil, as he permitted satan to attack Job. When this happens, God can bring good out of evil if you allow him. *On September 11, 2001, along with many others, James Cartier died in the destruction of the Twin Towers in New York City. In his memory, his six surviving siblings created a website which has brought James' love and selflessness to many internet viewers.*[7]

How do you respond with love when you encounter evil? Pray. When God seems deaf he may be acting as the Divine Physician who must wound in order to heal or who must force the sick to take medicine. Gregory the Great (Admonition 27) suggests that some of what seems evil is proof that God has not given up on humankind. "When a physician gives up hope for a patient, he allows him to have whatever he fancies; but a person whose cure he deems possible is forbidden much that he desires."

Instead of complaining that God is not granting your desires, thank him and try to discover what spiritual gift he has in store. Those who accept everything as God's will receive a holy joy that radiates and attracts others to them and, through them, to God. *On her first visit of the day, Willa paid a call on Mrs. Behan, a widow bedridden from arthritis. "I know I have it difficult," Mrs. Behan confided, "but I have got my daughter Clare to look after me. And I have this really interesting job being dispatcher for the police. The calls come in here, and I send the police cars out to those who need them. But look at poor Mrs. Somers. She has it worse than I do. She only has her husband to care for her, and he is not that strong." After a pleasant chat, Willa drove off to visit Mrs. Somers who also was bedridden from arthritis. Mrs. Somers was glad for the company. "Oh, I know I have it bad," Mrs. Somers smiled, "but look what I can do." She held up the colorful blanket that she was knitting. "I make these for the nursing homes. They love to get them. And," she smiled at her husband who was sitting nearby, "I have Dick to take care of me. But poor Mrs. Behan. Her husband is dead, and she cannot use her fingers like I can. She is much worse off than I am." Willa never forgot the holy joy of these two suffering women, each of whom had found the good and used her talents despite severe physical disability.* How much happiness comes by looking to God, nature, and others rather than focusing on self! "Look to him, and be radiant" (Ps 34:5).

Caring for Creation

Human beings have been placed in God's world to be good stewards of it. You cannot stop the ozone layer from thinning out, but you can use spray bottles instead of aerosols. You can car pool, combine errands to save on fuel, plant a tree, pick up trash, reduce air conditioning, recycle, compost, buy organic, avoid Styrofoam, and use natural pesticides and fertilizers. These things might seem inconsequential in the big picture, but that does not matter to God. He is concerned that you do what you can. Whatever you do makes a difference to "Mother Nature."

Being a good steward means realizing that God counts on the wise use of what he has given. Everything is his gift.

15
Patience

Patience is a virtue, but it is also a necessary quality of love. St. Paul lists patience as love's first quality. "Love is patient" (1 Cor 13:4). You need patience when, as Robert Burns stated in his poem, "To a Mouse," "The best laid plans of mice and men go oft astray." And they often do! Francis of Assisi noted that "We can never know how patient or humble someone is when everything is going well with him. But when those who should cooperate with him do exactly the opposite, then we can know. A man has as much patience and humility as he has then, and no more."[1] Everyone needs some "patience practice." One thing can be guaranteed: if you develop the virtue of patience, you will definitely make others around you more comfortable.

What causes you to feel impatience? Good legislation taking forever to be enacted? Waiting in line? Rainy weather on the day of your yard sale? Hunting all season but never once seeing the flick of a tail? A home improvement project falling behind schedule? A doctor's appointment at ten a.m. but being called into the office at noon? Pouring milk into your breakfast cereal, then having a long-winded neighbor call to harangue about the new zoning regulations? Every day, many times a day, opportunities to practice patience present themselves. Do you notice these as opportunities?

"When you are excited to impatience, think for a moment how much more reason God has to be angry with you, than you have for anger against any human being; and yet how constant is His love and forbearance,"[2] Elizabeth Ann Seton told the teachers in her schools. Certainly life can provide frustrations. But how much more do human pettiness and immaturity stand out in contrast with God's patience.

Where to begin? With prayer. Pray for patience. Ephraim of Syria composed a prayer for Lent that fits the circumstances of every day:

"Lord and Master of my life, take far from me the spirit of laziness, discouragement, domination, and idle talk; grant to me, thy servant, a spirit of chastity, humility, patience, love. Yea, my Lord and King, grant me to see my sins and not to judge my neighbor, for thou art blessed forever and ever. Amen."[3]

If you pray for patience, expect God to grant it. But you may not learn patience in exactly the way you expect. The following story is told of Philip Neri, who had been battling impatience for a long time: *One morning at Mass he gazed at the Crucifix and said, "O good Jesus! why is it that Thou dost not hear me? See how long a time I have besought Thee to give me patience! Why is it that Thou hast not heard me, and why is my soul disquieted with thoughts of anger and impatience?" The answer came in his soul: "Dost thou not ask patience of Me, Philip? Behold I will give it thee speedily on this condition: that, if thy heart desire it, thou earn it through these temptations of thine."*[4]

Patience comes like that — not by a magic touch from God that takes away your human nature but by practice in denying your impulsiveness and squashing your impatience. As your self-will weakens, you will become more patient. Most people have a vigorous self-will that weakens only when it is subdued. Subdued long enough, it eventually dies.

Controlling Anger

Everyone gets angry sometimes. Some of that anger is justified. Although Jesus had spoken often about the just uses of money, the moneychangers in the temple had ignored his preaching. Jesus wanted everyone to understand that greed harms others and impedes a relationship with God; therefore, mercenary transactions in a sacred place were especially reprehensible. When Jesus cleansed the temple of those interested in moneymaking instead of worship, he did not explode impulsively. Instead, his justifiable anger led Jesus to enter the temple with a whip of cords and to drive the moneychangers out, charging them not to make God's house into a robber's den (see Mk 11:15–17).

As Jesus' behavior shows, anger can be loving. When teaching or correction fails to eliminate an abuse, controlled anger might make a difference. Scripture does not record whether any moneychangers reformed, but Jesus' action made them think about it.

Often, however, anger leads to lack of control and overreaction. Anger drives people away from one another. Uncontrolled anger in those who are trying to act holy can also drive people from God. Since Jesus preached self-control and love, why would anyone but a religious hypocrite let anger spin out of control? To be loving, avoid contention; disagree without becoming disagreeable.

How can anger be controlled? The familiar advice about counting to ten works. If ten is too low a number, count to twenty or fifty before responding. Counting allows time to think, to cool off, and to respond with charity.

Meek persons who tend to avoid conflict may not say what needs to be said. Counting to ten or twenty or fifty may also provide time to fortify courage and speak up. Gregory the Great (Admonition 17) uses the example of Paul the Apostle. "Why," Gregory asks, "is it that, great master of the teaching art that he [Paul] was, in the present illustration of it he proposes the exercise of authority to the one [Titus], and patience to the other [Timothy]? Is it not that he sees Titus endowed with too meek a spirit, and Timothy with a little too zealous one? He inflames the one with zeal, the other he restrains with the gentleness of patience. He gives to the one what is lacking, he takes away from the other what is excessive. He aims at urging on the one with a spur, he checks the other with a bridle."

To calm someone who is angry, Gregory (Admonition 16) offers a few pointers. Let them alone "when their anger is actually seething; for when they are aroused, they do not perceive what is being said to them. But when they have been restored to their senses, they the more willingly accept words of counsel, as they blush for having been peacefully borne with." If, however, they are attacking others with their words, then they should be rebuked "sparingly with a certain respectful forbearance." Calm admonition to stop speaking so harshly is often effective. Never raise your voice when correcting those who are raising theirs. Calmness is like water to the fire of anger, but anger in response to anger is like throwing fuel onto flames.

Quelling Quarrelsomeness

Quarrelsome people find something wrong with everything. No matter how many virtues they may have have, the quarrelsome deceive themselves about their holiness. Jesus admonished you to love your neighbor, not argue with him or her. Gregory the Great (Admonition 23) says that knowing more than others is no excuse for quarreling with them. James the Apostle writes, "But the wisdom from above is first pure, then peaceable, gentle, willing to yield, full of mercy and good fruits, without a trace of partiality or hypocrisy" (Jas 3:17). Gregory notes how birds and beasts live together in flocks and herds, without quarreling. If animals can live in such concord, cannot human beings do even better?

Those who like to pick fights need to eradicate this tendency. What does it matter if another person does something in a particular way? Wears certain clothing? Holds a certain belief? Some things do matter, but many do not. If it does not really matter, let it go. Those who like to argue at least should exercise the courtesy not to do so in front of others. *Whitney and Maxine liked to quarrel. Although they seemed to get along and had been married for forty years, they often made others uncomfortable with their petty disagreements. At one dinner, they were arguing over how to cut the roast. To end the bickering, one dinner guest wanted to take the knife and cut the roast herself.*

Discord

Sowing discord means doing or saying things that cause others to argue. Whether out of fun or out of malice, some people like to provoke arguments. Whatever the cause, discord interferes with love. Gregory the Great (Admonition 24) notes that "In one single sin of malice [the sowers of discord] work innumerable others, since by sowing discord they extinguish charity…. Nothing is more esteemed by God than the virtue of charity, nothing is more desired by the Devil than its extinction. He, then, who sows discord and thus destroys charity in the neighbor, serves God's enemy, as if he were his familiar friend." Work to eradicate the bad habit of sowing discord. When poised to provoke an argument or to say something that will set people at odds, do not simply bite your tongue. Instead, say something that will bring people together. Consistently doing this will eliminate a nasty habit and make peace rather than destroy it.

Excessive Patience

It is possible to be too patient if someone needs correction, but you say nothing. Do not make the mistake of keeping peace at any cost. Your boss or your spouse may need correction, but may never learn how to yield gracefully unless you and others help. *Because Hildy had a learning disability, her mother always found fault with her schooling and her treatment. Everyone else had a problem, not Hildy. Being strong-willed and quick-thinking, the girl learned how to browbeat anyone who implied that she was wrong. She came to believe that everyone was against her and that she was always right. As a result, she could not retain a job because she considered all her bosses rude or incompetent. She had no regular physician because she could never find one who would accept her uncontrolled behavior. She lost friends because in her mind anyone who noticed even a single fault did not understand her. Hildy's whole life might have been happier had her mother weathered her child's tantrums and made Hildy take responsibility for her actions.*

To keep the peace, civilized societies need a police force. Police forces should ensure justice, truth, charity, and security to all in the society. "Do not give a false peace," wrote Benedict the monk.[5] A false peace pretends to agree with the thoughts, words, or deeds of others for the sake of "unity," but this can lead to accepting evil. Rather than live in cowardly collusion with evil, decent people will sacrifice their peace, even their lives, as they unleash "the wrath of God" against wicked abuses and deeds.

To avoid conflict, some people accept things that they should oppose. In reality, it can be doing others a favor to point out their real faults, but they may not think so. Before confronting anyone, steel yourself for a tongue-lashing. If you are afraid to confront someone alone, ask one or more friends with backbone to accompany you. In your own words, try to get across this message: "You are not perfect, and some of us disagree with you. Maybe you ought to reconsider your position." It is loving to provide such feedback even if the person confronted responds with anger or malice. You have a moral obligation to confront and correct evil or sometimes even imperfections that are making another less likable. Love is not always easy. It involves sacrifice, which sometimes requires disturbing the peace. No matter how the other person reacts, strive to remain peaceful. Even if your advice is rejected, continue to treat the person you have reproved as a beloved brother or sister.

Impulsiveness

Impulsiveness causes hasty decisions made without sufficient forethought. It can lead to regrettable actions that could cause lasting harm. *When Gina slapped her son in the face for saying something rude and insensitive, it hurt their relationship more than his cheek.* Prudence demands maintaining composure and trying to foresee the effects of your words and actions.

"Sticks and stones will break my bones, but words can never hurt me" is a false proverb. Both words and actions can harm. Any hurt can be forgiven, but the regret that impulsiveness can cause never fades away completely.

Whether harm is accidental or deliberate, others deserve an apology. *Bonita and Carl were given complimentary tickets to a dinner theater, with the explicit instructions that if they did not use the tickets the director would castigate Hector, the actor who provided them. After dinner, Bonita and Carl then felt like going home, so they turned in the tickets, asking the clerk to "give them to someone else who could use them." Discovering that the tickets were unused, Hector's boss lectured him in front of the entire cast for giving his complimentary tickets to people who "ate and ran." Bonita and Carl did not act out of malice but their action still caused Hector harm.*

Those who tend to be impulsive should practice looking before they leap. It has been said before, but it bears repeating: when you are asked to make a decision, say, "Let me think about that." Then be patient. Think for at least five minutes. The habit of thinking before speaking or acting provides the chance to foresee consequences. You may spare yourself and others a great deal of grief.

Bearing Pains or Trials Calmly without Complaint

Things that do not go your way are called "trials" because they "try" patience. The natural tendency is to complain during trials. But a better tendency is to thank God for them. Trials grow virtues — patience, strength, fortitude, courage, perseverance. Without trials, these virtues may never strengthen. Enduring trials by trusting God in them develops spiritual strength. The trials will not become less painful and may still cause you to complain, but they provide an opportunity to practice patience. God uses them to make those he loves more loving. *Anne Foose went through a disastrous time while trying to open Gianna's Prayer, a bookshop and pro-life pregnancy counseling center located next-door to an abortion clinic. Anne's business partner disappeared, leaving her with a floundering enterprise, a $136,000 debt, and three lawsuits filed by the abortionist next door. Anne decided to make the most of the situation. She enlisted neighborhood youngsters to pray for her business. She spoke to women who came into her store on their way to the clinic and convinced some to not abort their babies. She arranged several speaking* *engagements about her faith in God and how he had taught her virtue through her setbacks.*[6] *When she sold the bookstore several years later, she had developed the very virtues that she needed to begin a new youth ministry that would take her all across the United States.*[7]

Patience in Illness

Illness tests the patience of both the sick person and the caregivers. In times of health, Gregory the Great (Admonition 13) suggests using good health to do good works so as "not to set aside the opportunity of winning eternal salvation." One of those good works is caring for the ill. Gregory makes another pointed observation. "Men moan for having refused to serve God, when it is utterly impossible for them to serve Him and repair the losses due to their neglect." After a death, how many friends regret having never visited? If only they could roll back the years and make those visits! *Vanessa knew Mr. and Mrs. Flaxon, a gracious, elderly couple. When Mrs. Flaxon died, Vanessa promised herself that she would invite the widower over for dinner but never seemed to find the time to do it. When he died two years later, Vanessa felt remorse that she had never offered her invitation.*

Ill people face great trials and often regret their inability to perform the good works that they used to do. Gregory (Admonition 13) reminds them that "they are sons of God by the very fact that the scourge of discipline chastises them.... The stones for building the temple of God were hammered outside, that they might be set in the building without the sound of hammer (see 1 Kgs 6:7); so we are now smitten with scourges outside, that afterwards we may be set into the temple of God ... consider what great health of heart is bestowed by bodily affliction, for it recalls the mind to a knowledge of itself and renews the memory of our infirmity, which health commonly disregards." Sickness is a great reminder that humans are, after all, mortal beings.

The sick ought also to "consider how great a gift is bodily affliction, in that it both cleanses sins committed and restrains such as could be committed." What a novel insight! The sick cannot commit many of the sins they could when healthy, although they certainly need to avoid others such as impatience, despair, and faultfinding. They also frequently find themselves remembering the past and regretting its sins. Prolonged illness can become a great gift in the spiritual life, for it can foster repentance and perfect souls. *Years before she was diagnosed with cancer, Ariana had rejected faith in God. Through many painful treatments, some of which caused remission of the cancer for a period of time, she persisted in her atheism. She knew that her children were praying for her and told them not to bother. She was not about to convert. When the cancer reached its final stages, however, on her death bed Ariana agreed to see a member of the clergy and made her peace with God.*

"To preserve the virtue of patience, the sick are to be admonished ever to bear in mind how great were the evils endured constantly by our Redeemer at the hands of those whom He had created." Gregory's words echo those of countless other spiritual writers. A time-tested method of dealing with illness is to spend time reading the Passion of Christ in Scripture. When ill, unite your sufferings with those of Christ who, though totally innocent and totally good, suffered for love of you more than you could ever suffer for love of him. Offering up sufferings for others, as prayers of the body when unable to say many other prayers, brings good out of suffering. Suffering could be God's way of providing purification from sins and attachments to worldly things, thus preparing you for heaven. "No cross, no crown" is an old saying. Glory comes only after experiencing suffering which weakens the hold on ungodly things.

Forbearance

Some people must endure great trials and contradictions for long periods of time. Such trials strengthen forbearance, also called long-suffering. Prolonged trials provide powerful opportunities to foster patience. Parents of teens have years to practice this virtue. *Astrid, a mom of six children, wryly remarked that "the terrible twos last from eighteen months until twenty-two years."*

Parents need to remember that usually "time conquers all." Age generally solves most problems between parents and teens. Imagine a contentious teen when he or she is forty years old. By that time, for most people, life looks considerably different than it did twenty years earlier, and their ways of dealing with life change accordingly.

Living with addicts can be extremely trying. They cannot overcome an addiction until admitting to having one. Their families and friends must not make excuses for the addict, lie for the addict, or pretend that the addiction does not exist. Those behaviors and others keep the addict in denial and enable the addiction to continue. Alanon, a support group for families of alcoholics, offers those who live with an addict many ideas on how to help. Consider speaking to a counselor about staging an intervention, which sometimes can help an addict confront the problem. Aim toward convincing the addict that he or she has a problem. Only then can change begin.

Even after an addiction ends, many problematical behaviors still persist. Addicts need to attend support groups of recovering addicts for many years, often for a lifetime, and their family members may have to continue to attend similar groups as well. *The Jones family took in their niece Meg, a recovering drug and alcohol addict who also bore emotional scars from her abusive family. She attended AA and NA meetings while Mr. and Mrs. Jones attended Alanon. All parties needed support and advice in the recovery process.*

Bearing with someone who suffers mental illness can also be very trying. Many will not admit their illness. These victims may think and act in skewed ways. They may be unable to retain a job and often neglect or refuse the medication they need. Counselors can help such suffering individuals as well as those who support them.

Dealing with those who continually challenge patience demands prayer. Realizing that God gives strength by offering opportunities to practice forbearance provides strength for the day and for days to come. *Baxter's foster brother Percy suffers from mental illness coupled with alcoholism. He has made some poor choices including getting in trouble with the law and entering a homosexual relationship with a man who then deserted him. Baxter's approach has been to show Percy that he loves him by spending time with him but also by refusing to bail Percy out of the consequences of his choices. He prays for Percy daily and asks others to pray for him as well.*

Steadfastness

Steadfastness implies loyalty and faithfulness. God's love is steadfast in that it remains constant despite your imperfections and sins. That steadfastness is the model for loyalty to others. Those who constantly try your patience may tempt you to abandon them, but doing that may not be loving.

Through honest dialog and courtship, engaged couples must do their best, before taking the marriage vow, to determine whether they can form a permanent relationship. God calls the married to steadfast love and commitment. Of course, in an abusive marriage different parameters apply because partners must be steadfast in love for themselves and their children. No one deserves abuse. The most loving thing is to leave an abusive situation. Sometimes leaving will inspire the abuser to change. *Abby's husband Duane was sexually provocative and a viewer of child pornography. When he refused to change, Abby obtained a restraining order and filed for divorce. Duane was so shaken that he agreed to many months of counseling for sexual addiction. He also consented to having no unsupervised contact with his children.*

Steadfastness also involves commitment and loyalty to work and to groups. Fair-weather friends or employees lack steadfastness, unlike those who will stick with the team when the going gets tough. Evaluate work and groups to see if they are morally sound. If so, pray about staying with them. You may be the very person to help them overcome their trials.

Bearing trials is part of being steadfast. Wishy-washy love flees when trials come. Steadfast love remains. These trials can involve people or situations, but generally they involve both. *Some of the members of The Association of Devotees of Saint Silenius were sowing discord in the group. Sister Suzy, the founder, tried for months to make peace. Realizing that the situation was worsening, she and a few others took the advice of a religious superior and broke from the original foundation to begin the Association again as The Saint Silenius Sodality and to make peace among its members a requirement of membership. Since most members in the original foundation were unaware of the problem, the breakup unnerved nearly everyone. Some dropped out. Those who were steadfast in their devotion to Saint Silenius either stayed with the original foundation or joined the new one.*

Brooding over Injuries

In *The Way of Perfection* Teresa of Avila wrote, "Fly a thousand miles from saying, 'I was in the right; it was not right for me to suffer this; they had no right to do such a thing to me.' Do you think there was any question of rights when Jesus suffered the injuries which were so unrighteously inflicted on Him?"[8] Anyone who suffers no injuries in life must be dead! Every human being suffers — from others, from illness, from disaster. Which type of injury is more difficult to bear? The one you are suffering from now.

Accept injuries, mourn losses, and then move on with life. Forgive those people or situations that caused the injury because without forgiveness the injury never heals. Brooding over injuries is like picking at a scab. Even time cannot heal it because the wound never closes. Wholeness comes only by moving past the hurts. Praying for healing helps immensely. *Virginia was terribly hurt when Natalie, whom she considered a trusted friend, began to spread lies about her. She could not understand Natalie's motives. Of course, the friendship ended. Nevertheless, Virginia could not erase the hurt from her mind. Several years later, she decided that she had to stop brooding over Natalie's harm. She decided to pray for healing and asked others to pray for that intention. Shortly thereafter, Virginia finally felt able to release the pain.*

Waiting

A Spanish proverb states, "No matter how early you get up, you cannot hasten the dawn."[9] Waiting is part of life. Children want their gifts, but they have to wait for Christmas. Adults want a job or a spouse, but they have to wait to get hired or to get married. Parents want a bit of freedom, but they have to wait until their child is potty trained or goes to school or learns to drive. You anticipate that a job will take a certain amount of time to complete; then you must wait while another person takes longer than expected. You teach someone new skills and must wait while they learn to use them. You want to explain something quickly but must repeat it until the listener understands. Every day, whether in the grocery, at the bank, in the office, at school, on the road, or at home, you wait. Everyone has a certain tolerance for waiting. For some, that tolerance lasts only a few minutes. For others, it could last several hours or more. One good measure of your patience is your degree of tolerance when waiting.

The spiritual life also requires waiting. "Lord, give me patience right now," is a tongue-in-cheek prayer. But often people expect God to answer prayers at once or to come when called, as if he were a servant. Instant oatmeal can be bought, but not instant spiritual growth. "We must wait for God long, meekly, in the wind and wet, in the thunder and lightning, in the cold and dark. Wait, and he will come. He never comes to those who do not wait," F. W. Faber reminds us.[10]

Difficulty in waiting can be filled with diversions or activities. Read, pray, develop a hobby, make a phone call, clean, take a nap, or play some music. When waiting is likely, take something to do while waiting.

Whenever he goes to an appointment, Jerome carries along a book to read while he is waiting. Heather carries a sketchbook. Marianne takes along her knitting.

All waiting eventually ends. Remember other such moments. Thinking about them will provide perspective. Above all, be loving and understanding toward those who have no control over how long the wait might be. If kept waiting too long, speak charitably to the one in charge. Maybe speaking up will help to remedy the situation for others. When seen on time, thank the person in charge. A simple, "Thank you for seeing me on time" reinforces the commitment to keeping a schedule.

Becoming more lovable requires waiting, too, until some of the principles in this book become part of normal behavior. "Be patient with everyone, but above all with yourself," Francis de Sales advised. "Do not lose courage in considering your own imperfections but instantly set about remedying them — every day begin the task anew."[11] Today is the first day of the rest of your life. Begin now, again, to set things right.

16
Lovable You

Has reading this book made you more lovable? Putting into practice some of what you have read will make it so. But those who read without practicing the techniques "are like those who look at themselves in a mirror; for they look at themselves and, on going away, immediately forget what they were like," James the Apostle wrote (Jas 1: 23–24). It takes practice to become loving.

Some things can change but others will not, at least for now. The familiar Serenity Prayer of Alcoholics Anonymous contains much truth. "God, grant me the serenity to accept the things I cannot change, courage to change the things I can, and wisdom to know the difference." *Kathleen has a God Box, just a small, ordinary cardboard box. When feeling that she can do nothing about one thing or another, she writes it on a slip of paper and puts it into the God Box. Now that problem is God's worry, not hers.* Allowing God to be God over situations that you cannot handle is a powerful step toward treating yourself with love.

Finding a Counselor

Many times this book has mentioned finding a good counselor. At one time or another, you may feel that you need one:

- When you feel some aspect of life is unmanageable or out of control.

- When you are at your wits' end.

- When certain emotions or impulses are so strong that they frighten you.

    ❧   When you do not know how to respond.

    ❧   When you are pulled in so many directions that you feel fragmented.

    ❧   When someone or something is causing turmoil in your life.

These and other concerns could indicate the need for professional help. Find a few people who can be honest with you. Share your worries and ask, "Do you think that I ought to see a counselor?" If most agree, you probably could benefit from professional advice.

A good counselor can help you to develop more loving behaviors and can also suggest ways of dealing with difficult people, some of whom may need counseling, too. Because counseling requires a strong relationship of trust, find a good therapist. First determine if insurance will pay for all or part of counseling, and with whom. Some companies pay for certain therapists but not others. If insurance will not pay, consider a nonprofit counseling firm that offers a sliding fee. Find one near you by calling a local mental health agency and asking for referral.

Doctors can help, as well as members of the clergy, other professionals, or organizations of professionals. Ask such individuals to suggest a good therapist. Compile a list and see which names are repeated. They are probably the counselors whom professionals consider to be most competent. Eliminate any who have a close connection to a friend or family member or any who are counseling or have counseled someone who knows you. Your therapist should harbor no preconceived notions about you. Also eliminate anyone you might encounter outside of therapy. It is best to have a totally professional relationship with a counselor.

Telephone the therapists and study their websites. Do they belong to professional organizations? Which ones? What is their training and experience? What are their specialties? How long have they been counseling? Look for a therapist who has had intensive academic study (a master's degree or a doctorate) in mental health. Furthermore, find someone who has had a supervised clinical experience as part of his or her education and who is either certified, registered, or licensed as a therapist. Try not to select someone at either end of the experience spectrum. A brand new therapist may not be as competent as a more experienced counselor, but one about to retire may not have kept up with the latest theories or may retire in the middle of your therapy.

Leave your name, number, and a time to be reached with the receptionist or on the answering machine of the therapist who seems would best meet your needs. Do not discuss your problem. You need say only, "I would like to speak to the therapist." Ideally you will get a call back to make an appointment. You need not convince him or her to see you, nor should you discuss your problem over the phone.

After the appointment, evaluate the session. Did the therapist listen attentively while you talked? Did you do most of the talking? Were you comfortable? Could you be honest? Do you feel that whatever you share will be "safe" with this person? Did a secretary or another person disturb your session? Did the counselor take a phone call or see someone else during your therapy? Could you hear voices outside your room? Did the therapist remain non-judgmental and accepting? Did the therapist tell you anything helpful? Do the therapist's goals and time frame seem realistic? Can you set up regular appointments? Can you afford this person?

Abuse victims unconsciously may select an abusive therapist. If working with the therapist causes the same feelings that you experienced during the abuse, consider changing therapists. To become more lovable, you need to see yourself as worthy of love and respect.

Evangelization

The final way to be more loving, perhaps the primary way, is to witness by your life to the love God has for each person. Most people first think of using words to witness to the gospel, but actions unquestionably speak louder than words. A holy life makes a more lasting impression than hollow speech.

Gregory the Great (Chapter 40) admonishes those who want to spread the Good News. "Let them first rouse themselves up by lofty deeds.... Let them carefully examine themselves and discover in what respects they are idling and lagging, and make amends. Only then let them set in order the lives of others by their words."

In all things but love, practice moderation. You cannot love too much, but you can love unwisely. Unwise love is a masquerade of virtue. Are you loving because of what that love will gain for you, or are you loving because of what your love will give to another? True love involves sacrifice. If you turn your gaze to Jesus on the cross, you will understand the truth that love is willing to die for the sake of the beloved. Love to the extent that you are willing to give of yourself to another. May God grant you the grace to love wisely and well.

Notes

Preface

[1] Kuhl, *What Dying People Want*, 113.
[2] Halliday, *Psychosocial Medicine: A Study of the Sick Society*, 245.
[3] Kuhl, 111–18.
[4] Biblical references are taken from the New Revised Standard Version.
[5] Mother Teresa, *The Blessings of Love*, back cover.

1. God?

[1] Bonhoeffer, *The Cost of Discipleship*, 72–73.
[2] Benedict XVI, *Deus Caritas Est*, 10.
[3] Benedict XVI, *Deus Caritas Est*, 33.
[4] Wojtyla, *Love and Responsibility*, 73.
[5] John Paul II, Message for World Mission Sunday, October 2005.
[6] Benedict XVI, *Deus Caritas Est*, 1.

2. What Is Love?

[1] Thigpen, *Quotes from the Saints*, 135.
[2] Ibid., 136.
[3] Ibid., 135.
[4] Ibid., 136.
[5] Benedict XVI, *Deus Caritas Est*, 17.
[6] *To Be in Christ*, 13.
[7] *Les Miserables*, Chapter IV.
[8] 39. Cited in "Magnificat," January 2005 (6:1), 94.
[9] Saint Augustine, *The Works of Saint Augustine: A Translation for the 21st Century*, vol. III/15 *Expositions of the Psalms (1-32)*, 367.
[10] Ibid.
[11] Benedict XVI, *Deus Caritas Est*, 3.
[12] "Sermon on the Mount," in Crisostomo, *Commento al Vangelo di S Matteo*, 264, translation by Dom Julian Stead, OSB.
[13] Benedict XVI, *Deus Caritas Est*, 1.

3. How to Love

[1] *God Love You*, 56.
[2] Stevenson, *Home Book of Quotations*, 729.
[3] Lewis, *The Four Loves*, 87.
[4] Pepper, *The Harper Religious and Inspirational Quotation Companion*, 191.
[5] Benedict XVI, *Deus Caritas Est*, 14.
[6] Brainy Quote internet site, http://www.brainyquote.com/quotes/authors/m/martin luther king jr.html.

[7] Maximus, *Centuries* 1:42, 2:10.

[8] Ibid., 1:71, 2:30.

[9] ReligiousTolerance.org, "Shared Belief in Reciprocity," 12 January 2005.

[10] http://www.actsofkindness.org/inspiration/quotes.asp.

4. Compassion

[1] Celano, *First Life of Saint Francis*, XXIX.80.

[2] Mother Teresa, Nobel Prize Acceptance Speech, 1979.

[3] Tennyson, *Morte D'Arthur*, line 247.

[4] Margaret Preston (*Century*, vol. 32 [1886], 935) cited in Robertson, 137.

[5] *Blessings of Love*, 48.

[6] *Quotes from the Saints*, 88.

[7] McGeady, *"Please Forgive Me, God,"* 31–33.

[8] Koop and Schaeffer, *Whatever Happened to the Human Race?* 81.

[9] Benedict XVI, *The Yes of Jesus Christ*, 74.

[10] John Paul II, *Theology of the Body*, 28.

[11] "Parents defend treatment to keep girl child-sized." CTV.ca, updated January 5, 2007, http://www.ctv.ca/servlet/ArticleNews/story/CTVNews/20070104/ashley_treatment_070104/20070104?hub=TopStories.

[12] Chiara Lubich, *Christian Living Today: Meditations*, 20.

[13] "Word of Life," *Living City*, February 2005.

5. Honesty

[1] "Julian the Apostate." *Catholic Encyclopedia* on CD Rom, http://www.newadvent.org/cathen/08558b.htm and "Julian the Apostate." *Wikipedia*, 11 January 2007, http://en.wikipedia.org/wiki/Julian_the_Apostate.

[2] Peck, *People of the Lie*, 138-149.

[3] *Love Alone Is Credible*, 103.

[4] "Memorable Quotes from *Love Story* (1970)," http://www.imdb.com/title/tt0066011/quotes.

[5] Carnegie, *How to Win Friends and Influence People*, 134–43.

[6] "God Don't Make No Junk." Halo Benders, 24 June 1994. Funtrivia.com "General Chat." Hazardus01, 6 May 2006.

[7] "Popeye." *Wikipedia*, http://en.wikipedia.org/wiki/Popeye.

[8] Noonan, *When Character Was King*, 71, 158, 278.

[9] "4–H Centennial." History: 4-H in a New Millennium to "Make the Best Better" 1993–2002, http://www.4hcentennial.org/history/category.asp?catid=46.

[10] Wojtyla, *Love and Responsibility*, 28–31.

6. Promises

[1] "Discerning a Vocation." Sydney Archdiocese Vocations, http://www.cathcomm.org/vocations/discerning/riteOfOrdination.shtml.

[2] Noonan, *John Paul the Great*, 94.

[3] Boylan, *This Tremendous Lover*, 236.

7. Good Sportsmanship

[1] Groeschel, *The Virtue Driven Life*, 109–10.

[2] Osburn, *Love Walks by Faith*, 12–13, 35–38.

8. Thoughtfulness

[1] Dom Kunibert Mohlberg. Lecture at the Collegio Sant'Anselmo, Rome, Italy, 1956.

[2] Butler, *Lives of Saints*, 4.503–6.

[3] Ugolino, "The Life of Brother Juniper," Part 4 (226).

[4] Inspirational Quotes. The Random Acts of Kindness Foundation, http://www. actsofkindness.org/inspiration/quotes.asp.

[5] Yancey, *What's So Amazing about Grace*, 48–49.

[6] "Try to Remember," *The Fantastiks*, http://www.rockrecords.co.kr/mania/gasa/gasa show.asp?search=0&pge=2&sw=3&num=448.

[7] *Catechism of the Catholic Church*, 2270–2279, 2366–2379.

[8] Powell, Kara, "Mars and Venus: Men and Women Together in Ministry." Youth Specialties: 2003, http://www.youthspecialties.com/articles/topics/staff relationships/mars_venus.php.

[9] Story told by Father John Randall, "The Spirit and the Word" radio program. Providence, Rhode Island: WRIB 1220 Radio, n.d.

[10] Nancy Forest Kidd, "Letter to a Bride: Side Bar" ["Dorothy Day: Saint and Troublemaker." Lecture given at the Dorothy Day Conference, Marquette University, Milwaukee, Wisconsin: 10 October 1997], http://www.incommunion. org/forest-flier/jimsessays/dorothy-day-saint-and-troublemaker/.

[11] *God's Joyful Surprise*, 7.

9. Courtesy

[1] Fortini, *Francis of Assisi*, 314–15.

[2] Butler, *Lives of the Saints*, II, 550–51.

[3] Ibid., 551.

[4] See Benedict, *Rule for Monasteries*, chap. 23–28.

[5] *Apologia Pro Marcel Lefebvre*, Vol. 2, chap. xxix, "An Audience with Pope John Paul," Society of St. Pius X, District of Asia. Kansas City, Missouri: Angelus Press, Regina Coeli House, 18 November 1978.

10. Putting Others First

[1] Come Aside Retreat, Blackwood, New Jersey, July 12–14 1996.

[2] Marmion, Homily for Fifth Sunday after Pentecost, taken from *Christ, the Life of the Soul*, 361–62, http://www.fsspx.org/eng/spirituality/Marmion/Pentecost/ Pentecost5.htm.

[3] Bonaventure, *Major Life of St. Francis*, 6.1.

[4] Mother Teresa, *Meditations*, 28.

[5] West, *Theology of the Body Explained*, 31.

11. Respect

[1] Pepper, 313.

[2] King, *Strength to Love*, 69.

[3] Personal comment to the author.

[4] Pepper, 275.

12. Be Observant

[1] West, *Theology of the Body Explained*, 43.
[2] "Samuel Johnson," *Classic Encyclopedia*. Based on the 11th edition of the *Encyclopedia Britannica*, http://www.1911encyclopedia.org/Samuel_Johnson1911.
[3] *Complete Works*, 122.
[4] Guide to the Form of Life of the Private, Catholic Association of the Confraternity of Penitents: Constitutions XX: In Keeping with section 2 of the Rule.2g, http://www.penitents.org/statutesref.html.
[5] Ibid., VI: Purpose (Charism): Motto.
[6] Butler, *Lives of the Saints*, 3.487.

13. Self-Respect

[1] Meeting, Brothers and Sisters of Penance, Blessed Luchesio Chapter, Newport, Rhode Island, USA, 2 June 2002.
[2] Butler, *Lives of the Saints*, 3.427.

14. Good Stewardship

[1] Tertullian, *The Christian's Defense*, XXXIX.
[2] Hyde, "To Bill Gates, and Other Philanthropists," http://www.timesizing.com/1ceos.htm.
[3] Thigpen, *Quotes from the Saints*, 11.
[4] Ibid., 12.
[5] Mother Teresa, *Jesus, the Word to Be Spoken*, 29.
[6] See "Fine Artwork and Paintings by Portuguese Artist Joseph Matose," http://penitents.org/giftshopmp.htm.
[7] See James Cartier's website at http://www.jamescartier.com/index1.htm.

15. Patience

[1] Thigpin, *Quotes from the Saints*, 158.
[2] Ibid., 159.
[3] Knowles, *Catholic Book of Quotations*, 373.
[4] St. Philip's Suggestions for Idleness and Learning Patience, Activity Source: *Saints and Our Children, The* by Mary Reed Newland, P. J. Kenedy & Sons, New York; reprinted by TAN Publishers, 1958), Trinity Communications, 2007, http://www.catholicculture.org/lit/activities/view.cfm?id=247.
[5] Benedict of Nursia, Rule for Monasteries, 4.5.
[6] Gianna's Prayer, 55–56.
[7] Ann Foose in personal conversation with Madeline Pecora Nugent, Newport, Rhode Island, 2006.
[8] Knowles, *Catholic Book of Quotations*, 273.
[9] Knowles, *Catholic Book of Quotations*, 274.
[10] Ibid.
[11] Knowles, *Catholic Book of Quotations*, 274.

Works Consulted

Aelred of Rievaulx. *The Way of Friendship*. Edited by M. Basil Pennington. Hyde Park, New York: New City Press, 2001.

Aimsworth, Martha. "How to Choose a Competent Counselor," Metanoia.org (http://www.metanoia.org/choose/index.html), 1999.

Augustine. *The Works of Saint Augustine: A Translation for the 21ˢᵗ Century Series.* Edited by John E. Rotelle, O.S.A. © Augustinian Heritage Institute 1991. Hyde Park, New York: New City Press, 1991. Electronic version published by InteLex Corporation, 2001.

Benedict XVI. *"Deus Caritas Est" [God Is Love]*. Vatican City: Libreria Editrice Vaticana, 2005.

_____, (Joseph Ratzinger). *The Yes of Jesus Christ: Spiritual Exercises in Faith, Hope, and Love*. Translated by Robert Nowell. New York: Crossroad, 1991. Originally published as *Aus Christus Schauen: Einübung in Glaube, Hoffnung, Liebe* (Frieburg im Breisgau: Verlag Herder, 1989).

Benedict of Nursia. *St. Benedict's Rule for Monasteries*. Translated by Leonard J. Doyle. Collegeville, Minnesota: The Liturgical Press, St. John's Abbey, 1948.

Bonhoeffer, Dietrich. *The Cost of Discipleship*. Translated by R. H. Fuller, revised by Irmgard Booth. New York: Macmillan, 1971. Originally published as *Nachfolge* (Munchen: Chr. Kaiser Verlag, 1937).

Boylan, M. Eugene. *This Tremendous Lover*. 21ˢᵗ printing. Westminster, Maryland: The Newman Press, 1961.

Bonaventure, *The Major Legend of St. Francis, Francis of Assisi: Early Documents: The Founder, vol. 2*. Edited by Regis Armstrong, OFM Cap., J. A. Wayne Hellman, OFM Conv., William J. Short, OFM. Hyde Park, New York: New City Press, 1999.

Butler, Alban. *Butler's Lives of the Saints: Complete Edition*. Edited, revised, and supplemented by Herbert Thurston, SJ, and Donald Attwater 4 vols. (London: Burns and Oates, 1956). Reprinted Westminster, Maryland: Christian Classics, 1980.

Carnegie, Dale. *How to Win Friends and Influence People*. New York: Pocket Books, [1936] 1964.

Catechism of the Catholic Church. New York: Doubleday, 1995.

Celano, Thomas. *The Life of Saint Francis, Francis of Assisi: Early Documents: The Saint, vol. 1*. Edited by Regis Armstrong, OFM Cap., J. A. Wayne Hellman, OFM Conv., William J. Short, OFM. Hyde Park, New York: New City Press, 2000.

_____, *Second Life of St. Francis*. Ibid.

Christopher News' Note # 409: Healing Life's Hurts. New York: The Christophers, n.d.

Crisostomo, S. Giovanni. *Commento al Vangelo di S Matteo*. Translated from the Greek by Riccardo Minuti and Fiorenza Monti, vol.1, Rome: Città Nuova Editrice, 1966.

De Sales, Francis. *Introduction to the Devout Life*. Translated by John K. Ryan. Garden City, New York: Image Books, [1950, 1952] 1956.

Ellison, Sharon. *Don't Be So Defensive!: Taking the War Out of Our Words with Powerful, Non-Defensive Communication*. Kansas City: Andrews McMeel, 1998.

Fortini, Arnaldo. *Francis of Assisi: A Translation of Nova Vita di San Franceso*. Translated by Helen Moak. New York: Crossroad, 1981.

Francis of Assisi and Clare of Assisi. *The Complete Works*. Translation and introduction by Regis J. Armstrong and Ignatius C. Brady. New York: Paulist Press, 1982.

Gianna's Prayer: " Blessing in Disguise." Irving, Texas: *Catholic Marketing Network Trade Journal*, 2001, vol 2, issue 2, 55–56.

Green, Terri. *Simple Acts of Kindness*. Grand Rapids, Michigan: Revell, 2004.

Gregory the Great. *Pastoral Care*. Translated by Henry Davis, S.J. Vol. 11, *Ancient Christian Writers: The Works of the Fathers in Translation*. Edited by Johannes Quasten, S.T.D. and Joseph C. Plumpe, Ph.D. Washington, D.C.: New York: Newman Press, [1950] 1978.

Groeschel, Benedict J., C.F.R. *The Virtue Driven Life*. Huntington, Indiana: Our Sunday Visitor Publishing Division, 2006.

Gumbleton, Thomas J. "Twenty-Sixth Sunday in Ordinary Time." The Peace-Pulpit: *National Catholic Reporter* (NRConline.org). Kansas City, Missouri: *National Catholic Reporter*, 2004, http://www.nationalcatholicreporter.org/peace/gumb092604.htm

Halliday, James L. *Psychosocial Medicine: A Study of the Sick Society*. New York: Norton, 1948.

Hyde, Philip, CEO. "To Bill Gates, and Other Philanthropists." The Timesizing Wire, PO Box 622, Cambridge Massachustts 02140, c. 2000–02, http://www.timesizing.com/1ceos.htm

John Paul II. "Message for World Mission Sunday 2005." Libreria Editrice Vaticana, http://www.vatican.va/holy_father/john_paul_ii/messages/missions/documents/hf_jp-ii_mes_20050222_world-day-for-missions-2005_en.html

_____, "Salvifici Doloris" [On the Christian Meaning of Human Suffering]. Vatican Translation. Boston: Pauline Books and Media, 1984.

_____, *Theology of the Body: Human Love in the Divine Plan*. Boston: Pauline Books and Media, 1997.

Johnston, Francis W. *The Voice of the Saints*. Rockford, Illinois: Tan Books, 1965.

Kardong, Terrence G. *Benedict's Rule, A Translation and Commentary*. Collegeville, Minnesota: Liturgical Press, 1996.

Kidd, Sue Monk. *God's Joyful Surprise: Finding Yourself Loved*. San Francisco: Harper & Row, 1987.

King, Martin Luther, Jr. *Strength to Love*. Glasgow, United Kingdom: William Collins, Fount Paperbacks, 1977.

Knowles, Leo. *Catholic Book of Quotations*. Huntington, Indiana: Our Sunday Visitor Publishing Division, 2004.

Koop, C. Everett, M.D., and Francis A. Schaeffer. *Whatever Happened to the Human Race?* Rev. ed. Westchester, Illinois: Crossway Books, 1983.

Kuhl, David. *What Dying People Want: Practical Wisdom for the End of Life*. New York: Public Affairs, 2002.

Lee, Harper. *To Kill a Mockingbird*. Philadelphia and New York: J. B. Lippincott, 1960.

Lewis, C. S. *The Four Loves*. New York: Harcourt, Brace, & World, 1960.

Louth, Andrew. *Maximus the Confessor*. London and New York: Routledge, 1996.

Lubich, Chiara. *Christian Living Today: Meditations*. Hyde Park, NY: New City Press, 1997.

_____, "Word of Life." *Living City*, February 2005.

Maximus the Confessor. *The Four Centuries on Charity*. Translated and annotated by Polycarp Sherwood O.S.B., S.T.D. *Ancient Christian Writers*, vol. 21, Westminster, Maryland: The Newman Press; London: Green & Company, 1953.

_____, *Selected Writings*. Translated by George Berthold. *Classics of Western Spirituality*. New York: Paulist Press, 1985.

_____, "The Ascetic Life," "The Four Centuries on Charity," *Ancient Christian Writers #21*, Westminster, MD, 1955.

_____, "Opera Omnia," *Patrologia Graeca*. Compiled by Migne, vol. 90–91. Paris: 1865.

McGeady, Sr. Mary Rose. *"Please Forgive Me, God."* New York: Covenant House, 2001.

Nierenberg, Gerald I, and Henry H. Calero. *How to Read a Person Like a Book*. New York: Pocket Books, 1971.

Noonan, Peggy. *John Paul the Great: Remembering a Spiritual Father*. New York: Penguin, 2005.

_____, *When Character Was King: A Story of Ronald Reagan*. New York: Penguin Books, 2002.

Osburn, Charlie and Jeanne. *Love Walks by Faith*. Cincinnati, Ohio: Harvey Whitney Books, 2007.

Peck, M. Scott, M.D. *People of the Lie: The Hope for Healing Human Evil*. New York: Simon & Schuster, 1983.

_____, and Shannon Peck. *The Love You Deserve: A Spiritual Guide to Genuine Love*. Solana Beach, California: Lifepath Publishing, 2002.

Pepper, Margaret. *The Harper Religious & Inspirational Quotation Companion*. New York: Harper Collins, 1989.

Robertson, James. *Stonewall Jackson: The Man, the Soldier, the Legend*. New York: Macmillan, 1997.

Sheen, Fulton J. *God Love You*. Garden City, New York: Image Books, 1955.

_____, *The Power of Love*. Garden City, New York: Image Books, 1968.

Stead, Julian, O.S.B. *Saint Benedict: A Rule for Beginners*: Excerpts from the Life and Rule of Saint Benedict. Hyde Park, New York: New City Press, 1994.

Stevenson, Burton. *The Home Book of Quotations: Classical and Modern*. New York: Dodd, Mead, & Company, 1935.

Teresa, Mother. *The Blessings of Love*. Selected and edited by Nancy Sabbag. Ann Arbor, Michigan: Servant Publications, 1996.

_____, *In the Heart of the World: Thoughts, Stories, and Prayers*. Novata, CA: New World Library, 1997.

_____, *Jesus, the Word to Be Spoken: Prayers and Meditations for Every Day of the Year*. Compiled by Angelo Devananda and Angelo Scolozzi. Ann Arbor, Michigan: Servant Publications, 1999.

_____, *Meditations from a Simple Path*. New York: Ballantine Books, 1996.

Tertullian, *Defence of the Christians against the Heathen*. Trans. Alexander Souter, http://www.tertullian.org/articles/mayor_apologeticum/mayor_apologeticum_07translation.htm

Thigpen, Paul. *A Dictionary of Quotes from the Saints*. Ann Arbor, Michigan: Servant Publications, 2001.

Thomas Aquinas, *Summa Theologica*. New York: Benziger Brothers, 1948.

Twain, Mark (Samuel L. Clemens). *The Adventures of Huckleberry Finn*. Samuel L. Clemens, 1884.

Ugolino di Monte Santa Maria. *The Life of Brother Juniper [The Little Flowers of St. Francis]*. Translated by Raphael Brown. Garden City, New York: Hanover House, 1958.

van Zeller, Hubert. *To Be in Christ*. New York: Crossroad, 1981.

von Balthasar, Hans Urs. *Heart of the World*. Translated by Erasmo S. Leiva. San Francisco: Ignatius Press, 1979.

_____, *Love Alone Is Credible*. Translated by D. C. Schindler. San Francisco: Ignatius Press, 2004.

West, Christopher. *Theology of the Body Explained: A Commentary on John Paul's Gospel of the Body*. Boston: Pauline Books and Media, 2003.

Williams, Tennessee. *Summer and Smoke [Four Plays]*. New York: Signet, 1976.

Wojtyla, Karol. *Love and Responsibility*. Translated by H. T. Willetts. San Francisco: Ignatius Press, 1993.

Yancey, Philip. *What's So Amazing about Grace?* Grand Rapids, Michigan: Zondervan, 1997.

Love-Ability:
Group Discussion Manual

This manual may be used in a small group or classroom setting. Its sections correspond to the chapters in *Love-Ability* and provide a sixteen-session course on becoming more lovable. Each session is intended to last an hour and should begin and end on time.

Leadership should change from session to session so that every person gets a chance at being the leader. The leader asks the questions, keeps the discussion on the topic, and observes the session's time limits.

So that all have a chance to share, each discussion group should consist of no more than six people. If more than six are present, divide into smaller groups.

If desired, the session may begin with prayer (the Our Father is suggested) and end with intercessory prayers for the needs of the group.

In order to become more lovable, it is vital that participants do the reading and complete the assignments prior to each session.

The questions are to foster discussion but do not have to all be addressed. If a particular person does not wish to participate in a discussion or answer a question, his or her wishes should be respected with love.

Session 1:

1. Begin the session on time.
2. Select a leader for this session.
3. Select a time, date, and place to meet for Session 2.
4. Pass out copies of *Love-Ability* so that everyone has a personal copy.
5. Each person should write his or her name on the inside cover of the copy.
6. Going around the group, take turns reading orally the Dedication, Preface, and Chapter One.
7. Discuss all or some of the following questions:
   a. What do you hope to gain by participating in a sixteen session course on becoming lovable?

    b. What difficulties do you foresee in becoming more lovable?

    c. Chapter One discusses "God billboards." Can you think of any other slogans that would give an idea of God's love for us?

    d. How important is God to each member of your group?

    e. Discuss the idea of God being "the Ultimate Lover."

    f. What are some of God's greatest acts of love?

    g. What is the relationship between suffering and love? How does this relate to your life now?

8. End the session on time.

9. Assignment: Between Session 1 and Session 2, note any loving act of yours that involves suffering and be ready to share about it at Session 2.

10. Prepare for Session 2 by reading in advance Chapter Two of *Love-Ability*.

Session 2:

1. Begin the session on time.

2. Select a leader for the session.

3. Select a time, date, and place to meet for Session 3.

4. Discuss the Assignment from Session 1. How did your love involve suffering? What did you learn from this experience?

5. Review Chapter Two by discussing the following questions:

    a. How would you define love?

    b. How is love "maximum movement toward the Good"?

    c. How do we know what "good" is?

    d. What is fake love? How does it differ from real love?

    e. What is eros? Give an example.

    f. What is philia? Give an example.

    g. What is storge? Give an example.

    h. What is agape? Give an example.

    i. How is tough love an example of agape love?

    j. Where might you have to show tough love?

    k. Discuss Benedict XVI's statement that love is our "destiny."

6. End the session on time.

7. Assignment: Take a sheet of paper and divide it into four sections. Label one section eros, a second philia, a third storge, and a fourth agape. Categorize how you show love between Session 2 and Session 3. Record incidents of lovableness under the proper

category of eros, philia, storge, or agape. For example, if you take someone out to eat as part of a romantic date, write that under eros. If you go out to eat with a friend, write that under philia. If you are at a luncheon honoring a war veteran, write that under storge. If you give a sandwich to a homeless person, write that under agape.

8. Prepare for Session 3 by reading Chapter Three of *Love-Ability*.

Session 3:

1. Begin the session on time.
2. Select a leader for this session.
3. Select a date, time, and place to meet for Session 4.
4. Discuss how, between Session 2 and Session 3, your loving acts fell into the categories of eros, philia, storge, and agape. Do others agree with you? If not, why? Which categories were most often used in your group? Why might this be? Does your group have a good balance in showing love? If not, what can be done to improve?
5. Review Chapter Three by discussing the following questions:
   a. Why might the perfection of love be a perfection of friendship?
   b. Do you agree that "the best medicine in life is a friend"?
   c. What did Jesus say was the greatest commandment? What is your opinion of this and why?
   d. How do love and feelings differ?
   e. How is love akin to caring?
   f. Discuss this statement: "Love of self is the foundation for love of others."
   g. Do you think that it is possible to love everyone?
   h. How does the Golden Rule relate to love?
   i. What random acts of kindness have you experienced from others? How did those make you feel?
6. End the session on time.
7. Assignment: Between Session 3 and Session 4, do at least five random acts of kindness. Write them down and also record why you did them and how you felt about them. Be prepared to share on this at Session 4.
8. Read Chapter Four of *Love-Ability* before the next session.

Session 4:

1. Begin the session on time.
2. Select a leader for this session.
3. Select a time, place, and date for Session 5.
4. Each person should share at least one random act of kindness done between Sessions 3 and 4. How did this make you feel? Will you continue to perform random acts of kindness?
5. Review Chapter Four by discussing the following questions:
   a. Review the "People Attentiveness" exercise mentioned at the beginning of Chapter Four. Where and how might you do this? What difficulties do you foresee and how might you overcome them? You will be asked to complete this exercise before Session 5.
   b. This chapter mentions many ways to show kindness. What will be the most difficult for you and why?
   c. What do you consider to be evil? How might you combat it with love?
   d. Using the techniques in this chapter, how might you deal with the following people:
      i. A co-worker who calls out to you, "Hey, stupid!" every time that you walk past him or her.
      ii. An individual who has spread lies about you.
      iii. A person who has the annoying habit of burping while eating.
6. End the session on time.
7. Assignment: Before Session 5, complete the "People Attentiveness" exercise in Chapter Four. Be sure to do both the first and second parts of this exercise. Be prepared to share your experiences in Session 5.
8. Read Chapter Five before the next session.

Session 5:

1. Begin the session on time.
2. Select a leader for this session.
3. Select a time, place, and date for Session 6.
4. Discuss the results of your "People Attentiveness" exercise. What can you learn about others by careful observation? Did your

powers of observation improve? Did this exercise help anyone in the group to minister to another person?

5. Observe the members of your group. Each individual should make an insightful comment about every other group member based on observation. Briefly discuss the accuracy of these observations.

6. To review Chapter Five, discuss the following questions:

   a. Did you consider yourself to be an honest person before you read Chapter Five? How do you view yourself now?

   b. Why are well-meaning people often dishonest?

   c. Why is dishonesty unloving? Can it ever be loving?

   d. How might a person make restitution if he or she has robbed someone, not of goods, but of a good name?

   e. How can you distinguish between sinful thoughts and sinful actions?

   f. This chapter suggests sharing our thoughts in thirty to ninety seconds or less. What do you think of that suggestion? Practice it in your group sharing from now on.

   g. How might you make an honest response in the following situations?

      i. A friend asks you how you like her new coat which you consider to be hideous and immodest.

      ii. Your boss tells the employees that the company president is coming for a visit tomorrow. He wants everyone to say that everything is going well even though you, as company accountant, know that the company is facing great debts that it may be unable to pay.

      iii. You are expected to join your bowling team in going to a topless bar to celebrate a team member's birthday.

      iv. One of your acquaintances always believed you to be her friend, but when you were high school classmates, you often spread gossip about her. You don't do that any longer, but your past sins bother you.

      v. You don't want your children to know that your spouse is an alcoholic.

7. End the session on time.

8. Assignment: Before Session 6, complete the "Honesty with Yourself" exercise at the beginning of Chapter Five. Do you wear a mask? How can you be more honest with yourself and others? Be prepared to share on this exercise in Session 6.

9. Read Chapter Six of *Love-Ability* before the next session.

Session 6:

1. Begin the session on time.
2. Select a leader for this session.
3. Select a time, place, and date for Session 7.
4. Review the results of the "Honesty with Yourself" activity. What did it reveal? Do you need to change? How might the members of your group help you?
5. Review Chapter Six by discussing the following questions:
   a. Do you believe that God always keeps his promises?
   b. What problems do you have with making or keeping promises? How can these be rectified?
   c. Who or what must you obey? How do you feel about obedience?
   d. Have you ever been betrayed? How might you deal lovingly with the person(s) who betrayed you?
   e. Look over the various topics covered in Chapter Six. What area needs the most work in your life? How can you make improvements?
6. End the session on time.
7. Assignment: Between Session 6 and Session 7, work to improve the area that you named in 5e. Be prepared to share on how you made positive changes in your behavior.
8. Prepare for Session 7 by reading Chapter Seven of *Love-Ability*.

Session 7:

1. Begin the session on time.
2. Select a leader for this session.
3. Select a time, place, and date for Session 8.
4. Share on which area in Chapter Six you sought to improve. What changes did you make? How did you make them? Do you feel that the improvement will be long-lasting? How can you insure that it will be?
5. Review Chapter Seven by discussing the following questions:
   a. Do you accept correction graciously? If not, how might you improve?
   b. Are you tactful in offering correction to others? If not, how might you improve?

   c. Is there anyone whom you have trouble forgiving? How might you begin to forgive that individual?

   d. Can you relate God's forgiveness of our sins to the need to forgive others their offenses against us?

   e. To practice giving and receiving correction, and becoming a good loser and winner, do the following exercise.

       i. Each person in the group is to think of something to give away at the next session. This might be an item or an offer of time or work. The offering need not be expensive but it should have some meaning to the gift-giver. The leader of the session will record what each person will bring to the next session.

      ii. Once this has been done, the group will choose one of the following five challenges to be performed by all in the group. Each group member will participate in the challenge. The challenges are:

- Everyone draws a picture of the person on his or her immediate right OR
- Everyone sings one verse of a familiar song OR
- Everyone shares a joke or humorous experience OR
- Everyone performs a charade of an animal and the others guess the beast (remember, in a charade, body movements and expressions must indicate the character; use of the voice is prohibited) OR
- Everyone gives the most flattering description possible of the person to their right.

     iii. Take a secret vote on who has done the best with the challenge. The leader will announce the winner.

     iv. Everyone congratulates the winner, who will receive all the items brought to the next session. The winner accepts congratulations humbly.

      v. To complete the exercise, share on how you felt about the challenges, about voting, and about winning or losing. What did you learn about love from this?

6. End the session on time.

7. Assignment: Select one section of Chapter Seven to work on before the next session. Write how you sought to improve in this area and be prepared to share at Session 8.

8. Read Chapter Eight before the next session.

Session 8:

1. Begin the session on time.
2. Select a leader for this session.
3. Select a time, place, and date for Session 9.
4. Discuss the topics in Chapter Seven which each group member sought to improve. Was the effort successful? What suggestions can the group members make to help one another improve?
5. Present the winner of Session 7's challenge with the gift items brought by the other members.
6. Review Chapter Eight by discussing the following questions:
   a. How does thoughtfulness toward others begin with thoughtfulness toward ourselves?
   b. What is your opinion of Dorothy Day's advice, "If you can't meet your standards, lower your standards"?
   c. Practice listening and conversing skills by the following exercise: Choose one person to be the silent individual. That person should create imaginary biographical information about himself or herself. For example, he or she might pretend to be a government official, gangster, parent, member of the clergy, peasant, ruler, hobo, child, or whatever else comes to mind. The person is not to share this information, however. The others in the group will attempt to discover the mystery background by asking questions and listening to the responses. Allow ten minutes for this exercise, then reflect on the skills needed and practiced.
   d. Discuss how you can give advice, in love, to the errant individuals in the following situations:
      i. Your neighbor allows the dog to do his business on your property.
      ii. Your best friend thinks that piercing her navel is attractive.
      iii. Your boss has bad breath.
6. Review the various topics in Chapter Eight. Which three need the most work from you? Why?
7. End the session on time.
8. Assignment: Before meeting for Session 9, work on the topic areas mentioned in number 6. Write down how you sought to improve. Be prepared to share on this at the next session.
9. Prepare for Session 9 by reading Chapter Nine.

Session 9:

1. Begin the session on time.
2. Select a leader for this session.
3. Select a time, place, and date for Session 10.
4. Discuss the three topic areas worked on between Session 8 and Session 9. Share your success stories as well as any problems that you encountered. Share any advice that you may have for others
5. Review Chapter Nine by discussing the following questions:
   a. Discuss how courtesy is "one of the qualities of God" and "a sister to charity."
   b. Have you ever been guilty of ignoring the courtesy of a reply? How might you improve in this area?
   c. Discuss the following statement: "Good manners are an expression of love and charity. If you have the latter, you have the former."
   d. Review the section on manners. What other good manners might be added to the list?
   e. How might the world be different if everyone saw Christ's image in everyone else?
   f. How can you combat the following unloving characteristics?
      i. Jumping to conclusions
      ii. Moodiness
      iii. Assumptions
6. End the session on time.
7. Assignment: Before Session 10, make a list of twenty people whom you know and record what is unique about each. Also record what is unique about you. Be prepared to share this at Session 10.
8. Prepare for Session 10 by reading Chapter Ten.

Session 10:

1. Begin the session on time.
2. Select a leader for this session.
3. Select a time, place, and date for Session 11.
4. Without sharing the names of the individuals, share the results of the Assignment for Session 9. What are some unique traits in others that you may have overlooked? What is unique about you?

5. Review Chapter Ten by discussing the following questions:
    a. Discuss the terms "selfless sacrifice" and "self-sacrifice."
    b. How are selfish ambition and cowardice the opposites of selfless sacrifice?
    c. Review the section on "Acquiring Humility." What is your opinion of the suggestions offered there?
    d. What topics do you avoid addressing because of timidity or fear of confrontation? How might you address these?
    e. Chapter Ten discusses Nathan the Prophet's confrontation of David's sins by presenting to David a fictitious story about a poor man and his sheep. Reread that section orally. Then together devise stories that could be used to help the following individuals see their errors:
        i. Your brother-in-law cheats on his income tax.
        ii. A friend is planning to take her daughter for an abortion.
        iii. You are a preschool teacher and speak to a parent about her child biting the other youngsters, but she laughs and says, "Oh, he always does that."
    f. Share one of your faults with the others in your group. Each group member should respond in charity to your revelation. Discuss how you felt about this sharing.
    g. What most often causes you to complain? How can you control your complaining?
6. End the session on time.
7. Assignment: Select one section of Chapter Ten and follow or adapt its advice. Be prepared to share what you learned from this.
8. Prepare for Session 11 by reading Chapter Eleven.

Session 11:

1. Begin the session on time.
2. Select a leader for this session.
3. Select a time, place, and date for Session 12.
4. Share with the other group members your selection from Chapter Ten as requested in the Assignment from the previous session. How did you apply the techniques of this section? What were the results?
5. Review Chapter Eleven by discussing the following questions:
    a. What does respect mean to you?

b. What attitudes and behaviors are disrespectful? Chapter Eleven mentions several. What others can you add?

c. How should you deal with those who do not respect you? Give examples from your life, if possible.

d. Review Jesus' words (Luke 6:36-38), as shared in the "Be Merciful" section of Chapter Eleven. How might these be relevant to your life?

e. Do you know anyone who is possessive or controlling? Perhaps you are. How can you deal with possessiveness in yourself or others?

f. Practice saying "Thank you." Each person should compliment every other one in the group. Everyone who is complimented practices receiving the compliment graciously.

6. End the session on time.

7. Assignment: Between Sessions 11 and 12, become more aware of saying "Thank you." Look for opportunities to thank others. Write down fifteen situations in which you were able to saying "Thank you." Be prepared to share on these at Session 12.

8. Prepare for Session 12 by reading Chapter Twelve of *Love-Ability*.

Session 12:

1. Begin the session on time.
2. Select a leader for this session.
3. Select a time, place, and date for Session 13.
4. Share the group's experiences with Session 11's Assignment in looking for opportunities to say "Thank you." Was this difficult to do? How has this heightened your awareness regarding thankfulness?
5. Review Chapter Twelve by discussing the following questions:
   a. How can you increase your powers of observation?
   b. Why is observation often the first step toward love?
   c. As a group, do the exercise described under the "Seek the Good" section of Chapter Twelve. The group should name five unlikable public figures or enemies. What do you know about the pasts of these people that might have influenced them in a negative way? Brainstorm to discover ways that each of these people reveals truth, goodness, and beauty. What does this exercise teach you?

    d. Discuss the meaning of this statement: "I have chosen thee in the furnace of poverty."

    e. What are your phobias? How might you overcome them?

    f. How can each person in your group spread the message of God's love to others? What obstacles can you see to this? How might these be overcome?

6. End the session on time.

7. Assignment: Review Chapter Twelve. Which section needs the most work in your life? Work to improve yourself in that area. Be prepared to share on your progress during Session 13.

8. In preparation for Session 13, read Chapter Thirteen of *Love-Ability*.

Session 13:

1. Begin the session on time.

2. Select a leader for this session.

3. Select a time, place, and date for Session 14.

4. Share with one another the specific sections of Chapter Twelve that were worked on since the last session. Discuss how you profited from application of the techniques in those sections. What progress was made?

5. Review Chapter Thirteen by discussing the following questions:

    a. What is the difference between respecting God's image in another person and human respect?

    b. How can we respect others?

    c. How can we become respectable ourselves?

    d. What can you do to improve your physical well-being?

    e. What can you do to improve your spiritual health?

    f. How can you keep negativity from controlling your life?

6. End the session on time.

7. Assignment: Before the next session, do the exercise described in the "Making Changes" section. Bring the envelopes of "Things I Can Change" and "Things I Cannot Change" to the next session and be prepared to share on them.

8. In preparation for Session 14, read Chapter Fourteen of *Love-Ability*.

Session 14:

1. Begin the session on time.
2. Select a leader for this session.
3. Select a time, place, and date for Session 15.
4. Share with one another the things that you could change and those that you could not, as discussed in the Assignment for Session 13. Discuss the changes that you plan to make and how long these might take. Do you think that making the changes will be difficult? What did you learn about yourself from this assignment?
5. Review Chapter Fourteen by discussing the following questions:
   a. What are your talents? How can you use them to benefit others?
   b. Do you own anything that you can use to improve the world? How might you use these things well?
   c. What are alms? How may they be applied with charity? Name ten organizations or individuals that are in need of alms. Select one as a group, then take up a donation among the group members and send it to that charity as an alms.
   d. What evil have you experienced? How has God brought good from that?
   e. What other examples of evil do you recognize in the world? What good might God bring from these?
   f. What can you do to create a safer and healthier world?
6. End the session on time.
7. Assignment: Do the exercise on Money Management under the "Money" section of Chapter Fourteen. Once you have recorded how you use money, evaluate the categories and amounts. Do you need more balance or wisdom in managing money? How might you gain that? Be prepared to share on this experience at the next session. Prepare for Session 15 by reading Chapter Fifteen of *Love-Ability*.

Session 15:

1. Begin the session on time.
2. Select a leader for this session.
3. Select a time, place, and date for Session 16.
4. Review the Assignment from Session 14, but without divulging how much money anyone spends on each category. What categories for spending money are common to everyone in the group? Were any categories unusual? Evaluate how you spend your money. Do you need improvement? If so, how can you change?
5. Review Chapter Fifteen by discussing the following questions:
   a. Chapter Fifteen discusses many ways to exercise self-control. Why is self-control loving?
   b. Why is patience a virtue? How is it learned?
   c. What situations try your patience? How might you be more patient in these?
   d. Discuss the incident involving Philip Neri under the section titled "Patience." Have you ever had a similar experience of asking for a certain virtue and then immediately having to exercise it?
   e. What is the difference between righteous anger and self-centered anger? How can you tell the difference when you are angry?
   f. How might you deal with someone who sows discord or provokes arguments?
   g. What advice for enduring suffering could you give to the sick or to those suffering various other trials and afflictions?
   h. Do you have difficulty waiting? How might you be able to wait patiently?
6. End the session on time.
7. Assignment: Review Chapter Fifteen. Which virtues need work in your life? Write them down and then work to develop them. Also pray that God will help you. Should he present an opportunity for the virtues to develop, record it. Be prepared to share on this at Session 16.
8. Prepare for Session 16 by reading Chapter Sixteen of *Love-Ability*.

Session 16:

1. Begin the session on time.
2. Select a leader for this session.
3. Share the outcome of the Assignment for Session 15. What virtues have group members developed? Were there any unusual circumstances that helped to develop these virtues?
4. Review Chapter Sixteen by discussing the following questions:
   a. What is a God Box? How might it be a valuable addition to your home or office?
   b. Do you believe that many people need a counselor at some time?
   c. Do you have any prejudices against counseling or stereotypes of counselors? What might these be? How can you combat them?
   d. Why should you not have to reveal to a counselor, in advance of the first session, your reasons for requesting a meeting?
   e. How can your life be a witness to God's love?
   f. What are your thoughts about this: "In all things but love, practice moderation. We cannot love too much, but we can love unwisely."
   g. How might meditating on the crucified Jesus help us to understand the nature of love?
   h. Quickly review *Love-Ability* and the sessions you have spent together. What have you learned? What still needs work? How can you continue to grow more lovable?
5. Congratulations on completing the *Love-Ability* book and manual. May you become increasingly more lovable!

About the Authors

Madeline Pecora Nugent, a wife, mother of 5 children, and grandmother of two has written five other books and over 250 articles. A regular contributor to *True Girl* magazine, she is Minister General for the Confraternity of Penitents (www.penitents.org).

Julian Stead, O.S.B., a Benedictine monk and priest at St. Gregory's Abbey, Portsmouth, RI, has written *Saint Benedict: A Rule for Beginners*, as well as numerous articles on practical spirituality.